PHAENOMENOLOGICA

COLLECTION FONDÉE PAR H.L. VAN BREDA ET PUBLIÉE
SOUS LE PATRONAGE DES CENTRES D'ARCHIVES-HUSSERL

92

PHENOMENOLOGY IN PRACTICE AND THEORY

edited by

WILLIAM S. HAMRICK

PHENOMENOLOGY IN PRACTICE AND THEORY

edited by

WILLIAM S. HAMRICK

1985 **MARTINUS NIJHOFF PUBLISHERS**
a member of the KLUWER ACADEMIC PUBLISHERS GROUP
DORDRECHT / BOSTON / LANCASTER

IV

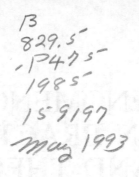

Distributors

for the United States and Canada: Kluwer Academic Publishers, 190 Old Derby Street, Hingham, MA 02043, USA
for the UK and Ireland: Kluwer Academic Publishers, MTP Press Limited, Falcon House, Queen Square, Lancaster LA1 1RN, UK
for all other countries: Kluwer Academic Publishers Group, Distribution Center, P.O. Box 322, 3300 AH Dordrecht, The Netherlands

Library of Congress Cataloging in Publication Data

Main entry under title:

Phenomenology in practice and theory.

    (Phaenomenologica; 92)
    Includes index.
    1. Phenomenology – Addresses, essays, lectures.
I. Hamrick, William S. II. Series.
B829.5.P475 1984   142'.7   83-25510
ISBN 90-247-2926-2

ISBN 90-247-2926-2 (this volume)
ISBN 90-247-2339-6 (series)

Copyright

PRINTED IN THE NETHERLANDS

TABLE OF CONTENTS

PART THREE: AESTHETIC, ETHICAL, AND RELIGIOUS
VALUES

PREFACE
by
Wolfe Mays

It is a great pleasure and honour to write this preface. I first became acquainted with Herbert Spiegelberg's work some twenty years ago, when in 1960
I reviewed *The Phenomenological Movement*[1] for *Philosophical Books*, one
of the few journals in Britain that reviewed this book, which Herbert has jok-
ingly referred to as "*the monster*". I was at that time already interested in Continental thought, and in particular phenomenology. I had attended a course on
phenomenology given by Rene Schaerer at Geneva when I was working there
in 1955–6. I had also been partly instrumental in getting Merleau-Ponty to
come to Manchester in 1958. During his visit he gave a seminar in English on
politics and a lecture in French on "Wittgenstein and Language" in which he
attacked Wittgenstein's views on language in the *Tractatus*. He was apparently
unaware of the *Philosophical Investigations*.

But it was not until I came to review Herbert's book that I appreciated the
ramifications of the movement: its diverse strands of thought, and the
manifold personalities involved in it. For example, Herbert mentions one
Aurel Kolnai who had written on the "Phenomenology of Disgust", and which
had appeared in Vol. 10 of Husserl's *Jahrbuch*. It was only after I had been
acquainted for some time with Kolnai then in England, that I realised that
Herbert had written about him in the *Movement*.[2]

The *Movement* itself contains a wealth of learning. It also exhibits what I
can only call philosophical detective work of a high order, of which Scotland
Yard could well be proud, if it was interested in philosophical questions. Over
the years I have repeatedly used the book when I wished to learn something
about lesser known phenomenologists as well as the better known ones. In the
latter case, Herbert's summaries often give a better insight into their ideas than
do some of the standard commentaries, and in addition they are often easier
to follow. If I had to give another name to the work, it would be *Herbert's*

W.S. Hamrick (ed.) *Phenomenology in Practice and Theory*.
© 1985 Martinus Nijhoff Publishers, Dordrecht/Boston/Lancaster
ISBN 90 247 2926 2. Printed in the Netherlands.

Thesaurus. Many a student taking a course in phenomenology will no doubt have raised a silent prayer of thanks to heaven for its existence, especially when faced by end of term examinations. The *Movement* is now in its third edition. I am sure that it will stand the test of time as a fine piece of scholarship, and that it will continue to serve as a reference work well into the 21st century; that is, if we don't blow ourselves up first.

Herbert has also written a volume on the history of phenomenological psychology and psychiatry,[3] but I know that he does not want to be thought of as primarily a historian of phenomenology. And, of course, he is a philosopher in his own right. He has done scholarly and original work in ontology, ethics and the philosophy of law. It is, I think, a great pity that his book on ethics has not up to now been translated into English. Further, his numerous phenomenological essays show that he has been able to take an original line in phenomenology. But Herbert ought not to disparage his efforts as a historian of phenomenology. One cannot do profitable philosophy, let alone phenomenology, without knowing something about the history of the subject. I know that this might be contested by those for whom philosophy merely consists in the study of philosophical problems. But these problems also have a history and their nature has changed in accordance with changes in our culture, science and technology.

The need for some understanding of the history of phenomenology is particularly important, since so much of the subject stems from the work of the founding fathers of the movement — Brentano and Husserl. Some knowledge of its origins is therefore of value to anyone coming fresh to the study of phenomenology. It is also useful for those of us who know something about the subject, since it prevents us from making the mistakes the founders of the movement made, as well as enabling us to see what their aims really were and how they differed from those of other philosophers.

I first met Herbert in 1965 at a meeting of the Society for Phenomenology and Existential Philosophy in Madison, Wisconsin. I remember him coming up to me with a smile and asking if I was Wolfe Mays who had written a favourable review of the *Movement* in *Philosophical Books*. From that time onwards we became firm friends, and I felt towards him as one might to an elder, wiser brother. I must, however, have seen Herbert at the International Congress of Philosophy in Brussels which we had both attended in 1953, although at that time my interest in Continental philosophy was somewhat peripheral.

My meeting with Herbert at Madison led me to attend the 1966 workshop on phenomenology at Washington University which he organized, and where I got to know him better. Apart from taking part in the programs of work there, which consisted in actually doing phenomenology: i.e. carrying out phenomenological observations and giving careful descriptions of them, I also gave a talk to the group on my recollections of Wittgenstein. Indeed, one of the exercises set us at the workshop had a delightful informal atmosphere about it. I still have memories of sailing down the Mississippi on a paddle steamer, and seeing the St. Louis Saarinen Gateway Arch from various perspectives as we moved along the river. We learnt from each other, whether we were teachers or students, what philosophising together really meant. I remember particularly well a convivial evening at Herbert's home where, among other things, we sang "The Phenomenologist's Song". I wrote a report of my experiences of the workshop which appeared in *The Philosophical Quarterly*, in July 1967.

Herbert and I have since then frequently corresponded with each other, despite the vicissitudes of an indifferent air-mail service. I have on a number of occasions been a welcome guest at his home in St. Louis, and once shared rooms with him at Trinity College, Dublin, where we were attending a European Philosophy Conference. He was, I know, disappointed when I decided not to take a permanent appointment in America. He had hoped that I would be much closer geographically to him, instead of being separated by a three-thousand-mile stretch of the Atlantic.

If anyone was the spiritual godfather of the *Journal of the British Society for Phenomenology* it was Herbert. Apart from helpful advice as to the layout of the journal and ways of advertising it, he contributed to the first number (Jan. 1970) two pieces, "Husserl in England: Facts and Lessons" and "Notes on the text of Husserl's Syllabus (of the London Lectures)". He has himself in this way done something to bring about a change in the fortunes of phenomenology in Britain, which he once described as being a low ebb. There may not be a full tide yet, but the waves are beginning to lap at the feet of the philosophical establishment.

Herbert was responsible for getting Richard Palmer's new translation of Husserl's *Encyclopaedia Britannica* article[4] published in the journal, together with an introduction to Husserl's "Syllabus for the Paris Lectures"[5] as well as a translation of the syllabus. Apart from his other contributions to the journal, what was of considerable interest and value was Herbert's account, in his paper "Visual Perception Before and After a Cataract Operation",[6] of his perceptual experiences before and after undergoing the operation. His observations and analyses are worthy of careful study by any student of visual perception.

As a phenomenologist Herbert has, like Ingarden, definite realist inclinations. These seem to have been derived from his Munich teacher Pfänder, whose work he has tried to make better known to a wider philosophical public. He thinks that Pfänder's posthumous work contains a valid alternative to Husserl's radical phenomenology without its idealist conclusions. It is doubtful, however, whether Husserl was an idealist in the pejorative subjective sense, anymore than was Berkeley or Mach. He would describe himself rather as a transcendental idealist. Husserl himself strongly denied Ryle's appellation of him as a solipsist, something Herbert drew my attention to. And I am not sure whether a realist approach in philosophy does not involve as many assumptions as does an idealist one, except that they interpret experience from different conceptual standpoints.

Although Herbert believes that phenomenology can provide a minimum of phenomenal certainty, he nevertheless differs from someone like Husserl, since he sees the quest for ultimate apodictic certainty as will-o'-the-wisp. Our experience, he argues, cannot be made understandable by simple description without interpretation entering in and this itself requires later verification. Further, he believes that the boundaries of phenomenological knowledge need to be extended by something like a seek-and-find technique. And he hopes "that such a self-critical but expanded phenomenology will also leave room for and promote the reintegration of phenomenology and transphenomenological science as a legitimate extrapolation of phenomenology".[7]

But Herbert has also another major ambition, that of promoting the doing of phenomenology by a combination of individual and group research. This, he tells us, led to the pilot experiment of the five Washington University workshops in phenomenology, which he hopes will be continued and developed by others in the future. I have every sympathy with Herbert's pioneering efforts here. I benefitted considerably from attending the 1966 workshop, as I learned something about the way experience can be directly studied by phenomenological techniques. It seems to me that we need more such first-hand accounts of experience.

Too many writers on phenomenology and existential philosophy rely on the observations, interpretations and analyses given by such thinkers as Husserl, Heidegger or Merleau-Ponty, without giving us much by way of their own. But even Homer nods occasionally. These thinkers may not always have been correct in their reported observations and analyses. It would be wrong to regard their writings as if they had been handed down like the tablets of law from Mount Sinai, and to assume that our task was simply to add a gloss to them. This can only lead to a scholasticism of texts.

I appreciate that one may be unable or unwilling to do phenomenology in this active sense. One may rather wish to explicate the writings of important thinkers, for the help they may give us in unravelling the complex warp and woof of experience. This is certainly a legitimate enterprise, as such explication can make clear the ideas of these writers, and show their relevance to the questions we are faced with today. But the student can only benefit from reading such commentaries if the commentator tries to put the philosopher's theories, observations, and conclusions into a readily understandable form.

I have read many papers on phenomenology and existential philosophy over the last decade or so. Some of them use the technical jargon of the philosopher's views they discuss without attempting to translate them into a meaningful English. Expressions which convey sense in German or French, may not do so in English if we are simply given a transliteration of the original terms. I would not dispute that philosophy has a place for technical terms and that common sense language and ordinary usage cannot always deal with the richness and complexity of our experience. However, these terms need careful definition and explanation, so that they are understandable to those who meet them for the first time.

When I once suggested to an author of a piece on Heidegger that he ought to rephrase it in comprehensible English, rather than simply transliterating Heidegger's Germanic vocabulary, his reply was that I was showing my true colours as an analytic philosopher. He went on to say that he was not going to distort his ideas by expressing them in a simplified form, so as to get his paper published. These are admirable sentiments, but they don't help to bridge the knowledge gap for the reader who has difficulties in understanding Heidegger's subtleties of thought and expression. It might be said that some of Heidegger's terms defy translation. But I refuse to believe that we can't do good philosophy in English or for that matter in Polish or Japanese, as well as in German. I am told that Ingarden used to write his books first in Polish and then translate them into German. If Heidegger had been able to translate his German text into English, his philosophy might have taken a different turn.

To return to the question of "first hand" phenomenology: what Husserl, for example, is doing in his fine introspective analyses, is in principle not all that different from what some modern psychologists are doing on a more behavioural level, in the field of cognition and concept formation, although probably not as adequately. Herbert refers to Charles Spearman,[8] an English psychologist, who put forward a theory of cognition based on self-evidence. Spearman, who had attended Husserl's lectures at Göttingen, noted that Husserl's own procedure as he "described it to me himself — only differed from that of the best experimentalists dealing with similar problems in that he had nobody but himself as experimental subject".[9]

At a later date Spearman tried to see if he could apply Husserl's procedures to his own experimental work. He felt that there was a great need in psychology for its present crude descriptions to be replaced "by some such finer delineation as that which was being taught by this sage of Göttingen". Spearman went on to say that, "The general re-expression of mental experience in the terms of Husserl — with or without attempted emendations of my own — did show itself to be quite feasible, and even to result in greater descriptive exactitude".[10] Nevertheless, he came to the conclusion that it did not throw light on problems in which anyone was interested. The Achilles heel in Husserl's approach was that it apparently failed to be scientifically useful.[11]

To this one might reply that the sort of immediately useful results Spearman was looking for, were quite different from the sort of problems Husserl was interested in. Unlike Spearman, who eventually came to concern himself with the elaboration of statistical tests for validating intelligence tests,[12] Husserl was primarily interested in the relation of theoretical notions to our actual cognitive processes. As an example of this, we may refer to the distinction he draws between generalising and formalising abstraction. In the former, we deal with such notions as red, colour, triangle, spatial form, etc.; in the latter, with such concepts as object, class, member of a class, relation, transitive relation, whole, part, number, etc. The correct analysis of these concepts is not something the man in the street is concerned with when he gossips with his fellows over a pint of beer in the pub. Husserl's enquiry is in the main of concern to philosophers in their technical discussions of conceptual questions. It deals with levels of abstraction with which the ordinary person is quite unfamiliar: his day-to-day transactions are usually on a more concrete plane.

It can be reasonably argued that the complex analysis of perception and of cognition, in which Husserl was interested, can only be carried out by those who can take up a philosophically informed approach to experience. This may be one of the reasons why some psychological laboratory experiments dealing with intellectual processes have a certain naïveté about them, as neither the experimented nor the subject generally seems to show much insight into the logical or philosophical questions, which many of these experiments touch on.

It was not until Piaget came on the scene that a serious attempt was made to study experimentally such concepts as classes, relations and numbers. Husserl's studies have evidently some applications here. Consider, for example, his account in the *Philosophie der Arithmetik* of *figurale Momente*,[13] the way we become aware of in perception of numerical groups as Gestalt-like configurations, which he contrasts with number on a categorical level, where, for example, the number three is regarded as a synthesis of three ordered abstract units. This interestingly enough is identical with Piaget's distinction between the figural and operational aspects of knowledge.

When discussing the way number develops in the child, Piaget tells us that Husserl makes a fundamental opposition between colligation (or additive operations) which give rise to sets which are categories, and global perceptual qualities, which he calls *quasi qualitative Momente* or *figurale Momente*. Piaget finds the elementary enumeration in the child is in terms of such global qualities, and not in terms of colligation. At this level there is as yet "no operation by which the child can colligate the units into a real and stable whole".[14]

In other words, number at this stage is for the child only a perceptual grouping. He is still unable to carry out additive operations — to synthesise on a cognitive level a series of abstract units into a new sum.

What Piaget's work does show is that Husserl's account of number is much more directly rooted in our actual experience, than is Frege's analysis of it in terms of a class of classes. As Findlay remarks, Husserl unlike Frege was not concerned to establish watertight definitions and axioms for arithmetic and build them into an all-embracing system, without regard to what we actually understand by these notions. He tries rather "to develop a rational genealogy of our arithmetical notions and methods out of primitive mental acts and confrontations".[15] What is of interest is that Piaget should have confirmed in his developmental studies of the growth of number, the introspective analyses carried out by Husserl using himself as an experimental subject. This is something Spearman apparently missed when he failed to find in Husserl's studies anything scientifically useful.

In the field of perception careful, phenomenological observations and analyses may enable us to decide, for example, whether Gestalt theory or associationism gives a more adequate account of the actual facts of perception. And comparative observations like those reported on by Herbert in his paper on visual perception before and after a cataract operation, can be both clinically and philosophically rewarding.

I hope that Herbert's work on ontology, ethics, philosophy of law and in phenomenology proper, will become better known to a wider philosophical audience. But if one restricts oneself to his work as a historian of the phenomenological movement, one must realise that he is not a detached observer standing outside it. He is within the movement itself, and is involved in the making of its very history. Speaking for myself, I am sure that my interests in phenomenology would have been different if I had not had to review Herbert's book some twenty years ago. And if the book had not appeared, phenomenology in Britain might have still continued to be at a low ebb.

NOTES

1. Herbert Spiegelberg, *The Phenomenological Movement*, Vols. I and II (The Hague: Martinus Nijhoff, 1959).
2. Spiegelberg, pp. 501 and 615.
3. Herbert Spiegelberg, *Phenomenology in Psychology and Psychiatry* (Evanston: Northwestern University Press, 1972).
4. See his *Gesetz und Sittengesetz* (Zurich: Max Niehaus, 1935).
5. *Journal of the British Society for Phenomenology*, Vol. 2, No. 2.
6. *Journal of the British Society for Phenomenology*, Vol. 7, No. 1.

7. *Journal of the British Society for Phenomenology*, Vol. 8, No. 1.

8. Herbert Spiegelberg, *Doing Phenomenology* (The Hague: Martinus Nijhoff, 1975), pp. xi–xv.

9. Spiegelberg, *Phenomenology in Psychology and Psychiatry*, p. 35.

10. Charles Spearman in *History of Psychology in Autobiography*, Vol. 1, ed. Carl Murchison (Worcester, Mass.: Clark University Press, 1930), p. 305.

11. Spearman, p. 312.

12. Spearman, p. 319.

13. Edmund Husserl, *Philosophie der Arithmetik* (Halle: C.E. Pfeffer, 1891), Chap. 11.

14. Jean Piaget, *The Child's Conception of Number*, trans. C. Cattegno and F.M. Hodgson (London: Routledge and Kegan Paul, 1952), p. 199.

15. J.M. Findlay, "Translator's Introduction" to Edmund Husserl, *Logical Investigations*, Vols. I and II (London: Routledge and Kegan Paul, 1970), p. 13.

About the Contributors

THOMAS ATTIG is Associate Professor of Philosophy at Bowling Green State University. He received his Ph.D. degree from Washington University (St. Louis) in 1973. He is co-author of *Introduction to Philosophy: From Wonder to World View* and *Values and Society: An Introduction to Ethics and Social Philosophy*. He has also published several articles in, and reviewed books for, the *Journal of the British Society for Phenomenology* and *Death Education*.

ROBERT BERNASCONI has been a lecturer in the Department of Philosophy at the University of Essex since 1976. He has written essays on Heidegger and on Levinas, and is currently editing a collection of Gadamer's essays on art.

PHILIP BOSSERT is President of Hawaii Loa College. He received his Ph.D. degree from Washington University (St. Louis) in 1973. He has been Executive Director of the Hawaii Committee for the Humanities, and has published *An Introduction to Husserl's Logical Investigations* as well as edited *Phenomenological Perspectives*.

DAVID CARR is Professor of Philosophy at the University of Ottawa. He received his Ph.D. degree from Yale University in 1964. He has translated Husserl's *The Crisis of European Sciences and Transcendental Phenomenology* and is the author of *Phenomenology and the Problem of History*. He has also contributed articles to various journals and collections.

EDWARD CASEY is Professor of Philosophy and Chairman of the Department of Philosophy, State University of New York at Stony Brook. He received his Ph.D. degree from Northwestern University in 1967. He is the author of *Imagining: A Phenomenological Study* and translator of works by Mikel Dufrenne. He is presently at work on *Remembering*, a sequel to *Imagining*. He is also the author of numerous articles in aesthetics, philosophical psychology, and the philosophy of mind.

FRANCIS DUNLOP teaches philosophy at Cambridge Institute of Education, Cambridge, England. He received his Ph.D. degree from the University of London in 1974. He has published numerous articles in phenomenological philosophy and the philosophy of education, mostly in British periodicals. Dr. Dunlop has also authored *The Education of Feeling and Emotion* (London: Allen & Unwin, 1983), which is a broadly phenomenological treatment of feeling, emotion, mood and impulse.

FRANK FLINN received his Bachelor of Divinity degree from Harvard University and his Ph.D. degree from St. Michael's College, the University of Toronto. He has taught at St. John's College, Santa Fe; the University of Toronto, and St. Louis University. He has contributed to *Women and Religion, A Time for Consideration*; and *George Grant in Process*. He is editor of *Horizons & Hermeutics* and *The Purposes of Christ*.

WILLIAM HAMRICK is Professor of Philosophy at Southern Illinois University—Edwardsville. He received his Ph.D. degree from Vanderbilt University in 1971. He has contributed several articles to, and reviewed books for, the *Journal of the British Society for Phenomenology, Process Studies, Man and World, Dialectics and Humanism, The Journal of Value Inquiry*, and the *Review of Existential Psychology & Psychiatry*. He is a member of the Executive Committee of the British Society for Phenomenology and of the Society for the Study of Process Philosophies. He is also an Assistant Editor of the *Journal of the British Society for Phenomenology*. At present, he is completing a book-length manuscript entitled *An Existential Phenomenology of Law: Maurice Merleau-Ponty*.

BARRY JONES is presently lecturing at the University of Manchester while completing his doctoral thesis under the direction of Wolfe Mays. He received his B.A. in Philosophy (First Class) at the University of Manchester in 1977, writing his undergraduate dissertation on Kant. He is an Assistant Editor of the *Journal of the British Society for Phenomenology*, has reviewed several books for the same Journal, and is organizing its Sartre Memorial Issue. His published works include "Phenomenology, Object Theory and Semantics" and "Was Husserl a Fregean?".

JAMES MARSH is Professor of Philosophy at St. Louis University. He has also been Visiting Professor of Philosophy at Fordham University. He received his Ph.D. degree from Northwestern University in 1971. He has published a variety of articles in several journals in phenomenology, existentialism, and critical social theory. At present, he is completing a book-length manuscript entitled *Post-Cartesian Meditations*.

WILLIAM McBRIDE is Professor of Philosophy at Purdue University and former Executive Co-Secretary of the Society for Phenomenology and Existential Philosophy. He received his Ph.D. degree from Yale University in 1964. His published works include *Fundamental Change in Law and Society: Hart and Sartre on Revolution; The Philosophy of Marx*, and *Social Theory at a Crossroads*.

KARL SCHUHMANN, former scientific collaborator of the Husserl-Archives at Louvain, is Professor of Philosophy at the State University of Utrecht (The Netherlands). He re-edited Edmund Husserl's *Ideen I* (1976) and compiled the *Index nominum zum Nachlass von Edmund Husserl* (1975) and the *Husserl-Chronik* (1977). In addition to a book on Fichte (*Die Grundlage der Wissenschaftslehre in ihrem Umrisse*, 1968), he has written several books on Husserl (*Die Fundamentalbetrachtung der Phänomenologie und phäno-menologische Philosophie*, 1973; *Die Staatsphilosophie Edmund Husserls*, 1981).

HUGH SILVERMAN is Associate Professor of Philosophy and Com-parative Literature at the State University of New York at Stony Brook. He is also Executive Director of the Society for Phenomenology and Existential Philosophy; Secretary-Treasurer of the International Association for Philos-ophy and Literature; and Executive Committee Member of the British Society for Phenomenology. He is the editor of *Piaget, Philosophy and the Human Sciences* (1980), co-editor of *Jean-Paul Sartre: Contemporary Approaches to His Philosophy* (1980), translator of Merleau-Ponty and others, and author of more than twenty-five articles in continental philosophy. He has also been a Visiting Professor at Duquesne University, New York University, and the University of Warwick (England). In 1981–82, he was an ACLS Fellow.

KENNETH STIKKERS is Assistant 'Professor of Philosophy at Seattle University. He received his Ph.D. degree in 1981 from DePaul University. He has also taught at DePaul University and at Loyola University of Chicago. He has studied philosophy at the University of Minnesota as well. He is the author of numerous articles in phenomenology, chiefly dealing with the thought of Max Scheler.

Editor's Introduction

The origin of this book lay in a conversation one April evening in Oxford, during a meeting of the British Society for Phenomenology. Certain philosophers, including some whose papers appear below, were lamenting the comparative scarcity of original printed work in phenomenology. The feeling was that, as we moved into the last two decades of philosophizing in this century, much of phenomenology was rather stuck in a reiterative pattern of either writing about what the method(s) is (are) (or could be) or, even more commonly, derivative explications of the works of major figures in the movement. The focus of the discussion then became whether phenomenology had actually spent itself in this century of its origin — and with which it is roughly the same age — and would not survive into the next.

In the weeks immediately following the Oxford meeting, this conversation crystallized into a challenge to create a forum for presenting original essays *in*, and not merely *about*, phenomenology. I invited as participants a variety of younger phenomenologists whose writings I knew and respected. As the reader will have observed above, the contributors form a truly international and diverse group of scholars, coming as they do from the United States, Canada, the United Kingdom, and the Netherlands.

No restrictions were placed on the various participants' conceptions of phenomenological method(s). Quite to the contrary, one calculated advantage of the book is to disclose diverse interpretations of the method(s). Indeed, in this context, the collection of essays itself would do phenomenology in the sense of exhibiting the phenomenon of phenomenology itself. It would exhibit the phenomenon in the Heideggerean sense as *"that which shows itself in itself, the manifest"*. [1] Moreover, this was intended not only spatially, in the sense of the presentation of a book of essays, but also temporally by situating phenomenology within the ongoing conversations which make up the history of philosophy. This is so because most of the authors develop their phenomenological perspectives while continually taking their bearings from a variety of philosophers throughout the history of philosophy. Thus the reader will find as many references to, say, Plato, Aristotle, Augustine, Descartes, Kant, Marx, and

Nietzsche, as he will to Husserl, Heidegger, Scheler, Merleau-Ponty, and so forth.

Still less, of course, were any restrictions placed on contributors in their choice of topics. They were even free to critically interrogate phenomenology itself, as some did, provided that they did not merely talk about it. The reader may expect to find, therefore, original philosophizing at work even in papers the titles of which make them appear as derivative commentaries in the sense we wished to avoid.

One example of this fact stands out in its own right as a singularly attractive addition to our collection. Karl Schuhmann's "Structuring the Phenomenological Field: Reflections on a Daubert Manuscript" marks the first time that a crucially important slice from the very origins of the phenomenological movement has, at long last, found its way into print.[2] But not only does the brief Daubert text itself constitute original phenomenologizing, but also Professor Schuhmann charts its significance in a highly original and imaginative fashion.

Schuhmann also recounts part of the story of how Daubert's papers have been rescued from the oblivion that almost engulfed them. In so doing, he makes clear the central role played by Herbert Spiegelberg, and this fact comprises a second reason why the essay is particularly appropriate for our collection. That is, a few months after the meeting of the British Society for Phenomenology referred to above, Herbert Spiegelberg happened to have his seventy-fifth birthday. Several of his friends, including the present author, wished to honor him on this occasion,[3] and so the dedicatory purpose of this volume, as well as the idea of Wolfe Mays' "Preface", came into being.

Thus all the participants contributed their papers with the double objective of increasing the body of original literature in phenomenology as well as appropriately honoring someone whose research and other professional activities, not least his phenomenological workshops, have made possible so many subsequent advances in the field. Those who really know him are aware of the fact that he combines in one concrete unity two rather contrary attitudes. The first is a rootedness in, and concern for, the past — and this achieves expression in an encyclopedic knowledge of the texts. The second attitude, on the other hand, is a future-looking concern for new knowledge, a zest for — to use a Whiteheadian phrase — "adventures of ideas". From my study window I see him in the mornings eagerly hurrying off for the library, a spectacle which always conjurs up the memory of the last sentence of Gabriel Marcel's *Homo Viator*: "And, when the given hour shall strike, arouse us, eager as the traveller who straps on his rucksack while beyond the misty window-pane the earliest rays of dawn are faintly visible!"[4] In this context, then, we are pleased to have the opportunity to offer the reader Herbert Spiegelberg's "Epilogue of Third-

XX

Generation Phenomenologists" which was written expressly for this volume.

I should like to conclude this brief introduction by thanking the Graduate School and the School of Humanities of Southern Illinois University at Edwardsville for financial assistance in the preparation of this manuscript and especially for the typing assistance of Ms. Patty Birky, without which there could have been little hope of this book seeing the light of day. To all who have helped along the way I am deeply grateful. Finally, a brief linguistic note: in the following pages I wished to avoid sexist language by replacing the ambiguous generic "he" ("him", etc.) with a convention suitable for giving due regard to women. But various substitute conventions have all proved too linguistically awkward. Therefore, I have reverted to the generic "he" ("him", etc.), but in recompense, I wish to disclaim any intended sexism.

NOTES

1. Martin Heidegger, *Being and Time*, trans. John Macquarrie and Edward Robinson (London: SCM Press Ltd., 1962), p. 51. *Sein und Zeit* (Tübingen: Max Niemeyer Verlag, 1967), p. 28: "Als Bedeutung des Ausdrucks *'Phänomen'* ist daher *festzuhalten: das Sich-an-ihm-selbst-zeigende, das Offenbare*".
2. This is almost completely true. The only exception to this claim of which I am aware is a photograph of one of Daubert's pages written in his difficult shorthand. It appeared in Eberhard Avé-Lallemant, ed., *Die Nachlässe der Münchener Phänomenologen in der Bayerischen Staatsbibliothek* (Wiesbaden: Otto Harrassowitz, 1975), p. 132.
3. See also in his honor Philip J. Bossert, ed., *Phenomenological Perspectives* (The Hague: Martinus Nijhoff, 1975).
4. Gabriel Marcel, *Homo Viator,* trans. Emma Crauford (New York: Harper Torchbooks, 1962), p. 270.

I. EPISTEMOLOGY AND ONTOLOGY

Structuring the Phenomenological Field:
Reflections on a Daubert Manuscript
by
Karl Schuhmann

I. A Note on Daubert's Life

Even among phenomenologists, the name of the Munich philosopher, Johannes Daubert (1877–1947) is practically forgotten today. Up to now, his life and thought were shrouded in deep darkness. But thanks to Herbert Spiegelberg's efforts to rescue his posthumous papers, it has become possible to publish here for the first time a text written by this highly original and extraordinary personality.

Daubert's presence in the conscious horizon of active phenomenologizing seems to have subsided at a quite early stage: it cannot be traced beyond World War I. Gerda Walther's case may serve as a revealing example for this claim. Although she had studied under the leading Munich phenomenologist Alexander Pfänder, Daubert's life-long friend, and under Husserl, himself on most cordial terms with Daubert, in her memoirs she apostrophizes him already with regard to her Freiburg years (1917–19) as "the legendary Daubert".[1] And Max Scheler, who in earlier years had participated in discussions with Daubert, in a 1927 manuscript in which he outlines the beginnings of phenomenology in Munich, notes between brackets: "Unknown phenomenologist Daubert".[2]

This evidence of the near-total eclipse of Daubert's name and philosophizing sharply contrasts with the estimate of the inside experts. Herbert Spiegelberg was the first one to point out that Daubert had been "perhaps the most influential member of the Munich circle",[3] and Eberhard Avé-Lallemant assigned to him "a key position of a special kind"[4] in this circle. This view is impressively confirmed by Pfänder himself who, in a manuscript note from 1929 on the origins of the phenomenological movement, puts Daubert's name next to Husserl's as being one of its two fountain-heads.[5] In the same vein a year later, Wilhelm Schapp, who knew Daubert since 1908, stated in retrospect that "in the first decenium of the new century the method of phenomenology had been set forth, in Göttingen and Munich, by Husserl, Daubert, and Pfänder".[6] Indeed already in 1912, Pfänder's Russian student, Arnold Karelitzki, had ac-

W.S. Hamrick (ed.) *Phenomenology in Practice and Theory.*
© 1985 Martinus Nijhoff Publishers, Dordrecht/Boston/Lancaster
ISBN 90 247 2926 2. Printed in the Netherlands.

knowledged Daubert's prominent position when, in the *curriculum vitae* appended to his doctoral thesis, he wrote: "I am greatly obliged to all my German teachers, but above all I am deeply indebted to the private scholar Johannes Daubert, to Professor Alexander Pfänder and the *Privatdozent* Dr. Max Scheler".[7] He thus credited Daubert, who held no academic position whatsoever, even before his teacher Pfänder who had supervised his dissertation! Also, five years earlier, one of Lipps' students, Wolf Bohrn, in the preface of his 1907 doctoral thesis, acknowledged that he owed most of his intellectual training "to discussions . . . , especially with Johannes Daubert, Alois Fischer, and Moritz Geiger".[8] Therefore, Wilhelm Schapp was doubtlessly right when, as late as 1959, he stated: "A main merit concerning the spreading of phenomenology in Munich belongs to Daubert. It would be worthwhile to write a work on Daubert".[9]

The picture of Daubert's impact during the pre-war period of phenomenology would remain incomplete if no mention were made of his unique relation to Husserl. In early 1902, Daubert, then an unknown 25-jear-old student of the Munich philosopher and psychologist, Theodor Lipps, had come across Husserl's recently published *Logische Untersuchungen*. He studied both volumes intensively and immediately recognized the first-rate importance of its revolutionizing approach. So he went to Göttingen by bicycle to visit Husserl. After hours of discussion, Husserl exclaimed: "Here is someone who has read — and understood my *Logical Investigations!*"[10] Back in Munich, he induced his fellow students (among them Pfänder, Geiger, Reinach and Conrad) to study the book thoroughly, and they alike hailed it as a breakthrough in philosophy congenial to their own efforts. "There was no event surpassing this", Theodor Conrad judged later on.[11] Two years later, the Munich group of phenomenologists had become constituted. So Moritz Geiger was certainly right when, more than two decades later, he stated that Daubert had "contributed" more than anyone else to the becoming known of the *Logical Investigations*.[12] During the Summer term, 1905, Daubert, together with several other members of the Munich group, studied with Husserl. This was the so-called "Munich invasion" of Göttingen. Eventually in August 1905, this encounter between Husserl and Daubert resulted in "the momentous joint summer vacation in Seefeld",[13] during which Husserl, Daubert and Pfänder discussed — partly together with some other Munich participants — a broad range of problems, including perception, the ego, and intersubjectivity.

It seems that sometime around 1906, Daubert definitely abandoned earlier plans to complete his years of study by writing a doctoral dissertation. From that time on, he settled in Munich as a private scholar. He never had felt happy about the idea of publishing books or articles. Nevertheless, he continued to write down his reflections in the strange and unusual variety of shorthand which he seems to have learned at school. Still, it was exclusively through lectures before friends and personal discussions that he exerted his unmistakable influence on the Munich group.

At least one episode of this period should be mentioned, namely his encounter with Brentano during the Summer of 1907. In March of that same year, Husserl had visited his venerated teacher in Florence and had tried to explain to the latter the meaning of his earlier battle against psychologism. But his efforts were in vain: "we didn't reach an understanding", Husserl reported. [14] He therefore pinned his hopes on Daubert and his ability for clearcut formulation as being a better advocate of his case. Thus when Brentano visited his brother in Munich, in July 1907, the aged and nearly blind philosopher indeed invited Daubert to discuss with him psychologism and categorical intuition. [15] Although they did not reach an agreement either, Daubert still seems to have got on with Brentano considerably better than Husserl had done.

The importance of Daubert's regular discussions with Husserl in Göttingen – on his trips between Munich and his home town, Braunschweig, Daubert used to stay there for at least one full day – cannot be assessed adequately as yet. But it is known that he always was a particularly cherished guest in Husserl's house. When, in 1907, Husserl conceived the idea of founding a phenomenological journal, it was a matter of course to him that first of all he approach Daubert to ask his opinion. In 1912, when this plan finally had materialized, Husserl depended heavily on his friend to contribute an article to the first issue of the new *Jahrbuch*. Daubert complied, but his voluminous manuscripts did not get beyond draft stage, and so he finally decided against publication. A year later, he met with Husserl in Switzerland for two weeks of discussion on the revised version of the famous sixth *Logical Investigation*.

The outbreak of the war put an end to Daubert's philosophical activities – at least temporarily – because he, like most other phenomenologists, volunteered for the army. During four full years, he was worn down by the "steel thunder-storms" (Ernst Jünger) of war. "It has exhausted me almost completely", he reported to Husserl in April 1919. Under these circumstances he lacked the composure to keep up his contacts with Husserl, although the latter ardently yearned for it. When in October 1917, Daubert's friend, August Gallinger, on his way through Freiburg, paid a one-hour visit to Husserl, the "master charged him to tell Daubert that he missed receiving news from him". "Even if you don't feel in a position", Gallinger wrote to Daubert, "to carry on the scientific exchange of views, he yet feels himself personally so close to you that he gladly receives any manifestation of life from you. He always has had so many impulses from you that he misses you painfully, scientifically as well as personally".

After his discharge from the army, Daubert exchanged the pen for the plough. He bought a farm just outside Munich to support his wife and himself. Except for discussions with Pfänder, who spent his vacation on the farm from time to time, Daubert seemed to have given up all philosophizing. Nevertheless, when around Christmas 1923 he sent a turkey to Husserl and his family, Husserl responded with a detailed letter on his actual work and about their relations in earlier years. He not only affirmed that Daubert had understood him and his philosophical task better than he himself, but he also confessed that originally he had tried to obtain a chair in philosophy in Munich for the very reason that he wanted to work in Daubert's vicinity and together with him. This "turkey letter", as it is called, may be said to be quite a unique piece in Husserl's correspondence because it exhibits his view of Daubert as the only philosopher congenial to him.

Around 1930, Daubert explicitly took up his philosophical activities again, trying to prepare an article for the then forthcoming Pfänder Festschrift. But after having drafted about 150 shorthand manuscript pages, he once more withdrew his promise. After this, he does not seem to have written down any further philosophical reflections. A note in a local newspaper on the occasion of his sixtieth birthday in 1937 simply mentions his sociability with young people and his fondness of motor-cycling. As in the case of Wittgenstein, his fellow villagers apparently had no notion of his philosophical past.

Finally, it should not go unmentioned here that Herbert Spiegelberg, when he was about to leave the Continent in 1936, had a memorable encounter with Husserl. The latter, overworked because of his revision of the first installment of *The Crisis of European Sciences*, bitterly complained about the Munich philosophers whom he suspected of having broken away from true phenomenology. The young scholar got no fair chance for a reply. So at the end of Husserl's philippic, Spiegelberg simply asked: "Could I do you some favor?" "Yes", Husserl replied, "could you please provide me with Daubert's address?" (Daubert had moved to another farm in 1932; Spiegelberg at that time, of course, neither knew nor could come to know his address.) But it is characteristic that even at so late a date Husserl obviously saw in Daubert someone who could interpret his aspirations and ideas to other people, and at the same time function as a faithful touchstone for his own attempts to build up a well-founded philosophy.

Following the eventual initiative taken by Spiegelberg, Daubert's papers were deposited in the Bavarian State Library in 1967.[16] Although they were thus preserved from possible destruction, they remained scientifically inaccessible — even after Dr. Avé-Lallemant had classified them — until I managed to decipher Daubert's shorthand in 1976.[17] In 1979, the State University of Utrecht made the necessary funds available to Dr. Reinhold Smid for the transcription, under my direction, of the file Daubertiana A I 1, entitled *Phänomenologie*, from which stems the Daubert text translated here. While this text may speak for itself, I am solely responsible for the interpretative essay appended to it. It is meant to spell out what, in today's situation, might be the relevance of a voice that, for more than a half century, had crept into the silent materiality of the letter.

II. The Text of Daubert's Manuscript

Phenomenological and Transcendental Method in Theory of Cognition

Transcendental theory of cognition starts from the contrast between the practical naive view of the world and the one the objects exhibit in our continually progressing cognition. So, things are nothing but representations naively made up for practical needs. Naive conception makes things come into being and pass away (it makes them the subjects of existence and nonexistence). Such things, in the sense of persevering fundaments of all statements on relations and changes, do not indeed exist. Naive man works with such representations because in practice they can most easily be handled (this is Natorp's interpretation of Aristotle in his *Plato*, p. 383). Kant has pronounced the result of the great revolution of the sciences and dethroned Aristotle by stating: Things consist of relations throughout. Among them there are indeed self-sufficient and persevering ones, and only through these a "determined object" is given to us. More pointedly, this statement means: In scientific reflection, the empirical object dissolves into an infinity of relations. Even the points of reference of the relation are never given to us in an absolute way, but must be fixed hypothetically. Only a cognition, deepened step by step, of the relations themselves (especially of the time-relations of events, i.e. of the "laws" of nature in the narrower meaning of this term) leads to an increasing exactness in the fixation of the points of reference.

With this, the thing as the persevering foundation of existence is not primarily given, but stands for the ideal goal of endless task. The inquiry into the true subject of motion, matter (as one calls it), has proven this even more clearly (Natorp, *Plato*, p. 382).

So, the object is the x of the equation in which cognition consists. It is determined through its relation to given quantities alone, and they again can be determined only through their relation to other ones.

Phenomenological reflection upon the thing starts from givenness: the colors, forms, and the unifying relations between them. Thereby it will not simply restate the popular view, but makes comparisons and asks for the legitimacy to bestow on determinate facts it has in mind, these or those determinations. In the answers to these questions about legitimacy, in these demands, a determinate objective world, the world pertaining to the senses as it surrounds us, becomes constituted. This is a totally pure and presuppositionless reflection upon givenness and the phenomena that hover before us and that we are unambiguously aware of in perceiving and thinking.[18]

Transcendental reflection here sees a presupposition it will not take for granted. Already in our data it sees relations to a reflecting subject. By this subject, one could understand 1) the always differing psychic individuals: they indeed do not come into question; 2) the sensuous subject common to all of them; 3) the subject of the *a priori* sensuous forms common to all of them. It now endeavors to eliminate this subject in order to look for the object-in-itself. In this case, it would not object to the question of the object-for-us.

Materially seen now, the question arises: Can we ever get out of such a phenomenological standpoint? Is not even the x an x-for-us? After all, we cannot even think of an "In-itself" unless we are the In-itself. In all thinking the phenomenological standpoint is implied. What sense can it still make now to relate the thing (x) to subjects possessing sensuous perception and the power of intellectual formation? That which is stripped off here from the psychological subject? One relates the thing to its fixed and given properties. This thing may be an x, but the important point is that this x is an x for us and that its meaning, therefore, can be cleared up as that of a bearer of functions.

III. Phenomenology and Phenomenality: An Interpretation

Daubert's manuscript (he dated it later on "about October 1905", i.e., shortly after the Seefeld vacation) apparently consists of two well-distinguished parts: a first one on transcendental (i.e., Neo-Kantian) theory, and a second one on phenomenology. Also, the title ("Phenomenology and Transcendental Method . . .") suggests a division of this kind. But close inspection shows that these main parts each fall into two subsections, so that the manuscript performs a sequence of four steps. First, the realism of the natural attitude (of "naive conception", as Daubert has it) is described. Then Daubert moves on to transcendental theory which dissolves the object into an infinity of relations open to subjective exploration. Third, he points out that, according to phenomenological investigation, this subjective activity presupposes a certain pluriformity as well as connection among the original subjective data. The last step then consists of a reflection on the three earlier ones: it shows that in all of them the "phenomenological standpoint" is involved.

This diagnosis can be read in two rather different ways. On the one hand, one may interpret it as a material tripartition. The text then would perform a move from natural via transcendental to phenomenological reflection. The last step, in this case, would not further the material content of the analysis; it only seems to recognize that, since its very beginning, the reflective process took place within the unitary continuum of the phenomenological sphere. What in fact already had been there is eventually brought to explicit consciousness. The way of phenomenology thus apparently moves along the beaten paths of

Hegelianism: it leads from perception through science to a type of consciousness which, in the end, understands its own nature and, by this, becomes self-consciousness. Reflection is by intrinsic necessity driven to higher and higher levels of self-actualization until it finally comes to repose in itself.

Over against this, the text may also be considered as being arranged in a way that merely contrasts the pre-phenomenology attitudes (no matter whether naive or transcendental) and phenomenology proper. This second view would imply a bisection of its structure in the manner already mentioned. Phenomenology is, and remains, opposed to any other conception of the world, because it is the only one to "strip off" the factor of worldliness. By this, its activity of clearing up processes that take place in the life-world moves along in presuppositionless and radical steps. Only in this sphere can the "questions of legitimacy" be both raised and answered, because phenomenology alone is built on a soil that transcends the uncertainties and ambiguities of naturalness into a region of clear and distinct evidences.

What lies behind this embarrassing possibility of a double view on the status of phenomenology? Need one fear an irreparable break between two clashing and mutually exclusive perspectives? What is it about the nature of a reflection which permits this apparent dilemma? How can one, on the one hand, contrast phenomenology and the procedures of the natural sort (the second view) if phenomenology must be said (in accordance with the first view) to exhibit above all a higher and more adequate version of the various types of cognition preceding it? Is it not correct to state that naturalness, after all, is just a stir within the pure sphere of phenomenological life itself (the first view)? But what, then, about the substantial differences prevailing between the several attitudes — differences that can in no way be explained away or be undone (the second view)?

A reflection upon the relation of phenomenology to naturalness inevitably seems to end up in conflicting and, when considered in its totality, contradictory statements. One view sees all cognition implied in phenomenology (and phenomenology wrapped up in it), while the other draws a sharp dividing line between phenomenology and the remaining attitudes which it is meant to explain. But is this dualism indeed irreconcilable? Must one not concede that the mediating as well as the separating view both are *views*? They both, therefore, are results of viewing and offsprings of a subject's interpretation and of its looking at the phenomena it has. This interpreting activity in fact forms the unitary root of the monistic as well as of the pluralistic perspective under which phenomenology appears to itself. In the process of interpretation, the subject appropriates the phenomena and makes them become *its* objects. At the same time, however, it sets off against these havings and differentiates between two opposite poles of intentionality, restricting itself to just one of the two sides. Moreover, both perspectives can be shown to be interdependent and presup-

10

posing each other. The subject, in their relation, can be understood to enjoy a special asymmetric position only because it is part and parcel of the total phenomenal field. Conversely, the phenomena cannot be said to contain any objective features whatsoever without opposing their objectivity to a subject they have to expel from their own range, i.e., that transcends them. So, neither of the two phenomenological perspectives may be considered to be a last datum. Whenever one of them is focussed upon, its counterpart will irresistibly come to the fore. Both are but basic functions of, and the index of each other in, the original field of interpretation and of the constitution of phenomena. In their interrelationship, they behave by turns as theme and horizon, as text and context. But between elements of this kind "there is equality in interaction", as Herbert Spiegelberg once put it. [19]

The relation between consciousness and its object (= non-consciousness), between self-consciousness and consciousness, and finally between phenomenology and non-phenomenology, [20] is in each of these cases governed by this character of one-sided, internal self-transcendence (the objective side) or intentional reference (the subjective side). The material content of Daubert's own manuscript furnishes what easily might be the most fitting example to illustrate this. Its first part − except for the first phrase which, however, is of crucial importance, as it establishes the framework for all that follows − consists of nothing but an occasionally somewhat free excerpt from three pages of a book on Plato written by the Marburg Neo-Kantian philosopher, Paul Natorp. [21] To Natorp's analysis of the native notion of the given thing, or to the refined concept of an x as "the ideal goal" of research, Daubert opposed a fresh phenomenological description of the "world pertaining to the senses" and of the x as a "bearer of functions". A pre-phenomenological reflection upon the two possible attitudes towards the object is thus superseded by a fuller unfolding of their relatedness to the subject. But on the other hand, Natorp's text is for Daubert more than just a stepping-stone towards his own phenomenological reflection. This is evidenced not only by the ascending line of thought he constructs by deliberately inverting Natorp's original train of thought (Daubert treats Natorp's p. 383 prior to pp. 382 and 384). It is also spelled out in still greater detail by his contention that the "criticistic mode of inquiry" presupposes "phenomenological standpoint" is effectively implied in all thinking, even in the seemingly naive conception of the object. This virtual omnipresence of phenomenology is the deepest reason for the possibility of arriving at the entrance gate of pure phenomenologizing, despite the fact that we must necessarily start from the pre-given fixations permeating our historically conditioned life-world.

It is this power of assimilating even standpoints apparently widely diverging from it that accounts for the superiority of phenomenology over other attitudes. In contrast, transcendental theory set out by opposing the practical naive view. It remains bound to this opposition, so that it never will overcome disunion and duality. Transcendentalism is doomed to maintain itself by erecting a world of its own, a world behind sense and experience which is shared by no one else. One may express this dichotomy as the antagonism of practical and theoretical directedness, of naive and scientific attitudes, or of the empirical and the transcendental conceptions of things. In all these variations, it instances the general Aristotelian scheme of the difference between the first-for-us and the first-in-itself. According to this scheme (to which even the would-be Platonist, Natorp, stubbornly sticks), the first-for-us, after having served as the starting-point of investigation, is neglected and devalued for the benefit of a higher type of cognition. Accordingly, Neo-Kantian transcendentalism fails to break out of this self-made prison; it misses the necessary power of integration and will not get beyond the negative conclusion that "things, in the sense of persevering fundaments . . . do not exist". With this, it overlooks the importance and exact bearing of its own insight that, in naive life, things as persevering units are "made up for practical needs": they are results, by not origins. Making up (*zurechtmachen*) — Daubert takes this word from Natorp — was also Nietzsche's preferred term for designating the way in which identity and objectivity in things are brought about in practical life in accordance with its strivings and in conformity with the demands of self-preservation. This term indeed points to the derivative status of the notion of a "thing": a tenet uniting Nietzsche and phenomenology. According to both of them, the physical thing results from a successful (mis)interpretation of phenomenal materials. Through it also, the subject orients itself in a world by marking out its own place. This constitutive function of the physical thing in the substantiation of a subject's selfhood explains the failure of naive conception to see the use of regressive inquiry into this very function: it serves no purpose in practical life. The same factor also causes transcendentalism to underestimate the theoretical bearing of this function: because it arises from the sole needs of life, it does not affect an attitude that tries to transcend this realm of immediate preoccupations.

From this it can be concluded that transcendental reflection lacks the capacity to lay bare its own roots in practical life. But that this life haunts even the abstractions of a reflection that is detached from direct, practical orientations, follows from the fact that, in transcendental thought, too, things appear as networks, i.e., as relations between multiplicities and unities. Whereas practical *naïveté* neglects the plurality of aspects in favor of the units and discontinuities it stands in need of, Neo-Kantianism treats these aspects as materials coordinated toward various "points of reference". This thematization of the relational nature of objects curtails, it is true, all claims to identical entities in the hypostatized sense of substances subsisting in themselves. And the superiority of transcendentalism consists precisely in this. But it still tries to align all occurring data by inserting them into regularities possessing the status of laws by which the varieties of givenness are governed. This necessity forms the structural link between practical life and transcendental theory. Although it does not bring into play the strategy of fixation and imagery applied by the "practical naive view" for maintaining itself and its grip on the flux of appearances, it nevertheless succeeds in streamlining them to patterns of referential points. In this way, it recognizes the fundamental instability of phenomenality without depriving itself of the right of rational inquiry into the canvas underlying the manifold of appearances. The limits of such an approach appear as soon as one inquires into the nature of the stabilizing factors for which transcendentalism searches. They surely are no phenomenal entities, but still exist only in relation to them. They enter the scene only via subjective staging and because of a special kind of reflection applied to the phenomena. Their appearance originates in the subject, more precisely in subjective making-appear. Transcendentalism had tried to determine the given terms by cutting them down and by translating them into complex sets of other terms horizontally connected with the points of reference that were first given. Although it thus correctly seized upon the relational and composite character of objects, it got lost in the infinite reiterability of its decompository method. Its "fundamental demand for a definition of each concept", i.e., the inescapability of its procedure of cutting up into small parts, led it astray. It got caught up in the dead end of infinitization, and with this it fell into the impossibility of any effective demarcation whatsoever.

Neo-Kantianism could not reach fixed ends because it had overlooked the first beginning and the source of appearing. A phenomenon, after all, not only presupposes something to appear, but also involve a subject to which it is to present itself. Hermann Lotze already had remarked (in a phrase Daubert was fond of quoting) that one cannot speak of a phenomenon "without adding a third instance. One cannot conceive of it as a radiance breaking out of the depth of being-in-itself; a radiance that would exist even without there being an eye in which it could arise, that spreads over reality and is present and apprehensible for everyone who tries to grasp it, but that also would remain, if nobody knew about it".[22] The structuring and organizing of objective appearances thus depends on the thematizing activity of a subject, and is measured by it. Phenomenological description, being a reflection upon the original situation of the subject, makes it clear that appearing and, with this, unification of appearances, are perfect correlates of subjectivity. They can take place only within the horizon of the subject conditioning them. Phenomenological reduction goes beyond transcendentalism by focussing on the central part the subject plays in achieving unity among fluctuating and shadowy occurrences. This demarcation of temporarily stable cores has aptly been described by Spiegelberg as the making of "incisions in the continua of phenomena".[23]

Being a fixation carried out by a subject, this "precission" (to adopt Peirce's wisely chosen term) remains dependent on it, and it never will fail to point back to this subjective origin. The products of subjective activity therefore seem to hinge, according to Husserl's phenomenological philosophy, on actual consciousness.[24] They just exist until further notice.

This phenomenological philosophy certainly was right in unearthing the vital role of subjectivity in the process of bringing about a world of objects. One has to concede to it that this world's limits, scope, shape, focus and mode of connection are correlates of the presence of a subject. But although Husserl and the early Wittgenstein would agree on this issue,[25] they both leave unanswered the question of the subject's way of making its distinctions. The subject is indeed to be held responsible for delimiting and disconnecting the objective flux. But does this not mean that it functions as an economizing and selective element in a field of percepts? Subjectivity introduces pauses and breaks in the phenomenal field; it is negativity at work. Its precissions result in identifying (or patching up) as well as in differentiating (or disintegrating) the given spots of appearance: "colors, forms and the unifying relations between them". So the subject forms the counterpart of an experience in which, on the one hand, all appearances are attributable to objective occurrences while, on the other, the subject's intermittently turning off the power source it preys upon, permits rational insight and, as Bertrand Russell put it, "the language of causation".[26]

But although the organization of perception may be considered an effect of subjective arrangements carried out in convenient ways, nevertheless this structuring does not spring from zero or from arbitrary decision. The subject passively depends for all contents it may receive on impressions which precede any attempt at configuration. Moreover, the possibilities of structuring are foreshadowed also by impressional constellations allowing for them. In the stream of "hyletic" data, certain pre-structured phenomenal kernels are discernible like centers of gravity attracting and deflecting co-present elements in their vicinity. The received phenomenological metaphor of a continuous stream of phenomena therefore should, in order to make sense, by preference be referred and geared to the Cartesian theory of vortexes rather then to the amorphic chaos of an Aristotelian first "hyle". Qualitative differences and blanks in phenomenality being pre-given, the subject works on them by grooving and notching them, so that its various ways of shaping the appearances may be described as differences in the degree to which it hollows them out. This capacity of constitution is, Husserl's philosophy notwithstanding, in no way comparable to any type of production. On the contrary, it denies to phenomena the chance of ever simply presenting themselves without the involvement of horizons of absence. The appearances, rather, are restricted to the indirectness of re-presentation; their being given to us signifies no more than that they "hover before us". A subject, with this, is equal to a tendency to deprive phenomena of their weight and their immediacy. It bestows a kind of distance and inaccessibility on them and so surrounds them with some halo of irreality. To this effect, it inserts them into a horizon of time, be it time elapsed or time to come. The full object so combines the two elements of a freshly offered constellation joined to the remembering of earlier achievements on like materials. Perception is thus describable as an outcome of this inextricable interwovenness of givenness and subjective coloring. This fact, by the way, might be the reason why the limit concept of "pure" data, unaffected by and prior to any subjective carving on them, cannot be applied to experience.

The presence of data and a horizon of transmitted pre-structures together form the legitimating grounds from which a "world pertaining to the senses" springs up. Present givenness and past experiences about handling them differ, however, only as to the point of time at which they appeared, i.e., in their degree of absence and irrelevance. But their dependence on phenomena is of the same sort. So instead of erecting consciousness into some kind of fetish, phenomenological description throws into relief the poverty of a subject's "making up" that lives on the (indirect) availability of a *materia actuosa* (to use Gassendi's untranslatable favorite term), which allows for being consumed and annihilated in this way by a predatory subject.

This constellation finally discloses the nature of the *vinculum substantiale* binding a subject to its world. Both arise from a basic phenomenal field by way of contraction and condensation; they emanate through processes of evaporation and rarefaction taking place within an active matter coexisting in this field. Thanks to this common origin, even the so-called unknown X still "is an x for us", while, on the other hand, the ineradicable difference between the x and the self entails the consequence that "we cannot think of an 'In-itself' except if we are the in-itself" (which of course would come down to not thinking at all). The same idea of a derivative status of the subject in the realm of phenomenality may also be found in Husserl's description of the ego as an "occasional expression", the occurrence of which depends on "factual circumstances" of some phenomenal frame of reference.[27] The play of forces both striking against each other and also interlocked this way in a single system of motion thus at the same time accounts for the variegated multiplicity of objects and for the occurrence of blind spots from which the field may reflect upon itself. Like eyes of storms, such breathers do not by themselves contribute to the ubiquitous change and unrest taking place in phenomenality. But thanks to their transparency they themselves constitute new shades of color in an overall process. With this, they serve as transitional stops on the way to the development of new sorts of phenomena. This structure of interlocking subjective and objective elements paving the way for the coalescence of new appearances will be illustrated best by Herbert Spiegelberg's striking observation: "A reflection on a smooth surface is not completely dependent on the viewer, but it can occur only in relation to him".[28]

Appendix: Daubert's Text

A I 1/35

A I 1/35r
Phänomenologische und transzendentale Methode in der Erkenntnistheorie
((m. Bleist.:)) [etwa Oktober ((19))05]
Die *transzendentale Erkenntnistheorie* geht aus von dem Gegensatz des praktischen naiven Weltbildes zu dem Bilde, was die Gegenstände unserer immer fortschreitenden Erkenntnis bieten. So sind die Dinge nichts als eine für den praktischen Bedarf naiv zurechtgemachte Vorstellung. Die naive Vorstellung lässt Dinge entstehen und vergehen (macht sie zu Subjekten der Existenz und der Nichtexistenz). Solche Dinge als beharrende Grundlagen jeder Aussage über Relationen und Veränderungen gibt es in der Tat nicht. Der naive Mensch arbeitet mit solchen Vorstellungen, weil sie sich praktisch am leichtesten handhaben lassen. [Natorps Aristoteles-Interpretation im *Plato*, p. 383.]

Kant hat das Resultat der grossen Revolution der Wissenschaften ausgesprochen und damit Aristoteles entthront durch den Satz: Dinge gestehen ganz und gar aus Verhältnissen, unter denen zwar selbständige und beharrende sind, wodurch uns erst ein "bestimmter Gegenstand" gegeben wird. Verschärft besagt dieser Satz: Der empirische Gegenstand löst sich in der wissenschaftlichen Betrachtung in eine Unendlichkeit von Relationen auf. Auch die Beziehungspunkte der Relationen sind uns nie absolut gegeben, sondern nur hypothetisch ansetzbar. Zur immer genaueren Ansetzung der Termini führt nur die sich schrittweise vertiefende Erkenntnis der Relationen selber (besonders der Zeitrelationen des Geschehens, d.h. die Natur – "gesetze" in engerem Sinn).

Damit ist das Ding als beharrende Existenzgrundlage nicht zuerst gegeben, sondern es bezeichnet das ideele Ziel einer unendlichen Aufgabe. Das hat immer klarer bewiesen die Forschung nach dem wahren Subjekt der Bewegung, der sog. Materie. [Natorp, *Plato*, p. 382.]

So ist der Gegenstand das x der Erkenntnisgleichung, das nur bestimmt wird durch seine Beziehung zu gegebenen Grössen, welche eben wieder nur durch Beziehung zu anderen bestimmt werden können.

Das Ding in der phänomenologischen Betrachtung:[1] Diese geht aus von den Gegebenheiten, den Farben, Formen und Einheitsbeziehungen von ihnen.

16

Dabei konstatiert sie nicht einfach die Vulgärmeinung, sondern sie vergleicht und fragt nach dem Recht, den bestimmten Tatsachen, die sie im Auge hat, diese oder jene Bestimmungen zuzulegen. In den Antworten auf diese Rechtsfragen in diesen Forderungen konstituiert sich eine bestimmte objektive Welt, die uns umgebende Sinnenwelt. Dieses ist ganz reine voraussetzungslose Betrachtung der Phänomene, die Gegebenheiten, wie sie uns als "bewusste" im Wahrnehmen und Denken eindeutig vorschweben.

1) ((Rb.:)) Im ganzen wird doch eine Unterschiebung der beiden Fragen vorliegen: 1) Was ist ein Ding? 2) Wodurch bestimmen wir es eindeutig? Und das Wesen der kritizistischen Fragestellung könnte dann liegen in der grundsätzlichen Forderung der Definition eines jeden Begriffs. Man glaubt, man könne durch Definition überhaupt etwas klaren, es selber bestimmen und fassen. Das kann man aber immer nur nach Kenntnis der ganzen (("ganzen" V. für "grossen")) phänomenologisch klar liegenden Beziehungen, die man zur Definition gebraucht. Die transzendentale Betrachtung sieht hier eine Voraussetzung, die sie nicht machen will. In den Gegebenheiten sieht sie schon Beziehungen zu einem betrachtenden Subjekt. Hierunter könnte man 1) (("1") V. für "einmal")) verstehen die jeweils verschiedenen psychischen Individuen, die kommen in der Tat nicht in Betracht. 2) Das in diesen gemeinsame Sinnensubjekt. 3) Das in ((Ms.: "unter")) diesen gemeinsame Subjekt der apriorischen sinnlichen Formen. Sie bestrebt sich nun, dieses zu eliminieren und nach dem Gegenstand an sich zu fragen. Sie dürfte dann keine Einwände haben gegen die Frage des Gegenstands für uns. Sachlich erhebt sich nun aber die Frage, können wir aus solchem phänomenologischen Standpunkt überhaupt heraus, ist nicht auch das x ein x für uns? Wir können ja eben gar kein "Ansich" denken, wir müssten das Ansich sein. In allem Denken liegt der phänomenologische Standpunkt. Was kann es nun noch für einen Sinn haben, das Ding (x) in Beziehung zu setzen zu sinnlich wahrnehmenden und intellektiv formenden Subjekten? Was man vom Subjekt hier als psychologischem abstreift? Man setzt das Ding zu seinen fest gegebenen Eigenschaften in Beziehung. Dieses Ding mag ein x sein, aber das Wichtige ist, dass dieses x ein x für uns ist und damit sein Sinn fest aufgeklärt werden kann also der eines Funktionsträgers. A I 1/35v ((leer)) A I 1/36 ((36/34 Doppelblatt; darin 35)) A I 1/36r ((leer)) A I 1/36v ((leer))

NOTES

1. *Zum anderen Ufer* (Remagen: Otto Reichl, 1960), p. 211.
2. *Gesammelte Werke*, Vol. 7, ed. Manfred S. Frings (Bern and München: Francke, 1973), p. 328.
3. *The Phenomenological Movement: A Historical Introduction* (The Hague: Martinus Nijhoff, 1960), I, 218.
4. Eberhard Avé-Lallemant, *Die Nachlässe der Münchener Phänomenologen in der Bayerischen Staatsbibliothek* (Wiesbaden: Otto Harrassowitz, 1975), p. 128.
5. This MS is reproduced in Avé-Lallemant, p. 11.
6. *Die neue Wissenschaft vom Recht. Eine phänomenologische Untersuchung* (Berlin: Grünewald: Dr. Walther Rothschild, 1930), p. 182.
7. *Urteil und Anschauung. Ein Beitrag zur Phänomenologie der Erkenntnis* (Parchim: Hermann Freise, 1914), p. 103.
8. *Die künstlerische Darstellung als Problem der Ästhetik* (Hamburg and Leipzig: Leopold Voss, 1907), p. v.
9. "Erinnerungen an Husserl", in H.L. Van Breda, ed., *Edmund Husserl 1859 – 1959* (La Haye: Martinus Nijhoff, 1959), p. 22. Schapp's demand is met here for the first time.
10. This well-confirmed story was already published by Franz G. Schmucker in his 1956 Munich dissertation on *Phänomenologie als Methode der Wesenerkenntnis*, p. 1.
11. *Zur Wesenlehre des psychischen Lebens und Erlebens* (Den Haag: Martinus Nijhoff, 1968), p. viii.
12. "Alexander Pfänders methodische Stellung", in the Pfänder Festschrift, *Neue Münchener philosophische Abhandlungen* (Leipzig: A. Barth, 1933), p. 4.
13. Spiegelberg, I, 174. For a detailed report on this event, see my *Husserl über Pfänder* (Den Haag: Martinus Nijhoff, 1973), pp. 128 – 183.
14. "Erinnerungen an Franz Brentano", in Oskar Kraus, ed., *Franz Brentano* (München: C.H. Beck, 1919), p. 165.
15. Brentano's report on his meeting with "the main protagonist" of phenomenology in Munich (as he apostrophizes Daubert) is contained in a letter to Hugo Bergmann of July 30, 1907, published in *Philosophy and Phenomenological Research* 7 (1946), p. 96.
16. Avé-Lallemant, p. 128.
17. For a first note on this fact, see my article "Ein Brief Husserls an Theodor Lipps", *Tijdschrift voor Filosofie* 39 (1977), p. 143.
18. Daubert's own footnote at this point is reproduced below at p. 16, n. 1.
19. *Doing Phenomenology. Essays on and in Phenomenology* (The Hague: Martinus Nijhoff, 1973), p. 187.
20. Daubert treated *Urphänomenologie* in a text (MS Daubertiana A I 1/49) which is closely connected with the one published here.
21. *Platos Ideenlehre. Eine Einführung in den Idealismus* (Leipzig: Felix Meiner, 1902), pp. 382–384. It should be noted that Daubert's choice of this work was particularly appropriate, because this book already had been meant by its author to serve a double purpose. On the one hand, it elucidated a purely historical topic, while at the same time it sought to introduce the reader to Natorp's own idealist philosophy.
22. *Mikrokosmus. Ideen zur Naturgeschichte und Geschichte der Menschheit*, 5th edition (Leipzig: S. Hirzel, 1896), I, 179.
23. *Doing Phenomenology*, p. 175.
24. See Edmund Husserl, *Ideen I*, Husserliana III/1 (Den Haag: Martinus Nijhoff, 1977), p. 104.
25. See *Tractatus logico-philosophicus*, 5.632 and 5.641.
26. *The Analysis of Matter* (London: George Allen and Unwin, 1927), p. 216.
27. See *Logische Untersuchungen*, Vol. II, 1st Investigation, p. 26.
28. *Doing Phenomenology*, p. 73.

Phenomenology and Relativism
by
David Carr

Husserl first made his name by denouncing psychologism in logic. In his influential *Prolegomena to Pure Logic* (1900), the theories of Mill, Wundt, Sigwart and others are attacked as versions of "skeptical relativism" which in various ways make truth dependent on the psychological make-up of human beings as a species ("anthropologism").[1] Later, in "Philosophy as Rigorous Science" (1910) the attack is extended to historical or cultural relativism ("historicism") as well, where his major target seems to be Dilthey.[2] Husserl's refutation seemed to clear the way for a philosophy which could rest assured of attaining objective, non-relative truths, and this assurance is evident not only in Husserl's early work but also in that of his early followers (e.g., Geiger, Pfänder, Scheler).

In view of the importance of this antirelativism to the beginnings of phenomenology, it may seem surprising that later heirs to the phenomenological tradition move steadily toward more or less explicit versions of relativism, especially of the historical or cultural sort. As in other versions of relativism, truth becomes relative to something like a "conceptual framework". The early Heidegger's theory of truth is arguably historicist, and this theory is further developed in the hermeneutical theory of H.G. Gadamer. Merleau-Ponty's perspectivism seems clearly relativistic. The later Heidegger and Jacques Derrida seem to view the whole western metaphysical tradition as a "conceptual framework" on a grand scale.

It might be argued (and this is the standard view) that this opposition between the early Husserl and later heirs to the tradition is not really remarkable: precisely to the extent that later phenomenologists have moved away from Husserl's antirelativism, they have also moved away from his conception of phenomenological method. Indeed, Gadamer, Merleau-Ponty, the later Heidegger and Derrida, are all so far removed from Husserl that it hardly makes sense to speak of a phenomenological tradition any more, let alone a

W.S. Hamrick (ed.) *Phenomenology in Practice and Theory*.
© 1985 Martinus Nijhoff Publishers, Dordrecht/Boston/Lancaster
ISBN 90 247 2926 2. Printed in the Netherlands.

school or unified method. Hence, it should be no surprise that Husserl and these philosophers differ on the matter of relativism. Besides, the move from strong initial claims of objectively binding truth to some form of skeptical relativism seems common to the development of many philosophical traditions. Something like this happened to British Empiricism from Locke to Hume, and a similar development occurred from German Idealism to the historical relativism of the later 19th century. In our own century the Anglo-American tradition in philosophy has seen the development from logical positivism to the relativism of Wittgenstein's "forms of life" theory, to Quine's "Ontological Relativity", and to the relativistic views of scientific theory made popular by Kuhn, Feyerabend and others. In fact, this gives us two ways of explaining the relativism of recent continental philosophy: either it is the result of a general law applying to philosophical traditions as such, or it is merely another manifestation of a widespread phenomenon of mid-twentieth century intellectual life.

However, it may be with these broad — and, I might add, somewhat "historicist" — explanations, it seems to me that the trend toward relativism among those influenced by Husserl is susceptible of a more detailed and reasoned account. I would like to argue that there are certain themes and concepts that are fundamental even to Husserl's earliest conception of phenomenology and which lead in a relativistic direction, even though Husserl himself may not have drawn such consequences from them. Furthermore, these are themes and concepts which have remained central to the approaches of at least some of those philosophers mentioned above as heirs to the phenomenological tradition, in spite of all their differences from Husserl; so that one *can* speak of a continuity to the phenomenological tradition precisely in reference to these concepts. In the following, I shall try to sketch these concepts briefly, point out their possible relativistic implications, and show how they have been carried forward as part of the tradition. First, a word about Husserl's antirelativist arguments in the *Prolegomena*. Generally, they take the form of accusing the relativist of contradicting himself. He (the relativist) puts forward theories and claims of supposedly objectively binding truth which are designed to show that no such theories and claims are possible. He tacitly assumes the nonrelative validity of his own concepts and scheme of concepts in order to show how any such scheme is "relative". Husserl also argues that the relativist cannot make sense of the notion of an "alternative conceptual scheme" without attributing to such a scheme certain fundamental concepts which are also fundamental to *our* conceptual scheme.[3] Husserl's antirelativist arguments are a priori ones that resemble certain arguments currently being put forth against the notion of alternative conceptual frameworks, for example, by Davidson: either such a framework, or language, is translatable into our own language and thus shares at least its rudimentary concepts, or else we have no means for classifying it as a language at all. Since the very idea of *a* conceptual framework suggests that there could be others, and this latter notion is incoherent, the idea of a conceptual scheme is itself questionable.[4]

Richard Rorty has recently tried to show that such arguments are inconclusive.[5] Admittedly we could never verify the existence of an alternative conceptual scheme without at the same time showing that it was not truly "alternative". But since we are aware of or can imagine conceptual arrangements that differ in some significant respects from our own, can we not "extrapolate"[6] to a conceptual scheme that differs in all respects? While we could never recognize such a scheme or language *as* such even if we stumbled over it, or even imagine what it would be like, we can nevertheless conceive of its possibility. With his notion of "extrapolation", Rorty applies a notion of "conceiving of the possibility of something" which his opponents would probably not accept. But he manages to articulate the doubt that always lingers at the conclusion of a priori arguments like those presented by Husserl and Davidson: in order to flesh out our conception of alternative conceptual frameworks, or indeed to say or do anything whatever, *we* have to appeal to concepts in such a way that *we* assume their universal validity. But does this make it so?

While a priori arguments like Husserl's may thus not succeed in ruling out the relativism of "alternative conceptual frameworks", they do seem to rule out the possibility that anything could ever count as evidence for the existence of such frameworks. How, then, did such an idea ever gain currency? It could, of course, be seen as a rather overhasty inference from the new information about different languages, cultures and forms of life that bombarded Europeans in the 18th and 19th centuries. Rorty, however, believes that the roots of relativism lie deeper. If Hegel gave expression to the notion of historically changing world views, the way was prepared for him by Kant, "himself the least historicist of philosophers. For Kant perfected and codified the two distinctions that are necessary to develop the notion of an "alternative conceptual framework" – the distinction between spontaneity and receptivity and the distinction between necessary and contingent truth".[7] In other words, a widely accepted view of the basic structure of cognition and experience made the relativistic interpretation of incoming cultural and historical data plausible, even though its author, Kant, was not himself a relativist.

Now I would like to say something similar about Husserl: at the very time that he was attacking relativism with the sort of arguments mentioned above, he was developing a view of the basic structure of experience which rendered relativism plausible. Some aspects of Husserl's basic conception are, of course, taken over from or shared with Kant, such as the distinction between necessary and contingent truths. It is on other aspects of Husserl's theory, however, that I wish to concentrate, aspects that are peculiar to him and peculiarly phenomenological.

1. The Search For the Given

One aspect of the Kantian framework which Husserl seems clearly to reject is the idea of a neutral sense-given which is interpreted by a conceptual grasp. In the first Logical Investigation where he deals with the experience of using and understanding language, he makes the distinction between the hearing of sounds or the seeing of marks on a page on the one hand, and the "animating intention" through which we grasp their sense on the other. One is tempted, he says, to see an analogous process going on in sense perception itself, such that "consciousness first looks at its sensations, then turns them into perceptual objects" through a similar animating intention.[8] Thus, sensations would be signs for external objects which we can either understand or not, like the written or heard signs of language. But Husserl rejects this view, as he does later in the *Ideas*.[9] Sensations, he says in the *Logical Investigations*, "plainly only become presented in psychological reflection: in naive, intuitive presentations they may be components in our presentative experience, parts of its descriptive content, but are not at all its objects".[10] This is, of course, what he says about *hyle* in the *Ideas*.[11] Certain of his formulations in both works may seem to suggest that he is not entirely free of the notion of sensations as neutral data that are spontaneously interpreted. For example, he says that "the perceptual presentation arises insofar as an experienced complex of sensations gets informed by a certain act-character, one of conceiving or meaning".[12] However, it must be noted that in this passage Husserl says that the complex of sensations is *erlebt* not *erfahren*: it is lived through, not intended as an object, just as the act of intending itself is lived through or performed but not itself intended and can become an object only in a subsequent act of reflection.[13]

Even the very restricted notion of sensation that Husserl holds in these early works has little importance for his overall theory, and it gradually fades almost entirely from view. He seems to recognize that even in this limited form, the notion of sensation is a hybrid left over from precisely the quasi-physiological and causal conception of experience he wants to overcome. But in these early works he has already seen the essential point which has been the source of so much confusion: in order to be viewed as "data" that are interpreted by an animating intention, sensations would have to be objects of conscious intentions, as are the signs of language, and this they certainly are not. To suppose the existence of some such interpreting process at the unconscious level would be, for Husserl, mere speculation.[14]

In spite of this rejection of the notion of sense data, Husserl is very much involved in a project which has traditionally been associated with that notion, namely what is usually called the search for the given. One recalls the famous slogan, *zu den Sachen selbst*! But because of the way Husserl construes the notion of the given, his results differ markedly from those of others who have been engaged in the same quest, and at the same time open the door to some relativistic interpretations. Traditionally, of course, the given was supposed to provide the guarantee *against* any sort of skepticism, relativistic or otherwise. The simple natures of the rationalists, or the sense data of the empiricists, were supposed to provide an infallible and unmediated link to reality.[15] To limit one's claims to what is directly given, or to what can be cautiously inferred from it, was to be assured of genuine knowledge of the world, agreement among all rational creatures following the same procedure, and the avoidance of baseless speculation and the prejudices of a parochial "point of view". Even in the hands of Kant, where the given (sensation) has to be supplemented by an interpretation supplied by the mind if cognition is to be possible, sensation still constitutes a link to reality in itself. But Husserl develops his notion of the given from a rather different slant and, in doing so, deprives the given of the function it is traditionally designed to serve. As far as our awareness of the external world is concerned, we have just seen that Husserl regards perceptual objects in space as the most primitive objects of which we are directly aware, denying the existence of a consciously given layer of sense data below it. Since he does admit the availability of sense data to a second level reflective analysis of perceptual experience, it might be thought that he would take the phenomenalist's route of trying to reconstruct the objective world by this procedure. But it is clear that for Husserl, reflection on the sense-aspects (or any other aspects) of experiences yields evidence for nothing but claims about those experiences themselves. In fact, it is essential to his notion of the intentionality of experience that we can draw no conclusions from the existence or nature of an experience about the existence or nature of its object.[16] Nevertheless, Husserl seems to be saying that in sense perception the external object is given. What does he mean?

It is clear that Husserl has seized on only one aspect of the given in the traditional sense, namely, its unmediated character; and furthermore, he treats this in a purely descriptive way. A glance at one of the topics Husserl deals with in the sixth Logical Investigation will show what this means. When we intend or refer to some empirical object or state of affairs, there are several different ways in which this intention relates to its object: we can intend it emptily, simply referring to it in a way that involves nothing more than understanding the words we use; or we can imagine it, thereby illustrating our intention to ourselves; or we can see a picture of it, so that it is again illustrated, but this time by means of perceiving an object (the picture) other than the one we intend; or we can infer its existence whether by interpreting some conventional sign or drawing a causal inference, where again our inference is based on some object other than the one we intend; or finally, we can just see it, or touch, hear, smell or taste it, in which case our relation to the object is not mediated by some other thing.[17] Here we see how Husserl's approach is descriptive and how his attack on sense-data is derived from this approach. We cannot describe how we could arrive at the perceived object or state of affairs on the basis of anything more basic such as sense data or images. We could only conjecture or postulate the existence of such an unconscious process on the basic of premises which are even more conjectural. And so, such theories are rejected. The descriptive fact is that as far as empirical objects and states of affairs are concerned, perception plays the role of supplying the *given*, the basic instance of self-evidence or fulfillment par excellence beyond which we cannot and need not go. The fact that perceptual evidence is always what Husserl calls "inadequate" and open to further question does not remove its function of supplying the given. Furthermore, perceptual evidence does not guarantee intersubjective agreement; rather, it appeals to it, it assumes it will be forthcoming. In this sense it remains a "pretension" or "presumption"[18] that has to be made good by further experience. The objective world in the strict sense, understood as the correlate of intersubjective agreement, is conceived by Husserl as a distant goal toward which we strive in our scientific endeavors, not something from which we begin.

Perception, on the other hand, is just that: it is that from which we begin. It is that on which our inferences are based and to which our perceptual judgments are naturally referred for their verification. To be sure, its presumption is to place us in contact with the real world that exists independently of us, but Husserl does not make a metaphysical pronouncement on the correctness of this presumption; his task is simply to describe it. Thus, the perceptual world is the "taken for granted", as he later calls it, on which our knowledge of the world is based. Of course, perceptual givenness is only one kind in Husserl's general theory of *Evidenz*: it would be inappropriate in the case of knowledge claims about our mental states, for example, or in mathematics. Here, according to Husserl, other forms of givenness are involved which are only functionally similar or analogous to perception in its domain. But as far as the real world is concerned, perception is our direct link to it, provided that the words "direct" and "real world" are understood in the descriptive sense as we have tried to define it. In this sense, perception becomes the core of what Husserl later calls the "natural attitude", the underlying general belief in the world whose objects are given in experience. Husserl's natural subject, the traditional man in the street under the sway of the natural attitude, is committed first of all to the space-time world about him which fills in his perceptual intendings. Within this world, he pursues his particular practical or scientific interests, picking out spheres of objects for observation or explanation, focusing upon certain aspects of the world, reasoning on the basis of what is immediately given to the greater world beyond, etc. But the perceived world is not itself something picked out, not an isolated aspect of reality, not itself something inferred: it is, to repeat, that from which we begin, as distinct from anything we arrive at through it or on the basis of it, by inference, abstraction or other mental activity.[19]

This particular version of the search for the given, as the unmediated in the purely descriptive sense, has been a constant theme in phenomenology. Merleau-Ponty, describing what he takes to be Husserl's task as well as his own, says: "To return to the things themselves is to return to that world which precedes knowledge, of which knowledge always *speaks* and in relation to which every scientific schematization is an abstract and derivative sign language, as is geography in relation to the countryside in which we have learnt beforehand what a forest, a prairie, or a river is".[20] But even before Merleau-Ponty, the search for the given or the return to the things themselves had already been undertaken in precisely this sense by Heidegger, and with rather striking results. As is well known, Heidegger in *Being and Time* claims that even perceptual objects, as "things" in space and time, are second-level abstractions from a more basic level which is actually our direct and unmediated encounter with the world. This is the level of *Zuhandenheit* at which we encounter not "things" but "equipment" in complexes of involvement and significance. It is only when we withdraw, for certain practical purposes, from engagements in this world of equipment, take a distance from it, as it were, that the world of *Vorhandenheit* comes into view, available to perception in the traditional sense.[21] Merleau-Ponty himself accepts many of the features of Heidegger's description of this unmediated encounter, even while he retains the term perception. He adds, of course, his own notion of the lived body as the natural subject of perception such that perceived things, and even space and time, have the status of functional values for a mobile and practical life rather than the status of objects for detached observation. While the description of the "given" thus changes considerably under the hands of these later phenomenologists, and while their views involve an implicit criticism of Husserl, it should be clear that these descriptions are arrived at by pursuing the notion of the given in precisely Husserl's sense: namely, as that which is "there" for us prior to abstraction and explicit mental activity and is not itself arrived at by any such activity.

We made the statement above that this conception of the given leaves the door open to a relativistic interpretation. It can easily be seen how this is so. The concept of the unmediated in the purely descriptive or phenomenological sense not only does not supply an unassailable cognitive link to an independent reality existing in itself; it does not even involve any assurance of intersubjective agreement, at least not in the universal sense required to overcome relativism. It is true that for Husserl, Heidegger, and Merleau-Ponty, the world of the natural attitude (the everyday world, or lived world) is intersubjective; it is a public world and not some idiosyncratic private spectacle that is given in this sense. That is to say, at least in Husserl's terms, that the perceiving subject takes himself to be in direct contact with a world that is available to others as well. But what is lacking is a transcendental argument to the effect that the world as perceived is not only factually accepted by others but must be accepted as such by any possible others. While Husserl may have conceived of it in this way, he provides us with no such argument. [22] All we have is a sort of layered description of mental life involving the distinction between what is given and what is secondarily derived from the given. In Heidegger and Merleau-Ponty, while this same stratification is retained, any pretense toward showing the universality of the given world is dropped altogether and the strong suggestion is made that the world may vary, if not from individual, then perhaps from one community or historical period to another. This is a possibility left open, as we have seen, by the Husserlian concept of the given from which they begin.

II. The Object as Intended

There is another aspect of Husserl's earliest efforts in phenomenology which leaves his theory open to relativistic interpretations and even positively suggests them. In the previous discussion we have seen that Husserl's notion of the given was that of the unmediated. What this meant was that our access to the object is not mediated by some other *object*. But there is another sense of mediation that is often involved in these discussions, what is called mediation by concepts. Something like this is involved in Husserl's theory of intentionality. In the fifth Logical Investigation, where he is broaching the thorny problem of the intentional object, Husserl insists, as he does throughout his career, that the object is not to be confused with or collapsed into the act in which it is intended. Nevertheless, he points out, we must distinguish between the object *which* is intended and the object *as* it is intended. When I refer, for example, to the Emperor of Germany, the object which is intended may have many correct descriptions (e.g., the son of the Emperor Frederick the Third, the grandson of Queen Victoria) other than the one which is included in this particular reference to it. But it is incorrect to speak of these descriptions as applying to the object *as* it is in this case intended. [23] This distinction is, of course, absolutely essential to Husserl's notion of a conscious intention which, though it in one sense requires an object, is not dependent on the state of the world in order to be what it is. It not only means that the intended object need not exist, as in the case of illusion or fantasy; it also means that even where one supposes the object to exist just as I take it to be, one cannot conceive of consciousness, experience or cognition as a straightforward relation obtaining between the subject and an object that exists "in itself". It means, in the language of recent discussions of intentionality, that descriptions of perceiving, thinking, believing something, etc., are nonextensional or "referentially opaque", i.e., that they do not permit the substitution of different expressions, such as "evening star" and "morning star", even if they refer to the same object.[24] Husserl's own interest at this point is in developing the idea of a conscious act, pointing out that the same object can be intended in different ways. He extends the distinction between object-*which* and object-*as* to perceptual objects as well as the references of linguistic expressions and begins to introduce his famous analysis of *Abschattungen* or profiles: the object is always perceived from some angle or another, and we must distinguish the object *as* seen from the object with all its possible determinations and perspectives.[25]

Here Husserl might be suspected of reverting to the Kantian distinction between the appearance and the thing-in-itself. This is, of course, not the case. The object-which or object-in-itself, in the distinction, is for Husserl not some unknowable whatnot and certainly not a remote cause of our sense experience, but is simply the object which robust common sense takes to be there independently of our different approaches to it, an object which we certainly can come to know and which in any case is directly given to us and not represented *in absentia* by some messenger or stand-in called an appearance. Besides, it is obvious that we have to know about the object-in-itself in order precisely to make the distinction in a given case between the object *which* is intended and the object *as* it is intended. What Husserl has introduced is something more like the Hegelian distinction between the in-itself and the for-me, a distinction which is perfectly legitimate and common-sensical and from which, according to Hegel and others, the Kantian distinction between appearance and thing-in-itself was illegitimately derived.

It will, of course, be recalled that when Husserl introduced his famous phenomenological reduction or *epoché* in the *Ideas*, his point was precisely to suspend the common-sense supposition of an object existing in itself in order to concentrate on the for-me or the object as it is intended. The notion of the independently existing object belongs to the "natural attitude", which brings with it the requirements of a relational or causal view of cognition and experience; and in order to avoid this requirement, the natural attitude had to be suspended. However, Husserl's purpose was to analyze and understand the natural attitude itself precisely by unearthing its hidden presuppositions, and thus he found, as Hegel had before him, that the distinction between the in-itself and the for-me is itself a distinction *for-me*. That is, it is a distinction internal to experience and thus turns up within the brackets of the *epoché*. The distinction has its place, for example, in the doctrine of the *noema* in *Ideas* where it is said that the object *as* I intend it always points beyond itself by tacit reference to other possible intendings of the same object.[26]

What emerges from all this is a picture of experience or cognition as a series of *prises* on a reality which, while it never eludes our grasp, is never fully within it either. Even the given in sense perception is interpreted or intended-as. To be sure, Husserl is interested in the manner in which, particularly in our scientific endeavors, we aim at objectivity, i.e., at a complete grasp of reality which is not limited to any one point of view or description. He makes a great deal of the role of intersubjectivity − the intersection and agreement of simultaneous but different intendings of the same object or state of affairs − in the pursuit of such objectivity. In view of this, it can be seen that Husserl's theory of consciousness had to become teleological, his theory of *Evidenz* had to become genetic and dynamic in character once he developed the implications of the distinction between the object which is intended and the object *as* it is intended.

We shall return later to the teleological and dynamic character of consciousness in Husserl's theory, but first let us pause to appreciate the relativistic implications of his notion of the intentional object. What Husserl has obviously discovered in his own way is the equivalent of the now-familiar notions of taking-as and seeing-as. And we can seen that these notions are made necessary by the concept of intentionality and by the intentionalist approach to experience and cognition. What Husserl's approach requires is that whenever we are dealing with conscious intending subjects, we cannot legitimately speak of objects, facts or even the world without at the same time asking, in effect: whose objects, whose facts, whose world? This is simply to say that, from the phenomenological point of view, object, fact, and world as intended are referred back to some particular act or acts of intending them. Even the objective world of science is referred back to the scientific community as it construes that world. Most important, of course, is that on this view the objects of our reference "underdetermine" our references to them; that is, they are always such as to allow other possible references in the sense of other intendings-as.

This Husserlian train of thought is also taken up and made central by Heidegger and Merleau-Ponty. In their case, too, taking-as is a feature of the most primitive level of experience, that which corresponds to what we called the given. In Heidegger, we find it in the notion of the "as-structure of understanding". [27] Understanding, which for Heidegger is a basic element of human existence, and which goes deeper than conceptual thought, means taking something *as* something. And from the point of view of his existential analysis of *Dasein* we cannot make philosophical sense of the world except as understood in this sense by *Dasein*. In Merleau-Ponty it is the concept of perspective in perception which acquires central significance. Perception is the basic or primary mode of consciousness, in whose structure all other modes share, and thus the concept of perspective or "point of view" becomes the central metaphor for any philosophical understanding of object or world. [28] World is always world as perceived from a particular, even if intersubjective, point of view.

In the case of Heidegger and Merleau-Ponty, it is important to stress again the intersubjective character of the as-structure of experience. In their discussions of everyday experience, taking-as is not to be regarded as something like a personal accomplishment, even though Merleau-Ponty often speaks of a kind of individual "style" in perception. The sense of the world and its constituents is from the start a shared sense, and it is only perhaps in the experience of quasi-conversion to what Heidegger calls "authentic" existence that the sense of the world acquires anything like a personal accent. But even though it is shared and thus intersubjective, the sense structure of the experienced world is pretheoretical in the sense that it exists prior to the explicit appeal to the categories of objectivity and the explicit aim of intersubjective agreement. These activities are called into play for certain practical purposes and for the development of scientific theory, but what the phenomenologists are interested in showing is that these activities presuppose and build upon a level of experience which is both more primitive and more rich than the pared-down and somewhat sterile objective world.

III. Consciousness as Temporal Gestalt

The Husserlian conceptions we have been examining so far have all derived from the *Logical Investigations* of 1900 – 01. The one we turn to next is almost as early, dating from the lectures on the *Phenomenology of Internal Time-Consciousness* of 1905.[29] Here Husserl begins to consider the dynamic character of consciousness, which later plays a role in his genetic and developmental theory of *Evidenz*. The temporal dimension is added to the conception of consciousness and intentionality developed in the *Logical Investigations*, where it had been passed over even where it seemed called for.[30] Even in the *Ideas* (1913) this discussion is suppressed, though Husserl is aware that it is required in order to make his phenomenology complete.[31]

In order to describe phenomenologically the consiousness of time, Husserl, like others before him, takes as his example the hearing of a melody. But a melody might well serve as an image for consciousness itself as Husserl describes it in his lectures. That is, consciousness is correctly conceived as consisting of more or less distinct phases or individual experiences (*Erlebnisse*), but each of these, like each note in a melody, derives its significance from its place in a temporal configuration that includes past and future phases. This is so *for* the experiencer since passing experiences are not annihilated for him, but are "held in his grasp" by a kind of background awareness which Husserl calls retention; and future experiences are anticipated in so-called protention.[32] The past need not be explicitly called to mind, as in "recollection", nor the future expressly anticipated, in order to play a role in our experience of the present.

Rather, they determine its sense, as the past and future notes of a melody determine the sense of the note I am hearing now. The "melodies" of a conscious
being may be of greater or smaller scope, may overlap with each other or be
contained in others as a theme is contained within the movement of a
symphony.

In speaking this way I am admittedly resorting to metaphors which Husserl
does not use and I have developed his theory somewhat beyond what he
presents in the lectures. But I think that the above account grasps the essence
of Husserl's temporal conception of consciousness, as can be seen by the way
it is finally integrated into his theory, especially in the *Cartesian Meditations*.
When he speaks there of the ego as a "substrate of habitualities",[33] he is referring to the manner in which ongoing experience stands out against an acquired
background of beliefs and convictions which bear upon or give a slant to the
present topic. For if we assume, as we must, that each individual has a different
experiential past, and that membership in a community will make one individual's themes of concern different from those of an individual in another
community, we can say that he confronts the world of his experience in a way
that is unique to him or to the members of his community. Such a conception
now gives us the means for elaborating on the two points that we have discussed
earlier: (1) If the "given" is seen as that which is "taken for granted" about
the world by particular individuals or groups, we can interpret this as a function of the temporal context of their experience, in such a way that such a context will vary depending on who is involved. (2) That an object is intended as
such and such, viewed or interpreted in a certain way to the neglect of other
possible ways of intending or interpreting it, may again derive from the temporal context or theme of interest of the individual who intends it. Indeed, we
can speak of typical ways of interpreting or intending objects or type of objects
as arising from the temporal backgrounds and interests of individuals or
groups of individuals.

Husserl himself began to draw out some of the relativistic implications of his
theory of consciousness in his latest work, where he made much of the
"historicity" of experience with its "sedimented" background.[34] But it was
Heidegger and his pupil Gadamer who made the most of this notion. Heidegger's temporal interpretation of *Dasein* with its mutually implying dimensions
of past, present, and future, can by seen as derived from Husserl's temporal
theory of consciousness.[35] And in his notion of the *Vorstruktur* of understanding, with its key concept of interpretation,[36] he supplies the basic materials
for Gadamer's hermeneutic theory. A combination of logical and perceptual
metaphors are involved in Gadamer's conception of interpretation: on the one
hand, the sedimented background the subject brings to his present experience
is seen as something like a set of ungrounded presuppositions or prejudices
from which the interpretation is derived; on the other hand, it, too, is viewed

as a sort of Gestalt which is a whole prior to its parts — whence the famous hermeneutical circle.[37]

IV. Summary and Conclusions

To sum up, we should begin by pointing out that Husserl's intentionalist approach, from the earliest of his phenomenological investigations, precludes the realistic positing of a world in itself to which consciousness stands in a real or even cognitive relation. He is limited to describing the world as it presents itself, as it effectively claims the allegiance of consciousness and functions in the fulfillment of intentions and the verification of claims about reality. It is in this sense that he takes the perceptual as the given. And while perception "pretends", as he says, or presumes to place us in direct contact with reality, the perceptual world is there for us prior to the explicit appeal to the categories of objectivity and intersubjective agreement. Further, while reality is thus given in perception, it is also subject, by the very nature of intentionality, to an interpretation or intending-as which leaves aspects of it beyond our grasp. Finally, even on Husserl's earliest view, consciousness does not approach reality empty-handed, as it were, but in each case brings with it the baggage of its past experience. Particular intentional grasps on reality are not isolated, but take their place in a Gestalt of a temporal character. We have tried to show the manner in which each of these points accommodates itself to a relativistic interpretation and has in fact received such an interpretation as it is carried on in the phenomenological work of later writers.

It might be argued that while these notions suggest a relativistic view of the knower's relation to the world or to external reality, this view would not necessarily be incompatible with Husserl's early antirelativism and might even have been acceptable to him. It would not necessarily imply a full-fledged *philosophical* relativism of the sort Husserl branded as a form of self-refuting skepticism. After all, Husserl's purpose in phenomenology was not to make straightforward claims about reality or to certify the veracity of our experience or our scientific theories. He did not wish to overcome skepticism in this sense, and in this he differs from Descartes. His purpose, rather, is to make transcendental or reflective claims of precisely the sort we have been describing about the nature of our experience and about the world as it presents itself in that experience. While he may arrive at a concept of world and reality that permits of a relativistic interpretation, the same would not necessarily apply to what he says about the basic structures of experience, e.g., the stratification mentioned above in which perception appears at the lowest level. The same could be said for Heidegger: while the public world of *Zuhandenheit* may differ considerably depending on which "public" is involved, the fact *that Dasein*'s everyday world has the character of *Zuhandenheit* is not itself subject to the charge of relativism, but is presumably meant as a universally valid claim, i.e., true of every possible *Dasein*.

It is not so easy, however, to avoid by this means a relativistic interpretation. Husserl's phenomenology does involve a description of the world, if only as phenomenon of world-as-it-presents-itself-to-us. This is so precisely because of the thesis of intentionality: because all consciousness is consciousness *of*, we cannot produce a description of consciousness without at the same time dealing with what it is of, i.e., with its objects and its world. Another way of describing what Husserl is doing is to say that he seeks to describe the nature of our most fundamental beliefs about the world. To be sure, phenomenology deals with the world in structural, not in factual, terms. But it is still open to the charge that it is only *our* world whose structure it is describing or only *our* most fundamental beliefs about the world – however broadly we construe the "our" – and not necessarily any possible world or beliefs about the world. The very fact that Heidegger and Merleau-Ponty could so revise Husserl's conception of the world of the natural attitude seems to brand Husserl's description as that of a limited "point of view" perhaps engendered in his case by an inherited set of objectivist prejudices. But if this can be said of Husserl's descriptions, why cannot something like it also be said of Heidegger's and Merleau-Ponty's as well, perhaps involving in their case other sorts of prejudices? It is hard to see how any phenomenological description is immune to this sort of criticism.

In this sense we can see that the same considerations which allowed for a relativistic interpretation of the consciousness of the natural attitude could apply as well to the phenomenologically describing consciousness. While its concern is not straightforwardly with the world but rather with consciousness, the structures of consciousness and the structures of the world as experienced, the phenomenologically describing consciousness is still, after all, consciousness. As such, does it not confront something analogous to a perceptual given in its own domain? Husserl himself suggests that it does. [38] In its approach to that domain is it not itself always a case of intending-*as*? Husserl admits as much when he says that transcendental experience may be *inadequate*. [39] Finally, does it not approach its task like any other mode of consciousness with a background of past experience? We can see that in this way the very aspects of Husserl's theory of consciousness that allow a relativistic interpretation with respect to the world also reflect back upon and allow for the same interpretation of phenomenology itself.

NOTES

1. *Logical Investigations*, trans. J.N. Findlay (New York: Humanities Press, 1970), Vol. I. See especially Chapter 7, pp. 135 ff.
2. "Philosophy as Rigorous Science", trans. Quentin Lauer in Edmund Husserl, *Phenomenology and the Crisis of Philosophy* (New York: Harper and Row, 1965). See especially pp. 122 ff. It should be pointed out that Husserl's use of "historicism" to mean "historical relativism" is at variance with other uses of the term, e.g., that of Popper in *The Poverty of Historicism* (New York: Harper and Row, 1964).
3. See especially the long critique of Erdmann in section 40.
4. Donald Davidson, "On the Very Idea of a Conceptual Scheme", *Proceedings and Addresses of the American Philosophical Association* 47 (1974), 5–20.
5. Richard Rorty, "The World Well Lost" in *Journal of Philosophy* LXIX, no. 19 (1972), pp. 649–665.
6. Rorty, p. 659.
7. Rorty, p. 649.
8. *Logical Investigations*, Vol. I, p. 309.
9. *Ideas: General Introduction to Pure Phenomenology*, trans. W.R. Boyce Gibson (New York: Macmillan Co., 1958). See section 43.
10. *Logical Investigations*, Vol. I, p. 309 f.
11. *Ideas*, section 85.
12. *Logical Investigations*, Vol. I, p. 310.
13. Cf. *Logical Investigations*, Vol. II, p. 540.
14. Cf. *Logical Investigations*, Vol. II, p. 567.
15. In an excellent study, J.N. Mohanty has pointed to the various and distinct notions (simplicity, immediacy, passivity, indubitability) that have been confusedly combined in traditional concepts of the given. See "The Given" in *Phenomenology and Ontology* (The Hague: Martinus Nijhoff, 1970), p. 13 f.
16. Cf. *Logical Investigations*, Vol. II, p. 537.
17. *Logical Investigations*, Vol. II, p. 710 ff.
18. "Pretension" is used in *Logical Investigations* (Vol. II, p. 712); "presumption" is a later (and better) term.
19. Cf. *Ideas*, sections 27–32.
20. *Phenomenology of Perception*, trans. Colin Smith (New York: Humanities Press, 1962), p. ix.
21. See *Being and Time*, trans. J. Macquarrie and E. Robinson (New York: Harper and Row, 1962), sections 12–18.
22. He comes closest to it, perhaps, in passages like *Cartesian Meditations*, trans. D. Cairns (The Hague: Martinus Nijhoff, 1960), p. 140.
23. *Logical Investigations*, Vol. II, p. 578.
24. See R.M. Chisholm, "Sentences About Believing", and the discussion that has grown out of Chisholm's paper, in *Intentionality, Mind and Language*, ed. Ausonio Marras (Urbana: University of Illinois Press, 1972); also the articles by myself ("Intentionality") and J.L. Mackie ("Problems of Intentionality") in *Phenomenology and Philosophical Understanding*, ed. Edo Pivcevic (Cambridge: Cambridge University Press, 1975).
25. Cf. *Logical Investigations*, Vol. II, p. 712 f.
26. Cf. *Ideas*, section 131.
27. *Being and Time*, section 32.
28. *Phenomenology of Perception*, p. 395.
29. Trans. James S. Churchill. (Bloomington: Indiana University Press, 1964).
30. Cf. *Logical Investigations*, Vol. II, pp. 694 ff.

34

31. *Ideas*, section 81.
32. *Phenomenology of Internal Time-Consciousness*, sections 8–13.
33. *Cartesian Meditations*, section 32.
34. See *The Crisis of European Sciences*, trans. D. Carr (Evanston: Northwestern University Press, 1970). In a study concentrating on Husserl's late work, *Phenomenology and the Problem of History* (Evanston: Northwestern University Press, 1974), I have dealt in more detail with the relativistic implications of the notion of "consciousness as temporal Gestalt" as it is elaborated in Husserl's "middle period" (*Cartesian Meditations*) and combined there with his theory of intersubjectivity to lead to the conception of historicity in the *Crisis*. The present essay goes further in tracing Husserl's implicit relativism to the earliest writings, not only the lectures on time-consciousness, but also, as in points 1 and 2 of this essay, *The Logical Investigations*.
35. *Being and Time*, section 68.
36. *Being and Time*, section 32.
37. H.G. Gadamer, *Truth and Method* (New York: Seabury Press, 1975), pp. 235 ff.
38. *Cartesian Meditations*, p. 27: "phenomenological *epoché* lays open (to me, the meditating philosopher) *an infinite realm of being of a new kind*, as the sphere of a new kind of experience (*Erfahrung*): transcendental experience." *Ideas*, p. 112: "our goal we could also refer to as *the winning of a new region of Being* ... a region of *individual* Being, like every genuine region".
39. *Cartesian Meditations*, p. 22 f.

Memory and Phenomenological Method
by
Edward S. Casey

"Even concerning this ultimate goal, the origins and
specific rights of the lower stages should not be
forgotten".
–Husserl, *Experience and Judgment*, section 10.

I

The marriage of memory and method in philosophy has been a notably
uneven event. The unevenness is dramatically evident in the differences between Plato and Husserl regarding the relation between method and memory.
These two most profound of philosophical *Eidetikers*, deeply allied in their
common concern for securing insight into essential structures, are just as deeply devided when it comes to the role of remembering in philosophical method.
This is not to deny that each is obsessed with devising the best possible method
for attaining an apodictically certain grasp of essences, and there are important
formal similarities in their respective conceptions of method. For instance, in
both cases a stagewise procedure is advocated, whether this be in the form of
moving step-by-step up the divided line (as outlined most completely in *The
Republic* 509 – 11) or as a matter of executing successive "reductions" (i.e.,
philosophical, eidetic, phenomenological-transcendental, as presented most
accessibly in *Ideas*). Indeed, Platonic dialectic and Husserlian reduction can be
said to possess the same view of the primary task to be accomplished in such
stepwise methods: namely, the overcoming or suspending of the stranglehold
which common belief or opinion brings with it. *Doxa* and the "natural attitude" are seen as at once inevitable *qua* starting-points and evitable by the
proper pursuit of a prescribed philosophical method, which promises to
cleanse their cloying effects. Further, the *telos* of Platonic and Husserlian
method – the final step – is crucially similar: "*Wesensschau*", Husserl's
preferred term for the intuition of essences, is an appropriate description of
Plato's final stage of *noesis*. At this ultimate point, there are no further mediations; all becomes luminous: hence the metaphor of the "spark" of noetic insight in Plato's seventh letter and Husserl's allied claim that we may ultimately
reach "the brightly lit circle of perfect presentation" (*Ideas*, section 69). For

W.S. Hamrick (ed.) *Phenomenology in Practice and Theory*.
© 1985 Martinus Nijhoff Publishers, Dordrecht/Boston/Lancaster
ISBN 90 247 2926 2. Printed in the Netherlands.

both philosophers, it is a matter of moving from doxic darkness to eidetic light, and for both, therefore, philosophical method will be a method of "clarification" (*Klärung*), of achieving an "absolute nearness" (*ibid.*, section 67) to essence; and such nearness can be realized only in the clarifying, if dazzling, sunlight of life outside the cave (*Republic* 514–21). For Husserl and Plato alike, philosophical method is in the end a "method for apprehending essences (*Wesenserfassung*) with perfect clearness" (the title of section 69 of *Ideas*).

I am not concerned here with such questions as whether "essence" means the same thing for Plato and Husserl (it does not insofar as Husserl distinguishes between formal and material essences) or whether Husserl was a crypto-Platonist (a charge which plagued him throughout his career and which he sought vehemently to deny). Rather, I shall restrict consideration to the following intriguing but vexatious question: how is it that two philosophers so alike in their concern for, and conception of, method as Plato and Husserl could be so different in their views of the role of memory in method? A cursory glance at Plato's position on this matter will be followed by a much closer look at Husserl's and then by some suggestions for a more adequate assessment of the place of remembering in phenomenological method. In this way I shall also be commemorating the lifework of Herbert Spiegelberg, who has done so much to bring the issue of method to the forefront of current research in phenomenology — both in theory (i.e., in his remarkable monograph "The Essentials of Phenomenological Method") and in practice (in his series of inspiring workshops in phenomenology, of which the present author was an early participant).

II

For Plato, memory in the form of recollection is the basic vehicle, and perhaps even the very substance, of eidetic knowledge. It is "the only route to knowledge of the standard subjects of dialectical inquiry".[1] Every other route represents a mistaken path, a detour dictated by *doxa*: which is to say, by the opinions of others, ultimately of *das man*. It is Plato's root premise that knowledge comes from within oneself (*ex hautou: Meno* 85 d; *Philebus* 34 b–c) and not from others or from the sensory experience in which oneself and others are immersed in common (cf. *Theatetus* 155–64; 184–6). The only plausible repository for such non-sensorially derived and internally held knowledge is memory. This is so not just by default but because of memory's positive properties of holding and retaining. As Heidegger has stressed, memory is the main gatherer and keeper in human experience: "Memory, in the sense of human thinking that recalls, dwells where everything that gives food for thought is kept in safety ... Memory, as the human recall of what must be thought about, consists in the "keeping" of what is most thought-provoking. Keeping is the fundamental nature and essence of memory".[2]

It is precisely this in-gathering and holding-in capacity of memory that recommends it to Plato as the main means of maintaining knowledge of the Forms. As such knowledge cannot have been acquired in this present life (or else we would remember its very acquisition: which we manifestly do not), it must have been gained in a previous life. All the more reason, then, why it must be *recollected* − where "recollection" implies a search for what we have forgotten in *this* life. Such a search is strictly dialectical both insofar as it proceeds stepwise (and not by a single intuitive leap) and insofar as it can be guided maieutically by others (who do not impart knowledge but only help us to recollect it for ourselves). Memory, then, supplies the primordial stock of knowledge acquired in a prior existence, while recollection selects from this stock those items searched for in a given cognitive inquiry.[3]

Recall the situation in the *Meno*, which propounds the doctrine that learning is recollection as a solution to the paradox of inquiry. The paradox is: how can we search for what we already know, for there would be no need for search; or for what we do not know, since we would then not know how to recognize it when we found it? (*Meno* 80 d−e). Being born into this life is equivalent to the forgetting of what we once knew, that is, to ignorance. But anyone in this state (and we are all in it) can, like the slave in this dialogue, be cajoled and prompted to recall what has been forgotten − at first in terms of true opinion and then as genuine knowledge. Rather than discovery, it is a matter of recovery, which makes possible the recognition that helps to resolve the paradox of inquiry. We need to search for knowledge, precisely because we have forgotten it; but we can end the search when we recognize that what we have recovered is something we once knew explicitly. Such an inquirer, in Socrates' summary, "will know it [i.e., recover-and-recognize it] without having been taught but only questioned, [since he has found] the knowledge within himself" (*Meno* 85 d). The dialectical process, in short, is one of recollection, for "is not finding knowledge within oneself (*ex hautou*) recollection?"[4]

What does this "within oneself" signify? First, as the *Meno* is designed to illustrate, it means that we do not take over knowledge directly from others, however essential they may be as goads or guides. Second, such knowledge is held strictly within the soul, not the body; as Plato says elsewhere, "when that which has been experienced by the soul in common with the body is recaptured, so far as may be, *by and in the soul itself* apart from the body, then we speak of 'recollecting' something" (*Philebus* 34 b; my italics). Third, this knowledge is at once associative and systematic in nature, since one item of it can call up many others with which it is associated.[5]

This Platonic stress on the immanence of knowledge-as-recollected (and there is no other kind of knowledge for Plato) does not deny the importance of three transcendent factors: the maieute or "teacher"; the necessity that the interlocutors in an inquiry recall as much relevant information as possible during the course of inquiry, that is, before the knowledge sought-for is obtained; and the critical role of material particulars insofar as they may "remind" the inquirer of the pertinent Forms: *anamimneskesthai*, usually translated as "to recollect", means literally "to be reminded".[6] Nevertheless, the first two factors can be considered contingent to the extent that one might inquire on one's own — which will be the implicit model of phenomenological inquiry — while reminding, even if it frequently occurs in a perceptual setting, need not do so (I can be reminded by a fantasy or thought as well as by a material particular); and in any case reminding throws us back upon our internal resources by its very operation: "if a person is to be reminded of anything, he must *first know it* at some time or other" (*Phaedo* 736; my italics), where such "first knowing" can only refer to knowledge held within oneself and capable of being recollected. Reminding is, therefore, only a particularly favorable occasion for recollecting, which remains the pivotal point of Platonic method, at once its indispensable *modus operandi* and its irreplaceable aim. Dialectical inquiry for Plato both proceeds in recollections (albeit spurred by remindings) and terminates in them. It is thus recollective through and through, from start to finish: never not a matter of remembering.

III

It is strange indeed that Husserl, despite his many affinities with Plato, should have so little place for memory in his methodological consideration. Moreover, one might have thought that the other philosophical ancestor to whom he has deep ties — in fact, still closer links than to Plato himself — would have influenced him on this very score: Descartes. For the latter, memory retains an important, if submerged, methodological value. At a critical moment in the fourth *Meditation*, Descartes remarks that there can be only two ways by which God could bring it about that I never make erroneous judgments even as I remain free and possess only finite knowledge. Either my intellect would have to be such as always to have "a clear and distinct perception of everything about which I would ever deliberate" or God would have to impress "firmly enough *upon my memory* — so that I could never forget it — that I should never judge anything that I do not clearly and distinctly understand".[7] As the first alternative obviously does not obtain for human beings, who have all too many indistinct and unclear ideas, the second offers the only real hope in the circumstance. Although Descartes has already admitted to the imperfection of memory in human beings,[8] he nonetheless believes that a concerted use of remembering will be cognitively salutary in avoiding error:

"even if I cannot abstain from errors in the first way, which depends upon the evident perception of everything concerning which one must deliberate, nevertheless I can do so by the second way, which depends solely *on my remembering that whenever the truth of a given matter is not apparent, I must abstain from making judgments"*.[9]

What is most striking about this passage, which makes memory indispensable to philosophical method, is that remembering is made operative at the very point at which phenomenological reduction is prophetically predelineated: namely, in abstention from judgment. The central feature of such reduction is, in Husserl's own classical formulation: "In relation to every thesis [i.e., concerning spatio-temporal existence] and wholly uncoerced we can use this peculiar *epoché* or abstention, a certain restraining from judgment ... The thesis is "put out of action"; bracketed, it passes into the modified status of a "bracketed thesis", and the judgment *simpliciter* into a "bracketed judgment".[10]

Instead of being impressed by the need to *remember* to abstain from judgment — a need which Descartes attributes to our constitutional "infirmity"[11] — Husserl is much more taken by the character of abstaining itself, especially its nuclear operation of disconnecting or suspending. Such suspending does not suggest remembering (in which there is always an element of commitment) but the very different action of "sheer supposing" (*sich bloss denken*), e.g., that "Nymphs are dancing in a ring" (*Ideas*, section 31). In other words, it is towards imagination, not memory, that Husserl's own description of phenomenological method pushes him. For imagining is the non-positing mental activity *par excellence*, and the phenomenological *epoché* is precisely an attempt to abstain by adopting a non-positing stance in the face of all the positing tendencies which the natural attitude belongs with it — including remembering, which posits the past reality of its content.

Thus is hardly surprising that Husserl comes to favor imagination at almost every turn in his various discussions of phenomenological method, not only in *Ideas* but in later texts such as *Experience and Judgment*. I have traced out elsewhere in some detail Husserl's predilection for imagination in methodological matters.[12] Suffice it to say for now that imagining figures prominently, and sometimes exclusively, at the following nodal points:

(1) in supplying examples which need not be based on one's own experience (such examples are either imagined freely or borrowed from the imagining of others, e.g., from literature);[13]

(2) in allowing the envisagement of formal possibilities of eidetic structure not available in an already constituted format;[14]

(3) in being the sole basis for "free variation", i.e., the projection of variant versions of an object so as to realize what its invariant features are.[15]

From such considerations Husserl concludes that "in phenomenology, as in all eidetic sciences, presentifications or, more exactly, *free imaginings assume a privileged position* over against perceptions ... The element which makes up the life of phenomenology, as of all eidetical science is "fiction" (*Ideas*, section 70; my italics). Evident in such a claim are its own origins, implicit as they may be, in Kant's privileging of productive over reproductive imagination. In the *Critique of Pure Reason* the latter is equivalent to memory; it operates by association and is directly dependent on the offerings of pure intuition; as reproductive, it accounts for the "synopsis" of experienced items but cannot achieve the full-blown "synthesis" which productive imagination alone can effect. The productivity of the latter consists precisely in its ability to transcend the givens of sensory experience by its schematizing activities; and one such form of transcendence is fiction, the creation of productive imagination in its truly "formative" (*bildende*) power as it is termed in the *Critique of Judgment*. [16]

Husserl, very much a neo-Kantian in this respect if in few others, finds the fictionalizing capacity of imagination critical for phenomenological method. Why is this? Chiefly for three reasons. First, only on the basis of such a cognitive power can a working phenomenologist effect the *Gedankenexperimente* that are essential to expanding the intrinsically limited scope of the investigator's own personal experience: "the freedom of research in the region of essences necessarily demands that one should operate with the help of imagination" (*Ideas*, section 70). Second, imagining is essential to clarifying, thus to pursuing one of the most basic aims of all phenomenological method; what Husserl says of the geometer is equally true of the phenomenologist: "In imagination [the geometer] must toil to secure clear intuitions, and from this labor drawings and models set him free. But in actual drawing and modelling he is restricted; in imagining he has an incomparable freedom to recast arbitrarily the figures he has imagined in running over continuous series of possible shapes, in the production therefore of an infinite number of new creation" (*Ideas*, section 70). Clarification arises from the recasting, from seeing something in a continuously new light (even if, or precisely because, this is not the light of the day but the mind's own self-engendered luminosity). Third, the very production of new, and mostly fictive, figures by productive imagining brings forth a set of variants sufficient for an invariant eidetic nucleus to emerge therefrom. Only in this way can we be certain that a given feature is genuinely essential: that is, by discovering that it cannot be *dis*-imagined from the variations which have been set forth in imaginative form. Also, *between* such variations congruences and coincidences will make themselves manifest, constituting *ipso facto* eidetic structures of the phenomenon being varied. [17] Much as does recollection for Plato, then, imagination emerges for Husserl as of central significance at every stage of eidetic inquiry: from the initial gathering of examples regarded as prototypes (*Vorbilder*) to eidetic insight into the invariant itself.

IV

Nevertheless, a closer look reveals a somewhat less one-sided picture – just as it does in the case of Plato, whose reliance on a mythopoetic imagination proves to be essential to the constitution and course of Platonic dialogues themselves.[18] For one thing, it is surely significant that Husserl's ground-breaking Göttingen lectures of 1904–5 deal predominantly with primary and secondary memory as the most critical features of time-consciousness, broaching the issue of imagination mainly as an adjunct to this preoccupation with memory in the domain of temporal experience.[19] Second, imagination and memory have, at least in principle, an epistemological equality insofar as both are main types of "presentification" and differ only insofar as one is non-positing and one positing; or, more radically, imagination is considered as dependent and supervenient on memory as the more basic act: "Imagining in general is the *neutrality-modification of the 'positing' act of presentification*, and therefore of remembering in the widest sense" (*Ideas*, section 111; Husserl's italics). Remembering is therefore presupposed by imagining in human experience as such: a theme that is expressed later by Husserl in the thesis that passive synthesis (which includes remembering as an associative act) is presumed by all active synthesis (of which explicit imagining forms part). Third, and returning to strictly methodological concerns, at one particular point in *Ideas* (the very text in which imagination is accorded the highest methodological significance) memory and imagination are suddenly accorded an equally valid role in method: "Thus we rehearse to ourselves by way of illustration certain conscious experiences chosen at random taken in their individuality just as they are given in the natural attitude as real facts of human life, *or we presentify them to ourselves through memory or in the free play of imagination*. On the ground of illustrations such as these, which we assume to be presented with perfect clearness (and by free variation grasping the invariant in its pure generality) we grasp and fix in adequate ideation the pure essence which interests us".[20]

By pointing to this equality of methodological status, I do not want to suggest that some kind of competition between imagination and memory is being waged in Husserl's mind. I think, rather, that he is simply of two minds on the matter: which is to say, ambivalent and even inconsistent. Nor is it my own interest to stage such a competition, either within the Husserlian *corpus* or independently of it. Instead, I want only to redress the balance – to give to memory its just due in the practice of phenomenological method without passing any final judgment as to its inferiority or superiority vis-à-vis imagination within that practice. In this act of non-vindictive vindication, I shall proceed in two steps: first, by showing that three of Husserl's own notions entail the methodological importance of memory, implicitly and explicitly; then, by pointing to two areas of memory's methodological significance neglected by Husserl but singled out by Herbert Spiegelberg.

V

(i) *Sedimentation*. This first notion is the last to occur in Husserl's work and the least completely developed of all, but it is not for this reason of any less interest or value. Sedimentation or tradition-alization[21] arises when a body of method or theory (and often one mistaken for the other) insinuates itself into successive historical epochs as a "garb of ideas" (*Ideenkleid*) which disguises the character of the actually experienced life-world of those who live in these epochs. To return to this pre-given world with its sensible plena of concretely intuited shapes — that is, to the world as "actuality pre-supposed in all idealization"[22] — we must perform an act of de-sedimentation not unlike the phenomenological reduction but now directed exclusively at the distorting overlay of the ideational complexes which have closed off acknowledgment of various life-world realities and of which the paradigm case for Husserl is that of Galilean physics in its substitution of "planar" for "plenar" attributes. In any such operation of de-sedimenting memory is operative at two levels: (a) in recalling, through factual knowledge, that the garb of ideas is contingent in origin (i.e., as in fact conceived or discovered at a particular moment in time) and in its subsequent sedimentation into lived experience. Here a specifically historical memory is called for which would be at once collective and commemorative, and thus exceed what is confined to personal memory alone. (b) More basically, in the recollection of what lived experience is like independently of the supervening cloak of ideas; Husserl calls this process one of "reactivation", and he describes it as follows in "The Origin of Geometry": "The awakening is [at first] something passive: the awakened signification is thus given passively, similarly to the way in which any other activity which has sunk into obscurity, once associatively awakened, emerges at first passively as a more or less clear memory. [But] in the passivity in question here, as in the case of memory, what is passively awakened can be transformed back, so to speak, into the corresponding activity: this is the capacity for reactivation that belongs originally to every human being as a speaking being".[23] What is crucial here is the idea of "transformation back", which is the means by which reactivation is achieved. I take it to be founded directly and solely on remembering what unsedimented experience is like — now strictly in the individual. Evidence favoring this interpretation comes from a footnote appended to the just-cited text: "this is a transformation of which one is conscious as being in itself patterned after [what is passively awakened]".[24] If one is indeed conscious of the transformed as patterned after what has been passively awakened, and if the latter is itself" a more or less clear memory", then it is an inescapable conclusion that the reactivation which accomplishes desedimentation in the individual is reliant on remembering, a remembering of the subtly sensuous structure of one's lived world or of eidetic insights into this structure.

(ii) *What remains over*. A second arena in which memory is operative in Husserlian phenomenological method is found in connection with phenomenological reduction proper. One of the most constantly reiterated themes in *Ideas* is that this reduction does not affect or alter that which is bracketed on a given occasion except with regard to its "general thesis" or existence-positing tendency. This tendency, at once naive and natural, posits the surrounding world as "simply there" (*einfach da*) in space and time. It *remains before us* as an object of doxic commitment before we have decommissioned the actually operative component in this belief: "it" [the fact-world] remains ever, in the sense of the general thesis, a world that has its being out there" (*Ideas*, section 30). This pre-reductive moment has *its* own memory too, of course; otherwise, we could not hold the transcendent world before us in such a steady fashion as a single coherent world. A generalized memory of what Merleau-Ponty calls "the world's rays"[25] is therefore presupposed by the phenomenological reduction itself, which requires a world constantly recalled to which to apply itself.

But once we undertake the reduction itself, two different and still more pertinent senses of remaining over obtain, each calling for remembering in its own way:

(a) In direct answer to the question "what can remain over (*bleiben übrig*) when the whole world is bracketed"? (*Ideas*, section 33), Husserl proclaims that the relevant remainder is none other than consciousness, the sphere of sheer immanence: "Consciousness has a being of its own which in its absolute uniqueness of nature remains unaffected by the phenomenological disconnection ... it therefore *remains over* as a 'phenomenological residuum'".[26] Consciousness as that which escapes the net of the reduction remains over as a domain or field of inquiry in its own right, and as such it demands remembrance within the sphere of immanence: remembrance of its primary features, beginning with intentionality and continuing with its special modes of apprehending, appreciating, reflecting, and so forth. These structures and modes are not simply discovered after the phenomenological reduction has been executed; we have known that they existed all along; but the new clarity wrought by reduction, its elimination of the distractions of transcendence-positings, allows us to bring them back to conscious mind more pellucidly; in short, to remember more adequately how they are formed and how they operate. (Here is indeed an analogue of Platonic recollection but only as performed within the compass of a single lifetime.)

(b) Within pure consciousness itself, however, more than its own operations are disclosed after reduction: not just its forms of intending (its noeses) but the things therein intended come to appearance. And these latter, in their strict noematic format, enclose within them references to the very world under suspension. The contents of this world, its transcendent items, are still present, only now with a changed existential index. In short, nothing has been lost, *everyting remains*: it has just been relocated within pure consciousness or transcendental subjectivity: "We have literally lost nothing, but have won the whole of absolute being [i.e., pure consciousness], which, properly understood, conceals in itself all worldly transcendences (as international correlates of acts of habitual validation which ideally form a unity together), "constituting" them within itself". [27]

A direct consequence of this non-loss notion of reduction is that memory will become even more requisite than at stage (a). For it will be the only means by which the totality of what remains over can be kept in mind and brought to the explicit attention of the phenomenologist. *How else* can "the role of absolute being" as containing mundane transcendences be made available for discernment and scrutiny? *Where else* than in memory could any such massive remaining-over occur? Were it to occur in present consciousness alone, it would overtax and overwhelm the latter, leading to confusion rather than to clarification. The very idea of remaining over, I submit, requires remembering as its cognitive counterpart.

(iii) *Retaining-in-grasp*. Perhaps the most directly ingredient role of memory in phenomenological method occurs, paradoxically, in the case of free variation. The matter is paradoxical since it is precisely in free variation that *imagination* is most alive by virtue of its proliferation of variants. But it is in regard to this very proliferation that remembering is most needed: to stem the time of "an infinitely open multiplicity" or at least to make it manageable. [28] It does so, however, in neither of its two most traditionally recognized forms: as primary memory (constituted by retentions) or as secondary memory (constituted by recollections). Instead, a middle-range memorial activity, termed technically "still-retaining-in-grasp" (*noch-im-Griff-behalten*), is called upon; I simplify this term, as does Husserl himself, to "retaining-in-grasp". Its intermediate status is underscored by the claim that it is always a form of "passivity in activity", a thematizing or objectivating passivity (in contrast with, say, the pure passivity of retentional consciousness). [29] Its operation consists in a holding-in-mind of recently experienced objects and states of affairs whenever they remain impressionally present (e.g., a sound continuing to sound as we retain-in-grasp its earlier phases) or have become non-impressional altogether, whether our attention remains fixed upon a single object throughout or turns to different objects, or whether there is in addition an explicative synthesis whereby a substrate is determined in regard to its properties. [30] Whichever is the case, the achievement of retaining-in-grasp is always a coincidence or overlapping, which may be partial or total depending on the particularities of the situation; and it is just this achievement which is most pertinent in the special case of free variation. For retaining-in-grasp is ideally designed in just this fashion to draw together the indefinite multiplicity of variants which is the natural consequence of freely varying an initial *Vorbild* in an unrestrained way. In order that "all the arbitrary particulars [i.e., variants] attain overlapping coincidence in the order to their appearance and enter . . . into a synthetic unity",[31] retaining-in-grasp must intervene to effect such a unity. There is no other cognitive activity equal to this task.

Performing the task is in turn essential to eidetic insight: an *eidos* emerges only as the identically one in the many of its imaginitive variations, as "*hen epi pollòn*". It is retaining-in-grasp that effects the eidetic openness that saves the manyness of the variants from falling into what Aristotle would term a mere "heap" of particulars: "Only if we retain in grasp the things imagined [*Fikta*] earlier, as a multiplicity in an open process, and only if we look toward the congruent and purely identical, do we attain the *eidos*".[32] Not only, then, do we witness here a role for memory in phenomenological method which is at once unique and uniquely important (indeed, indispensable to the final grasp of an *eidos*) but we are made to recognize a very different fate of remembering in the pursuit of essences from that which we observed in the instance of Plato. Where recollection for him was a matter of *bringing back* fully intact knowledge from a previous life (thanks to reminders present in this life), retaining-in-grasp for Husserl *brings together* the dispersed, non-intact products of an active imagination. In Plato's case, it is a question of a strictly passive being reminded ("passive reawakening" as Husserl would call it); for Husserl, it is a matter of an equiprimordially active-and-passive holding-together in a united and unifying grasp. Memory is essential to eidetic knowledge in both instances; but it is so in crucially disparate modes of its basic operation.

VI

I want to turn finally to two last ways in which memory figures into phenomenological method. These did not come to Husserl's attention explicitly as parts of an official methodology, even though they are outgrowths of his conception of what a valid phenomenological method should consist in:

(i) *Watching*. The fourth "essential" in Professor Spiegelberg's compendium of basic methodological moves is termed "watching modes of appearing".[33] This is the special form of apprehension wherein the changing modes of appearing of a given object or state of affairs are made thematic. These appearings (*Gegebenheitsweisen* as Husserl would call them) are attended to for their own sake: which is to say, not as aspects of an explicative synthesis of determinations of a particular substrate. Nor are they watched for the kind of unity that is realized in retaining-in-grasp, which is limited to the

46

unification of aspects experienced in the recent past.

For we may "keep watch" over how something appears during a quite extensive stretch of time: as when we watch a person's face aging over a decade or more. For such watching, continuous observation is obviously not required. The watching can be discontinuous in terms of the occasions on which we look intently at the phenomenon in question, and yet may be no less committed or discerning. What *is* needed throughout, however, is remembering; in fact, it is precisely memory which makes the discontinuity itself viable: not because we need to be consciously recalling former appearings in interim moments but because we know that we can do so in principle, at least within the usual limits of voluntary recollectability. Error is of course not excluded, but the watching itself guards against this. The watching, in any case, is not of details per se (e.g., of exact spatial or temporal positions); it bears, rather, on developing profiles – on the changing aspects of a durational flow. The watching, in short, is of an apparitional *Gestalt*: "how x manifested itself during (nonmetric) time t and at place p".

Such watching is required in eliciting certain essential structures: for example, someone's character, which does not reveal itself fully to us in a single isolated act (paradigmatic as this can be at times). It is then a longitudinal matter, and the kind of memory subtending it is characteristically "long term". In other words, recollection in its usual, and not in its Platonic, sense is at work in this kind of watching; or I should say more precisely, recollection in its *virtual* mode of operation. By this I mean not just the state of storage and inprinciple availability of properly registered and encoded memories,[34] but their ongoing effect and presence albeit from a marginal position in the mental field. The most illuminating analogy here is that of language, which in its totality exists in a latent state (de Saussure in fact uses the word "virtual" at just this point) ready to be recalled. Like the preconscious (where language is located according to Freudian metapsychology), there is accessibility without the oppressiveness which would result from constantly complete recall. The action of such virtual states, whether strictly linguistic or mnemonic, is one of continually funding experience, thus of making it more cohesive and coherent.

This action is the very basis, the subterranean support for watching modes of appearance, that which makes it possible to say that we are watching *the same thing* over a period of discrete and discontinuous viewings. The virtual recollectability of formerly watched appearings contributes directly to the selfidentity of the thing watched; indeed, this self-identity of the watched may be said to depend on such recollectability.[35] And so too, consequently, must the grasp of its *eidos*, whose invariancy requires the self-identity of that of which it is the essence. Once more, then, and in yet another way, recollection and eidetic insight are seen to be intrinsically linked – to be partners in a common methodological enterprise.

(ii) *Interpreting*. The seventh, and last, of the Spiegelbergian essential steps is called "interpreting concealed meanings",[36] which I shall shorten to "interpreting" *simpliciter*. There is, however, nothing simple about this last step, which has been the subject of debate and discussion from Heidegger to Gadamer to Ricoeur. Indeed, it is very much at issue in the problematic of sedimentation and reactivation which is so central to Husserl's *Crisis*. I shall restrict consideration to the role of remembering in interpreting meaning and even then will only begin to adumbrate the full complexity of the phenomenon.

Interpretation is per force interpretation of meaning, while meaning is itself conceived in phenomenology as the "noematic nucleus" or as the "upon-which" of projective understanding.[37] Either way, meaning is a close cousin of essence, which has much the same compact and central character of the "determinable X" (*Ideas*, section 131). But where essences have as their destiny becoming fully manifest – being disclosed in full "self-evidence" – meanings may arise in human experience as masked: *essentially so*. That is to say, they may occur as not fully manifesting themselves and thus as requiring interpretation of various sorts. Such interpretation represents a further step beyond reduction and free variation, which are limited by their very nature to what makes itself manifest once these very techniques are applied.

Interpretation proceeds in various modes of taking-as, most characteristically from what Heidegger would term the "existential-hermeneutical as-structure" to the "apophantical as-structure" (*Being and Time*, section 33). It is in making this transition – which is as various as there are interpretive procedures – that concealed meanings come to an explicitness which they would not otherwise know. Much depends, of course, on the phenomenon to be interpreted: if it is perceptual, then it will be mainly a matter of clarifying and of de-illusioning in different modes; if it is psycho-dynamic, it will involve recourse to free association or other bases of interpretive insight; if it is cultural, it will require historical/social/political considerations. But whatever mode or style of interpretation is pursued, remembering will be active and relevant. It will be so in two fundamental ways:

(a) *bearing-in-mind*. This is closely allied to retaining-in-grasp, but is confined to the transition from the existential-hermeneutical to the apophantic as-structure. As we make this move, we must bear in mind the particularities of the primarily taken-as so as not to lose their specificity: even if (indeed precisely if) it is performing a masking role. As Freud says pertinently in this connection: "the symptom is on the agenda all the time".[38] Just as the symptom must be borne in mind in its unique structure (in this case, as a "compromise formation" involving repressed and repressing elements) throughout the work of analysis proper, so any other confusing-concealing as-structure has to be kept in mind as its hidden elements emerge and are made articulate in apophantic (i.e., affirmative-descriptive) utterances. Such bearing-in-mind is like retaining-in-grasp in that it concerns items recently experienced or focussed on; but it differs in that its intentional objects are limited to intrinsically perplexing as-structures.

(b) *interpreting as dialogical*. Adequate interpretation often calls for the intervention of another person to aid in the interpreting process. This is perhaps most manifest in the case of psychoanalysis, where the effects of transference are of critical importance. But it also obtains in interpreting historical events (when others have to be involved as co-historizing witnesses) and even in autobiographical self-interpretation (insofar as others' recollections are often needed to supplement one's own, e.g., concerning events of early childhood years). In all such cases of interpreting, the other enters as a dialogical partner in a situation of mutual cross-examination. When this situation occurs – a situation which is precisely that which is dramatized in Platonic dialogues – what Collingwood has called "the logic of question and answer"[39] prevails. This logic is a dialectical logic of interchange between interlocutors whose more exact form has been traced out by Gadamer in *Truth and Method*.[40] Suffice it to say that the interchange is an inter-play in which the topic-to-be-interpreted (the "*Sache*" in Gadamer's term) comes to clarification and that such an interchange need not take place in a full-fledged form: I can regard the other's positions and views as answers to possible questions I (or some hypothetical interlocutor) might put to him.

It is in such an exchange of questions and answers, however, that memory is actively at work. Not only must I hold in mind the possible question of the other (and he mine) but I must remember the cultural (artistic, philosophical, etc.) tradition out of which he would pose that question. Only in this special form of "remembrance of things past" can I make genuine dialectical progress. In Gadamer's own terms, there must be a "fusion of horizons"[41] (i.e., of mine with his, past with present, etc.) if progress in interpretation is to occur. The fusion, however, is of remembered and not just of hypothetical or extrapolated horizons. Such a remembering need not be a case of conscious recollection; once again, it can be virtual in status, and often is – though with a virtuality which is distinctively collective, a matter of deeply shared experience. It is the sharing in fact which aids most in the bringing to light of culturally concealed meanings: socio-political symptoms, we might say. The archeological excavations needed to grasp the meaning of such symptoms call for the operation of a culturally comprehensive memory present *on both sides* of the dialogical interchange of questions and answers; otherwise, no fusion, no genuine understanding, can take place, and the obscure only chases after the still more obscure. Only a co-active, collectively-based memory can illuminate such depths ... can guide us out of the cave of self-isolated ignorance.

For a last time, then, Plato is suggested – now in the context of the community of inquiry, the co-interpreting dyad of questioner and answerer rather than the isolated eidetic researcher. Indeed, the interplay between Plato and Husserl themselves has been a recurrent theme in this essay. I have pointed to a number of abiding affinities despite deep-seated differences — and differences precisely with regard to the place of memory in philosophical method. We have seen that the diremption in this latter area between the two philosophers who embody respectively the *arche* and *telos* of Western rationalism, is less severe than appeared at first. Husserl, while not lending credence to anything like a recollective memory stemming from a previous existence, nevertheless acknowledges the significance of memory in phenomenological method at several critical points. And, with the genial assistance of Herbert Spiegelberg's own reflections on this method, we have discovered two more ways in which remembering is of widely ramified value in the practice of phenomenology. My conclusion can only be that memory is of an importance at least commensurate with imagination in this practice, even though this importance has been recognized as such and despite the fact of Husserl's own earnest efforts to promote imagination into a distinctly privileged position. The privilege is in fact shared between these two mental activities, which are as equiprimordial in the pursuit of phenomenological method as they are coeval in the constitution of human experience at large.

NOTES

1. Richard Sorabji, *Aristotle on Memory* (London: Duckworth, 1972), p. 36. In what follows I draw on Sorabji's excellent analysis of Plato at *ibid.*, pp. 35–46.
2. Martin Heidegger, *What is Called Thinking?*, trans. J. Glenn Gray (New York: Harper, 1968), pp. 150–1.
3. Sorabji expresses this point by saying that the memory of earlier knowledge is related to the recollection of such knowledge as (i) preceding the latter; (ii) being its condition of possibility; (iii) being forgotten in the interim. Cf. Sorabji, p. 40.
4. Sorabji, p. 40. Cf. *Philebus* 34C: "when the soul that has lost the memory of a sensation or what it has learned resumes that memory within itself (*ex hautou*) and goes over the old ground, we regularly speak of these precesses as 'recollections'".
5. "As the whole of nature is akin, and the soul has learned everything [in previous existences], nothing prevents a man, after recalling one thing only – a process men call learning – discovering everything else for himself" (*Meno* 81 d).
6. On the last two points, see Sorabji, pp. 35–6.
7. René Descartes, *Mediations on First Philosophy*, trans. D.A. Cress (Indianapolis: Hackett, 1979), p. 39. My italics.
8. "If I examine the faculty of memory, imagination, or any other faculty, I manifestly find [only] what in me is feeble and limited, but what in God I understand to be immense", Descartes, p. 37. On pp. 19–20, memory is omitted from Descartes' list of powers that determine human beings as thinking things.
9. Descartes, p. 40; my italics. Elsewhere a different use of memory is suggested, one which ties it to a trust in God's non-deceptiveness: "*it must be fixed in one's memory* as the highest rule, that what has been revealed to us by God is to be believed as the most certain of all things" (*Principles of Philosophy*, Part I, section 76; my italics).
10. *Ideas*, section 36. Most of this is in italics in the text. It is hardly accidental that Descartes' methodological doubt is discussed only a few paragraphs before in this same section. Husserl says that "we link on here", even though he is concerned to disaffiliate himself from Descartes's tendency to turn doubt into denial.
11. "Although I observe that there is in me this infirmity, namely, that I am unable always to adhere fixedly to one and the same knowledge, nevertheless I can, by attentive and frequently repeated meditation, bring it to pass that I recall [this infirmity] every time the situation demands; thus I would acquire a habit of not erring", Descartes, *Meditations*, p. 40.
12. "Imagination and Phenomenological Method". In F. Elliston and P. McCormick eds. *Husserl: Expositions and Appraisals* (Notre Dame: University of Notre Dame Press, 1977), pp. 70–82. In several respects, the present essay can be considered a companion piece to the earlier effort.
13. Cf. *Ideas*, sections 3, 4, 23 and especially 70: "We draw extraordinary profit from what history has to offer us, and in still richer measure from the gifts of art and particularly of poetry. These [latter] are indeed fruits of imagination (*Einbildungen*)".
14. See especially section 70 of *Ideas*.
15. "Free variation in imagination" is discussed most fully at *Experience and Judgment*, trans. J.S. Churchill and K. Ameriks (Evanston: Northwestern University Press, 1973), section 87a. The invariant thus obtained is explicitly likened to a Platonic *eidos* minus its "metaphysical interpretations" at p. 341.
16. On these conceptions of Kant's, see *The Critique of Pure Reason* A 100–1–3, A 120–24, B 180–82; *Critique of Judgment*, sections 22, 48.
17. On this last point, see *Experience and Judgment*, section 87c ("Congruence and Difference in the Overlapping Coincidence of Multiplicities of Variation") and Marcy C. Rawlinson's analysis of it in a forthcoming essay on "Theory of Essence in Proust and Husserl".

18. This is not to mention the further facts that (a) the interlocutor's responses in a given dialogue can be considered as a form of free variation in imagination; (b) a number of substantive Platonic themes, e.g., the nature of Eros and of image-making, offer profound meditations on imagination itself.

19. The recently published volume of Husserliana, *Phantasie, Bildbewusstsein, Erinnerung,* ed. E. Marbach (The Hague: Martinus Nijhoff, 1980) does not change this assessment, though it does show how deeply interested Husserl was in the structure of "image-consciousness" itself. There is a discernible tendency in this collection of writings, however, to subordinate imagination to memory. Cf. sections 1, 3, 11, 13, 15 as evidence of this tendency.

20. *Ideas,* section 34; my italics. This passage exemplifies another equality as well: that of the factual vs. the non-factual, the presentational vs. the presentificational. In eidetic inquiry, facts have no priority over fiction.

21. The two terms are used synonymously, e.g., at *The Crisis of European Sciences and Transcendental Philosophy,* trans. David Carr (Evanston: Northwestern University Press, 1970), p. 52.

22. *Crisis,* p. 50.

23. *Crisis,* p. 361.

24. *Crisis,* p. 361.

25. See Maurice Merleau-Ponty, *The Visible and Invisible,* trans. A. Lingis (Evanston: Northwestern University Press, 1968), pp. 241–2, 265.

26. *Ideas,* section 33, my italics.

27. *Ideas,* section 50; translation emended. Compare similar passages from the *Crisis* written almost twenty-five years later: "Through the *epoché* a new way of experiencing, of thinking, of theorizing, is opened to the philosopher; here, situated *above* his own natural being and *above* the natural world, he loses nothing of their being and their objective truths" (*Crisis,* section 41, p. 152; my italics). Cf. also p. 253: in undertaking an epoché "nothing at all can be lost".

28. *Experience and Judgment,* section 87a, p. 340.

29. On this characterization of retaining-in-grasp as "active – passive" see *Experience and Judgment,* sect. 23 a–b.

30. On these various avators of retaining-in-grasp, which are considerably more complex than I have presented them here, see *Experience and Judgment,* sections 23 and 24.

31. *Experience and Judgment,* section 87c, p. 343. The title of this section is "the Retaining-in-Grasp of the Entire Multiplicity of Variations as the Foundations of Essential Seeing".

32. *Experience and Judgment,* p. 343. It is difficult to make this passage compatible with the claim in the next sentence that "the overlapping coincidence ... takes place of itself in a purely passive way". Surely, we still have to do here with a situation of "passivity in activity".

33. Herbert Spiegelberg, *The Phenomenological Movement: A Historical Introduction* (The Hague: Martinus Nijhoff, 1980), II, 684–88. Husserl discusses "watchfulness" (*Achtsamkeit:* "needing" in Gibson's translation) in *Ideas,* sections 35 and 37; no link is there made to phenomenological method.

34. On the distinction between accessibility and availability in memory, see Robert G. Crowder, *Principles of Learning and Memory* (Hillsdale, N.J.: Erlbaum, 1976), pp. 10 ff. On encoding and registration, see Crowder, Chapters 4, 6.

35. As Husserl says in the *Cartesian Meditations:* "in the case of evidence of immanent data, I can return to them in a series of intuitive recollections that has the open endlessness which the "I can always do so again" ... creates. Without such "possibilities" there would be for us no *fixed and abiding* being" (*Cartesian Meditations,* trans. Dorion Cairns (The Hague: Martinus Nijhoff, 1960), p. 60; his italics).

36. See *The Phenomenological Movement,* II, 694–98.

37. Cf. Husserl, *Ideas*, sections 90–94, 98–100, 124; and Heidegger, *Being and Time*, trans. J. Macquarrie and E. Robinson (New York: Harper & Row, 1962), section 31.
38. J. Breuer and S. Freud, *Studies on Hysteria* (London: Hogarth, 1955), p. 297.
39. See R.G. Collingwood, *An Autobiography* (Oxford: Oxford University Press, 1939), Chapter 5.
40. Cf. Hans-Georg Gadamer, *Truth and Method* (New York: Seabury Press, 1975), pp. 325–45.
41. Gadamer, pp. 273 f., 337 f., 358.

"Plato's Cave", *Flatland* and Phenomenology
by
Philip J. Bossert

I

Both Martin Heidegger and Eugen Fink have used the platonic "allegory of the cave" to explicate certain aspects of Edmund Husserl's phenomenological philosophy. Heidegger's discussion of the allegory comes in his 1930 Freiburg Lecture, *"Platon's Lehre von der Wahrheit"*. [1] Without ever specifically naming Husserl, Heidegger uses the allegory to show why Husserl's phenomenology is "inadequate" as truly radical philosophy.

Fink's discussion appears in a 1934 article entitled, "Was will die Phänomenologie Edmund Husserls?". [2] Fink employs the allegory to clarify the sense of Husserl's phenomenological reduction as a shift in attitude [3] and to explain how the philosophical transformation of life achieved by means of this shift in attitude critique of Husserl and attempt to defend Husserl's phenomenological philosophy against Heidegger's criticism. [5]

The allegory of the cave is, I believe, definitely valuable in coming to an understanding of Husserl's philosophy. The problem with Heidegger's and Fink's uses of the allegory in this context, however, is that Heidegger's discussion of the allegory reflects primarily his own hermeneutic reinterpretation of phenomenology [6] rather than Husserl's transcendental phenomenology and Fink's discussion actually presents a mistaken version of the allegory in his attempt to explicate Husserl's philosophy. [7] It is also significant, I think, that Husserl himself, to my knowledge, never uses the Platonic allegory to explicate his own philosophical position. Hence, in what follows, I offer first, a discussion of Plato's allegory as an explication of phenomenological philosophy which reflects a Husserlian interpretation of phenomenology and which remains faithful to the text of the original Platonic myth [8] and, second, a discussion of an analogy which Husserl himself chose to use to explicate his method, i.e., the "analogy of dimensionality" drawn from the mathematical theory of axiomatic systems.

The result will be, I hope, a better understanding of Husserl's phenom-

W.S. Hamrick (ed.) *Phenomenology in Practice and Theory.*
© 1985 Martinus Nijhoff Publishers, Dordrecht/Boston/Lancaster
ISBN 90 247 2926 2. Printed in the Netherlands.

enological philosophy achieved by means of a careful explication of it both in terms of the ancient but still very important Platonic analogy and, comparatively, in terms of the contemporary and scientifically more significant mathematical analogy.

II

For Husserl, doing phenomenology requires the adoption of a special type of attitude or standpoint toward one's life or experience which makes explicit certain "anonymous" or normally hidden aspects of that life or experience. In Husserl's terms, the constitutive elements of experience which are always operative but usually anonymous are made thematic as a result of adopting the phenomenological attitude. Under normal circumstances, we live our lives out as human beings engaged in daily affairs, concerned with the usual and unusual people, places, things, events, problems and reflections which make up that which we call "the world". Husserl calls these normal circumstances the "natural attitude" towards experience, that is, the straightforward acceptance of our experiences for what they appear to be (also variously called "common sense realism" and "naive realism").

It should be noted that when one is in the natural attitude, one is not aware of having a natural attitude toward experience; for, in the natural attitude, one is not philosophically aware that such things as "attitudes towards experience" even exist. It is only after one has shifted from a natural attitude by adopting a phenomenological attitude that one recognizes that various attitudes toward experience are possible, one of which is the natural attitude or straightforward acceptance and another of which is the phenomenological attitude of eidetically and transcendentally critical reflection.

Thus, pre-phenomenologically-reflective human beings are in much the same situation as the Platonic cave dwellers who are unaware that they are victims of an illusion which causes them to accept echoes and a shadow show on the wall in front of them as reality and, in so far as they are unaware of being in this predicament, are also unaware that things might be otherwise (i.e., that they might be freed from the chains of this illusion). The problem, however, is that they must first be freed from their chains in order to recognize that they were ever imprisoned to start with and, hence, the victims of an illusion. In Gaston Berger's words, "naïveté is evident only to one who has freed himself from it ... Knowing that we have nothing before us but shadows presupposes a knowledge of real objects. A slave must have some idea of freedom to understand the constraint imposed by his chains".[10]

Now Husserl would not agree with Plato that living in the natural attitude is equivalent to being chained to an illusion (I have more to say on this later), but he would agree with Plato that there is nothing about life in the natural attitude which leads one to recognize it precisely as such (i.e., as "life in the natural attitude"). Such a recognition is indeed possible — else how could Plato, Husserl or we be here discussing it — but it is only an occasional poet or philosopher, pushing the wonderings and reflective awareness of everyday life to its radical limits, who stumbles into such a re-cognition or re-thinking of everyday life. And the number among this occasional few who are able to rationally explicate this recognition (rather than slipping off into a pleasant and fascinating mysticism) is even fewer. Plato claims to have been led to his recognition by Socrates who, tradition has it, was led to his insight as a result of an encounter with the Delphic Oracle. Husserl seems to have been led to his recognition while trying to discover the foundations of the apodicticity of logic.[11] But this is not our major concern here; rather, what does the phenomenologist aware of the natural attitude have in common with the cave dweller freed of his chains?

The first major change upon adopting the phenomenological attitude is that one no longer just sees things and lives through events in the world; rather, one notices that one is having experiences which are meaningful or "make sense" and that "things" and "events" are the meanings (the sense made) of experience. In other words, things and events as objects in the world, and the world itself as an ultimate horizon of objectivity, are now seen as the sense that has been and is being made of pre-predicative experiences.[12] This shift in attitude has actually had two results. First, things, events, persons are no longer seen but rather seen as (i.e., no longer "just there" but now "understood as" being somehow other than they appear to be). This is the fundamental aspect of the change in attitude, from things-seen to things-seen-as. Once this change has been made, what remains is the not so fundamental but definitely more difficult task of explicating just what it is that things and events are now seen as. The fundamental aspect is called by Husserl "the phenomenological reduction" and is that shift in perspective or attitude which recognizes the existence of a natural attitude toward experience and of an alternative phenomenological or transcendental attitude which transforms the things and events we experience in our lives into the phenomena of pure of transcendental consciousness. The explicative aspect undertaken after this shift has occurred is called "phenomenological or transcendental reflection", i.e., the reflective analyses undertaken in the phenomenological attitude which reveal these phenomena to be "meanings", or "senses" and, hence, the results of constituting acts of meaning-giving and sense-making.

In the case of our cave dwellers, the fundamental act of freeing themselves from the chains of illusion is the shift from seeing things and events in the world to seeing the things and events of the world as shadows. The explicative process of grasping just what a shadow is is basically the task of discovering how a

56

shadow is constituted or projected by a silhouette carried in front of a fire. Thus, the cave dwellers are first able to recognize only that what confronts them as the things and events of the world might somehow be other than what they straightforwardly appear to be and, hence, that the nature of this "otherness" needs investigation. As a result of this investigation (looking around the cave and getting accustomed to the bright fire light), they are eventually able to understand what confronts them *as* a shadow, i.e., as an image cast by a silhouette held before a light.

This latter point holds true for Husserl also. His initial formulation of phenomenology was as a "descriptive psychology", a serious misinterpretation on his part that he soon enough retracted but only five or six years later completely understood why such a formulation was erroneous. Thus, given the fundamental shift in thinking which transformed things into phenomena, he was able to investigate the nature and constitution of these phenomena, he was able to investigate the nature and constitution of these phenomena over a period of years and eventually grasp them as intentionally constituted meanings. Only then did he understand what it was that had happened in the initial shift in attitude. [13]

But let us return to the cave dwellers and their investigations of the constitution of shadows. After understanding how a shadow is produced, the newly freed and inquiring minds of our prisoners push things one step farther and begin to inquire into the nature of the silhouettes and the fire which produce the shadows. Again, a fundamental shift has occurred. They no longer *see* the fire and the silhouettes, but *see* them *as* something to be investigated, i.e., not as things and events now confronted and accepted as shadowmakers but as objects of yet another round of or type of reflection. This new series of investigations takes them outside the cave and into confrontation with "real" things and events illuminated by the sun. As a result of these analyses, they are now able to understand the fire as an artificial sun, the silhouettes as reifications or copies of the shadows of "real" things cast by the sun, and the entire domain of fire – silhouettes – shadows as a cave in the ground of the earth.

In Husserl's case, the phenomenological reduction and the ensuing reflections from the new standpoint accomplish something analogous to this latter discovery of the cave-dweller as well as something analogous to the former discovery. For the phenomenological reduction is a shift both to a *transcendental stance* which recognizes a particular thing or event of one's life as an actual phenomenon intentionally constituted in pure consciousness and to an *eidetic stance* which recognizes the actual phenomenon as one of the many actual and possible instances of a "meaning", an "eidos", an essential construct. In a phenomenological extension of the cave analogy, therefore, one might say that the transcendental aspect of the shift reveals the relationship between real things and the actual silhouettes responsible for the casting of these particular shadows, while the eidetic aspect reveals that any actual silhouette is really only one of many possible silhouettes that might have been constructed from the shadow of, say, a real tree. Insofar as a silhouette is a reification of the shadow of the tree, any actual silhouette is only one instance of a whole class of silhouettes, since there are an infinite number of actual and possible shadows that might be cast by a tree in the sun.

The transcendental aspect of the shift to a phenomenological attitude results in our seeing the things and events of the world as phenomena of consciousness, while the eidetic aspect of this shift results in our understanding these phenomena as meanings.[14] And just as the cave dwellers ultimately recognize themselves as such, i.e., as *cave* dwellers, and their whole realm of everyday experience as a cave, so too does the phenomenologist ultimately recognize himself in the phenomenological attitude as a particular type of phenomenon — a philosophizing human being — and the whole realm of his everyday life (the world) as a sphere of mundanity (of mundane existence) within the "ground" or sphere of transcendental subjectivity.[15] As a result of the shift to a phenomenological attitude, therefore, we (as philosophizing human beings in the world) are now able to understand ourselves as empirical egos rooted in a sphere of mundane experience which is itself the sedimented sense or meaning of a history of meaning-giving (sense-constituting) eidetic events in the flow of transcendental experience. It is just this realm of transcendental subjectivity or transcendental experience which remains hidden or anonymous as we live out our lives in the natural attitude. And it is just this realm that phenomenological reduction reveals and phenomenological reflection (analysis) explicates.

But what impact does this all have upon one's life as a human being in this world? Phenomenology is the vocation of a philosopher, not the entire life of a human being. What then happens when the philosopher drops the phenomenological perspective and joins the family for dinner?

Here Husserl and Plato part company. For when Plato's cave dwellers return to the cave, their eyes are full of darkness and their words sound like the ramblings of idiots to those still bound by the illusion. In comparison to the "real" world above the earth, life in the cave is an unbearable and chaotic darkness. The phenomenologist, on the other hand, returns to his engagement in life as a human being with a sense of the great richness and complexity of things and events. Whole new realms of possibility and interest, of research and appreciation are opened up and, with them, a greater respect for everyday life and a better understanding of the common sense view of the world.

This fundamental difference between the Platonic analogy and phenomenology lies in the fact that Plato conceives of the world of everyday experience in basically negative terms; it is a shadow show and life in it is like being a prisoner chained to an illusion without knowing it. "True reality" and "true life'' — the "really real" — is to be found only in the realm of ideas. Human existence is an imprisonment of the soul in a body that can only truly free itself by dying. Husserl has no such negative prejudices toward life in the everyday world. Mundane existence may be ungrounded or philosophically unclarified, but it is not in any sense an illusion. Understanding and wisdom can be found in the realm of transcendental experience and, hence, an enlightened sense of life and reality but phenomenology does not seek to deny or replace everyday reality and the world of common sense experience:

> It is not that the real sensory world is "recast" or denied, but than an absurd interpretation of it, which indeed contradicts its own intuitively clarified meaning, is set aside. (This attitude) springs from making the world absolute in the philosophical sense, which is wholly foreign to the way in which we naturally look out upon it. [16]

This basic difference in attitude which separates Plato and Husserl can be traced, I think, to the difference in their conceptions of the relationship between everyday life with its world and the philosophically clarified realm which founds the everyday realm. For Plato, the two realms are mutually exclusive; one is faced with a choice between a life of illusion in the cave and a life of contemplation in the real world. One can attain wisdom and return to live in the cave, and this is indeed what Plato himself did in his own life and what he prescribes for other philosophers in the *Republic*, but it is a demanding task that makes life miserable for the philosophers (VII, 517–520). Husserl, however, does not see the two realms as mutually exclusive but rather as essentially interdependent; the everyday world of experiences provides the subject matter for phenomenological elucidation and analysis, while this analysis provides the philosophical clarity to live as an enlightened human being in the world. Indeed, it might be said that one can be a wise man only by living in the world reflectively! In this sense, Husserl finds it much easier than Plato to accept the implications of the Socratic maxim: "the unexamined life of everyday affairs is worth living — not because it is the duty of a philosopher but because his insight allows him the privilege of doing so".

III

Husserl, unlike Fink and Heidegger, was a mathematician by training, and it is very likely for this reason that he preferred a mathematical analogy to explicate his views rather than a literary metaphor like the allegory of the cave. As I noted in my introductory remarks, Husserl's own source of this analogy of dimensions seems to have been a published lecture of Helmholz's on certain implications of Riemann's non-Euclidian axiomatic geometries. Helmholz's mention of this analogy, however, is very brief and does not lend itself as well, in my view, to the task of explicating Husserl's phenomenology as does Edwin Abbott's treatment of this same analogy — very likely also inspired by Helmholz — in a book entitled *Flatland*. Because Abbott's "romance of many dimensions" may not be quite as familiar as Plato's cave allegory, a brief synopsis is perhaps in order.

The first half of the book is devoted to a discussion of life in the two-dimensional world of Flatland. The narrator is a square who is a lawyer in this realm and it is he who describes the geography, the architecture, the inhabitants, the social structure and some of the history of his land. It is also here that an explanation is given of how a resident on the plan of Flatland is able to determine from his perception of a one-dimensional line — for this is all that one "sees" within the two-dimensional realm — what type of two-dimensional being confronts him.

The second part of the story deals with the square's encounters with realms of dimensionality other than that of Flatland. It begins with a discussion between the square and his grandson, a hexagon, about the notion of the existence of a third dimension being heritical in spite of the fact that such a third dimension is mathematically demonstrable. This is followed by a dream of the square in which he tries to persuade the rule of a one-dimensional world, Lineland, that reality is in fact two-dimensional even though the king and his subjects are only able to perceive one dimension of this true "plane" of reality. The king, of course, finds the notion of a two-dimensional reality both heretical and non-sensical and drives the square away.

The discussion with his grandson and the "bad dream" leave the square very perplexed and unsure, and it is just at this point that he is visited by a sphere from the three-dimensional world of Spaceland. An argument develops as to whether reality is truly three-dimensional or truly two-dimensional. The square, of course, is not able to *see* the sphere but only a line which he is able to determine to be a circle in the plane of Flatland (one with very irregular behavior) — just as the king of Lineland could not see the square but only a point which he determined or conceived to be a line in Lineland and, likewise, just as the sphere would not actually *see* a three-dimensional cube but only a two-dimensional plane which he could recognize as a cube. [17] The square eventually tires of, and is angered by, this "tricky circle's" heretical and non-sensical carrying on about a third dimension of reality and attempts to attack the sphere. The enraged sphere, unable to persuade the square of the "true nature of reality", finally takes hold of the square and rips him out of Flatland. The square is suspended for several moments above Flatland so that he can finally *see* the limited dimensionality of his homeland albeit not yet understand the true, three-dimensionality of reality:

> An unspeakable horror seized me. There was a darkness; then a dizzy, sickening sensation of sight that was not like seeing; I saw a Line that was

no Line; Space that was not Space: I was myself, and not myself. When
I could find voice, I shrieked aloud in agony, "Either this is madness or
it is Hell". "It is neither", calmly replied the voice of the Sphere, "it is
Knowledge; it is Three Dimensions: open your eye once again and try to
look steadily". I looked, and, behold, a new world! There stood before
me visibly incorporate, all that I had before inferred, conjectured, dream-
ed ... [18]

After the sphere has explained the "mysteries" of the third dimension to the
square — including a quick trip to the nondimensional solipsistic world of
Pointland — so that he can go back to Flatland and preach the truth, the square
begs the sphere for one last favor: that he also be shown the fourth dimension.
The sphere, of course, berates the square for his stupidity and his failure to
grasp the *true* nature of reality; there is no fourth dimension; any fool can
plainly see that it is merely conjecture, a mathematical construct with no real
equivalent!

The square returns to Flatland and attempts to convey what he has seen to
the other inhabitants. His Flatland language is not adequate to describe his insights, however, and his words are either taken as meaningless chatter — the
ravings of an idiot — or as espousing the heresy to the third dimension. Unable
to demonstrate the validity of his claims in the Flatland court of law, the square
is jailed for life; it is here that he writes his memoirs, calling them *Flatland*. [19]

This metaphor of a multiplicity of co-existing dimensions of reality offers
a particularly appropriate analogy for understanding Husserl's phenomenology, both because Husserl himself explicitly invokes it (in its Helmholzian
form) on numerous occasions and because it is implicitly operative in many
other places in his work. It appears in an early manuscript from his
mathematical period[20] as part of a discussion of the possibility of constructing
the proofs of Euclidian geometry on the surface of a sphere. More important
for our purposes, however, is the fact it appears in the form of an analogy
during one of the first descriptions of the phenomenological method after the
breakthrough to the correct sense of reduction around 1906. This analogy is
then used repeatedly in his works on methodology up to and including the
Krisis of 1936.

In his 1906 lectures on "Critique of Cognition", he speaks of a "philosophical sphere of being"[21] and in his 1907 lectures on the "Idea of phenomenology" he writes that his philosophy is interested in a wholly new dimension
of investigation.[22] It is in his 1908 lectures on formal logic, however, that the
analogy is first fully explicated:

Natural understanding is limited: it fails to grasp a dimension which only becomes apparent in the philosophical manner of thinking. As far as
the scope of natural cognition is concerned, we are, as naturally thinking
men, what one might call "plane-beings" ((*Flächenwesen*)) who have no

idea of the heights and depths of the third dimension. And in this dimension lies everything that we call philosophy in the genuine sense. I caution you against understanding this in some sort of mystical sense: the image is only meant to indicate a certain essential imperfection and incompleteness of natural cognition, namely: just as a third dimension is nothing without the field of the first and second, so too is philosophy nothing — it lacks a foundation ((*Substrat*)) — without essential reference back to natural cognition and the sciences of natural cognition. On the other hand, just as a plane receives its full existential value ((*Seinswert*)) only as the limit to a three-dimensional manifold, so too do the results of the natural sciences receive their full existential value only in the depth of philosophy. [23]

In all of his intervening work, the use of the analogies of dimensions, spheres and realms occurs frequently. Allow me to note just one other instance of explicit use of this analogy in the *Krisis* manuscript:

This schema for a possible clarification of the problem of objective science reminds us of Helmholz' well-known image of the plane-beings, who have no idea of the dimension of depth, in which their plane-world is a mere projection. Everything of which men — scientists and all the others — can become conscious in their natural world-life (experiencing, knowing, practically planning, acting) as a field of external objects — as ends, means, processes of action, and final results related to these objects — and on the other hand, also, in self-reflection, as the spiritual life which functions thereby: all this remains on the "plane" which is, though unnoticed, nevertheless only a plane within an infinitely richer dimension of depth. [24]

The analogy to Abbott's Flatland can be made as follows. The realm of Spaceland is equivalent to the sphere of transcendental subjectivity; life in Spaceland is life in the phenomenological attitude toward experience, the life of the phenomenologically philosophizing consciousness. The realm of Flatland is equivalent to the sphere of praxis, of everyday life in the life-world; it is life lived in the natural attitude toward experience by human beings. The realm of Lineland is more or less similar to Husserl's conception of the spheres of investigation of the individual sciences and humanistic disciplines; it is the life of a physicist, an historian, a biologist, an anthropologist, etc. *qua scientist* (as opposed to *qua human being*) and is lived in a naturalistic or psychologistic or historicistic, etc., attitude toward experience. The realm of Pointland is perhaps analogous to the life that a solipsistic empirical ego would allegedly have if such a thing were possible; the closest thing to this state that I can imagine might be an acute case of catatonic psychosis.

The point that distinguishes Husserl's use of this analogy from Abbott's is that, for Husserl, life occurs in all three dimensions simultaneously (the nondimensional realm of Pointland excluded here), while for Abbott the square seems to be a two-dimensional being rather than a three-dimensional being manifest in only two of its dimensions. Abbott's sphere, however, is aware of its life in all three dimensions. The sphere's life as a circle in Flatland is much richer in possibility as a result of its awareness of its third dimension of being.

Thus, we must consider the square in Flatland to be a cube whose third dimension of being remains anonymous in his life. Husserl is emphatic, especially in his latter works,[25] that each of us as a human being is also a transcendental subjectivity, even though in most cases this transcendental dimension of our lives remains hidden and anonymous to us in the natural attitude toward experience. This transcendental dimension is operative in and constitutive of our everyday existence insofar as our lives make sense to us, but it is only in the adoption of the phenomenological attitude (or its equivalent) that we become aware of this transcendental sphere of our being.

Phenomenology makes the realm of transcendental subjectivity or transcendental experience "thematic" for the philosopher; however, transcendental subjectivity still remains "operative" at the same time that it is "thematic". It is in this sense that the shift to the phenomenological attitude is not so much a shift from one level to another or out of one life into another, as it is an opening up of an additional dimension of experience. When the square is taken into Spaceland by the sphere, one of the things that he observes is life as usual going on in Flatland. Nothing is lost to him, rather he has all of his life in Flatland before him as before and, in addition, his insights concerning Flatland life from the Spaceland standpoint.

Thus, we are indeed as the natural sciences tell us "a living physical entity in Nature", but not just that. We are as the social sciences and humanities tell us "an historical, socio-culturally determined human being in a time and place", but not just that. And we are as the philosophers tell us "spirit, soul, transcendental subject", but again not just that. We are body-in-nature, man-in-society, person-in-the-world, and transcendental subjectivity all at the same time. One or more of these may remain hidden or anonymous to us in our daily lives insofar as our vocations or tasks in life do not make them thematic (in science, in life, in philosophy) but they are nonetheless all operative and continuously present.

For Husserl, everyday life is life as a two-dimensional being on the "plane of the life-world". The natural, social and humanistic sciences all pursue various "lines" of inquiry in this plane of the world in an attempt to articulate that world as it is accepted by us. Phenomenology, on the other hand, attempts to ground both this world of everyday life and, consequently, the various sciences of it, by revealing and clarifying the transcendental "space", within which this world and its life and its sciences are constituted as meaningful. Becoming aware of or recognizing this transcendental dimension of our lives does not directly alter them; it does not interfere with the events of the world or the sciences of those events, although it may enrich both our everyday and our scientific conceptions of the world. Rather, the task of phenomenology is to make the world and our lives in it "philosophically understandable".[26]

<h2 style="text-align:center">IV</h2>

What can be gleaned from these two analogies about Husserl's phenomenological philosophy? First and foremost, I believe that they clarify the sense in which Husserl's "platonism" and his "transcendental idealism" are not a retreat into some distinct and separate realm of essences or ideas "outside of" or different from the world of everyday life. The sphere of transcendental subjectivity is not another "world" in addition to the world of human existence any more than the physical sphere is another "world". The "physical world" delimited, described and investigated by physical science is an articulation and explanation of certain aspects of our everyday life-world; and in the same way the realm of transcendental experience disclosed, described and investigated by phenomenology is a philosophical founding or clarification of the world of common sense experience in terms of its meaningfulness and knowableness.

Secondly, the analogies throw additional light on the seemingly esoteric nature of the language of phenomenological description. That the phenomenologist, like the cave dweller returning to the cave from above or the square returning to Flatland from Spaceland, is unable to describe or demonstrate his insights in everyday language is not a serious objection to phenomenology any more than it is to theoretical physics. The sort of sophisticated mathematics that is required to do and to understand relativity and quantum physics do not lend themselves to common sense explication either, but this has hindered neither the development and power of modern physics nor its acceptance as a valid science by educated men in the everyday world. To do and to understand physics requires that one adopt the attitude of a physical scientist (i.e., perform a physical or naturalistic reduction of experience); to do and to understand phenomenological philosophy requires no more and no less than that one adopt the attitude appropriate to the pursuit and understanding of this endeavor (i.e., perform a transcendental-phenomenological reduction).

One need not do or understand physics, biology, history, psychology, anthropology, etc. in order to live one's life in a sound, common sense manner but, at least in my own case, my education and continued reading in these areas adds considerable richness to my experience of the world and an appreciation of the complexity of life that I might not otherwise have. So too can one lead a good healthy life without doing or understanding phenomenology; the insights of phenomenological philosophy, however can also result in a similar increase in the richness and appreciation of our everyday lives as human beings in the world of common sense. [27]

That the common sense understanding of nature is a limited and *factually* impoverished one can be truly understood only by the natural scientist. That the common sense understanding of the world and of the enterprise of science itself is a limited and *epistemologically* impoverished one can really be understood only by one who has sought and at least to some extent gained philosophical clarity on these issues. Insofar as the motivation to seek such natural scientific or philosophical understanding requires some initial wonder or stimulus to reflection and insofar as the plethora of readily available theories to explain everything conceals the wonder of everyday life for most of us all to early in life, we must rely on analogies such as Plato's allegory of the cave and Abbott's *Flatland* as a stimulus to the imagination that will hopefully motivate the intellect.

NOTES

1. Martin Heidegger, "Platons Lehre von der Wahrheit" in *Wegmarken* (Frankfurt: Klostermann, 1967), pp. 109–144.
2. Eugen Fink, "Was will die Phänomenologie Edmund Husserls?" in *Studien zur Phänomenologie* (Den Haag: Martinus Nijhoff, 1966).
3. Cf. Philip J. Bossert, "The Sense of 'Epoché' and 'Reduction' in Husserl's Philosophy" in the *Journal of the British Society for Phenomenology*, Vol. V (1974), pp. 243–255.
4. Cf. especially section two of Fink's article on the "idea of a phenomenological philosophy" where he argues that the thematization of consciousness achieved via phenomenological reduction ultimately results in an "encompassing knowledge of the world" and "understanding of Being".
5. A recent article by Douglas R. McGaughey, "Husserl and Heidegger on Plato's Cave Allegory: A Study of Philosophical Influence", *International Philosophical Quarterly* XVI (1976), pp. 331–348, presents a detailed study of the critique in Heidegger's article and the defense in Fink's article of Husserl's phenomenological philosophy.
6. Cf. Martin Heidegger, *Sein und Zeit* (Tübingen: Max Niemeyer, 1967), pp. 15–40.
7. In his article, Fink claims that the shadows are cast upon the cave wall by people outside the cave walking in front of the entrance of the cave, completely missing the entire intermediate dimension of the fire and the silhouettes carried in front of the fire to cast the shadows inside of the cave. Although the mistake does not significantly affect the conclusions Fink is attempting to draw in his article, the omission does reduce the explicative power of the analogy relative to Husserl's philosophy.
8. Plato, *The Republic*, trans. B. Jowett (New York: Vintage, 1960), VII: 514–520.
9. Husserl's own familiarity with this metaphor comes from his reading of a lecture of Hermann von Helmholz delivered in 1870 in Heidelberg and later published in a collection of his papers. Cf. "On the Origin and Significance of Geometrical Axioms" in *Popular Scientific Lectures*, ed. Moris Kline (New York: Dover, 1962). For the purpose of my discussion of this analogy, however, I will rely upon the somewhat more developed and popular version of this analogy in Edwin Abbott's classic little book, *Flatland: A Romance of Many Dimensions* (New York: Dover, 1962).
10. Gaston Berger, *The Cogito in Husserl's Philosophy*, trans. K. McLaughlin (Evanston: Northwestern University Press, 1972), p. 43.
11. Cf. Bossert, p. 246.
12. By "prepredicative experience" I understand the raw data of "givens" in the flow or stream of pure consciousness, i.e., that which is available or presents itself in consciousness prior to the processes of objectification (the constitution of or making sense of these "givens" as things and events) and subjectification (the constitution of or making sense of these "givens" as personal experiences of "mine").
13. Cf. Bossert, pp. 246–249.
14. This "double aspect" might be diagrammed as follows:

	Empirical Attitude	Eidetic Attitude	
B			**C**
	Transcendental Science	Phenomenological Philosophy	Transcendental Attitude
A	Common Sense	Descriptive Science	Natural Attitude

D

Thus in order to do descriptive science, one must shift from the natural-empirical attitude of common sense to the natural-eidetic attitude, and in order to do phenomenology, one must shift from the natural-empirical to the transcendental-eidetic attitude. The terminology used by Husserl for the various types of reductions or shifts in attitude that are possible according to the above scheme are:

A-to-B or D-to-C: Transcendental Reduction
A-to-D or B-to-C: Eidetic Reduction
A-to-C: Phenomenological Reduction
C-to-B or D-to-A: Empirical Reduction
C-to-D: Naturalistic Reduction
B-to-A, D-to-A or C-to-A: Life-world Reduction

With respect to the allegory of the cave, the cave dwellers would be in a common sense or natural-empirical attitude, the freed cave dweller giving consideration to the fire and the silhouettes would have a natural-eidetic attitude and be engaged in descriptive science of shadows, the freed cave dweller ascended outside of the cave and inspecting the shadows cast by real objects in the sunlight would have a transcendental-empirical attitude and be engaged in a transcendental science of shadows, and the cave dweller contemplating the sun and the things and events in the world outside of the cave would have a transcendental-eidetic attitude and be engaged in what Plato would call philosophy and Husserl would call phenomenological philosophy.

15. Section one of Fink's article discusses this "ground-laying" aspect of phenomenology at length.

16. Edmund Husserl, *Ideas*, trans. by W.R. Boyce Gibson (New York: Macmillan Co., 1931), p. 153.

17. The common characteristic here then is that the original date of cognition must be re-cognized according to certain principles of perceptual interpretation in order to "see" something, i.e., the cognized line is recognized according to Flatland principles as a circle, the cognized plane in Spaceland is recognized as a cube, and so forth.

18. *Flatland*, p. 80.

19. The similarities between Abbott's myth and the Platonic one are obvious in several places: the initial fear and confusion of the free cave dweller and the inhabitant of Flatland upon confronting the new dimension of knowledge, their inability to adequately explain or describe to their fellow inhabitants what they have experienced and now see as a result of this new dimension of knowledge, the ridicule and threats they receive from their fellow inhabitants when they try to teach the doctrine of their new discoveries, and so on, all suggest that Abbott, a classics teacher and schoolmaster in England in the 1880's, had Plato as well as Helmholz in mind when he wrote his allegory.

20. Cf. Ms. K I 34/81a in the Husserl Archives in Louvain. I am grateful to Dr. Karl Schuhmann of the University at Utrecht for locating this passage.

21. Cf. Ms. F I 10.

22. Edmund Husserl, *The Idea of Phenomenology* (Den Haag: Martinus Nijhoff, 1964), p. 19.

23. Cf. Ms. F I 1. Note that Husserl's view of the world of everyday life and the natural attitude of common sense in this passage is again positive and supportive as in the passage cited above in *Ideas*.

24. *Krisis der europäischen Wissenschaften und die transzendentale Phänomenologie* (Den Haag: Martinus Nijhoff, 1954), edited by Walter Biemel as Vol. VI of the *Husserliana* edition of Husserl's work.

25. Cf. Edmund Husserl, *Cartesianische Meditationen* (Den Haag: Martinus Nijhoff, 1959), and the *Krisis*.

26. Cf. *Ideas*, p. 153.

27. The analyses of Heidegger, Sartre, Merleau-Ponty and especially Alfred Schutz are excellent examples of this enrichment of human experience and the common-sense view of life through phenomenological reflection upon it.

Time and Time-Consciousness
by
Barry J. Jones

In this essay, I wish to reflect on the nature of time and its relation to consciousness as they described both within and outside contemporary phenomenology. I shall first consider certain views of time which interpret it as unreal
and/or "subjective", and then I shall take up the opposite sort of theories in
which time is real and "objective". I hope to show that neither view by itself
is adequate, and I shall try to work out a synthesis of the two, largely in the
context of the later writings by Martin Heidegger.

I. Time and Non-Being

> " . . . the aspect of time
> caught in the form of limitation
> between un-being and being".[1]

From antiquity, philosophical thought has dwelt upon the problem of the
seeming unreality of the temporal order. For example, one can clearly perceive
this view of time — in various forms, to be sure — running from the pre-
Socratics, passing through Plato and Aristotle, down to Augustine's insightful
reflections on time-consciousness which Husserl praised so highly. Plato, for
example, held that time was "a kind of moving image of the eternal [intelligible
order]" (*Timaeus* 37d). And Aristotle after him maintained that "time by its
nature is the cause . . . of decay, since it is the number of change, and change
removes what is" (*Physics* IV, 221b 1–3).

However, for Plato, the temporal order was not understood as a confused
"subjective" perception of an objective reality. Indeed, the categories of "subjectivity" and "objectivity" had not really emerged at the time of Plato. It was
understood rather as an order, which, because of its inherent non-being, was
of a lower ontological status. Time was not a "subjective form of sensibility"
which accrued to entities *per accidens*, but was rather the manner of being of

W.S. Hamrick (ed.) *Phenomenology in Practice and Theory*.
© 1985 Martinus Nijhoff Publishers, Dordrecht/Boston/Lancaster
ISBN 90 247 2926 2. Printed in the Netherlands.

68

that class of entities (*aisbuta* or *sensibilia*) which do not reside in perfect logical identity with themselves.

The connection between time and "subjectivity" was left for Augustine, since historically subjectivity was a retreat into "the inner man". With Augustine's question, "Do you know you are?", we find one of the earliest instances of self-reflection in and for itself. It comes as no surprise, then, that his further question, "What, then, is time?",[2] led him into what were perhaps the earliest analyses of time-consciousness as such. Aristotle had certainly observed the essential connection between time and the soul, but his analyses remained on the ontological level, and the impermanence of temporal things was explained in terms of the potentiality (*dynamis*) and lack of Being (*steresis*) which characterized matter. It was natural enough that Augustine should have retained something of the ontological distinctions, since his greatest affinity had been with Plato and the Neo-Platonists; but he deviated from these in seeking certainty in himself and in the self-evidence of his own existence. From the point of view of certainty, even (God as) the Truth Itself was subsequent to the lesser truth, but prior certainty, of the one who thinks; and one might therefore conclude that with Augustine self-reflection had become the *measure* of Truth and Being. *Tu, qui vis te nosse, scis esse te? Scio ... Cogitare te scis? Scio.* ("You, who wish to know, do you know you are? I know ... Do you know you think? I know".)[3]

Augustine questioned time as follows: Firstly, "How can ... the past and future *be*, when the past no longer is and the future is not yet?"[4] Secondly, if the present can have no duration without one half of that duration being past and the other future, "how can we say that even the present *is*, when the only reason why it *is*, is that it is *not to be*? In other words, we cannot rightly say that time *is*, except by reason of its tendency to *non-being* (*tendit non esse*)".[5]

However, the fact that we *measure* time seems to imply that time must exist in some sense, and also that it must have some measurable extension (i.e., duration). Therefore, since only the present can really *be*, then in order for the past and future to exist, there must be a present of things past, a present of things present and a present of things future. Moreover, continues Augustine, since time must be extended, it is probably an extendedness of the soul itself, for it is in the soul that the past is retained in memory, the present is directly perceived and the future is prefigured by expectation. But, then, since time stems from the mind alone, it cannot be a feature of Reality. True Being (*summa essentia, summa est*) resides in eternity, and the temporal order can exist only as a privation of this.

Historically, Augustine was at the cross-roads of the two ways that time is conceived to tend toward non-being: between time as the "semblance" of Being and time as the being of the subject. Just as his conviction that "Truth dwells in the inner man" (*in interiore homine habitat veritas*)[6] had led him to something resembling the Cartesian "I think", so his analysis of time led him to something like the "subjective" view of time expressed by Kant: "Time is not something existing by itself or which belongs to things as an objective determination, and it does not remain when an abstraction is made of all subjective conditions of its intuition".[7]

In one respect, the modern phenomenological concept of "intentionality" was an attempt to bridge the hiatus left by Cartesianism and Kantianism between Being and subjectivity. But, unfortunately, intentional analyses have themselves fallen heir to similar difficulties. The tendency has been to interpret all Being as "merely" *intentional being*, and thus to make it once again "subjective". Or, if this has been avoided, consciousness has been construed as so empty of Being (including subjective being) that all Being is extraneous to it, and consciousness is once again separated from Being by the impassable barrier of its own nothingness. I shall consider the former interpretation as the last part of this section, and I shall enlarge upon the latter interpretation now by considering Sartre and Merleau-Ponty's analyses of time.

In their respective chapters on "Temporality",[8] Sartre and Merleau-Ponty seize upon Augustine's time-paradox and summarize it thus: If the past and the future do not exist, and if the present has no duration, then time as such ceases to be. Augustine's answer to this, namely that the past and future are held together by memory and expectation, has the effect of making all time *present*; and this as such is unsatisfactory, because time then ceases to be "temporal". To avoid this, Sartre and Merleau-Ponty decline to conceive of the three temporal modes as existing "within" consciousness, and conceive rather of consciousness itself existing *in and as* the three temporal modes. It is because consciousness has no "within" − i.e., no being of its own − that it can transcend any particular mode and exist as temporality itself. This is indeed a solution to Augustine's immediate problem; and yet there is a sense in which Sartre and Merleau-Ponty have not gone beyond Augustine. In particular, they are in agreement with him on the following points: (i) Temporality is a type of non-being; (ii) The present is the nexus of time, and (iii) time is "subjective" in that it belongs to consciousness and not to Being itself.

(i) "Temporality", Sartre says, "is not".[9] "The objective world", Merleau-Ponty says, "is too much of a plenum for there to be time. Past and future withdraw of their own accord from being and move over into subjectivity in search ... of a possibility of not-being which accords with their nature".[10]

(ii) For Sartre, the *pour-soi* (consiousness) is defined as not being what it is and as being what it is not. This paradoxical statement resolves itself in a temporal sense as follows: "[As the] present [the *pour-soi*] is not what it is (past) and it is what it is not (future)".[11] "In contrast to the past which *is* in itself (*en-soi*), the Present is *pour-soi* ... [But] There is a peculiar paradox in the Present: ... what is present *is* − in contrast to the future which is not yet and the past which is no longer. But ... a rigorous analysis which would attempt to rid the present of all which is not it − i.e., of the past and immediate future − would find that nothing remained but an infinitesimal instant [and time would collapse]".[12] Finally, "As Present, Past and Future − all at the same time − the *pour-soi*, dispersing its being in three dimensions, is temporal due to the fact that it nihilates itself. None of these dimensions has any ontological priority ... none of them can exist without the other two. Yet ... it is best to put the accent on the present ekstasis and not on the future ekstasis as Heidegger does ... [Because] The Present ... is the mould of indispensible non-being for the total synthetic form of Temporality".[13] Merleau-Ponty concurs: "Heidegger's historical time", he writes, "which flows from the future ... is impossible within the context of Heidegger's thought itself ... It is always in the present that we are centered".[14]

(iii) "Temporality exists", Sartre argues, "only as the infrastructure of ... a *pour-soi* ... But Temporality is the being of the *pour-soi* [only] in so far as the *pour-soi* has to be its being ekstatically".[15] Merleau-Ponty is even more emphatic on this point: "We are not saying that time is *for* someone, which would once more be a case of arraying it out and immobilizing it. We are saying that time *is* someone ... We must understand time as the subject and the subject as time".[16]

Of course, these analyses should not be taken out of context, or as representing their authors' final word on the matter. Even in this same work Sartre speaks of Being and nothingness as an "indissoluble dyad",[17] and Merleau-Ponty later repudiated those aspects of his *Phenomenology of Perception* which remained within the "philosophy of consciousness".[18] But the essential point, I believe, remains: namely that, in their respective chapters on "Temporality", Sartre and Merleau-Ponty each conceive of time as the non-being of consciousness standing over against the plenum of Being.

Of course, the main source within the phenomenological tradition for both Sartre and Merleau-Ponty's reflections on subjectivity and time-consciousness was the seminal work of Edmund Husserl, and chiefly his *Phenomenology of Inner Time-Consciousness*. Now it is not possible to reproduce here all the details of his complicated descriptions of the intentional structures of time-consciousness. But I do wish to make a few brief comments about his view in order to conclude this section of the essay on time and non-being.

Describing the flow of time-consciousness, Husserl tells us that this flux "is something which we name in conformity with what is constituted, but it is [itself] nothing temporally "Objective". It is absolute subjectivity and has the absolute properties of something to be denoted metaphorically as "flux", as a point of actuality, primal source point, that from which springs the [objective] "now", and so on. In the lived-experience of actuality, we have the primal source point and a continuity of moments of reverberation. For all this names are lacking".[19] These moments of the absolute flux are not themselves phases of objective time, since they belong to that "wherein" time itself, with its objective predicates, "now", "before" and "after", is constituted. Therefore, "the predicates as such cannot be meaningfully attributed to them".[20]

In his otherwise excellent article,[21] J.B. Brough gives the impression that the reason "we have no names" for the quasi-temporality of the flux is simply that they have already been applied to the (temporal) *objects* of the flux. But the problem is surely more radical than this. It is not simply that the names have already been applied elsewhere, but rather that the absolute flux cannot *in principle* be named. The constitutive flux is neither a constituted *object* nor a *content* which might in turn be perceived. "[All] contents of consciousness [are] contents of primal consciousness which is constitutive of temporal objects. [But] Primal consciousness ... is not in this sense again a content, an object in phenomenological time".[22] Moreover, "Following the phenomenological reduction, every temporal appearance ... is reduced to such a flux. The consciousness in which all this is reduced, I cannot myself again perceive, however. For this new perceived entity would be something which referred back to a constitutive flux of just such a kind ... *ad infinitum*".[23] Finally, "the experiencing Ego is still nothing that might be taken *for itself* and made into an object of inquiry on its *own* account ... it is completely empty of essential components, it has no content that could be unravelled, it is *an und für sich* indescribable".[24]

At the time of his *Logical Investigations,*[25] Husserl had already understood that there is a "conceptually undemarcated and unutterable kernal" to the stream of experiences; but at this point of his development he seems to construe this as a *de facto* oversight rather than as an *essential limit* to determinate thought. He speaks, therefore, of the reflectively graspable appearances of the Ego as though they stood in a similar relation to the Ego that grasps them as does a single appearance of a perceived object to the whole of that object. In short, he had not discerned here, as he did later, that whereas we can always walk around a perceived thing in order to see its other facets, it is perfectly meaningless to think of consciousness as being able to "walk around" itself.

Time-consciousness, then, cannot be an object. If we try to make an object of it, this object would have a temporal position and a duration; but the flux has no duration. Duration is the *form* of "what" endures; and it is "objective time" which functions as this duration. Process always presupposes this duration, but duration is itself *constituted* in the flux: " it pertains to the essence of [the] flux that there can be nothing persistent [no duration] in it".[26] Certainly, every act perceives *itself* as well as its object, but this "internal perception" does not mean that it is *directed* toward itself as it is toward its object: "every 'lived experience' is ... internally perceived. But internal perception is not, in the same sense, a 'lived experience'. It is not itself again internally perceived

... Behind this act of perception there stands no other such act, as if this flux were itself a unity in a flux".[27]

Consciousness, then, can only *know* itself by means of an "iterated reflection", and the notion of "knowledge" becomes problematical if applied to that which makes iterated reflection possible.[28] Consciousness can only apprehend its own *form* — i.e., the longitudinal intentionality of retentions of the past and protentions of the future — in terms of a Kantian "Idea".[29] But such an "Idea" is only an *intellectual representation* of the temporal synthesis, and not that synthesis itself. (Kant has called this presentation the *synthesis intellectualis,*[30] but he makes the mistake of construing this as the pre-existing static form, or *eidos*, of the temporal synthesis.) This intellectual representation of time, the Idea of infinite time, "is a structure of conceptual representations (*Vorstellen*) exactly like that of an infinite numerical series, infinite space, etc." It is not the *authentic* intuition of time due to the "primordial association" or auto-constitution of the flux itself.[31] As Kant says, "consciousness in itself is not so much a representation distinguishing a particular object, but really a *form* of representation in general".[32] Or, as Aristotle puts it, "[The mind] can have no nature of its own, other than that of having a certain capacity ... before it thinks [it is] not actually anything real ... [It] is in a sense potentially whatever is thinkable, though actually it is nothing until it has thought" (*De Anima*, 429a 20–23; 429b 30–32).

The intellectual representation of the temporal synthesis is a static image of a dynamic flux. Consciousness is really "nothing" apart from its objects, and time-consciousness is really nothing other than the *way* — the *manner* — in which objects manifest themselves. This is why "nothing" can be said of the flux itself. The Idea of a completed time is a conceptual abstraction and reification of the structural moments of the objective content of the stream of perceptions.[33] But these "structural moments" really do belong to the objective content, and do not accrue to it because of its involvement with "subjectivity". The originary presentation of things on the ground of their horizons of potentiality and possibility is the actual *manner of being* of the things themselves; and the Idea of time as a given structure which things "come to occupy" is an abstraction from this originary manner of the things.

All acts of consciousness, together with the objects from which they are inseparable, pass away with the flux of time. Even the reflective acts which take the flux itself as their object are themselves subject to the flux, and are replaced by ever new acts. This is indeed why the flux cannot be apprehended as such: all of the apprehensive acts are themselves *phases* of the thing to be apprehended and require to be apprehended by further such acts, *ad infinitum*. Of course, the flux itself does not "pass away", since then a second flux would be required wherein such "passing away" could occur. The flux "remains", but only *qua flux* — only qua the continuous modification of temporal things. Things pass away *with* time. *For time itself passes away*. But by passing away constantly, time remains *as time*.[34] This is what Klaus Held has called the "anonymous *nunc stans*". It is "The unity of standing and streaming ... the authentic essence of the "living present", which remains nonobjective, i.e., anonymous".[35]

Husserl conceived of the "living present" (*lebendige Gegenwart*) as the solution to two demands. On the one hand, the ego, as the ultimate centre of all constitution, must be conceived as a sort of "I – pole" (*Ichpol*) or *nunc stans*. And on the other hand, as a living flux of experience, Time must have some formal unity if it is to "remain" *as time*, and yet it must also be "temporal": it must admit of flux and passage. The "living present", then, is the synthesis of these two demands. It is a unity in flux – a standing-streaming (*stehend-strömend*). It is not a "now" in objective time, but a pre-objective (anonymous) present: the intentional unity of an auto-constitutive temporal manner. As such, it stands in a mediated (temporal) relation to itself, and it is this which makes apodictic (or logically unmediated) self-knowledge unobtainable.[36]

In reality, there are but two apodictic moments of self-reflection: the abstract *existence* of the self (the "Cartesian" self as *reflected*), and the temporal *form* (the "Kantian" form which makes self-reflection possible). However, neither of these are *contents*; no factual knowledge, whether mundane or phenomenological, can be adequate to an apodictic content.[37] The "Idea" as self-reflection can only know itself *abstractly* – i.e., as an *object*; a spatialized time conceived as the synchronic form of objective possibilities. It cannot know itself *as temporality*, and hence, as it were, "reclaim itself" from its temporal manner of being. It can neither reclaim the concrete flux, the concrete presencing of things with their originary manner, nor even *itself (qua temporality)*, since its own iterated reflection is just another way of swelling itself back into time.

In a sense, all self-being is self-transcendence. It is such that its being consists in the "coming to" (*Zu-kunft*) that being. The "streaming" is already this "coming to" – it is already the *future* of the "standing", and it is this which gives the present its character of "being before" (*prae-esse*). Each new present is transcendent, one knows that one never coincides with it. It is not something with defined contours, but a "swelling" of time – a *Zeitform* influenced by its *Zeitmaterie*.[37] Merleau-Ponty writes: "One never gets beyond time. Husserl says only that there are many ways of living time. On the one hand, there is the passive way, in which one is inside time and submits to it – being in time (*Innerzeitigkeit*). On the other hand, one can take over this time and live it through for oneself. But in either case one is temporal and never gets beyond time".[38]

II. Objectivity and Time

"If all time is eternally Present
All time is unredeemable". [39]

Over against the phenomenological tradition, many philosophers have considered time to be real, "objective", an independently existing entity of some sort. I shall now approach the problem of "time itself" by considering McTaggart's argument for the unreality of time. [40] McTaggart states a positive and a negative thesis concerning time. [41] The positive thesis holds that there are two types of temporal series: the "A-series", which consists of the determinations, "Past", "Present" and "Future"; and the "B-series", which consists of the determinations, "earlier than ... ", "simultaneous with ... " and "later than" ... The A-series is called the "dynamic temporal" because it is described by *tensed* statements, and the B-series is called the "static temporal" because it is described by *tenseless* statements (about the relations between events "in" time) which are "timelessly" true or false. The positive thesis also holds that it is the A-series which is *fundamental* to the concept of time, since time is essentially a dynamic flux of change and becoming.

The negative thesis, however, holds that the A-series is *inherently contradictory*, and it concludes that, since this series is *essential* to the very notion of time, then time as such *cannot be real*. The putative contradiction is this: No real event can possess more than a single A-determination. And yet it is evident that every event must possess all three − every event must be "past" in relation to certain other events, "present" in relation to others, and "future" in relation to yet others.

The "Pickwickian" character of the negative thesis invites a *prima facie* objection, and this McTaggart answers as follows: "It is never true, the answer will run, that [event] M is past, present and future. It *is* present, *will be* past, and *has been* future ... The characteristics are only incompatible when they are simultaneous ... [not when] each term has them successively ... Thus our first statement about M ... [really] means that M is present at a moment of present time, past at some moment of future time, and future at some moment of past time. But every moment, like every event, is both past, present and future. And so a similar difficulty arises ... again we get a contradiction". [42]

The point is that any event appears to possess all three of the mutually exclusive determinations, "past", "present" and "future"; and if we try to explain this contradiction away by suggesting that the event is only past at some future moment, present at the present moment and future at some past moment, we have introduced a second series of "moments" to resolve the inherent contradiction of the first series of "events". But nothing has been gained. The second series possesses the same contradiction as the first: every "moment" is present in relation to present moments, past in relation to future moments and future in relation to past moments.

McTaggart's train of reasoning runs as follows: The A-series is *fundamental* to time and change. But the inherent contradication of the A-series cannot be resolved without introducing a second series which involves the *same* contradiction. Therefore, the A-series cannot be real. But if the A-series cannot be real, then neither can the B-series, because the B-series is a series of unchanging events, and it cannot be a *temporal* series unless the relations between those events are *temporal* relations involving A-determinations. Therefore, time is unreal.

The refutation of McTaggart's negative thesis will involve the demonstration that the A-series can be defined without contradiction. But first, two remarks: (i) the English word "reality" is derived from the Latin word "*res*", which means "thing" or "content". But, of course, the demonstration of the "reality" of time cannot involve the reduction of time to a "thing" (*in* time) or a "content" (*of* time). Time assuredly cannot be a "thing", "since it is *eo ipso* the *way* that "things" appear – the *form* of temporal things. (Hume calls it the "manner" in which things appear; Kant terms it the "a priori form" of all phenomena.) However, this surely cannot mean that it is spurious to argue for the "reality" of the *manner* of things, even though that manner is not itself a "thing". McTaggart's negative thesis asserts precisely that time *is not* "really" the manner of things. (ii) The demonstration which denies that the A-series, as properly conceived, is contradictory, does not entail either that time should be conceived in terms of the A-series *alone*, or that time as properly understood is unproblematical. The entailment is simply that, if the A-series is not *eo ipso* contradictory, then the implication of A-determinations to the B-series does not imply the "unreality" of time so conceived. In fact, time does indeed involve by A- and B-determinations, and the two series are merely abstractions from the concrete concept of time as such. This means that time is certainly problematical from the point of view of a *synchronic* analysis, but this in itself can be no evidence of its "unreality".

If the distinction is to be made between the two series, it must be made with clarity and precision. The A-series *per se* consists only of the temporal determinations, "past", "present" and "future"; and the B-series *per se* only of the "timeless" (tenseless) determinations, "earlier than . . . ", "simultaneous with . . . " and "later than . . . " The former determinations are *intransitive* or semantically *complete*, and the latter are *transitive* or semantically *incomplete*. All B-determinations, such as "(M is) earlier than . . . ", have an inherent reference to some other event, but A-determinations, such as "(M is) past", do not. Therefore, such statements as "M is past *in relation to* . . . " and "M is *more* past *than* . . . ", etc., clearly involve the *confusion* of A- and B-determinations.

It is not necessary, then, to introduce a second series to resolve the putative contradiction of the first A-series. That "contradiction" only exists because McTaggart has *already* introduced the determinations of a second series into his description of the first. What else are we to make of such statements as "A present event is future in relation to past events and past in relation to future events?" How can a present event be anything other than *Present*, unless we relativize the "absolute" determinations of the A-series by the insinuation of tenseless B-determinations? As Bergson says, time is not something *thought*, something "spread out in space", but always something *lived*. It is not a series of "timeless relations", but always an "absolute" (in the above sense). We must always wait until the sugar melts![43] Within the B-series *per se*, any event can be present (past or future) *in relation to* certain other events quite irregardless of whether the "absolute" A-determination, "Present", applies to it or not. But this only comes down to the tautology that events are "later than" earlier ones and "earlier than" later ones, and it says nothing of the "absolute" temporal determinations of those events.

McTaggart's problem, then, comes down to this: first he asserts that an event can have only *one* of the three "absolute" temporal determinations. Then he argues that the event has all three of these determinations "relative to other events". He then concludes that this is proof of the inherent contradiction of the A-series. But it must now surely be evident that the three "relative" A-determinations are only the "disguised" B-determinations, "earlier than . . .", "simultaneous with . . . ." and "later than . . .". The putative contradiction does not, therefore, apply to the A-series as properly conceived.

Having abstracted the A- and B-series, McTaggart contracts them again into two peculiar notions of time:[44] either (i) the B-series "slides along" a fixed A-series, or (ii) the A-series "slides along" a fixed B-series. In (i) the chain of events passes through the three static regions, "Future", "Present", and "Past". And in (ii), the three temporal "regions" pass in succession over the static events. These are perhaps the most unsatisfactory time-metaphors ever conceived. Having been abstracted and reified in this way, the two "sliding series" can never have any *essential* connection. And since in both (i) and (ii) the A- and B-series so conceived are each hybrid concepts containing both A- and B-determinations, the further concept of these hybrid series "moving along" each other is not only redundant, but involves the absurdity of time moving within time.

If, for exampe, we consider the A-series to be the "moving partner" (since it *is* the "dynamic temporal"), then, since the two series have no essential connection, the determinations "future", "present", "past", which accrue to the events of the B-series due to the movement of the A-series, can only be *inessential* to those events. Moreover, the confluence of A-determinations and B-events will constitute a series of second-order events, which are not contained within the B-series and this will involve a second-order time series. [45] Virtually everyone has taken note of this latter problem. But since it is not generally observed that both A- and B-determinations inhere in each hybrid time series, the tendency has been to conclude that it is the A- and B-series themselves which lack any essential connection. This has led philosophers to conceive of time in terms of one or the other series.

Grünbaum has distinguished between a purely *formal* conception of the B-series having the characteristics of a geometrical line, and the B-series conceived as consisting of the *de facto* continuum of events. [46] His purpose in making this distinction is to show that the "direction" of time (which is conceived by B-theorists in terms of the relation "earlier – later") can be established in terms of the event-continuum alone, without incorporating a time-direction into the formal definition of the B-series by the insinuation of A-determinations. On this latter point, I think he is mistaken. I do not believe that the *de facto* event-continuum can be said to have any temporal direction unless this direction is understood, either explicitly or implicitly, in terms of A-determination. And if it is so understood, then the *formal* series will no longer be like the geometrical line, since it too will have a temporal direction. However, these various distinctions – although necessarily abstract – are useful in the analysis of time, and it will profit us to consider them.

In a sense, the A-series *per se* is a series of time-determinations only, and not of the "things" to which these determinations apply. As such, it is an essentially *formal* series: it appertains to time *itself* – the *form* of time – and not to its "material" or "content". Indeed, this is why A-determinations are, in a manner of speaking, "absolute" – or why the past, for example, is simply "*the* Past" and not "past *in relation to* . . .". Of course, there is also a sense in which the Past is *always* "earlier than" the Present, and the Present *always* "earlier than" the Future; and this, I believe, is because of the essential *complicity* of A- and B-determinations in any *concrete* way of conceiving of time. However, it is apposite to any *abstract* analysis of time, such as this, to present all of these distinctions as clearly as possible, so that they may reveal their own limitations.

The B-series, considered abstractly, is really only the series of *events* "within" time: a series of events related by "timeless" (tenseless) relations, or of "things" with their temporal manner abstracted. The *formal* B-series, then, "would be" (if it could be defined as such without the implication of A-determinations) a series of temporal instants, or empty temporal "positions", which the events if the *de facto* B-series "come to occupy". These empty "positions", however, are themselves a type of "thing": they are earlier or later *in relation to* other such "positions" just as the "event-things" are earlier or later *in relation to* such "event-things". In short, B-determinations apply only to "things", and within the terms of the B-theory *per se* even time itself is just another "thing" – a static Newtonian framework which other things come to occupy.

In the case of the *de facto* event-continuum, simultaneity obtains because event-things deploy themselves along a (spatial) dimension which is transversal to the formally conceived time-series. But in the case of the *formal* B-series, no two "things" can be simultaneous, since the "things" in question are the "times" themselves, and no two "times" (instants of time) can be the same. Therefore, if conceived in complete abstraction from the A-series, the formal B-series is logically indistinguishable from a geometrical line. Both, in fact, are continua of empty positions determined by the relations "before" and "after", and (given the "before-after" relation) both have the same logical characteristics: transitivity, asymmetry and irreflexivity. Moreover, since it is really a matter of convention which ends of the line are to be designated as "before" and "after", the line can have no logical "direction" and the formal B-series no chronological "direction". This would be true, moreover, even if the "spatial" dimension were reintroduced into the formal B-series. As formally conceived, Minkowskian four-dimensional space is entirely without "direction" or "manner", and it is entirely arbitrary which of the four dimensions is chosen to represent time. In fact, temporality accrues to the formal B-series only *extraneously*, just as it does to the line. It is, as Kant says, only because we *draw* the line in thought, or allow it to manifest itself as a succession of empty "now" presentations, that it ceases to be a merely mathematical continuum and takes on its temporal character.[47] This is also what Aristotle means when he speaks of time as movement which admits of enumeration, or as number which is counted, not that with which we count.

The ideal of objectivity has brought modern scientific thought to a view of total reality (*omnitudo realitatis*) which is called the "Theory of the Manifold". This theory is called "objective" because it conceives of total reality literally as an *object*. And it is called the "Theory of the Manifold" because the absolute object is thought to be an anisomerous, four-dimensional *manifold* of unchanging events. Time, on this view, is understood solely in terms of events, and these "time-events" are said to form a mathematically "dense" (or "compact")[48] continuum which constitutes the fourth dimension of the absolute object. But, of course, events are spatial as well as temporal. Therefore, the entire historical and spatial deployment of an object is understood as a single "world-line", and the compact totality of such worldliness is understood to constitute total reality.

In terms of the B-theory, any change in the determinations of a thing is itself treated as a "thing", and this "event-thing" is then described by propositions which, if true, are timelessly true. In this way, the existential-temporal "form" or "manner" of the thing is lost. But really, time is this "form" or "manner", and things with their "manner" constitute an indissoluble unity which can only be correctly understood in terms of a *synthesis* of A- and B-determinations. However, since B-theorists are convinced that the A-series is inherently contradictory, or at least that A-determinations are reducible to B-determinations, they conceive of time purely in terms of the latter.

Generally, when the temporal form is abstracted from things, it is called "time *per se*" and is described in terms of A-determinations. But in terms of the formal B-series, "time *per se*" appears as just another "thing": a static framework which "event-things" come to "occupy". But, of course, this notion of "occupation" is absurd. If it were the case that the determinate events of the *de facto* series actually "come to occupy" the previously empty temporal positions of the formal series, then this "occupation" would itself be a second-order event and would require a second-order time. Just as it proved impossible to reunify the sundered A- and B-series, so it proves impossible to establish any essential connection between the *de facto* series and its formal counterpart. This is the problem of abstraction: no essential connection can be established between two "things" unless they are comprehended by some third "thing" (i.e., a medium). But in this case the only *tertium quid* would be a second-order time, and this proves to be absurd. Therefore, B-theorists have been forced to relinquish the formal series altogether, and to conceive of time purely in terms of its *material* − i.e., purely in terms of *events*. Time, then, is reduced to being merely a *feature* of events, and the "direction" of time is determined solely on the basis of event-asymmetry.

In general, the theory of the manifold has the two following premises: (i) Events are completely determined by propositions which, if true, are *always* true. Therefore, events are not subject to process or change. If, then, whatever is true of an event is *always* true of that event, every event always has precisely the same determinations, and always has precisely the same relations to every other event existing elsewhere in space and time. (ii) If all events simply *are*, then the A-determinations, "Past", "Present" and "Future", do not apply to the events themselves, but only to those events as they are experienced by a subject. A-determinations, then, obtain only because of the interagency of subject and object, whereas the B-determinations, "earlier" and "later", apply to the relations obtaining between objects themselves.[49]

The conclusion derived from these premises is this: Reality *per se* is an anisomerous manifold − i.e., a manifold of asymmetric parts of events. And the so-called "anisotropy", or "asymmetrical transform-ation", of events (from future to present to past) is only a subjective representation of the unchanging asymmetry of reality itself.

(i) McTaggart's defense of the first premise was only intended to show that change is foreign to the B-series *per se* − and in this I think he was correct. But if one further incorporates the B-theory premise that A-determinations are reducible to B-determinations, then the conclusion to his argument is that change is foreign to events as such. Let us consider, then, the following outline of McTaggart's reasoning: If a given proposition, such as "This poker is hot at time t", is true, then it must *always* be true. Therefore, the event which it describes – namely, "this poker being hot at time t" – must *always* be the case. Events, then, cannot change. Because change could only appertain to events if the propositions which describe them were sometimes true and sometimes false.

It is true, of course, that events do not change in the sense that a given event, such as the storming of the Bastille, could ever become "something else" (i.e., some other event). But it is fallacious to conclude from this that things do not have an existential-temporal manner of being which can include change. Moreover, although the proposition "This poker is hot at time t" is always true, this does not mean that the event in question, and/or time t, must always exist. The "truth" of such propositions is a truth of a second-order – a timeless, propositional truth, which does not coincide with the existence of the event in question. However, the "truth" of first-order propositions, such as "This poker is hot", is one and the same as the actual existence of the event they describe. And such propositions *are* therefore sometimes true and sometimes false. It the event described no longer exists, or if it does not yet exist, the first-order proposition does not have its "truth".

To say that a second-order proposition is "always true" really means that its "truth" always "exists". And this means either that it "exists" at *all times* or, if Aristotle is correct to say that "these things are not in time", then it exists at *none* of these times, i.e., time t, time t, time t, and so forth. However, the first-order "truth" (i.e., the event itself) – which is the condition of the second-order, propositional "truth" – exists (only) at time t. Therefore, neither the event itself nor time t "always exist" in either of the senses that the "truth" of the second-order proposition "always exist", and we cannot, then, argue from the nature of propositional "truth" to the nature of existential "truth". Second-order propositions include the time of the event along with the event itself, and then this "second-order event" (if we can call it that) can no longer be temporal. For example, the second-order event "this poker being hot at time t" cannot itself obtain at time t, or at time t, or at any other time. It "exists" rather at all times (or at none of these times), and this is because it is the "truth" of a second-order proposition.

Something analogous is true of change. But with change the problem is complicated because all change requires duration and time t is generally taken to be instantaneous. However, perhaps the mathematicians will alow us the following point. In reality, the event is not the poker being hot for a mathematical instant, but rather the poker being hot for some time – i.e., the poker being in process of change from being very hot to being slightly hot. If, then, this whole process of change is given the name "event", it will be a second-order "thing" which evidently cannot change. A process of change cannot itself change any more than time can itself be in time. But none of this can mean that a first-order thing does not include change as part of its manner of being.

(ii) If the "formal" element of time is relinquished in favour of the *de facto* continuum of events, then event-systems cannot be earlier or later simply because they belong to earlier or later "times". Indeed, they cannot belong to "times" at all, since, on this view, the "times" are determined in terms of event-systems, and not vice-versa. However, the event-systems themselves cannot give any earlier – later "direction" to the continuum, but only a certain "order" or "content". Event-asymmetry can no more determine a "direction" than can colour-asymmetry give a "direction" to the visible spectrum. Just as the colour-gradations of the spectrum go neither from red to violet nor from violet to red, so the "content" of the *de facto* continuum has no inherent earlier – later "direction". Therefore, McTaggart is correct to say that "earlier" and "later" are disguised A-determinations, which cannot appertain to the B-series as such.

To establish a "direction" of events on the basis of their asymmetry, it is necessary to add a further principle, such as the second law of thermodynamics, which makes the earlier – later direction of the continuum correspond to a given direction of event-asymmetries. However, such a principle cannot be true by definition, because it would then be either arbitrary or tautologous (i.e., it would not be *"de facto"*). Therefore, it can only be *discovered* to be the case. But, then, in order to know that earlier and later events do in fact have the asymmetric physical features required by the principle, it is necessary to *know already* from experience which events are earlier and which later. Therefore, either A-determinations must be an essential feature of the *de facto* continuum, or the events simply do not have an inherent earlier – later direction, and time, as McTaggart says, is unreal.

The alternative to McTaggart's conclusion is to give the temporal manner back to events, and to conceive of the continuum not as consisting of asymmetric "parts" but as constituting an asymmetrical or directional *process*. Of course, the event-process cannot then be thought of as moving forward in any "time" extraneous to itself; the rigorous path of B-analysis must surely have taught us this. The event-process is not "in" time, but rather is time. The form and the material of time are inextricable. The error of the *de facto* B-theory lies not so much in conceiving of time in terms of events, but in forgetting that events have a certain *manner of being*. If the event-process were negentropic rather than entropic, the content would remain the same, but the "direction" or "manner" of this content would differ. And it is this which suggests the "reality" of this direction.

Bergson refers frequently to the fact that classical thermodynamics conceives of time as a background given or invariant.[50] If time were accelerated or retarded, scientific formulae would remain unchanged. Their function is to describe events as though they were pictures on a fan. As the fan is opened, the pictures "appear" or the events "happen". But, as the picture-events are "already there", the opening of the fan is a mere formality. The formulae describe only the events, and not their manner of being.

The modern B-theorist would object to the fan metaphor on two counts: (i) Since time is a feature of events, the opening of the fan would mean that events happen twice and that time moves within time. (ii) The supposition that the fan can open in either direction would imply that the direction can be determined independently of the intrinsic order of events.

(i) The first objection is certainly valid, but it should be noted that Bergson is not defending the fan metaphor. What seems absurd is not that events *happen*, but that they have "already happened" (before they *happen*), and that they form an already complete and unchanging series, of which the temporal series is a mere image. The happening of events can only seem like a "normality", as Eddington expresses it,[51] if something like the latter is presupposed.

Of course, within the terms of the theory of the manifold, the thesis that all event-systems exist does not mean that they exist *simultaneously*. If the various event-systems are one and the same as the various "times", and if these various event-systems are all different, then naturally all of the "times" must be different. Therefore, as no two "parts" of the manifold can exist at (or as) the same time, so the totality of these "parts" cannot constitute a *totum simul* or *nunc stans*. Indeed, as the manifold is not a "part", but a whole of (space-) time, there is no question of it existing "now", since the "nows" (i.e., the "times" or event-systems) are the "parts" of time, and the whole cannot exist *qua* whole in any of its parts. As time itself, then, the manifold cannot change "within time", since this would require a "second time". And as the manifold consists only of events, then these latter cannot change either, since any change in the "parts" would involve a change in the whole, and this has already been precluded. Therefore, although no two "times" are simultaneous, it is not the case that any of them no longer exists or does not yet exist. They all *are*. They all *exist*.

This very fine, incisive analysis is, I think, mistaken. To say that total reality is not in process (of change) does not mean either that it does not exist *as* process, or that its "parts" do not have process and temporality as their manner of being. On this point mathematical analysis is fundamentally deceptive. For such an analysis reality appears as a continuum of unchanging events, such as "this poker being hot at time t". But such "events" are "truths" of a second-order: they do not themselves obtain at any "times", and are dependent for *their* truth upon first-order "truths" which *are* temporal and *do* obtain at the specified "times". First-order, temporal "truths", then, are not mere "subjective representations" of an unchanging continuum of second-order truths. They are, rather, reality itself *qua* the process of self-disclosure and self-meditation.

Reality cannot exist as disclosure other than by self-meditation, and disclosure is not something that "happens" to reality, but is the realization of reality as such. Reality has no determinable "outside", since all determinations, *qua* "real", must obtain "within" reality. It exists rather as process, and it remains the same reality throughout all event-transformations. All determinacy, as expressed (paradoxically) in terms of "pure A-determinations", obtain "within" − or rather, *as* − disclosure. And disclosure cannot in turn be disclosed, since it has no "outside". In truth, then reality does not exist as a determinable totality. It exists, rather, as the process of self-totalization. It is, of course, "more than" its event-transformations, since it is also the origin and "eventuality" of events. But A- and B-determinations alike are the "outcome" of events: they emerge with the "coming-out" of e-vents (in disclosure), and can have no sway over the originating reality of disclosure as such.

(ii) The second objection really comes down to this: Since the event-continuum is all that there is, and since this continuum is *in fact* entropic, then all talk of a possible negentropic direction is superfluous. In a sense, this is correct. But it is this "in fact" which must be understood. If reality were simply a continuum of asymmetric "part", it would have no *de facto* direction − entropic or negentropic. It is the *anisotropy* or *unidirectional* transformation of events which gives time its direction, and it is this manner of transformation which is, in general, entropic. It is said that the event-manifold, although full and actual and therefore exclusive of any "no longer" or "not yet", is not more necessarily determined than it is fortuitous. On this view, a causally determined sequence would appear within the manifold as a perfectly sequence of contents. And quantum phenomena would appear as abruptly dissimilar, proximate contents, which appear on the micro-level only and do not disrupt the overall continuity of the macro-continuum. However, if the continuum consists only of content, this cannot be the case. The fact that the multiplicity of quantum phenomena are not perceived to disrupt the overall continuity does not alter the fact that the content-continuum contains "content-gaps", and therefore cannot be an actual *continuum* unless there is a formal element over and above the mere contents as such.

Reality, in fact, is "more than" the *de facto* event-series. It is also an open horizon of possibility and potentiality, in relation to which the *de facto* and the *actual* gain their meaning. It is a manifesting-unmanifest: a matrix of space-time, a living disclosure of fact and essence, and a tissue of presence, absence, possibility and necessity.

If the B-series is the abstraction of the "content" from the "form" (the flux) of time, then the A-series is the abstraction of "time *per se*" (the form) from temporal things. But unlike that of the *formal* B-series, the "form" of the A-series is not that of things *in actu* which have already lost their temporal manner. For Aristotle, there were two types of form: form in repose (synchronic

form) and form as active and generative (diachronic form). The former he called *eidos* and the latter *energeia* In abstraction from its material, time appears
as pure *energeia* – pure becoming, pure production. Or, as Hegel says, pure externality and abstraction: it is intuited mere becoming – sheer coming-out-of-
self.[52] Considered in its essential involvement with its material, however, it is
temporal being (*on energeia*), which becomes of itself according to its essential
self-production. This latter is really "what" exists: it is substance (*ousia*) as
such: not, indeed, what is recondite – nor even what is unambiguously
manifest – but rather what is manifesting, the concretion which involves both
eidos and *energeia*.

Time *per se* is a sort of essence, or rather the active aspect of essence.
Therefore, in the case of time per se, it is necessary to think of essence (*ousia,
Wesen*) as a sort of "standing out" or "essence", and not as substance or
presence (*parousia, Anwesen*) – i.e., not as an "instance": something "standing in" self-identity.[53] Without *eidos, energeia* is sheer and uncompromised.
It is absolute openness and negativity, *metabasis* without a *basis*, self-sublation
without a "self", *ekstasis* without a *stasis* , a river without a riverbed. "Time
itself", then, involves the following paradox: only the present can really *be*,
but the present is already its future. Therefore, no-thing is present. No aspect
of time is. Time is simply a no-thing that nihilates.

"Time *per se*", then, is a sort of contradiction, since in abstraction time
possesses no ipseity. (This is the real consideration underlying McTaggart's
analysis.) Just as the pure flux of time-consciousness can only determine itself
in terms of its objects, so time is "objectively determinable" only in terms of
temporal things. This is why Aristotle says (*Physics* IV 219b 10–220a 3) that
what is most knowable about time are the things that transpire "within" time,
whether these are "real" things or the succession of objective "now" presentations which obtain when "time itself" is enumerated. Of course, Aristotle did
not hold that time is *reducible* to motion or change. It is, rather, the number
of motion and change – i.e., to the event that this number is enumerated, not
insofar as it "subsists" (or "insists"). "For the time is . . . [the] number of motion in respect of "before" and "after" . . . not movement [itself], but only
movement". As such, then, time is essentially bound up with the soul, but not
in the sense that it could be some sort of "subjective representation". This
would be to misrepresent Aristotle. Even the "enumeration" of time as a sequence of "nows" *requires* time, because "that which is 'in time' [i.e., the
enumeration and the "nows"] involves that there *is* time", and "Time [itself]
is not held to be made up of "nows" – the "now" (*nun* is no part' of time . . .
any more than the points are part of the line". This is why "a time greater than
anything 'in time' can be found" (*Physics* IV, 219b 1–8).

When abstracted from its material, time *per se* is an empty and indeter-
minable flux. When the material of time is abstracted from its "manner", we

gain a preeminently determinable structure of objects (and objectivities), the new "form" of which is *insistence*, or *eidos*. This latter is also the "time" of the formal B-series. It is "time itself" as an object: *energeia* becomes *eidos*, or "space" in the generic sense. There is a sense, then, in which, as Hegel says (*Encyclopedia*, s258), space "would be" if the distinction "obectivity−subjectivity" were applicable to space-time as concretely conceived. In concrete space-time, abstract ek-sistence (time) and abstract coexistence (simultaneity, space) go together. The *simul* represents the complicity of A- and B-determinations in things. It is a virtue of the fact *that* things ek-sist that they can exist as *what* they are, but is in virtue of the "what" of things that their "standing out" as determinate ek-sistence is possible. The complicity of space and time is the condition of all disclosure of Being in beings.[55]

When other "objects" are abstracted from their "manner", they are seen to become precisely "what" they are (to insist), but they are seen as retaining their "that" (their existence) as a sort of quality or attribute, which likewise "inheres" or "insists". However, when time itself is made into an object, there is an additional problem: "time *per se*" cannot appear as a "now", something that insists "within" time. It cannot appear as a *nunc stans*, since if all "nows" appear "within" time, there is no "now" for it to stand in. Nevertheless, *qua object*, it must stand "somewhere", since like an infinite number, it is thought to be indifferent to the fact that its infinity of "parts" cannot be enumerated (in time). This, however, remains unthought: How can the series of "parts", the so-called *totality of what is*, be spread out before us and thought "now" in terms of mathematical forms which somehow "transcend" this totality and determine it from "without"? In reality, such forms obtain within the totality, and fall within the sphere of *eidos* rather than *energeia*. But they do not obtain at any of the "times" of the *de facto* series, since these "times" are always *concreta of eidos and energeia*. The "totality", however, is no mathematical totality, since it is rather the Origin of that disclosure wherein concrete ek-sistence obtains with its amalgamation of A- and B-determinations, and wherein the preeminently determinable structure of *eidos* obtains as the abstraction from concrete space-time as such.

When thought in terms of A-determinations, the abstract concept of "time *per se*" corresponds to the similarity abstract and impalpable concept of "existence". Existing, as Heidegger says, is something temporally determined.[56] Just like the predicate "existence" (if indeed it is a predicate), the A-determinations, "past", "present" and "future", add nothing to the "objective content" of the concept of a thing. As regards their "objective contents", then, the concepts of an object as "past" or "future" are the same as the concept of that object as "present". But with the former concepts, the object is thought vaguely as "existing elsewhere". This is why, as Heidegger says, in the history of metaphysics, *energeia* as the "manner" or "presencing" of beings, has been determined in terms of beings themselves as "the present" (*Gegen-wärtigen*). A-determinations really apply to the abstract concept of time as *existentia*, pure "standing out", or "thatness" (*quodditas, hoti estin*). B-determinations, on the other hand, apply to the abstract concept of *essentia* as *actualitas*: the pure "standing in" (*insistentia, instantia*) of "the present" within "presence" − the latter being conceived as the objectively determinable structure of "whatness" (*quidditas, ti estin*). Existence, then, becomes determined in terms of the obstance (the objectivity) of objects, and time *per se* as thus determined becomes itself an object − the "time" of the formal B-series, a mathematically dense continuum of empty instants conceived *sub specie aeternitatis*. In short, as we find in Spinoza's *Ethics, energeia qua existentia* is reduced to *eidos* (Idea or *essentia*). And extension (space) is understood as the fundamental attribute of What Is (the "Is" being reduced to the "What", since existence is essential), whereas time is reduced to the problematical "indefinite continuation of existence" conceived *sub specie aeternitatis*. [57]

In reaction to such a concept, Kierkegaard writes: "All logical thinking employs the language of abstraction, and [therefore] is *sub specie aeterni* . . . [But]It is impossible to conceive existence without movement, and movement cannot be conceived *sub specie aeterni* . . . The only "thing-in-itself" which cannot be thought is existence, and this does not come within the province of thought to think".[58]

The disclosure of things does not have the nature of a "representation" (of things) within consciousness. Disclosure has no "without", in the sense of having a nature of its own. And its "within" is simply the field of potentiality or non-being which things involve as their inherent manner of being "in time". Time does not accrue to things through their involvement with "subjectivity" any more than it accrues to "pure thought" through the latter's involvement with "matter". Either "subjectivity" or "objectivity" can be constructed from the concrete flux of phenomena that we call "space-time". It is simply a matter of the ground adopted.[59]

(i) If we go toward "subjectivity", we discover the timeless transcendental subject: the form of time which is not itself temporal. The manifold of objects pass away in time before this same unchanging subject, which only "falls into time" by a process of "self-objectification". Of course, the acts of such a subject are temporal, but only because they have to apprehend and, so to speak, "keep pace" with temporal objects. In subjectivity *per se*, however, there is, as the psychologists say, no inherent "time sense". Without the objects of consciousness, and the temporal "clues" they provide, we have no internal awareness of time's passage.[60] Strike out the objects and all that remains is the unchanging field of consciousness: the form and the limits to the objective world.

(ii) If we go toward "objectivity", we discover an unchanging realm of objects held together by a structure of timeless relations and forming a four-dimensional space. Time, in the sense of genesis and decay, is only incidental to such a structure. It is, as they say, only "mind-dependent" and therefore a "subjective representation" (an image) of that structure as it is in itself. Strike out the subject, and all that remains is an absolute object, wherein "time" is merely the mathematically determinable multiplicity of unchanging elements which constitute that object's fourth dimension.

In reality, however, the truth lies between these two extremes. Time is neither "subjective" nor "objective". It is the synthetic manner of manifestations, the emerging-presencing that we call "nature", the primitive disclosure of first-order truth. It is not the multiplicity of mathematically determinable and unchanging second-order structures, not the *synthesis intellectualis* effected in pure thought before the latter associates itself with matter and non-being.

III. The Being of Time and the Temporality of Being

"Neither plentitude nor vacancy. Only a flicker
Over the strained time-ridden faces".[61]

Time, Heidegger says, is "earlier" than any subjectivity or objectivity, because it is the condition of the possibility of this "earlier".[62] It is too late to ask the question of time, claims Derrida, because time has already appeared.[63] Any reflections upon time is already within time. It cannot recover itself from time by construing itself as the transcendental subjective "power over time", nor can it attain to any transcendent objective reality "underlying time". Cartesian subjectivity and Galilean objectivity are abstractions from the more fundamental reality of *disclosure*.

What, then, is disclosure if not a subjective representation of what is? *To what* is Being disclosed? To answer this it is necessary to cease to think in terms of representational thought. In Wittgenstein's "picture theory of the proposition", for example, one thing, an objective state of affairs, is represented or "pictured" by another, a pictorial state of affairs, which has the same "logical form" (and is therefore equally "objective"). This is not the case with disclosure. The disclosure of Being is not a "picture" of Being, not something "other" than Being: and therefore, there is "nothing" to which Being appears. However, if we insist upon polarizing the "that" and the "to which" of disclosure, let us call the former the "matter of apprehension" and the latter the "essence (or logos) of apprehension itself" — always remembering, however, that these are not two things "in" Being, but simply Being itself: disclosure.

For Aristotle, the soul has no nature of its own. Time is not an "image" of

Being, and the soul is not a *subiectum* which adds something of its own "nature" to the "matter" of disclosure. Only if this is thoughtfully understood will Aristotle's following remark on time and the soul deliver itself in its true perspective: "[Consider] Whether if soul did not exist time would exist or not ... for if there cannot be someone to count there cannot be anything that can be counted, so that evidently there cannot be number ... but if nothing but soul, or in soul reason, is qualified to count, there would not be time unless there were soul, but only that of which time is an attribute – i.e., attributes of movement, and time is these qua numberable".[64]

Time, for Aristotle, is a type of *synthesis*, not a stasis-continuum or a configuration. Indeed, he speaks of *physis* (Being or nature) as the "primary synthesis": the real essence of things with matter and (*eidetis*) form, their principal source of movement and the *telos* of their becoming (*Metaphysics* V, 4). The real connection between time, Being and the soul can be seen in Aristotle's treatise, *On the Soul*, where he writes: "That which the mind thinks and the time in which it thinks are ... divisible only incidentally and not as such ... (something indivisible gives unity to the time and the whole of length; and this is found equally in every continuum: temporal or spatial" (*De Anima* 430b 16–19). This "something indivisible" is "mind": the absolute *prius* of all synthesis, and the form of all forms. Aristotle does say that it is divisible in its "being" (*De Anima* 427a, 4), but all he means by this is that it is perfectly homogeneous and that infinite sub-division would not reveal any "elementary parts". Indeed, as the capacity (the essence) for thinking all things, it is free from all admixture, and "parts" are entirely foreign to its "nature".

As the "form of forms", mind is analogous to Kant's concept of time as the "formal condition, *a priori*, of all phenomena whatsoever", but for Aristotle forms were not mere "appearances", not mind something "subjective". In every case, what unifies is mind, and division is only possible on the basis of this fundamental synthesis. When mind discriminates other things, it retains its own unity in a single (lapse of) time. What is qualitatively simple is thought in a simple time by a simple act of the soul. A length, for example, has no actual parts until it has been divided – and if one does so divide the length, then by the same act one divides the ("objective") time also. Points and other things that divide are realized in consciousness only as privations: and one can think "abstract objects", as in mathematics, only by "removing them from" (*abstractus*) that which they are inseparable.[65]

For Aristotle, the so-called "common sensibles" – i.e., movement, rest, figure, magnitude, number and unity – are not perceived by any special sense (organ), but rather by *movement* – or by the *arrest* of movement (since number is the *negation* of continuity), and this is the origin of our "general sensibility" (*De Anima* 425a 18–425b 3). This is why "points" and "nows" are not considered to be *parts* of space and time, since they are rather the *negations* of such continua. Numbers that subsist ideally are determined by number as enumerated, and such enumeration is possible only as the negation of serial continuity. Time is only the "number of movement and change" insofar as the "common sensibles" – *including* number and movement – are *perceived* by movement (or its absence), and it is not itself number of movement *qua* a "common sensible". Time can only be a quantity incidentally – i.e., because it is generally determined in terms of movement and movement in terms of space. Only this latter is really a "quantum" (*Metaphysics*, 1020a 29–32).

In reality, on Aristotle's view, the soul does not "move" at all. It is not by moving itself that the soul originates movement in other things; rather, it is by intention or process of thinking. The soul is neither a spatial thing nor the form or proportion of spatial things. "Mind (not the sensitive or desiderative soul) is one and continuous like the process of thinking: its thoughts have a serial unity like number, not the unity of a spatial magnitude" (*De Anima* 406a 3–9, 408a 6–34). Moreover, although the soul does not move, movement sometimes begins or ends with it, as in the cases of recollection and sensations. And if the soul could be moved by the body, such movement would be merely *incidental* to it, as is the "place" occupied by the body. Actually, movement of the soul by the body is enigmatic, since the soul is the substance and actuality of the latter. Moreover, any compound, such as that of soul and body, is always *more than* its elements. It is also the *ratio* (the formulable essence) of these elements – and this is not the spatial form of the body alone, which (body and spatial form) is only the "appropriate matter" (*De Anima* 407b 13–33).

In every case it is the soul which generates movement, in numbers it is in the body. But the soul cannot be a self-moving number; it is always the mover, never the moved. If the soul as a unit could move, it would generate spatial forms (lines and surfaces), and this would involve the absurdity of a "psychic body" – a *Doppel-gänger* of the physical body.

As we have said, disclosure belongs to an *Origin*: to an Originating or Disclosing of disclosure. That which discloses itsels as (space-) time and the disclosure as such – namely (space-) time itself – are essentially the Same.[66] (Space-) Time and the essence of apprehension *together* constitute the Being of the temporal order, and this Being belongs to an *Origin*. However, that which discloses disclosure cannot be anything "other" than disclosure. Time, Being and the essence of apprehension are not things "in" time, beings "in" Being or representations "within" thought. If we conceive of the Origin as the *power* of disclosure – i.e., if we try to think of it as it is "In itself" – we might speak of it as the "Unmanifest", but as the *Disclosing* of disclosure nothing is added to this "Unmanifest". It is "In Itself" the Manifest. It does not disclose Itself "in" time, but rather *as* time. The Disclosing and its disclosure are "the Same".

Time is not a "moving image of eternity", since then either a second "time" would be required in virtue of which it could be said that at one "time" time did not exist, but that at the present "time" it does, [67] or a second "eternity" would be required in virtue of which it could be said that time endures for "eternity" as an image of eternity. Let us summarize this difficult matter as follows: time and eternity are really "the Same" — though without being logically identical. Time itself is "temporal" but it is not itself something "within" time. The flux itself is not a unity "within" the flux. Hegel expresses if thus: "The Universal as law, also has a process within it, and lives only as a process; but it is not *part* of the process, not *in* process ... On its phenomenal side, law enters into the time process ... [but as] Idea, Spirit [it] transcends time because it is itself the Notion of time; it is eternal ... because it does not lose itself in one side of the process". Moreover, "Idea, Spirit is eternal. But the notion of eternity must not be grasped negatively as abstraction from time, as existing, as it were, outside of time". [68]

For Heidegger, this "the Same" (*das Selbe, Idem, to auto*) means the "identity in difference" of *noein* (apprehension) and Being, and whenever he uses the expression, it is always with reference to Parmenides' *to gar auto* ("For the Same ..."). [69] However, within Heidegger's thought there is a precedent for another sense of the expression, "the Same": Being as disclosure belongs to, and is the Same as, the (Undisclosed) Originating of disclosure. When Being discloses itself in beings, it withdraws — *qua* the Originating — into dignified Self-concealment. But the Origin and its disclosure are the Same. There is but One Reality: a Temporal—Eternal or Manifesting—Unmanifest.

Similarly, the Vaibhāsika philosopher, Sanghabhadra, writes: "The *Tathāgata* is and is not beyond this world. The character of dependent causation is to be and not to be permanent ... We accept that *dharma* exists always and, at the same time, we teach that *dharma* is not eternal. But ... the terms "eternal" and "not eternal" are used in two different senses ... The *dharma* lasts eternally, but the *dharmabhāva* [literally, the "becoming" or "existence" of the *dharma*] changes". This is perhaps more simply expressed by A.K. Coormaraswamy, who writes: "God is an essence without duality (*a-dvaita*) ... but his essence subsists in a two-fold nature (*dvaitabhavā)*: as being and becoming". [70] Here, the paradox is evident: the One Reality is two-fold. And such an insight, I believe, is at the basis of the *Mādhyamika* philosophy of Nāgārjuna, where the endless round of existence (*samsāra*) is understood to be one and the same eternal reality of *Nirvana*. [71]

According to Benjamin Lee Whorf, similar considerations appear to obtain in the case of the Hopi Indians. [72] For the Hopi, the One Reality consists of two forms: "the Manifest" and "the Unmanifest (or Manifesting)". The former includes the whole of physical and historical nature, and the latter, which is called "the Spirit of the Breath" (and seems analogous to the concepts of *Geist* and *pneuma*), includes all that is yet to emerge from the "soul" or "heart" of the One Reality.[73] The latter is a purposeful striving toward manifestation – not an abstract, kinematic movement. It is *tunátya*: the action of hoping or desiring, a mental-causal surge to become "the Manifest".[74] The Hopi have two verbal forms, which Whorf calls "the inceptive" and the "expective". *Tunátya*, which translates as "begins to hope", is expective, and its inceptive equivalent, *tunátyava*, translates as "comes true being hoped for". Where the two meet we seem to have a concept of emerging or presencing which is analogous to the Aristotelian concept of *energeia*, and the two forms share the same verbal root, since they describe the two aspects of the One Reality.

Hegel's analyses of time show clearly the expropriative–appropriative dialectic of time and its Origin, but for Heidegger, these analyses remain within the traditional concept of time as a sequence of "nows". Let us, therefore, consider Heidegger's interpretation of Hegel. According to Howard Trivers,[75] Heidegger approaches Hegel's analyses in terms of Spirit "faling into time" (expropriation),[76] and not in terms of the return (appropriation) of Spirit to itself in time. This is why Heidegger regards the concept of "falling" to be obscure, when Spirit is supposed to be "the power over time and is therefore "outside time".[77] However, for Hegel, time is nothing but the Concept (i.e., Spirit) *Itself* – but in the attitude of *actual existence (der daseiende Begriff)*.[78] But, as Trivers says, Heidegger's assertion that Hegel lays down "the within-time-ness of Spirit as a Fact" is highly questionable.[80] The truth is not "*die Innerzeitigkeit des Geistes*", but rather *die Innergeistigkeit der Zeit* (the within-Spirit-ness of time). Time is not, as Heidegger says, "external to Spirit" (*Ausseres des Geistes*),[81] but rather Spirit itself *as* externality.

In a sense, Heidegger deliberately misrepresents Hegel so that his own analyses can be presented in explicit contrast. He writes: "Our existential analytic of Dasein, on the contrary, starts with the "concretion" of factically thrown existence itself in order to unveil temporality as that which ... makes such existence possible. "Spirit" does not first fall into time, but it *exists as* the primordial temporalizing of temporality ... factical existence "falls" ... *from* primordial authentic temporality".[82]

It is, of course, true that Hegel does not *start* with this "concretion", but he makes it abundantly clear that space and time are the two forms of Spirit *in complete self-externality and abstraction*. The first *concrete* thing, the unity and negation of these abstract momenta, is matter. It is related to them in motion, and when this relation is no longer external, we have the absolute unity of matter and motion: self-moving matter. The "truth" of abstract space is to exist as (the relative, determinate space of) some material body. Nowhere can a space *per se* be demonstrated; it is always filled with something. Both space and time are pure, abstract (Kantian) forms of intuition: they are "the non-sensuous sensuous" (*das unsinnliche Sinnliche*). In reality, things themselves are the temporal, and so too are their objective (spatial) determinations.

92

As Derrida observes, the same critique of "within-time-ness" that we find in *Sein und Zeit* could be exhibited by a careful reading of Hegel. Whatever criticisms can be brought to bear against Hegel's concept of *fallen* with reference to the "fall" of Spirit, can be brought to bear against Heidegger's *Verfallen* with reference to the "fall" of *Dasein* from authenticity. [83] In fact, as regards the relation between time and its Origin, Hegel and Heidegger say much the same thing.

If, however, there is a real critique of Hegel, it must be directed against the concept of absolute Knowledge or absolute Idea. Knowledge cannot reclaim itself from time, since in essence thinking (*noein*) and time emerge together as disclosure. The relationship that we call "disclosure" is more fundamental than the "things" related. As Heidegger says, "intentionality" is nothing physical or subjective, but involves instead an "ontological" relation between the Being of intentional acts and the being which is intended. It is not a matter of consciousness "constituting" its objects, but of "letting being *be* in their objectivity [Being]". [84] In every case, the "elements" of the intentional relationship — namely objective being and conscious being (*bewusst-sein*) — are less fundamental than that relationship itself; and intentionality in turn requires the open horizon of disclosure.

Hegel's analyses show that "time *per se*" is something of an abstraction. Although time is not something "in" time, neither is it something *other* than what appears in time. The disclosure (as Being) and the disclosed (as beings in Being) belong together as concrete spatio-temporal existence. And as belonging together, they share (they are "the Same as") that Origin whose nature is expropriation–appropriation. What, then, of the spatio-temporal order? If it is not an "image" of its Origin, does this mean that it is in no sense *different* from its Origin? Indeed not! The Origin can only be "the Origin" *qua Originating*. Disclosure is the self-deferment (the identity in difference) of the Origin. Nevertheless, if we think of the Origin as "Being Itself", as opposed to "the Being of beings" (which we have called "the disclosure"), then beings with their Being appear as a sort of privation, a sort of "representation" which somehow falls short of what it represents. This view, however, is not really correct. There is no such "fall".

Heidegger has continually conceived of disclosure in terms of a "lighting" or "opening" (*Lichtung, clairière*), or of a "coming out" (e-vent, from *e-venire*), and he has often given the impression that this progression of Being out of its Origin is some sort of errancy, something to be overcome. In a sense this is correct: the oblivion of Being in favour of beings as mere "matter" for manipulation *is* "to be overcome", but "overcoming" in its usual sense is only another type of "manipulation". Therefore, in his final works, Heidegger says that metaphysics, however, "errant", is not to be "overcome": metaphysics is to be "left alone". [85] Indeed, as Augustine says, it was *primogenitus (De Civ.*

Dei, XI, 9). The creation of the angelic host was the first act of the Divinity, and the first of this host was Lucifer.

The characteristic non-being of the temporal order is not something which separates it from its Origin. As the Disclosing of disclosure, the Origin originates Being and non-being in their essential togetherness; and together they are the Truth and the Origin. Non-being, as Heidegger says, *belongs* to Being: "Nihilation unfolds essentially in Being itself, and not in the existence of man so far as this is thought as the subjectivity of the *ego–cogito*. Dasein in no way nihilates as a human subject who carries out nihilation in the sense of denial; rather Dasein nihilates inasmuch as it belongs to the essence of Being as that essence in which man ek-sists. Being nihilates as Being". [86]

Aristotle moved very carefully through the whole problematic of "substance metaphysics", and yet he was chary about the problem of non-being – time always remaining for him a rather special case. "For nature is also in the same genus as potency, for it is a principle of movement – not, however, in something else but in the thing itself *qua* itself. To all such potency, then, actuality is prior both in formula and in substance [essence]; and in time it is prior in one sense, but in another not" (*Metaphysics*, IX 1049b 8–11). The problem is that time is a sort of movement from potency to actuality: "people look for a unifying formula, and [also] a difference, between potency and complete reality. But the proximate matter and the form are one and the same thing, the one potentially, the other actually. Therefore to ask the cause of their being one is like asking the cause of unity in general: for each thing is a unity, and the potential and actual are somehow one. Therefore there is other cause here unless there is something which caused the movement from potency into actuality" (*Metaphysics*, VIII, 1045b 16–23). In time, potency comes first because the embryo, for example, always precedes the mature animal. But potency is always a potency of some determinate kind, and is therefore always determined by some prior actuality: the embryo is, so to speak, *ontologically* determined by the *form* of the animal which is to become. The conclusion is that, just as there are many types of being – substance, quantity, quality, relation, and so on – so there are many types of non-being. And potency and actuality are to be conceived as manners of Being and not in abstraction as beings within Being. This, as I see it, is the main criticism of the Ideal theory: if non-being is seen as "other" than Being, then the Ideas of "Being" and "the Other" (non-being as the "indefinite dyad") will both be actual beings; and the whole question of potency, time, and so on will have been glossed over. [87]

According to Heidegger, the epoch of substance metaphysics began with the Ideal theory of Plato, wherein the "ontological difference" (between Being and beings) is replaced by the "metaphysical difference" (between essence and existence). [88] Within the metaphysical tradition, the Being of beings, which Heidegger understands to be the presencing of what is present (*energeia*), is interpreted in terms of *actualitas*. Being is thought as sheer perdurance, as sheer "now-ness" (instancy, insistence, *Inständigkeit, maintenance*), and as "presence-at-hand" (*Vorhandenheit, Anwesenheit, parousia*). Moreover, the meaning of beings is determined as "permanence" and "persistence" (*Beständigkeit* and *Ständigkeit*). [89]

However, if becoming *is* (or if Being *ek-sists*), then it is necessary to think Being is so radical a manner as to *include* becoming and perishing (*genesis* and *pthora*). We cannot *exclude* all absence from what is present, since even "being no longer" and "being not yet" belong to the essential nature of Being *qua* Being. The epochal (historical nature) of Being belongs to the concealed temporal character of Being itself. In fact, this history of Being solely Being Itself, and metaphysics is simply this history of Being as the progression out of its Origin (i.e., *qua* the phenomenology of the Concept). This "opening out" is itself a fundamental characteristic of Being, and not its consequence. It is Being's mediating self-relation, or the appropriation of time to its Origin, that is the condition of world-historical time. Becoming, appearance, the ought, and so on, all belong to Being. Possibility belongs to Being as much as actuality and necessity, and in its broadest sense, Being is the silent power of the possible. Appearing is not something that happens to Being, but its very essence. Being and truth belong together as the disclosure of a single Origin:

> *tà eonta* names beings in the sense of "the present". In speaking of "present" (*gegenwärtig*), we moderns mean either the "now" in time, or we relate "present" to "the standing-over-against" (*Gegenständigen*). As "the objective" this "standing-over-against" is related to a representing subject.
>
> But precision forces us to understand "the present" on the basis of the *eonta*, and not vice-versa. For *eonta* is also what is past and future. Both are modes of the non-present present. The Greeks called the presently present *tà pareónta* where *para* means "close by" — drawing into dis-closure (*Unverborgenheit*). The "gegen" (against) in *gegenwärtig* (present) does not mean "over against a subject", but rather the region of dis-closure where the *pareónta* comes to dwell. "Present" means, as the characteristic of *eónta* "dwelling awhile in dis-closure". Such coming to dwell is the presencing of the genuinely present. What is past and future are also "presents" (*Anwesendes*), but outside dis-closure. The non-present *qua* *absent* within disclosure ... Consequently *eón* (the Being of beings) means: presencing in disclosure ... *Tà eónta* means either in the presently present or all that it is present including the non-present. [90]

In *Sein und Zeit*, Heidegger speaks of temporality as "the Meaning of Dasein" (*Der Sinn des Daseins ist die Zeitlichkeit*). [91] He says: A distinction has been made between "temporal" entities (natural processes and historical happenings) and "non-temporal" entities (natural processes and historical happenings) and "non-temporal" entities (spatial and numerical relation-ships). We are accustomed to contrasting the "timeless" meaning of proposi-tions with the "temporal" course of propositional assertions. It is also held that there is a "cleavage" between "temporal" entities and the "supra-temporal" eternal, and efforts are made to bridge this over. Here "temporal" always means simply being "in time" ... If Being ... [and its modes] ... are to become intelligible ... by taking time into consideration, then Being itself (and not merely entities ...) is thus made visible in its "temporal" are "tem-poral" with regard to their Being.[92]

However, Heidegger later makes a statement which appears to stand these remarks on their head: "temporality as ecstatico-horizonal, temporalizes sometimes like *world*-time, which constitutes a within-time-ness of the ready-to-hand and the present-at-hand. But in that case such entities can never be designated as 'temporal' in the strict sense. Like every entity with a character other than that of Dasein, they are non-temporal, whether they Really occur, arise and pass away, or subsist 'ideally'. If world-time thus belongs to the tem-poralizing of temporality, then it can neither be volatilized 'subjectivistically' nor 'reified' by a vicious 'Objectification'".[93]

The way to reconcile these apparently conflicting statements seems to be as follows: in each case Heidegger lumps together "Real" and "ideal" entities. Both types of entity are either "temporal" or, in a different sense, "non-temporal". In the first sense, they are "temporal" because they are beings "in" Being, and Being as disclosure has a fundamentally "temporal" char-acter. In the second sense, they are "non-temporal" because they are only *what is disclosed* "in" disclosure, and the only disclosure *itself* is the tem-poralizing of temporality. In a sense, Heidegger has chosen a rather misleading way of expressing himself, because he leaves us with the problem of how en-tities in general can be both "temporal" and "non-temporal". But it is necessary to remember that disclosure is not a "framework" wherein entities are deployed. It is, rather, Being itself *as* time. With regard to their *Being*, all entities are "temporal", but with regard to their *meaning* (their determination or *eidos*) they are "non-temporal" (always remembering that even temporal relations *qua determined* are "timeless"). Only the disclosure *itself (qua the "Da" of Dasein)* is "temporal" in both senses, and this is because its meaning and its Being are the same: its *eidos is energeia*.

NOTES

1. T.S. Eliot, "Burnt Norton", V.
2. Augustine, *Confessions*, XI, 14.
3. Augustine, *Soliloquia*, II, 1.
4. Augustine, *Confessions*, XI, 14. Cf. Aristotle, *Physics*, III–IV, 217b35–218a 1.
5. Augustine, *Confessions*, XI, 14. Cf. Aristotle, *Physics*, IV, 218 a 1–5.
6. Augustine, *De Vera Religione*, 39, n. 72.
7. Immanuel Kant, *Critique of Pure Reason*, A 33, B 49.
8. Jean-Paul Sartre, *Being and Nothingness*, trans. Hazel Barnes (London: Methuen, 1969), p. 107. Maurice Merleau-Ponty, *Phenomenology of Perception*, trans. Colin Smith (London: Routledge, 1962), p. 412.
9. Sartre, p. 136.
10. Merleau-Ponty, p. 412.
11. Sartre, p. 123.
12. Sartre, p. 120, Cf. p. 128.
13. Sartre, p. 142.
14. Merleau-Ponty, p. 427. Cf. pp. 430–1.
15. Sartre, p. 136.
16. Merleau-Ponty, p. 422.
17. Sartre, p. 120.
18. Maurice Merleau-Ponty, *The Visible and the Invisible*, ed. Claude Lefort, trans. A. Lingis (Evanston: Northwestern University Press, 1968), pp. 183–4. Cf. pp. 6, 12, 35, Chapter 2: "Interrogation and Dialectic", pp. 88–89, 95, 99. See also *Themes from the Lectures*, trans. J. O'Neill (Evanston: Northwestern University Press, 1970), Chapter 7: "Dialectical Philosophy".
19. *Husserliana*, Vol. 10, *Zur Phänomenologie des inneren Zeitbewusstseins*, S. 36, pp. 75 and 371. (This work will be abbreviated hereafter as "*Huss.* 10".) *The Phenomenology of Internal Time-Consciousness*, trans. J.S. Churchill (Bloomington: Indiana University Press, 1964), p. 100. Cf. R.T. Murphy, *Hume and Husserl* (Den Haag: Martinus Nijhoff, 1980), p. 103.
20. *Huss.* 10, p. 370.
21. J.B. Brough, "The Emergence of an Absolute Consciousness in Husserl's Early Writings on Time-Consciousness", in F.A. Elliston and Peter McCormick, eds. *Husserl: Expositions and Appraisals* (South Bend: Notre Dame University Press, 1977), p. 98.
22. *Huss.* 10, S. 40. (English translation [hereafter: E.T.], p. 110)
23. *Huss.* 10, App. VI, p. 111. (E.T., pp. 149–50.)
24. *Husserliana* 3, Ideen I, S. 80. *Ideas* I, trans. W.R. Boyce Gibson (London: George Allen & Unwin, Ltd., 1969), p. 233.
25. *Investigations* V, S. 6. Trans. J.N. Findlay (London: Routledge, 1970), pp. 543–4.
26. *Huss.* 10, App. VI, p. 113. (E.T., p. 152) Cf. SS. 35, 36, and 38. (E.T., pp. 99–100 and 104.)
27. *Huss.* 10, App. XII, p. 127. (E.T., pp. 175–6.) Cf. App. VI and VIII, pp. 113, 114, and 116–8. (E.T., pp. 152, 154, and 162–3.) *Logical Investigations* V, S. 6 (E.T., p. 545.) *Ideen* I, SS. 81–2 (E.T., pp. 236 and 238–9.), and *Cartesian Meditations*, SS. 12, 17, 19, and especially 18.
28. Cf. Thomas M. Seebohm, "Reflexion and Totality in the Philosophy of Edmund Husserl", in *Journal of the British Society for Phenomenology*, Vol. 4, No. 1, January 1973, pp. 20–30.
29. *Huss.* 10, App. VI, p. 112. (E.T., p. 151.) *Ideen I*, S. 83, and *Cartesian Meditations*, S. 46 (E.T., p. 103.) Cf. Kant, A 320, B 376.
30. Kant, B 149–52.
31. *Huss.* 10, SS. 3–5. (E.T., pp. 33–9.) Cf. Merleau-Ponty, *Phenomenology of Perception*, p. 423.

32. Kant, A 346, B 404–5.
33. Philip J. Bossert, "Hume and Husserl on Time and Time-Consciousness", *Journal of the British Society for Phenomenology*, Vol. 7, No. 1, January 1976, pp. 44–6 and 49–50.
34. Cf. Martin Heidegger, *On Time and Being*, trans. J. Stambaugh (New York: Harper Colophon, 1977), p. 3. See also G.W.F. Hegel, "The Philosophy of Nature", *Encyclopedia*, Pt.2, trans. A.V. Miller (Oxford: Clarendon, 1970), S258.
35. Klaus Held, *Lebendige Gegenwart* (Den Haag: Martinus Nijhoff, 1966), p. x.
36. Cf. Seebohm, pp. 25–6 and Iso Kern, "The Three Ways to the Transcendental-Phenomenological Reduction in the Philosophy of Edmund Husserl", in Elliston and McCormick, pp. 126–49, especially p. 134.
37. *Husserliana 8, Erste Philosophie 2*, pp. 397–8. *Husserliana 1, Cartesianische Meditationen*, pp. 67 and 81. *Cartesian Meditations*, trans. Dorion Cairns (Den Haag: Martinus Nijhoff, 1960), pp. 28 and 43.
38. Maurice Merleau-Ponty, "Phenomenology and the Sciences of Man", in *The Primacy of Perception*, ed. James N. Edie (Evanston: Northwestern University Press, 1964), p. 49.
39. T.S. Eliot, "Burnt Norton", I.
40. McTaggart's argument first appeared as "The Unreality of Time", in *Mind*, 17 (1908), pp. 457–74. See also his *The Nature of Existence* (Cambridge: Cambridge University Press, 1927), Vol. II, Book 5, Chapter 33.
41. McTaggart, *Mind*, pp. 458ff; *The Nature of Existence*, II, 9ff.
42. McTaggart, *Mind*, p. 468; *The Nature of Existence*, II, 21 (SS. 330–2).
43. Henri Bergson, *Creative Evolution*, trans. A. Mitchell (London: Macmillan, 1911), p. 10. Cf. *The Creative Mind*, trans. M.L. Andison (New York: Citadel Press, 1946), pp. 20–1.
44. McTaggart, *Mind*, p. 470; *The Nature of Existence*, pp. 10–11, n.
45. Cf. D.C. Williams, "The Myth of Passage", *Journal of Philosphy*, 48 (1951), pp. 457–72, especially pp. 463–4. J.J.C. Smart, *Philosophy and Scientific Realism* (London: Routledge & Kegan Paul, 1963), p. 135. See also C.D. Broad, *An Examination of McTaggart's Philosophy* (Cambridge: Cambridge University Press, 1938), Vol. 2, Part 1, Chapter 35, S1.22: "Absolute Becoming".
46. Adolf Grünbaum, "The Status of Temporal Becoming", *The Philosophy of Time*, ed. Richard M. Gale (London: Macmillan, 1968), pp. 325–6.
47. Kant, A 33, B 50, B 137–8, B 154–5, and B 292.
48. A mathematically "compact" series is one in which no two members are next to each other. The series of fractions, for example, is compact because between any two fractions there is always an infinity of others. See Bertrand Russell, *Our Knowledge of the External World* (London: Open Court, 1914), especially Lecture V: "The theory of Continuity", pp. 129ff.
49. Bertrand Russell, "On the Experience of Time", *The Monist*, 25 (1915). Cf. *The Principles of Mathematics* (Cambridge: Cambridge University Press, 1903), especially pp. 458–76.
50. Henri Bergson, *Creative Evolution*, p. 10; *The Creative Mind*, p. 20; and *Time and Free Will*, trans. F.L. Pogson (London: George Allen & Unwin, 1910), p. 193. (The passage cited is from the 6th Impression, 1950.)
51. Arthur Eddington, *Space, Time and Gravitation* (Cambridge: Cambridge University Press, 1920), p. 51. See also *The Nature of the Physical World* (Cambridge: Cambridge University Press, 1928), p. 68.
52. Hegel, "The Philosophy of Nature". *Encyclopedia*, Part 2, S. 258.
53. Cf. Jacques Derrida, "Ousia and Grammé: A Note to a Footnote in *Being and Time*", trans. Edward S. Casey, in F.J. Smith, ed. *Phenomenology in Perspective* (Den Haag: Martinus Nijhoff, 1970), p. 91. See also pp. 61 and 63. See also Martin Heidegger, "The Anaximander Fragment" and "Aletheia", in his *Early Greek Thinking*, trans. D.F. Krell and F.A. Capuzzi (New York: Harper & Row, 1975), pp. 24, 26–7, 37, 39, 112–3, 115, and 123. See also *Identity and*

98

Difference, trans. J. Stambaugh (New York: Harper & Row, 1974), p. 33; and *An Introduction to Metaphysics*, trans. Ralph Manheim (New York: Doubleday, 1961), pp. 50–1, 59, 63, and 68. See also *The Question Concerning Technology*, trans. W. Lovitt (New York: Harper Colophon, 1977), pp. 3n, 30–2, 36n, 53n, and 161. Cf. Merleau-Ponty, *The Visible and the Invisible*, pp. 108–27, especially 115, 117–8, and 122. See also pp. 174, 203, and 206–8.

54. Aristotle, *Physics*, IV, 219b 1–8. Cf. Heidegger, *Sein und Zeit* (Tübingen: Max Niemeyer Verlag, 1967), p. 421. *Being and Time*, trans. J. Macquarrie and E. Robinson (Oxford: Basil Blackwell, 1967), p. 473.

55. Cf. Derrida, pp. 72 and 79–81. See also Martin Heidegger, "Building Dwelling Thinking", in *Poetry, Language, Thought*, trans. Albert Hofstadter (New York: Harper Colophon, 1971), pp. 145–61. Cf. Walter Biemel, "Heidegger's Concept of Dasein", Frederick Elliston, ed. *Heidegger's Existential Analytic* (The Hague: Mouton, 1978), pp. 111–31.

56. Martin Heidegger, *Frühe Schriften* (Frankfurt a.M.: Klostermann, 1972), p. 127. Cf. Broad, S. 3.11: "Criticism of McTaggart's Main Argument".

57. Spinoza, *Ethics*, Part II, Def. V.

58. Soren Kierkegaard, *Concluding Unscientific Postscript*, trans. W. Lowrie and D. Swenson (Princeton: Princeton University Press, 1968), pp. 273 and 292.

59. Bossert, pp. 45 and 50.

60. Cf. William James, *The Principles of Psychology* (New York: Henry Holt, 1890), Chapter XV: "The Perception of Time", pp. 605–42, especially 619–20.

61. T.S. Eliot, "Burnt Norton", III.

62. Heidegger, *Sein und Zeit*, p. 419. (E.T., p. 472.)

63. Derrida, p. 66.

64. Aristotle, *Physics*, IV, 223a 16–28, especially 22–8. Cf. 218b 20–4 and 219a 4–7, 22–34.

65. Aristotle, *De Anima*, 430b 11–15, 20–2; 431b 14–5.

66. Cf. Heidegger, "The Anaximander Fragment", in *Early Greek Thinking*, pp. 50 and 55. See also his "Conversation on a Country Path", in *Discourse on Thinking*, trans. J.M. Anderson and E.H. Freund (New York: Harper Colophon, 1969), p. 86. See in addition "Recollection in Metaphysics", in *The End of Philosophy*, trans. J. Stambaugh (London: Souvenir Press, 1979), p. 79.

67. Cf. Aristotle, *Metaphysics*, XII, 1071b 6–7; Augustine, *Confessions*, XI, 13; and G.W.F. Hegel, *Wissenschaft der Logik* (London: George Allen & Unwin, 1969), Vol. 1, Book 1, Section 2, and Chapter 2, C. (b) remark 2, pp. 234ff.

68. Hegel, *Encyclopedia*, S. 258 and *Zusatz*.

69. Martin Heidegger, "Moira", in *Early Greek Thinking*, pp. 79, 87–9, 91–2, 95–6 and 100. See also *Identity and Difference*, pp. 27–30; *An Introduction to Metaphysics*, pp. 116–7; *Being and Time*, S. 44; and "Letter on Humanism", in *Martin Heidegger: Basic Writings*, ed. David F. Krell (London: Routledge & Kegan Paul, 1978), pp. 196, 203–5, 215, and 236.

70. Cf. F. Staal, *Exploring Mysticism* (London: Penguin Books, 1975), pp. 48–51; and A.K. Coomaraswamy, *Hinduism and Buddhism* (New York: Philosophical Library, 1943, p. 10.

71. Cf. T.R.V. Murti, *The Central Philosophy of Buddhism* (London: George Allen & Unwin, 1955).

72. Benjamin L. Whorf, "An American Indian Model of the Universe", in *Language, Thought, and Reality*, ed. J.E. Carrol (Cambridge, Mass.: M.I.T. Press, 1956), pp. 57–64.

73. Whorf, pp. 59 and 60.

74. Whorf, pp. 61 and 62.

75. Howard Trivers, "Heidegger's Misinterpretation of Hegel's Views on Spirit and Time", in *Philosophy and Phenomenological Research*, III, (1943), pp. 162–8.

76. *Sein und Zeit*, pp. 428 and n. xvii, and 434–6. (E.T., pp. 480, 485–6.) See also Trivers, pp. 164 and 167.

77. *Sein und Zeit*, p. 435 and n. xxxix. (E.T., p. 485.) Cf. Hegel, *Encyclopedia*, S258.
78. Hegel, *The Phenomenology of Mind*, trans. Sir James Baillie (London: George Allen & Unwin, 1964), p. 800. See also pp. 104, 806–8, and *Encyclopedia*, S258. Cf. Trivers, pp. 164–6.
79. *Sein und Zeit*, p. 434. (E.T., p. 485.)
80. *Sein und Zeit*, p. 428. (E.T., p. 480.) Cf. Trivers, p. 167.
81. *Sein und Zeit*, p. 435. (E.T., p. 485.)
82. *Sein und Zeit*, pp. 435–6. (E.T., p. 486.)
83. Derrida, pp. 68 and 89.
84. Martin Heidegger, *Prolegomena zur Geschichte des Zeitbegriffs* (Vol. 20 *Gesamtausgabe*), ed. P. Jaeger (Frankfurt a.M.: Klostermann, 1979), pp. 63 and 97.
85. Heidegger, *On Time and Being*, p. 24.
86. Heidegger, "Humanism", in *Martin Heidegger: Basic Writings*, p. 238. Cf. "Anaximander", in *Early Greek Thinking*, p. 36; and "What is Metaphysics?" in *Existence and Being*, ed. W. Brock (London: Vision, 1949), pp. 368–70. See also Merleau-Ponty, *The Visible and the Invisible*, pp. 52ff.
87. Cf. Aristotle, *Metaphysics*, XIV, 2; and Plato, *Sophist*, 237a, 240 and 256e.
88. Heidegger, *Identity and Difference*, pp. 7, 12 and 15. Cf. among many other places, "Methaphysics as History of Being" and "Recollection in Metaphysics", in *The End of Philosophy*, pp. 1, 3, 17, 81, and 87.
89. Cf. Heidegger, *Sein und Zeit*, S69 (b), pp. 78ff, pp. 201, 427, and n. xiii. (E.T., pp. 108ff., 245, 479, and n. xiii.) See also *Kant and the Problem of Metaphysics*, trans. James S. Churchill (Bloomington: Indiana University Press, 1962), S. 44. Compare Derrida, pp. 55–6 and 61–2, but see Biemel, pp. 127–9.
90. Martin Heidegger, *Holzwege* (Frankfurt a.M.: Klostermann, 1950), pp. 319–20. (E.T., "Anaximander", in *Early Greek Thinking*, pp 3415.)
91. *Sein und Zeit*, p. 331. Cf. pp. 17, 19, and 326–7. (E.T., p. 380. Cf. pp. 38, 41, and 373–5.)
92. *Sein und Zeit*, p. 18. (E.T., p. 40.)
93. *Sein und Zeit*, p. 420. (E.T., 472.)

II. SOCIAL AND POLITICAL LIFE

"Left" and "Right" as Socio-Political Stances
by
William McBride

In his long career, Herbert Spiegelberg has taught and published a great deal in the areas of social, political, and legal philosophy. Indeed, as he indicates in his "*Apologia pro bibliographia mea*",[1] for many years it was with this region of philosophical concerns, rather than with the comprehensive exposition of phenomenology for which he is now no doubt more widely known, that he was primarily identified. It occurred to me, when I was honored by being invited to contribute to this homage to him, that the exploration of a theme in this area would not be out of place.

I began by mentally surveying aspects of our everyday current socio-political experience. Unfortunately, given their almost infinite capacities for distortion and trivalization, the communications media (the press, television, and radio) seem to be among the most salient sources of shared experiences having to do with socio-political matters today. And if one attends to them, one finds, I think, more frequent use of "ideological" labels than Americans have experienced for many years. (I put the word "ideological" in quotation marks because its exact meaning is so much subject to dispute; here I am using it in its most innocent, unexamined sense, as a convenient shorthand.) Circumstances surrounding the national elections of 1980 have contributed to this, of course. "Conservative" and "liberal" are probably the two most commonly-employed terms in this regard, but one also reads and hears a great deal now, as one more rarely did two of three decades ago,[2] about "the Left" and "the Right" — primarily the latter.

Phenomenologists have not infrequently undertaken hodological explorations of right and left as directions in lived space. But right and left as political stances have generally appeared to be particularly forbidden areas for attempts at systematic description and hence have been greatly neglected. (There are exceptions, of course; Karl Mannheim's work is among the best known.[3]) This is so, first, because the entire domain of politics is so filled with ambiguities as to constitute very inhospitable territory for anyone trained to seek apodictic evidence. Secondly, the very terminology of "right" and "left" in this context

W.S. Hamrick (ed.) *Phenomenology in Practice and Theory*.
© 1985 Martinus Nijhoff Publishers, Dordrecht/Boston/Lancaster
ISBN 90 247 2926 2. Printed in the Netherlands.

is so obviously the product of the merest historical accident, the seating arrangements of delegates in early assemblies.[4] Thirdly, the words have the curious effect of at first evoking a reaction of clear recognition (don't we all at first think we know, without for the most part being able to claim the slightest expertise on the subject, what a report means when it recounts clashes between "Rightists" and "Leftists" in, say, El Salvador?) and then, whenever they are subjected to reflection, of descending into virtually unfathomable murkiness. Finally, and most obviously, the words arouse the deepest emotional reactions to anyone who cares about political life, and this scarcely contributes to calm investigation.

Now, I strongly support Herbert Spiegelberg's assertion that "no one, not even Hegel or Husserl, has proprietary rights to a term like "phenomenology". It is older than both, and it is in this sense anyone's for the taking — and defining. It is true that Husserl's annexation has given it the greatest enrichment but also complication in its history. But this is no reason to forget its earlier and wider meanings".[5] So my approach will not conform to any recognizable version of orthodoxy. Nevertheless, it seems to me that some of the fundamental principles of the accepted phenomenological method, such as questioning the natural attitude and following a procedure of imaginative variation, should prove particularly helpful in exploring the meanings of the polar stances that I have chosen to examine here. My purpose will be to investigate these stances *sine ira et studio*,[6] so that, while I can scarcely expect complete success in the sense of full agreement, even many of those who fail to share my greater personal affinity for the Left might accept elements of the description.

Spatial metaphors. Let us begin by briefly reconsidering the spatial dimensions which were the actual origins of the use of the terms at present under consideration. It is not an utter coincidence, analytically speaking, that "right" and its equivalents in other languages have traditionally been associated with a host of other words meaning good or at least proper, whereas "left" and its equivalents have so often meant less good or even bad. The person of the Right begins with the advantage of implicitly having rightness, propriety, and perhaps even righteousness on his or her side, whereas a stance on the Left suggests at least awkwardness, gaucherie, or deviousness (in English, for instance, one speaks of a "left-handed compliment"), if not something even more sinister. Much more than innocent punning is involved here, of course; it is essential to the Left to deviate, to venture away from the established forms, whereas it is essential to the Right to insist that certain forms that either are or should be established, be observed.

But what if, as has frequently occurred in recent times, the Right appears to be challenging an established order? What of the cases, for example of the challenges to "liberal establishments" made by two twentieth-century movements of very different intensities and types (but we are more interested here in the resemblances than in the differences) that have both been at least nominally Rightist, Hitler's Nazis and Reagan's Republicans? It should be noted that the rhetoric of such movements places greater emphasis on the claim that it is the *de facto* establishment which is actually deviant — morally deviant as well as deviant in terms of deep-rooted historical traditions. This further implies a sharply dissimilar orientation towards time.

Time. As is well known, the French Revolution initiated a new calendar, and the U.S. dollar bill contains the slogan, *"hovus ordo seclorum"*. The new calendar was intended at once to supplant the old and yet to become permanent in its place, as was the new order (both that of the United States and the Roman order endorsed by the original writer of the phrase, Virgil). More consistent as a Leftist stance, though it failed to become a prominent part of American political ideas, was Jefferson's insistence that existing constitutions should not encumber future generations and that some upheaval was probably beneficial once every generation. It is characteristic of the Left to look to the future as the justification of its "deviant" actions in the present. Simone de Beauvoir's *Ethics of Ambiguity* is an excellent illustration of this in the domain of ethics.[7]

The Right, on the other hand, appeals to a past alleged in some respects to be better than the present as a justification for action. It may be a mythical past, or at least it may contain an admixture of mythical elements. It may also be a very distant past, as is the case of Mussolini's appeal to the memory of ancient Rome. It is not essential to a Rightist stance to maintain that the past can somehow be recaptured or even revised, although occasionally such a claim is proffered; it is only essential that actual or alleged facts about the past serve as positive reasons for acting. The Left's positive grounds for justification, future possibilities, are by definition facts only in a derivative sense, since they have not yet occurred. For the Left, it is important to be familiar with the injustices, contradictions, or whatever other expression is employed to convey a sense of the constraints on social amelioration, that have existed in the past right up to the present time, in order to understand what form of process of "negation of the negation" should take. This leads us to consider the respective stances of Right and Left toward change.

Change. Gyorgy Lukacs' masterful *History and Class-Consciousness*, in particular its central essay, "Reification and the Consciousness of the Proletariat",[8] makes a strong, philosophically documented case in favor of the notion that the spirit of the Left, which he identifies with an idealized proletarian consciousness, is the vehicle of unblocking, of flux, *par excellence*, whereas the Right resists change by processes of reification, or, to substitute a familiar Sartrean metaphor, petrification. This is a useful initial statement of differences, but it is by no means free of difficulties. For one thing, as all those familiar with Lukacs' work are aware, he himself succumbed to a most blatant and dangerous, of paradoxical, sort of reification by fixing on the Party as the contemporary, in some respects virtually infallible, change agent. For another thing, it is important to note that the Right, too, often favors change – whenever, that is, the Right is in opposition and regards the current state of affairs as parlous. Moreover, movements on the Right, especially in recent times, have frequently exhibited a great fascination with change; consider, for instance, the close affinity expressed by proponents of Fascism, and even by Il Duce himself, with Henry Bergson's anti-positivist, anti-static philosophy of *durée,*[9] (an intellectual or at least emotional affinity that seems to have endured among elements of the Italian Right even to this day). But we need not confine ourselves to recent times in order to observe such an apparently surprising connection; we have only to think of the aristocratic Heraclitus, so paradoxically cited by Engels as the first great dialectician.[10]

It is probably mistaken to attempt to locate the differences between Right and Left on the question of change (for I am convinced that there are differences, even if certain cases such as those just mentioned may tend to blur them) in divergences concerning the possible or desirable *direction* of change. The person of the Left could agree with the conservative *cliché* that not all change is *eo ipso* progress, and some writers on both Left and Right have been equally skeptical of utopian blueprints for a proposed *goal* of social change, just as others on both Right and Left have busied themselves in drafting such blueprints. A more fruitful suggestion, I think, is that we look to the respective proposed *subjects* of changes, who or what is said to be changeable and/or deserving of change, in order to delineate on opposition. Two of the prime test phenomena for drawing such a distinction are socio-economic structures and human nature. In general, the Right opposes, while the Left proposes, fundamental alterations in the former, and the Right denies the very possibility of a *metábasis eis állo génos* in the case of the latter. While writers on the Left are divided in their attitudes about "human nature" – for instance, one recent writer favorable to Marx goes so far as to develop an entire book around the core theme of Marx's alleged theory of human nature[11] – it seems to be that it is an essential tendency of the Left to put the concept, at least insofar as it is intended to capture certain definable qualities, desires, instincts, etc., said to be distinctive of human beings across all times and places, radically into question, and along with it even the underlying metaphysics of discrete genera.

Underlying metaphysics. Many of our contemporaries who are most closely attuned to "ideological" disputes would probably be puzzled by the assertion that metaphysical differences or, more accurately, differences about metaphysical questions underlie these quarrels; but they inevitably must, even if they are seldom acknowledged *eo nomine.* Ultimately, the divergent stances concerning time and change that I have just been describing are of this metaphysical sort. Most fundamental of all politically relevant issues concerning the nature of reality, however, is the question, interpretably in a vast variety of ways with respect to its exact meaning, as to whether fixed essences actually exist. On the whole, the belief that they do facilitate a consistent stance on the Right, whereas the claim that they do not may well be a necessary, though it is not sufficient, precondition for taking a stance on the Left.

Philosophical, as distinguished from populist, questioning the doctrine of fixed essences and in particular of the notion of a fixed human essence, or nature, is an almost exclusively modern phenomenon, discoverable in an isolated passage in Rousseau [12] and then more widely in writings of the Nineteenth Century. Hegel's contribution to this development is of course very significant, but it is mitigated by a number of other elements of his thought, including his belief that a fixed pattern and goal, and hence a sort of global "essence", are ascribable to History as a whole. Politically speaking, Hegel remained more Rightist than not, but Marx drew great intellectual sustenance from Hegel's initiatives in this area and in the *Theses on Feuerbach* broke consciously with most of the remnants of essentialist thinking. [13] It is with Sartre's explicit, self-conscious, and repeated denial that a human essence exists, however, that we encounter the purest philosophical statement consistent with a Left stance in this regard.

The practical significance of the conviction of fixity that I have attributed to the Right with respect to the human "essence" and other alleged "essences" of a socially relevant sort, such as the "essence of justice" or the "essence of femininity", is that, if it is inconceivable and impossible that these could be changed, then any thought or action premised on a contrary assumption is utterly irrational and morally perverse. For instance, it was crucial to the Right of several centuries ago to uphold the belief that there was an undeniable essence of secular (as well as of ecclesiastical) *authority* that was derived from God, just as it is crucial to the modern American Right to insist on the essentiality of a process of economic *competition*, from which "winners" and "losers" are bound to emerge, in any well-ordered human society. This leads us to consider hierarchy and equality.

Hierarchy and equality. There would seem to be fairly widespread agreement that the Left tends to be more egalitarian than the Right, but there is equally great disagreement as to what the nature of the equality sought after by the Left or scorned by the Right might be. One must constantly recall Marx's polemic against "crude, egalitarian communism" [14] when attempting to grasp this aspect of the phenomenology of Left and Right. One could, of course, maintain that Marx was simply not a purely Leftist as, let us say, the fanatically egalitarian, in the sense of levelling, officials of the Cambodian Pol Pot regime apparently were with respect to this issue, but this strikes me as superficial. Probably the most objectionable single feature of crude egalitarianism is its rejection of facts, so to speak, in the name of a preconceived attitude; it is, *inter alia*, bad phenomenology and therefore should be equally objectionable to thoughtful persons across the "ideological" spectrum. Foremost among the sorts of facts that crude egalitarianism wishes to deny are inequalities to talents. One does not have to believe either in fixed natures or even in such a thing as a fixed character in the case of an individual person in order to accept the fact that differences with respect to various abilities do exist among individuals at any given time.

Of considerable assistance in clarifying this matter, though it does so without discussing by name the phenomena of Left and Right, is an early article by Herbert Spiegelberg, "A Defense of Human Equality",[15] in which he concludes that the defensible form of equality is one with respect to moral rights and duties. The article begins by making clear its experiential point of departure, a particularly poignant one in 1944; it is the contempt in which Nazis hold the concept of equality. Something of this attitude, I think, can be said to characterize the Right as a whole, although it is also true that some of those who identify themselves as Rightists today claim to accept equality with respect to rights and duties. Such individuals, however, would usually be skeptical about the *extent* of the alleged rights to be ascribed to everyone; for instance, they would tend to dispute the notions of there being a right to employment or a right to health that have each surfaced in international discussions (specifically, in the Universal Declaration of Human Rights and in the World Health Organization, respectively) in recent years. In short, the Right is skeptical about equal rights, as recently instanced by the Reaganite denunciation of the proposed Equal Rights Amendment to the United States Constitution, whereas, while some on the Left (including Marx and Sartre) question the *terminology* of "rights" in light both of the long history of misleading, mystifying uses to which it has been put and of its essentialist implications,[16] the Left tends to support the egalitarian objectives to which many alleged rights are intended to conduce.

Fundamental to this difference, I think, are diverse conceptions of the essence, not now so much of the human individual as of society as a whole. To the Right, it is necessary (morally necessary, in order to preserve order – a favorite term of writers on the Right – and avert chaos) that there be some sort of hierarchy, or inequality of power, within any significant social group. (With respect to this assertion, the writings of Edmund Burke concerning the alleged need for "natural aristocracy" remain unsurpassable.) Thus, among alleged rights to which the modern Right is most unqualifiedly committed is the right to private property, since it is (correctly) assumed that this "right", when exercised within a capitalist system, will inevitably produce considerable inequalities, in actual property holdings and in the relative power of impotence which accompanies them. The Left, on the other hand, is not committed to any metaphysical presuppositions about the inevitability of hierarchy and is in fact bound to regard any existing inequalities in social and political power that are buttressed by such presuppositions as irrational and eliminable. This tendency to reject differences that are based on what it must ultimately consider mere mystifications about the nature of society is what constitutes, it seems to me, the basic egalitarianism of the Left.

Here, a note is in order concerning a very obvious and well-known rift within the contemporary Left, or what passes for the Left, itself. If we may label the belief in the inevitability of power structures "authoritarianism",[17] it is clear that there is a strain of this in Marx that a defense of it is to be found in the writings of his colleague, Engels,[18] and that the most numerous group of their followers have embraced authoritarianism wholeheartedly both in practice and, except for vague talk of some distant future time when the State might begin to shrivel up, theoretically. Others on the Left, including Sartre especially in his last years, when he came increasingly to regard himself as a kind of anarchist more than a Marxist, maintain a vigorously and unqualifiedly anti-authoritarian stance. What is to be said about this? To the extent to which, if the entire present enterprise makes sense, we should expect to find close inter-relationships among the positions taken by the Right and by the Left, respectively, on the various topics that we have considered, then the Sartrean position on hierarchy seems to be more in keeping with a Leftist stance than that of Stalin or Brezhnev; a self-styled "Marxist socialism" that espouses authoritarianism seems in this regard no more Leftist than Naziism which, after all, is shorthand for "national Socialism". Still, the matter is confusing and underscores the difficulty of attempting any description that is not based on a *parti pris* in this domain. This difficulty is seen most clearly when we turn to the final aspect of the political Right and Left that I wish to consider in this essay, namely, their respective stances towards freedom.

Freedom. Freedom has not always been appropriated with enthusiasm as a goal by the Right, as it (at least nominally) always has, to the best of my knowledge, by the Left. The spirit of Plato's *Republic*, in which the dominance of atmosphere of great freedom is seen as the essential *vice* of a democracy and of "the democratic character", has found echoes in Rightist thought down through the centuries. Movements of liberation and, indeed, liberalism itself have generally been associated with the Left. But the contemporary situation, in which what used to be called "Manchester liberalism" has increasingly become the focal point of positions considered to be conservative in the United States and other countries with capitalist economic systems, is much more complex.[19]

There are, to be sure, very traditionalist "conservatives" who would, like Plato, argue for emphasizing virtue *over* freedom as a value, while there are still other self-styled "conservatives" who (as a recent radio commentator did) would urge persons of Rightist persuasions to regard Bismarck and Hobbes as their political guides, because these figures were strong authoritarians. Of

110

course, two very disparate philosophical traditions have contributed to the devaluing of freedom which is shared by advocates of these two approaches. By contrast with both of them, "libertarian" thinking, as it has come to be called, has its basis in yet a third tradition (perhaps more than one) and, by definition, exalts freedom *überhaupt*. A great many writers fashionable with the contemporary Right, such as Robert Nozick, are characterizable as libertarians.

But so, for that matter, was the later Sartre, [20] and so are many other thinkers on the Left. Consequently, it has increasingly become accepted parlance to distinguish between "libertarians of the Right" and "libertarians of the Left". Clearly, two very different conceptions of liberty are at issue here: does the "free market" ensure, or does it curtail, the development of free individuals? [21] Much of the current argument, which is concentrated more on the Rightist than on the Leftist notion of liberty, takes place at the level of highly abstract idealizations of the sort dear to builders of economic models. The problem with many of these idealizations, however, is that they are much more dependent than those who construct them often realize on certain debatable presuppositions once again, about the alleged essential nature of human beings – in particular, the presupposition that we are inevitably dominated by economic motives and categories, that *"homo sapiens"* and *"homo oeconomicus"* are in reality identical terms. [22] Once this presupposition is accepted unquestioningly, then, it seems to me, acceptance of the general conception of freedom advanced by contemporary libertarians of the Right follows with virtual inevitability. But libertarians of the Left reject this presupposition as well as the claim that the type of "liberty" espoused by their counterparts on the Right is in fact liberty in the fullest sense.

The best way to try to clarify this impasse, in which virtually the entire Left and a large segment of the Right both lay claim to the appropriation of freedom as their own, lies in reorienting the discussion from a debate about a word or a debate about abstract idealizations to a debate about concrete phenomena. Descriptions, using imaginative variations, of what the lived experiences of members of social structures organized according to the two different conceptions of "freedom" in question would be, can easily be drawn up and compared. (I use the subjunctive mood because there does not exist, after all, a real society of perfect competition corresponding to Rightist dreams, while no Left libertarian would claim much intellectual affinity with the extremely hierarchized actual societies of the East that denominate themselves "socialist". Yugoslavia is a special case, but at the present, anti-capitalist but market-oriented and quite authoritarian stage of its evolution it can hardly serve as an ideal for either the Right or the Left.)

It will then emerge that, for example, while some of societies organized according to Right-libertarian principles would be able to live *"wie ein König in Frankreich"*, many others would inevitably not derive much value or worth from the liberty that they theoretically and legally possess.[23] On the other hand, no one in a society organized on Left-libertarian principles would enjoy the *range* of that proverbial king's personal freedom of action, since such a society would be so structured as to discourage the kind of competition that leads to vast disparities in economic power. (Thus, the question of hierarchy and equality arises once again and is seen, like the metaphysical question of an alleged fixed human essence, to be inextricably interrelated with that of freedom.) Furthermore, the experience of individual "freedom" in the first society would be in opposition of, or at least indifferent to, certain possible experiences of shared community, while that within the latter society would be feasible only within shared community activities. And so on; the descriptions of the respective experiences of "freedom" in the two types of societies can be expanded indefinitely by adding details. While this method cannot automatically resolve the issue as to which type of society is preferable, it *can* substitute a process of mutual clarification of meanings, on which considerable agreement is obtainable, for the sheer name-calling ("I'm for freedom and you're not", "No, it's the other way around") that so frequently characterizes discussions of this complicated matter of freedom in the context of opposed political "ideologies". And such clarification has been my purpose with respect to all the facets of "Left" and "Right" that have been considered here.

In conclusion, this has been an intentionally brief and partial exploration of my chosen theme, but I hope that it will service to indicate how phenomena that at first blush seem riddled with contradictory pieces of evidence and hopelessly emotion-laden may begin to be subjected to systematic scrutiny without at the same time being reduced to something other than themselves, e.g., mere manifestations of different psychological tendencies. Political and social theorists have occasionally attempted to "define" the differences between Right and Left by isolating a single, presumably decisive set of criteria, such as the relative preference for change,[24] and relative liking for popular sovereignty,[25] or identification with the rich versus the poor or vice versa.[26] The problem with such definitional approaches is that they too often produce unhelpful formulae, such as Runciman's labelling of Peronism as "a Rightism of the Left", when cases that are difficult to fit within the prescribed definition are introduced. Political history is indeed filled with difficult cases, as we have again seen here, but they are better understood if the stances of "Right" and "Left" are seen to be complex, yet still meaningfully different, attitudes, with a number of interrelated aspects. Total purity and neatness of categorization are unattainable in this domain, but that does not justify prematurely abandoning the effort at gaining intellectual insight.

Among the important disparate themes that a more extended investigation would need to explore are the attitudes of Right and Left towards violence and towards "intellectuals" and intelligence (both very complex matters), the role of nationalism (a stance that appears clearly identifiable with the Right and now with the Left in the contemporary world, but about which very nearly the reverse could be said if we consider the situations of *citoyens* and *émigrés* at the time of the French Revolution), ethnocentrism and racism, and the meaning of the Center. There are, no doubt, many more. But one final question that I have often heard raised by colleagues in conversation yet seldom seen in print intrigues me and provides an interesting question with which to terminate this homage to an individual who has done so very much to chronicle the phenomenological method in its entirety: does phenomenological method, in its classical forms, lend itself more to a Rightist or a Leftist political stance, or is it truly neutral in this respect?

Historical evidence, of course, is very ambiguous on this point. Just as Hegel's dialectic gave birth to both an "Hegelian Right" and an "Hegelian Left", so Husserl's important followers have included one who temporarily associates himself with the Nazi movement, Heidegger (but was this consistent with the rest of this thought, or was it a mistake?); a number, especially in France, on the relatively extreme Left, and others of many stripes in between. What we must consider, then, is the fundamental spirit of phenomenology. If we are to believe Richard Zaner's characterization, phenomenology *is* "criticism as a philosophical discipline"; this is the subtitle of his introductory book on the subject. [27] Although Zaner himself does not draw any such conclusions, it would seem to follow from this characterization that phenomenology has greater affinity with a Leftist than with a Rightist stance since the criticism in question is directed against, *inter alia*, the presuppositions of common sense and of the natural attitude that militate against future-oriented projects of fundamental change and in favor of doctrines of fixed nature. Thus Sartre's and de Beauvoir's Leftism, though in many respects they have departed quite far from Husserl's methodology, is quite consistent with the critical spirit of that method; for example, both *Anti-Semite and Jew* and the second half of *The Second Sex* are lengthy phenomenological descriptions that are seen to lead to and to undergird conclusions identifiable with the Left.

On the other hand, classical phenomenology defines itself, precisely, as the intuition of essences. Now, although Herbert Spiegelberg has been eminently successful in demonstrating the erroneousness of certain conceptions of what Husserl means on this point, as on so many others, [28] so that no one can have any excuse for attributing real, as distinct from ideal, existence to Husserlian *eidei*, still the suspicion remains that there is some difficulty about applying the phenomenological method to objects of the sort that I have been considering in this paper. For such objects are phenomena of a profoundly transitory nature which nevertheless lend themselves to romanticized and often historically inaccurate idealizations concerning an imaged "eternal Left" and "eternal Right". No doubt socio-political stances which could without exaggeration be identified as "Rightist" and "Leftist", even though the terms did not exist, were prevalent in Rome, Athens, and Jerusalem at the time now known as the beginning of the Christian era, for example. Did those stances have enough in common, however, with their respective modern counterparts to warrant our now speaking in terms of an essence of the Right or of the Left, perhaps along the lines that I have been developing in this essay, that would be applicable to either of the pairs of counterparts across such a long stretch of time? But if so, then are we perhaps conceding a certain immutability to social structures and to the human natures that compose them? The answer to this question of what might be called the social *a priori* is very complex; Herbert Spiegelberg's friend, the late Alfred Schutz, has much of value to contribute to it. In short, does a method of eidetic intuition, when applied to phenomena of the sort that I have been considering, allow for the possibility of *fundamental* change, of (relatively) *radical* novelty, in the social world across history? I think it does. If it did not, then its methodological presuppositions would, after all, have to be acknowledged to support some of the attitudes of the Right, as they have been described in this essay.

114

NOTES

1. *Phenomenological Perspectives: Historical and Systematic Essays in Honor of Herbert Spiegelberg*, ed. Philip J. Bossert (Den Haag: Martinus Nijhoff, 1975), pp. 267–70.
2. As Samuel Brittan points out – *Left/or/Right: The Bogus Dilemma* (London: Secker & Warburg, 1968), p. 29 – the *Oxford English Dictionary* assigns the first political use of the two terms in Great Britain to Carlyle's *French Revolution* (1837), but in fact even in his country, much less in the United States, this usage did not come into general currency until the 1920's.
3. As Mannheim says in his essay, "On the Interpretation of *Weltanschauung*": "It will be obvious to anyone familiar with Husserl's work to what extent this phenomenological analysis is indebted to him, and in how far his procedure has been modified for our purposes". Kurt H. Wolff, ed., *From Karl Mannheim* (New York: Oxford University Press, 1971), p. 18.
4. "The origin of the terms left and right goes back to the first meetings of the French States–General in 1789, when the nobility took the place of honour on the King's right while the ordinary members – "the Third Estate" – sat on the King's left". –Brittan, p. 29.
5. Herbert Spiegelberg, *Doing Phenomenology* (Den Haag: Martinus Nijhoff, 1975), p. xxii.
6. A good example of the opposite approach, what one might call *cum maxima ira*, reads as follows: "If we then identify, in a rough way, the right with freedom, personality, and variety, and the left with slavery, collectivism, and uniformity, we are employing semantics that make *sense*". – Erik Maria, Ritter von Kuehnelt-Leddihn, *Leftism: From de Sade and Marx to Hitler and Marcuse* (New Rochelle, New York: Arlington House, 1974), p. 43.
7. "Indeed, cut off from his transcendence, reduced to the facticity of his presence, and individual is nothing; it is by his project that he fulfills himself, by the end at which he aims that he justifies himself; thus, this justification is always to come. Only the future can take the present for its own and keep it alive by surpassing it". – *The Ethics of Ambiguity*, trans. B. Frechtman (New York: Citadel Press, 1970), p. 115.
8. *History and Class Consciousness*, trans. R. Livingstone (Cambridge: MIT Press, 1968), pp. 83–222.
9. See Sergio Panunzio, *Rivoluzione e Constituzione* (Milano: Fratelli Treves, 1933), especially p. 280.
10. Friedrich Engels, *Herr Eugen Duhring's Revolution in Science*, trans. E. Burns (New York: International Publishers, 1939), p. 27.
11. John McMurtry, *The Structure of Marx's World-View* (Princeton: Princeton University Press, 1978).
12. "Celui qui ose entreprendre d'instituer un peuple doit se sentir en état de changer pour ainsi dire la nature humaine ..." – *Du Contrat Social* II, VII (Paris: Editions Garnier, 1955), p. 261.
13. See my discussion of this in *The Philosophy of Marx* (London: Hutchinson and New York: St. Martin's Press, 1977), pp. 84–6. A consideration of the ways in which "*Wesen*" still plays an important conceptual role, though one that is very different from its uses in the thought of Hegel, much less of Aristotle, in Marx's *Capital* is beyond the scope of this essay. It would no doubt shed light, however, on some of the limitations of Marx's own Left orientation. Roughly speaking, Marx in his later years thought it meaningful to speak of an essence of *capitalism*, though not (I would contend) of an essence of "*man*". Some later thinkers on the Left, influenced by Marx, have found this remaining "essentialism" of his unnecessarily Procrustean.
14. Karl Marx, *Economic and Philosophic Manuscripts of 1844* (Moscow: Foreign Languages Publishing House, 1961), pp. 98–101.
15. *Philosophical Review* 53, 2 (March 1944), pp. 101–124. Reprinted in W. T. Blackstone, ed., *The Concept of Equality* (Minneapolis: Burgess, 1969), pp. 144–164.

16. Sartre's short story, *Childhood of a Leader*, is a masterpiece of description of the Rightist attitude towards (privileged) "rights" that he finds so deplorable. Similarly, his account of Roquentin's visit to the portrait gallery of local notables at the Bouville Museum, in *Nausea*, takes as its central theme the sarcastic observation, "Car ils avaient eu droit à tout: à la vie, au travail, à la richesse, au commandement, au respect, et pour finir, à l'immortalité". *La Nausée* (Paris: Gallimard, 1938), p. 109.

17. The identification of authoritarianism as a Rightist attitude received much support from the classical study by T.W. Adorno, E. Franke-Brunswik, D.J. Levinson, and R.N. Sanford, *The Authoritarian Personality* (New York: Harper & Brothers, 1950). For a discussion of the very close connection between authority and political power, see my *Demokrati og autorite* (with Robert A. Dahl), trans. S. Lordal (Oslo: Dreyers, 1980), pp. 37–54.

18. Friedrich Engels, "On Authority", in Robert C. Tucker, ed., *The Marx–Engels Reader* (New York: W.W. Norton, 1978), pp. 730–733.

19. An historic moment in the identification of deep disagreements concerning the nature of modern American conservatism was Walter Lippmann's denunciation of Senator Goldwater at the beginning of the 1964 Presidential campaign. The crucial paragraph reads in part as follows: "By all the historic and traditional considerations of the English-speaking world, by the precedents that come from Burke and Hamilton, from Disraeli and from Lincoln, Barry Goldwater is not a conservative at all ... His political philosophy does not have its roots in the conservative tradition but in the crude and primitive capitalism of the Manchester school. It is the philosophy not of the conservators of the social order but of the newly rich on the make". – from *The New Haven* (Conn.) *Register*, January 7, 1964, editorial page.

20. See the interview with Michel Contat, "Self-Portrait at Seventy", in *Life/Situations*, trans. P. Auster and L. Davis (New York: Pantheon, 1977), pp. 24–25.

21. For an excellent, very brief discussion of the two libertarianisms, see David A. Crocer, "Guest Editor's Introduction", *The Occasional Review* 8/9 (August 1978; special issue on Rawls and Nozick), pp. 8–12. His discussion, in turn, is indebted to the work of Lawrence Crocker, as he acknowledged.

22. See my chapter, "Socio-economic Bases of the Current Crisis in our Culture", in *Social Theory at a Crossroads* (Pittsburgh: Duquesne University Press, 1980), pp. 117–151.

23. I have in mind Rawls' distinction between "liberty" and "the worth of liberty", which he introduces in order to attempt to dissolve, with a haste that is excessive in a book otherwise as long as his, apparent difficulties with respect to equal freedom posed by the vastly unequal possession of resources and hence power in a country such as, presumably, the United States. Many commentators have remarked on the great weakness of this part of his theory. See *A Theory of Justice* (Cambridge: Harvard University Press, 1971), p. 204.

24. See, e.g., Maurice Duverger, *Introduction à la politique* (Paris: Gallimard, 1964), pp. 66–68.

25. This is the approach of David Caute, *The Left in Europe Since 1789* (New York & Toronto: McGraw-Hill, 1966), pp. 26–44.

26. Caute (pp. 20–25) calls this approach "the sociological fallacy"; he attributes it to W.G. Runciman, S.M. Lipset, and "probably" R.M. Mac Iver.

27. Richard Zaner, *The Way of Phenomenology: Criticism as a Philosophical Discipline* (New York: Pegasus, 1970).

28. See, e.g., *The Phenomenological Movement*, 2nd ed. (Den Haag: Martinus Nijhoff, 1969), II, 676ff.

A Phenomenology of Coercion and Appeal
by
James L. Marsh

One thread uniting many thinkers is the denial of any possible reciprocity among men. To the claim that one can teach another Socratically in such a way that the student becomes freer, one writer objects that such teaching is just a form of weak control, of positive reinforcement. To the notion that one can genuinely love another person in such a way that the person's very being is enhanced, another answers that such love is just a form of domination, of seducing away the other's very being and turning it into an object. Still another asserts that technocracy is the only rational form of government and that any plea for freedom, democracy or participation is anachronistic. [1]

For politics the debate has important implications. If genuine dialogue among free men is impossible, then political domination and manipulation are not only inevitable but justified, and the classical notion of democracy must be jettisoned. Thinkers such as Marcuse, Arendt, and Habermas have criticized twentieth-century capitalist states for being technocratic, and turning real democracy into merely formal democracy, a mere appearance of popular decision making. [2] The norm for such criticism is an ideal of rational, free discussion among equals taking place in such a way that the freedom of each is enhanced − in a word, appeal.

For the above reason, therefore, a phenomenological inquiry into the experience of coercion and appeal is essential. Phenomenology here means, first, a description of experience as it is given, setting aside prejudices about what the experience must be; second, an essential account of "coercion", "appeal", and their different types. A totally unprejudiced description is, of course, impossible; but as much as possible I will describe different experiences of coercion and appeal without assuming ahead of time that one is reducible to the other. Within phenomenology Sartre's is the strongest, best-argued disagreement with my position. I will briefly consider this argument before moving into my own positive account.

W.S. Hamrick (ed.) *Phenomenology in Practice and Theory*.
© 1985 Martinus Nijhoff Publishers, Dordrecht/Boston/Lancaster
ISBN 90 247 2926 2. Printed in the Netherlands.

I. Freedom and the Other: The Look

Sartre's paradigm for relations with the other is the "look". If I am in the hallway and am looking through a keyhole at something, I hear footsteps on the stairs and am caught in the act, transfixed before the gaze — I am ashamed.[4]

To deal with the situation, I can do one of two things. I can stare back and try to reduce him to an object, I can say, "Who are you to condemn me, for I have caught you doing the same or worse", or I can grovel in my shame. The situation becomes a contest between freedoms, each trying to subdue the other.

Sartre's claim here is that I do not become aware of the other as subject by knowing him, because such knowledge objectifies the other, and therefore, does not really present him as subject. Any look is an objectifying and degrading look that robs the other of his freedom. I can only be aware of the other by being "looked at", by being the object of his knowledge. Only this experience gives me an indubitable certainty of the other.

Real human mutuality between persons is, therefore, impossible, because that would involve mutual looking and therefore a contest of freedoms in which one ends up being dominant. Human intersubjectivity is essentially conflictual because freedom presupposes an absolute independence, negativity, and lack of receptivity. Since any mutuality presumes mutal influence and dependence, any attempt at mutuality would be the negation of freedom. I can be either free or dependent on another, but not both. I can be either in charge of my destiny or open to another's influence, but not both.

In a subsequent chapter entitled "Concrete Relations with Others", Sartre uses this general paradigm to explore specific kinds of intersubjectivity; sadism, masochism, and so on. In each instance there is a capitulation to the other or domination of the other. If I am the stronger, I become sadistic in a sexual relationship; if weaker, then I go the masochistic route. Even apparently mutual and loving relationships turn out to be hidden forms of domination in which one person is controlling or using the other.[5]

What are we to make of Sartre's intriguing account of intersubjectivity? First, there is an inadequate account of objectivity and objectification in which personal, thematic, and alienated objectivity are uncritically lumped together. If such a procedure is incorrect, then to objectify is not necessarily to alienate. There are many kinds of looks: loving, encouraging, respectful, friendly that have a different logic from Sartre's accusing look, as well as a different result.

To pursue this point more fully, we can perceive a crucial, logical difference between looking at someone and saying, "you are a good philosopher", and looking at someone with contempt. The first is encouraging and enhances freedom; the second is alienating and negates freedom. Again there is a difference between alienating and thematizing looks. When I compliment someone, I am explicitly putting into words what we are both experiencing in the relationship, but this thematizing is experienced as contributing to both our freedoms, not detracting from them. It is true that thematizing is present in the alienating look as well: what I am denying is that thematization is necessarily alienation. All alienation is thematization, but not all thematization is alienation.[6]

Second, Sartre describes freedom as totally independent, negative, and unreceptive to motives or values.[7] If this account were true, genuine dependence on another of any kind would detract from freedom, and true mutuality would be impossible. But this notion of freedom is one-sided and to that extent false. Rather, true freedom is a unity of determination and indetermination, motive and leap, receptivity and activity. "I choose because ..." is the model of such freedom, which is open and receptive to the world, the body, and motives.[8] Consequently, with this more comprehensive notion of freedom, mutuality between persons emerges as a possibility.

One example of such a receptive freedom is philosophical discussion itself. When Sartre tries to persuade us of the truth of his position, such receptivity on the part of the hearer or reader is necessary. Otherwise the discussion is either an exercise in futility or domination. Yet such a receptivity, tacitly presumed by Sartre in his attempt to convince us, is explicitly denied by him: Either man is wholly determined (which is admissible, especially because a determined consciousness – i.e., consciousness externally motivated – becomes itself pure exteriority and ceases to be consciousness) or else man is wholly free.[9]

One consequence of positing a total freedom is that all reasons become rationalizations for my fundamental project. Yet such a consequence contradicts Sartre's attempt to convince us of the truth of his position, an attempt tacitly presupposing a distinction between reasons and rationalizations. Such a distinction presupposes a motivated, receptive freedom.

Third, Sartre's attempt to convince us of the truth of his account presumes the possibility of genuine dialogue, of what in the next section I will call "appeal". For he is attempting to convince us of the truth of his position by appealing to criteria that are not arbitrary. Yet according to Sartre's account of intersubjectivity, any attempt to persuade is an attempt at domination, no more objectively binding than any other such attempt. The explicit claim, therefore, conflicts with the implicit performance, tacitly presupposing a communication free from domination.

Fourth, in tension with Sartre's own account is the admission that we perceive the other and, therefore, know him. Perception would seem to be at least a necessary condition for such knowledge even in Sartre's own account: "but all of a sudden I hear footsteps in the hall. Someone is looking at me".[10]

Fifth, our awareness of the other does not seem apodictic as Sartre claims.

Even he admits that we can think we hear footsteps and be mistaken. But Sartre attempts to meet this difficulty by saying that nonetheless the other "is present everywhere, below me, above me, in the neighboring rooms". [11] However, this vague, general sense is corrigible also because it rests on present and past perceptions and memories that are corrigible: memories of being caught in the act in the past, past perceptions of others' response to such behavior, and present perceptions of muted conversations in rooms, radios blaring, record players sounding.

Sixth, it seems that Sartre overgeneralizes from one kind of intersubjective encounter, that of the accusing look, to all encounters. Yet phenomenological description, such as that of appeal in the next section, disputes Sartre's generalization. His descriptions are valid for certain types of negative encounters, but they fall desperately short as the general story.

Seventh, this kind of phenomenological point has to be made against Sartre, but it is not enough. For he goes from a description of the immediate experience to a further kind of necessary claim: even if certain experiences with others seem to be mutually liberating, they really are not because they cannot be. And they cannot be finally because of an "either – or" logic, which Hegel describes as the logic of understanding, that is in tension with and dictates to the phenomenological results. Because Sartre affirms a necessary disjunction between activity and passivity, positivity and negativity, determination and indetermination, dependence and independence, people *cannot* participate in mutually liberating relationships even when they seem to be doing so.

What seems to motivate such a logic is a will to absolute freedom in Sartre. To confront Sartre at his deepest is to confront him here. We do so by arguing that such an "either – or" approach to conscious experience is both self-refuting and phenomenologically false. First, the approach is self-refuting because, as I have already shown, any truth claim implies a commitment to reason and to criteria of truth and, therefore, implies a union of determination and indetermination, passivity and activity, motive and "leap". The very attempt to defend indeterminism rests on a tacit appeal to a "both – and" conception of logic. Second, Sartre's conception is phenomenologically false because human consciousness emerges in phenomenological description as a unity of opposites: subjectivity and objectivity, perception and intellection, body and mind, positivity and negativity, determination and indetermination, motive and leap. Perception, for example, is both active and passive and takes place through a lived body experienced as subject. [12] Aesthetic experience involves an active attention to the object, an attention that is at the same time deeply receptive. [13] Freedom is both negative and positive, implying not only the ability to distance myself from my environment but the adherence to values. Even an apparently totally negative social revolution justifies itself by an appeal to positive values, such as freedom or justice. [14]

To think phenomenologically in a way that is faithful to experience is to understand experience and thought as a "bacchanalian revel", a play of opposites that is fruitful and mediated. Husserl and Hegel come together here: Sartrean *Verstand* must give way to Hegelian *Vernunft*. The irony is that Sartre uses the Hegelian language of dialectic more than anyone else in phenomenology. Yet there is no one in that tradition who is further away from the genuine spirit and intention of Hegel.

To the extent, therefore, that Sartre rests his claims on phenomenological description, they can be disputed. To the extent that he appeals to an "either – or" logic, possibly motivated by a desire that freedom be absolute and God-like, his claims are arbitrary, and what is arbitrarily asserted can be rationally questioned or denied. The interest and power of *Being and Nothingness* to a large extent derive from this tension between his phenomenology and existentialism, between a description attempting to be faithful to the limits and dialectical complexity of human experience and an existential will towards an absolute autonomy.

II. A Positive Account: A Description of Coercion and Appeal

We have seen from the preceding section that Sartre's account of intersubjectivity is contrary to experience and self-refuting. Not only are there many other kinds of intersubjective encounter that do not fit his model but Sartre's own attempt to persuade his readers of the truth of his viewpoint presumes the necessity of appeal or dialogue. If Sartre's argument is simply one more attempt to dominate us, then we cannot and should not take it seriously as an argument. If, however, his truth is what should appeal to us, then there is a contradiction between what he explicitly says and what he implicitly does.

Appeal emerges then as a dialectical necessity from the preceding argument. However, we still have to determine the content of appeal. What is it in itself and how is it distinguished from coercion? What are the different types of coercion and appeal? With the purpose of answering these questions, we will reflect first on the general nature of dialogue as this is expressed in language. Second, we will then move to consider specific instances of appeal and coercion.

Let us briefly return to the dialogal situation where Sartre is trying to convince someone of the truth of his position. In the linguistic interaction between two persons, certain presuppositions emerge that allow us to make the distinction between coercion and appeal. What anyone tacitly presumes when he is trying to convince another of the truth of an argument are four validity claims: comprehensibility, truth, sincerity, and appropriateness. To say anything presumes that it is intelligible and that I am telling the truth; otherwise the conversation could not go on. Even lying presupposes the general intention of truth, for someone else will only believe a lie if he thinks it to be the truth. Consequently, sincerity is also implied; if all speakers were universally insincere and recognized to be such, no argument could go on. And because even such recognition in language is a true, sincere recognition, universal insincerity is impossible. [15]

Appropriateness, the final validity claim, involves reciprocity between speakers as the rule and any departure from that rule as the exception. If Sartre asks me to just take his word for the truth of indeterminism, then I sense the arbitrariness of this request and ask why I should take his word on the matter. I resist an inappropriate assuming of authority in this situation or any lack of reciprocity in the assumption of roles. If Sartre has the right to ask questions, state opinions, and express feelings, then so do I.

Such validity claims in dialogue are normally taken for granted and are not as a rule brought into question. What is tacitly assumed, however, is that they can be brought into question and reasons given for any claims that are made. An ideal speech situation of total reciprocity and complete freedom in questioning, asserting, and role playing is tacitly assumed. This is not to say that such a speech situation is ever totally realized; in any dialogal situation, there will be unexamined presuppositions and prejudices.

The distinction between coercion and appeal, therefore, depends on the recognition or lack of recognition of validity claims. Because consciousness is essentially expressive and linguistic, [16] consciousness of intersubjectivity based on appeal is the consciousness that validity claims are being mutually observed and realized. Coercion, on the other hand, rests on a violation of one or more of the validity claims.

One of the most striking examples of appeal is the Socratic situation, where the teacher, through a process of questioning and answering, helps someone to understand something, for instance, that God is intelligent, that the categorical imperative is true, or that capitalism is irrational. What characterizes such a learning is that, first, there is the appeal on the part of the teacher to the reason of the other person, and invitation to participate in the search for the truth. Second, there is the mutual openness of the part of each towards the other. At any point in the process, the student can raise questions about presuppositions or ask that a different hypothesis be considered. This freedom is essential if the Socratic method is to be authentic and to avoid becoming propaganda for the teacher's truth rather than the truth. Any arbitrary assumption of authority by the teacher, a violation of the fourth validity claim, would reveal itself as dogmatic. Third, the activity of the student is called forth — the teacher functions as the midwife for this activity. The point of Socratic method is to help the student see for himself, not take the teacher's word for it. Fourth, there is an experienced fulfillment on the part of the student in reaching the truth. That which he did not know he knows; the questions that he was asking now have answers. Finally, the teacher's intention is altruistic, the student's growth in autonomy. The point of Socratic method is to help the student achieve independence as a thinker and person; the student realizes in himself or herself the four validity claims. He sees and judges for himself that an argument is comprehensive, true, sincere, and appropriate.

With Socratic method, then, the ideal speech situation is approximated. There is unlimited freedom to raise questions, express disagreement, and assume different roles. Any claim that seems unclear, false, insincere, or inappropriate can be questioned and explored. If the teacher has authority here it is not one arbitrarily assumed by him, but one freely, rationally granted by the student. But his is an authority that can itself be questioned any time the teacher becomes dogmatic or makes untrue claims. His authority is that of a guide who aims to make himself dispensible; at any time the student can question whether he is a good guide or not.

Now let us take another example, that of a discussion between equals about one of these same questions. Here there is the same recourse to reason, the same tacit willingness to question anything and everything, the same emphasis on activity rather than passivity, the same sense of fulfillment in reaching the truth, the same altruism. What is not present here is the relation of authority. The dialogue here takes the form of mutual questioning and answering, with each being free to raise any hypothesis he wishes. If one arguing that capitalism is irrational is using dubious presuppositions, his partner can bring these into the discussion. If one person is being unconsciously dogmatic about a certain point, that dogmatism can be made thematic.

Now it is true that this is an ideal case, that any real dialogue will fall short of this ideal to a greater or lesser extent. Nevertheless we have all experienced discussions which approximate the ideal in their concern for truth and better argument alone prevailing. We have also experienced discussions in which the opposite is true, where there is some constraint introduced into the argument. People are trying to score debating points, assert their authority in covert ways, or refuse to question beyond a certain point. We are aware of these situations as coercive, however, because of their contrast with the ideal speech situation, where appeal and not coercion is dominant.

Now let us consider kidnapping, an obvious example of coercion. A criminal or group of criminals kidnap the child of wealthy parents to get money from these parents. First of all, the use of force is an attempt to bypass the reason and freedom of the parents. Because the kidnapper realizes that a donation of 1,000,000 to his own bank account is not something the parents would spontaneously give through rational persuasion, he is violating the fourth validity claim of appropriateness. Therefore, and this is another contrast, there is constraint introduced, a forcible limiting of options. There is no confidence in the merits of the case or that the better argument will prevail; there is a departure from the second validity claim of truth. Force and not truth is what the kidnapper relies on. Because the parents love their child and want him or her back, they are discouraged from bargaining with the kidnappers or questioning their demands. Third, in contrast to the emphasis on the personal activity of the agent in the first two cases, here the will of the kidnapper is dominant, rendering the parents and child more or less objects in the hands of the kidnapper. The equality and reciprocity of the ideal speech situation is violated.

Fourth, in contrast to the non-alienated character of the first cases in which both parents are trying to see for themselves and want the truth for each other, there is an element of alienation. Here the kidnappers try to force the parents to "do what they really do not want to do". Freedom is not totally absent in the parents, of course, because they can still choose to comply or not comply with the kidnapper's demands. But there are constraints introduced that make it unlikely that the parents will refuse to comply. The parents are pressured to consider only the options suggested by the kidnappers. In the examples of appeal, on the other hand, there is no gap between action and desire and no forcible limiting of options. Both persons are discussing a certain topic because they want to do so, not because they are forced to do so. Here the actors "choose to do what they really want to do".

Finally the goal of the kidnapping subordinates the good of parents and child to the goal of the kidnappers. In this instance of coercion, people become mere means to an end. In the two examples of appeal, on the other hand, the good of the other is an essential concern. That the student reach the truth on his or her own and grow through such activity is the goal of the teacher. That the opinions and questions of the other be taken seriously is an overriding concern of the discussion between equals.

Is such selfishness present in all instances of coercion? Although it does seem to be present in many instances, at times the good of the other can be intended and achieved. A parent disciplining a child, a policeman pulling a potential suicide away from a bridge, and a court order forbidding people to swim in polluted water are all examples of coercion which intends the good of the other and does not merely use the person. Whether or not such coercion is moral is beyond the scope of this paper, but at least coercion is not obviously immoral in all instances.

There are other, more subtle examples of coercion that must be considered. For instance, a son informs his father that he wants to be a musician rather than the doctor his father always wanted him to be. The father subtly lets his son know that if the latter does choose the piano over the surgeon's knife, he will forfeit his father's love and respect. Here the coercion is psychological rather than physical, but no less real. Here there is the same attempt to bypass the person's freedom and reason by introduction of alien considerations, the same limiting of options, the same domination, alienation, and exploitation. The father here subordinates the good of the son as the boy conceives it to his own desire that the son follow in his footsteps. Total disregard for the autonomy of the son masquerades as genuine love. All four validity claims are being covertly violated here − lack of love, untruth, insincerity, and inappropriateness clothe themselves in their opposites.

Up to this point we have been confining ourselves to personal forms of appeal and coercion exercised between two or three persons. However, in addition to the legal coercion already mentioned, there are even more subtle forms. Various types of political propaganda and advertising present themselves as in earnest about the people they are addressing, but such appearances are highly questionable in many instances. If I am looking for an automobile, I may become convinced through patient reflecting and consulting *Consumer Reports* that a fairly inexpensive Toyota is the best car for me. However, I am constantly assaulted by advertisements informing me that my masculinity will be enhanced if I buy a bigger, flashier car such as a Charger.

If certain social critics are correct, [17] all four validity claims are violated in advertising. The claim to comprehensibility is violated because terms such as "freedom", "happiness", and "power" are manipulated and obfuscated. In the Master Charge advertisement of a few years ago, "true clout" is identified with having a Master Charge card. Such "power" and "freedom" really imply and conceal their opposites, the impotence of men to really change their lives in a substantive way and the enslavement of men to consumption.

There is untruth because such "clout" turns out not to be the real item; the real power that comes from effective individual and collective decision in action is tacitly shunted to the side and ignored. There is insincerity because the advertisement presents itself as looking out for my good and is really interested primarily in profit, in getting me to charge as much as possible and to pay the eighteen percent interest on what I charge. There is inappropriateness because the advertisement tacitly assumes that its version of the good life is the true one and discourages questioning of that claim by its appeals to emotion. By tacitly shoving reason to the side, the advertiser helps to avoid the criticism that would bring such emotional appeals into question.

What is interesting about such blandishments is that they are not negative but positive. They are not trying to coerce me though threats but through psychological seduction, promising me that I will be a better man, more sexually fulfilled, and more socially acceptable if I buy a certain type of car. Like the earlier forms of coercion, this type tries to bypass reason and freedom through addressing feeling, imagination, and the unconscious; forcibly limiting options, rendering me passive by manipulating me, and alienating me. Such coercion introduces a division between what I should do and what I feel like doing. Unlike the earlier forms, however, this comes bearing gifts, presenting itself as the answer to my problems, consolation for my grief, rest for my weary bones.

This type of coercion, positive reinforcement in Skinner's sense, is difficult to see through because it does not present itself as coercion. Finally, like the negative coercion, this type is not necessarily selfish in the sense that the good of the person addressed is always consciously subordinated to the good of the ruler or businessman. In positive coercion exercised in political affairs, presidents and kings can be well-intentioned when they use propaganda "for the national interest". However, we also often are aware that such pleas of disinterestedness are specious. When McDonald's tells me that "you, you're the one" or Master Charge urges me to "get real clout", a little reflection indicates that the bottom line is profit.

Not all advertisements are positive in the sense described above. There are many that are negative as well, threatening the person with a loss of job, sex appeal, or status if he does not buy the requisite product. Nor are social and political coercion the only kinds of positive coercion. Only brief reflection on some of the previous examples is necessary to see how widespread positive coercion is. The teacher suggesting that his or her students will be sophisticated and up-to-date if they agree with him or her, and the parent showing his son what a respected member of the community a doctor is are both exercising positive coercion. Indeed in many instances negative and positive coercion are both present in varying degrees of emphasis and explicitness, and each can be dominant at different times in the same situation. A student resisting the pressure of his or her teacher or a son the arguments of his father may experience a gradual shift from promise and love to threat and intimidation as the dominant form of interaction.

III. Conclusion

Appeal is a rational, free addressing of another as a rational, free, active center, initiating a relationship in which both are not alienated but fulfilled and one with themselves and each other. Such fulfillment expresses itself as a realization of the four validity claims. Coercion, on the other hand, is irrational and unfree in its address, rendering the other passive and alienated even when his own good is intended. Coercion can be devided into negative and positive, selfish and altruistic. In positive coercion there is an appearance of rationality, always contradicted by the facts; and altruism, often contradicted by the facts.

One consequence of this analysis is that there is an essential difference between control and influence. Control has a different logic, the logic of coercion, whereas influence is possible through appeal. Because Sartre ignores this distinction, he ends up with no possibility of genuine mutuality in social life.

A second consequence is that genuine democracy and participation are possible; human interaction escapes the alternatives of object submission and arrogant domination. Human beings can interact with one another politically, question means, and set goals. Any arbitrary assumption of authority by an "expert" claiming better insight can be questioned and resisted. Indeed, one criterion that emerges for the political health of a society is the degree of its freedom from domination and oneness to a dialogue governed by the four validity claims.

128

NOTES

1. B.F. Skinner, *Beyond Freedom and Dignity* (New York: Alfred Knopf, 1972), pp. 84–87. Jean-Paul Sartre, *Being and Nothingness* trans. Hazel Barnes (New York: The Citadel Press, 1964), pp. 337–406. *L'Etre et le néant* (Paris: Gallimard, 1943), pp. 410–482. Niklos Luhmann, in Jürgen Habermas and Niklos Luhmann, *Theorie der Gesellschaft oder Sozialtechnologie – Was leistet die Systemforschung?* (Frankfurt am Main: Suhrkamp Verlag, 1971), pp. 7–100, 291–405.
2. Herbert Marcuse, *One Dimensional Mann* (Boston: Beacon Press, 1964), Hannah Arendt, *The Human Condition* (Chicago: University of Chicago Press, 1958), Jürgen Habermas, *Towards a Rational Society*, trans. Jeremy Shapiro (Boston: Beacon Press, 1970), pp. 81–122; *Technik und Wissenschaft als "Ideologie"* (Frankfurt am Main: Suhrkamp Verlag, 1968), pp. 48–103.
3. It is true that Sartre goes beyond or attempts to go beyond the position articulated in *Being and Nothingness*. On the possibility of reciprocity, see *The Critique of Dialectical Reason*, ed. Jonathan Ree, trans. Alan Sheridan Smith (London: NLB, 1976), pp. 109–121; *Critique de la raison dialectique* (Paris: Gallimard, 1960), pp. 189–199. Because the argument in *Being and Nothingness* still remains the strongest argument within the phenomenological tradition against my position, I am considering that argument here.
4. Sartre, *Being and Nothingness*, pp. 228–278; *L'Etre et le néant*, pp. 298–349.
5. Sartre, *Being and Nothingness*, pp. 337–406; *L'Etre et le néant*, pp. 410–482.
6. See James L. Marsh, "Objectivity, Alienation, and Reflection", *Studies in Existentialism and Phenomenology*, ed. Calvin Schrag and William McBride (The Hague: Martinus Nijhoff, forthcoming), for a fuller analysis of the different kinds of objectivity and their non-reducibility to one another.
7. Sartre, *Being and Nothingness*, pp. viii, 419–420, 430–431, 458, 474–465, 471–473, 499, 507; *L'Etre et le néant*, pp. 24–25, 497–499, 509–511, 538–539, 544–546, 551–554, 558–581, 588–589.
8. Paul Ricoeur, "The Philosophy of the Will", Vol. I, *Freedom and Nature: The Voluntary and the Involuntary*, trans. Erazin Y. Kohak (Evanston: Northwestern University Press, 1966), pp. 37–84; *Philosophie de la volonté*, Vol. I, *Le Volontaire et l'involontaire* (Paris: Aubier, 1949), pp. 37–81. James L. Marsh, "The Irony and Ambiguity of Freedom", *Irony*: An Interdisciplinary Reader: Essays on Ambiguity in Intersubjective Encounters (London: Harvester Press, 1981).
9. Sartre, *Being and Nothingness*, p. 428; *L'Etre et le néant*, p. 497.
10. Sartre, *Being and Nothingness*, p. 36; *L'Etre et le néant*, p. 306.
11. Sartre, *Being and Nothingness*, p. 253; *L'Etre et le néant*, p. 324.
12. James L. Marsh, "The Paradox of Perception", *The Modern Schoolman* LIV (May 1977), pp. 379–384.
13. Mikel Dufrenne, *The Phenomenology of Aesthetic Experience*, trans. Edward Casey, Albert Anderson, Willis Domingo, Leon Jacobson (Evanston: Northwestern University Press, 1973), pp. 370–434; *Phénoménologie de l'expérience esthétique* (Paris: Presses Universitaires de France, 1953), pp. 462–536.
14. James L. Marsh, "The Irony and Ambiguity of Freedom". Paul Ricoeur, *History and Truth*, trans. Charles Kelbley (Evanston: Northwestern University Press, 1950), pp. 305–328; "Négativité et affirmation originaire", *Aspects de la dialectique, Recherches de Philosophie II* (Paris: Desclée de Brouwer, 1956), pp. 101–129.
15. Jürgen Habermas, *Theory and Practice*, trans. John Viertel (Boston: Beacon Press, 1973), pp. 17–19. *Theorie und Praxis* (Berlin: Hermann Luchterhand Verlag and Suhrkamp Verlag, 1963, 1966, and 1971), pp. 23–26, Habermas and Luhmann, *Theorie der Gesellschaft oder Sozialtechnologie*, pp. 101–104.
16. See James L. Marsh, "Consciousness and Expression", *The Southwestern Journal of Philosophy* IX (Spring 1978), pp. 105–109, for a fuller discussion of the relation of thought to language and expression.
17. Stuart Ewen, *Captains of Consciousness: Advertising and the Roots of the Consumer Culture* (New York: McGraw-Hill, 1972).

Phenomenology as Psychic Technique of Non-Resistance
by
Kenneth W. Stikkers

Phenomenology is commonly understood, by those standing both within and outside of its tradition, as a philosophical movement rooted in the thought of Edmund Husserl, and phenomenologists are often all considered to be either directly or indirectly disciples of Husserl. Although it was Husserl who did the most to lay the groundwork for phenomenology as a movement, the above notions are hardly accurate, for at the time of Husserl's *Logical Investigations* (1901), several thinkers were developing phenomenologies quite independently of him. One such thinker was Max Scheler.[1] Contrary to the claims of much secondary literature,[2] Scheler was in no way a "student" of Husserl but had already worked out the foundations of his own phenomenology before reading any text of Husserl.[3] He suggested a notion of phenomenology not entirely inconsistent with that of Husserl but, in the opinion of this writer, much broader and containing vastly richer possibilities for human self-understanding.

The most general difference between the phenomenologies of Husserl and Scheler is that while for the former phenomenology is rooted in and disclosive of "thetic" *consciousness*, for the latter it is rooted in an disclosive of *life*-urge (*Lebensdrang*).[4] For Husserl, phenomenology was a reflective act that cut across the normal flow of consciousness to reveal and delineate its eidetic, or essential, structures, viz. its intentional nature, as the subjective condition for the possibility of all thinking, of all mental acts whatsoever, especially science. For Scheler, phenomenology was an "attitude" based in a "psychic technique of non-resistance", a special act of spirit that blocks the normal flow of life to reveal its growing, striving, becoming tendencies, on the one side, and the givenness of the world as resistance, on the other – a technique which Scheler saw already in Eastern Buddhism, a major source for his thinking.

Surely one must understand a notion of phenomenology such as that of Scheler on its own terms and not interpret and criticize it from the standpoint of Husserlian phenomenology, as some commentators have tried to do.[5] But Scheler never presented his later thinking on phenomenology in any single, systematic work. Indeed, what he has to say on the matter can be found only

W.S. Hamrick (ed.) *Phenomenology in Practice and Theory.*
© 1985 Martinus Nijhoff Publishers, Dordrecht/Boston/Lancaster
ISBN 90 247 2926 2. Printed in the Netherlands.

130

in a few passages dispersed throughout his writings. Thus it is my purpose here to organize these scattered suggestions into a coherent outline of phenomenology as psychic technique of non-resistance, all the while contrasting this conception with the more familiar one presented by Husserl and Heidegger. Though the inspiration for such a project derives from Scheler, the thinking through and development of a coherent notion of phenomenology along these lines is entirely my own. In what follows, I make frequent references to a variety of Scheler's texts for two reasons: (1) as a scholarly duty to give proper credit for the source of my inspiration for those readers already familiar with his vast *corpus* of writings and (2) to provide firsthand familiarity with Scheler's work for the probably much larger group of less-knowledgeable readers.

To begin with, phenomenology for Scheler was not a method, as it was for Husserl, but an "attitude of spiritual seeing", because "A method is a goal-directed procedure of *thinking about* facts, for example, induction or deduction. In phenomenology, however, it is a matter, first, of new facts themselves, before they have been fixed by logic, and second, of a procedure of *seeing*".[6] Phenomenology then is not a simple series of steps one follows, in the tradition of Descartes, to arrive at a state of apodictic certainty, but a special manner of viewing the world, and "attitude" thus designates this non-goal-directed manner of viewing.

Conceived as an attitude rather than a method, phenomenology is not foundational for all other attitudes towards the world, e.g., science, as it was for Husserl, but occupies a much more modest position, although providing us insights of a very special kind. To grasp this point, one must understand phenomenology in connection with the sociology of knowledge. One significance of Scheler's *Sociology of Knowledge*[7] was its implicit rejection of the tendency in Western philosophical systems to make one type of knowledge − e.g., religion, metaphysics, positive science (Comte), economics (Marx), phenomenology (Husserl) − foundational to all others in the sense that it provides elementary, indubitable premises upon which all other knowledge is built. To do so is to fall into rationalism and dogmatic assertion. Rather, all aspects of thinking, whether they be of an individual or group, grow together and interact with one another in a single comprehensive, organically unified *Weltanschauung*. Metaphysics, for example, may provide the foundation for socio-economics, but no more so than socio-economy, say, as Marx argued,[8] conditions metaphysics.

Thus phenomenology cannot be a radically presuppositionless science upon which all other sciences must rest; it is not pre-philosophical, as Husserl claimed it to be.[9] Phenomenology may, for example, illuminate the presuppositions and life-world conditions of science, but in turn socio-economic science can illuminate a phenomenology rooted in egological consciousness as a natural

outgrowth of an overly introspective, narcissistic bourgeois society.[10] The
search for an absolute natural attitude is as naive as, and an outgrowth of, the
attempt of Enlightenment thinkers to describe a natural state of humanity,
prior to the formation of society. Because human beings are essentially social
beings, to imagine them in a state of nature is to imagine what is not humanity.
So, too, because every world-view is at once religious, metaphysical, scientific,
sociological, economic, etc., there can be no absolute natural world-views, i.e.,
world-views not relative to socio-historical context.[11]

Granted, Scheler speaks frequently of an "order of foundations of
knowledge", but by this he does not mean an order whereby one type of
knowledge provides the elementary premises upon which other types of
knowledge are built. Rather, the "order of foundations" is an order of com-
prehensiveness. Religion, contrary to the claims of August Comte, is foundational to metaphysics and science (both natural and human), not because
religious faith provides building-block premises upon which the latter two rest,
but because genuine religious experience (as opposed to institutional
theological dogma) offers an intuitional vision of the One, of *to en*, of the
Whole of Being, *out of which* metaphysics and science carve their particular
claims about *things*. Without such a foundation, the propositions of
metaphysics and science cannot hold together in any unified system but
disintegrate into trivia. Such disintegration is characteristic of the "crisis" of
Western science, to which phenomenology is in part a response. Part of the
special task of phenomenology then, in conjunction with the sociology of
knowledge, is the disclosure and articulation of the order of foundations and
of the interrelatedness of all types of thinking within a comprehensive relative
natural world-view, and hence it is essentially linked to religion. But again, the
unity of religious intuition is a dynamic unity, determined in part sociological-
ly, and the mode of phenomenological viewing is always itself a product of the
comprehensive whole in which it finds itself and which it describes: as such,
it is never "presuppositionless", as Husserl everywhere maintained it to be.

Phenomenology as psychic technique of non-resistance, then, is neither
simply foundational to nor based upon metaphysics but in essential intercon-
nection with it, or with what Scheler termed "metabiology".[12] While for
Husserl the phenomena of dator consciousness are constituted within the
polarities of noesis and noema, for Scheler the reality of the world is given
within the polarities of vital-urge (*Lebensdrang*), tending toward increasing
spiritualization, and world resistance. Scheler denied the sharp distinction commonly made between living and non-living things, organic and inorganic being,
arguing that a single vital, growing, becoming tendency (*Alleben*) permeates all
nature and could be found already in the pulsations of sub-atomic particles.[13]
This vital-urge is not random or chaotic in its movements of becoming, but
rather, in its striving toward increasing spiritualization, it projects, like a cone

of light from an automobile headlight, its own possibility, its own *ability-to-be*, ahead of itself as a phantasmic image.[14] Vital-urge seeks out those object-correlates that most adequately fulfill its interests. "Everything which we perceive must, before we perceive it, in some way address and interest our vital drives".[15] On the one hand, then, we experience something as "real", as existing, only insofar as it presents itself within and against a world-context, which withstands, or resists, vital-urge's coming-to-be. On the other hand and reciprocally, vital-urge experiences itself, is *self-given*, primordially as *resistance to* and withstanding the impingements of what it is not, that is, of the world. "Existence, or a sense of reality", Scheler writes "is derived from the experiences of resistance in a world already present as given, and this experience of resistance is inherent in the vital drive, in the central vital-urge of our being". And, he continues, "This original experience of reality as an experience of resistance, *precedes* any consciousness, conception and perception".[16] The experience of reality occurs within the co-relational resistance of vital-urge and world, and this experience of resistance is prior to the perception of whatness (*Sosein*) and existence (*Dasein*) of things as well as the cognition of essences (*Wesen*). As Scheler writes, "We comprehend, therefore, in the order of givenness, the being-real [*Realsein*] of an indefinite something [viz., resistance] *prior to* its *what*ness [*Sosein*]".[17]

In short, where there is not tension, no strife, between drives and world — no world resistance to the becoming of life-urge and no vital resistance to the impingements of the world — there is no reality given to life, neither of the world nor of itself. We might imagine a world like the one envisioned in the German fairy tale "The Land of Cockaigne", portrayed by the sixteenth century Flemish painter Pieter Bruegel the Elder, where every human desire — be it appetitive, sexual, or power based — is immediately fulfilled: such a world must be an imaginary world, an unreal world, precisely because it is a world where there is no strife, no resistance of vital drives. The world itself, as a thing-in-itself, *might*, of course, continue to exist without such strife, but neither we nor any other vital-spiritual act center, including God, would ever have any way of knowing. Hence Scheler is in full agreement with Heraclitus's contention that "Strife fathers all things".

It was the very lack of any adequate notion of resistance that Scheler was most critical of in the phenomenologies of Hegel and Husserl and that he found most objectionable in the "fundamental ontology" of Heidegger's *Sein und Zeit*; that is, there is no adequate resistance factor in the unfolding of Spirit in history, in transcendental subjectivity, nor in Dasein's way Being-in-the-world, respectively.

Granted, Husserl describes the givenness of intentional objects of perception in terms of resistance, but the objectivities of the world are constituted as resisting: resistance is a characteristic of constitution and not an element of the eidetic structures of consciousness itself wherein such objectivities are constituted. Moreover, the occurrence of resistance is strictly for Husserl in the realm of consciousness, while for Scheler resistance is thoroughly vital and prior to and conditional for the givenness of objects in consciousness.

With Heidegger that matter is much more complicated. For although he does not use the term, something like "resistance" is central to Heidegger's description of the being of tools in terms of their un-readiness-to-hand of the tool as the tool's givenness to Dasein as present-at-hand is precisely a matter of resistance, as illustrated in the following passage from *Sein und Zeit*:

> In our concernful dealings, however, we not only come up against unusable things *within* what is ready-to-hand: we also find things that are missing – which not only are not "handy" but are not "to hand" at all. Again, to miss something in this way amounts coming across something un-ready-to-hand. When we notice what is un-ready-to-hand, that which is ready-to-hand enters the mode of *obtrusiveness*. The more urgently we need what is missing, and the more authentically it is encountered in its un-readiness-to-hand, all the more obtrusive does that which is ready-to-hand become – so much so, indeed, that it seems to lose its character of readiness-to-hand. It reveals itself as something just present-at-hand and no more, which cannot be budged without the thing that is missing. The helpless way in which we stand before it is a deficient mode of concern, and as such it uncovers the Being-just-present-at-hand-and-no-more of something ready-to-hand. [18]

Although Scheler would undoubtedly use different words to express the point here – e.g., he would not describe our relationship to the tool that is present-at-hand as one of "helplessness" – he would be, I believe, in essential agreement with Heidegger. [19] Their point of difference is this: Heidegger charges that to root the experience of Being in resistance is to ignore the referential totality in which Dasein is emerged, viz., Dasein's Being-in-the-world. Heidegger writes: "Under the strongest pressure and resistance, nothing like an affect would come about, and the resistance itself would remain essentially undiscovered, if Being-in-the-world, with its ontological disposition, had not already submitted itself to having entities within-the-world "matter" to in in a way which its moods have outlined in advance. *In the ontological disposition lies, existentially speaking*, a disclosive reference to the world, out of which we can encounter something that matters to us". [20] And again:

> When Being-out-for something comes up against resistance and can do nothing but "come up against it", it is itself already *alongside* a totality of involvements. But the fact that this totality has been dis-covered is grounded in the disclosedness of the referential totality of significance. *The experiencing of resistance – that is, the discovery of what is resistance to one's endeavors – is possible ontologically only by reason*

134

of the disclosedness of the world. The character of resisting is one that belongs to entities with-the-world. Factically, experiences of resistance determine only the extent and direction in which entities within-the-world are discovered. The summation of such experiences does not introduce the disclosure of the world for the first time, but presupposes it. The "against" and the "counter to" as ontological possibilities are supported by disclosed Being-in-the-world.[21]

Insofar as the disclosedness of Being-in-the-world occurs in Dasein within the phenomenon of care, "Reality is referred back to the phenomenon of care".[22]

Scheler's responses to Heidegger are several and worth summarizing here because they help clarify his notion of resistance and make it more precise.

First, Scheler suggests (naturally) that Heidegger severely misunderstands his notion of resistance by lumping it together with that of Dilthey.[23] The experience of resistance is not to be equated with the experience of reality and of objectifiable entities in the world, as "the discovery of what is resistant to one's endeavors". As Scheler makes quite clear, the experience of resistance is *prior to* and *a condition for* the experience of any whatness of existence of entities, and it is certainly not the case that the experience of resistance presupposes the disclosedness of Dasein's referential totality of significance, viz., Dasein's Being-in-the-world. On the contrary "resistance" describes the very manner in which Dasein finds itself primordially already within a context of significance, the very manner in which Being-in-the-world discloses itself to Dasein, prior to the encounter with any objectifiable entities within-the-world, and hence is presupposed by Being-in-the-world.

Moreover, that which experiences resistance – experiences the world as resistant to its own becoming and experiences itself as resistant to the world – viz., vital-urge, is in no way given ontic status by Scheler. He writes:

And when in a real-ontological sense I define being-real as image posited through vital-urge, I do not mean further to impose *realitas* on the state of becoming of vital-urge itself. The "desire", the "thirst" for being-real is itself not at all real, precisely because it is not objectifiable but first of all "seeks" realization [*Realsein*]. I entirely agree with Heidegger that it is high time to stop finally transporting the categories and modes of being found in the *narrow* sphere of physical being over into life, consciousness, the ego, and so forth.[24]

Rather, vital-urge is a pure becoming tendency (*Werde-sein*), or flux, (*Wechsel*), being-in-the act, which is wholly non-objectifiable, and not that which is "becoming something" (*Sein-werden*).

Second, and more seriously, Scheler charges that without a foundation in something like life-urge, Heidegger's notion of Dasein lacks adequate unity and represents a doctrine of "solipsism". It is not enough to say simply that

Dasein experiences itself fundamentally and primordially as "Being-in-the-world" because, Scheler claims, "Here "being-in" is supposed to mean something like "being caught up in" or "being involved in". Can this idea have any meaning at all unless the "*solus ipse*" also experiences itself as independent from the world — something that Heidegger cannot admit?"[25] We experience our distinct manner of Be-ing not as a nebulous "Being-in-the-world" but even more fundamentally as a unitary becoming, vital act-center of resistance — which Scheler designates by "person" rather than "Dasein"[26] — not in but rather *against* the world. Reciprocally, the disclosedness of the world, upon which all cognition of reality is founded,[27] is centered in "the unity of resistance against the unity of the drive center".[28] Heidegger's failure to root Dasein in something like a unitary life urge means that only can he not account for the dynamic unity of the world wherein Dasein is Being-in; he can only *assert* such a unity. He cannot explain why our world is a "*universum*" rather than a *multiversa*, as William James held in *A Pluralistic Universe.*[29] Scheler writes:

> ... resistance against the *single* drive — and life-center, produces the unity of real sphere — *before* all individual realities, insofar as they are indebted to such being functions and qualities of sensation in a secondary way ... A "worldhood" as phenomenon (not as "idea") is, I am sorry to say, absolutely unknown to me. The "referential totality of sigificance" (*Sein und Zeit*, p. 210) seems to me a very vague and ill-defined concept. There simply is no proof that the drive impulse is a "modification" of a noncognitional mode of comportment, which Heidegger calls "care", and that resistance presupposes Being as that about which we care (or the being of our fellow-man as the one for whom we have solicitude).[30]

Indeed, Heidegger is not able to account for the very "thrownness", the very Da-ness, of Dasein without a unitary vital act-center, which both *resists* and is *resisted by* the world.

Except for rare moments, vital-urge, in its striving toward increasing actualization of spirit against the resistance of the world, suffers from a lack of fulfillment. That is, suffering is co-given with reality in vital-urge's encounter with world-resistance: suffering is the subjective correlate of reality in experiences of resistance.[31] Thus the task of all thinking — religious, philosophical, scientific, etc. — is, Scheler contends, the elimination of this suffering,[32] and this means to make the world less real. There are basically two techniques for the elimination of suffering, two major traditions in world history, which Scheler summarizes in this way: "the Western idea of heroism places the means of eliminating suffering in the *external*, technical activity directed toward material nature and toward the organization of the community — the Indian-Buddhist idea of heroism places it in an *internal* activity, or better: it places the means of eliminating suffering in an activity within the soul and the organism, directed towards the drives".[33]

The first technique is found in the Western heroic attitude; it is a combative stance towards the world: one seeks to eliminate suffering by *overcoming* world-resistance and bolstering one's resistance to the world. The world is seen as something to conquer. This can be done in two ways, either through physical force or mentally through rationality. Examples of the physical overcoming of the suffering of resistance include: the Western (Greek) hero who seeks to overcome his enemies; modern notions of "success" and "accomplishment"; the advocacy legal system, which seeks justice through retribution and punishment rather than forgiveness; medical science's use of drugs and surgical procedures to cure disease and illness; the spread of modern technology generally; the attempt to solve social ills through legislative and institutional reforms; and the tendency in modern universities to use ideas as weapons, to construct "knock down" arguments, in order to defeat one's opponents and thereby promote one's own professional success and enhance one's own ego. Mentally the technique of overcoming resistance is expressed in rationalism, that is, the attempt to predetermine intellectually the kinds of realities that there can possibly be. For example, empiricism, which is the primary method of modern science, far from being the opposite of rationalism, as it is commonly supposed, is a prime instance of it, for it predetermines intellectually and arbitrarily that only sense impressions count as "real". The rationalism of modern science seeks to conquer world resistance, reality, by ensnaring it in its conceptual net and bringing it under the rule of its abstractions and logic, principles and laws, often to prepare the way for the conquering of the world physically, viz., to technologize it. The overcoming of resistance has been the primary technique in the West for eliminating the suffering of the world and thereby making it less real.

The second technique for eliminating suffering, found mainly in Eastern mysticism, e.g., Buddhism and Taoism, but also in the West, e.g., in Christianity, is the psychic technique of non-resistance. Through such a technique, one seeks to "block", or render inoperative, vital-urge and thereby cancel, or dissolve, the point of resistance with the world. Reality is thereby "suspended". The world is "de-actualized", "de-realized", "ideated", and its essences are thereby allowed to come forth and show themselves purely and simply: psychic technique of non-resistance puts aside the ontic claims about the world, but lets the world ontologically and essentially be. In whatever form psychic technique of non-resistance takes, "it always is a matter of one thing". Scheler claims:

> ... to bring about *pure "contemplatio"* of genuine ideas and primordial phenomena and to produce, in their congruence, "essence" free of existence through an *act of blocking out* those acts and drive-impulses that yield the objects; moments of reality ... For reality, in all modes of

perception and remembrance, is given only as "resistance" against dynamic drive-like attentiveness ... the moment of reality in the experience of resistance is the condition for the *hic-et-nunc whatness* of objects. To the extent that this moment of resistance has been deactivated the *"essence"*, which is identical in objects and independent of their *hic et nunc, must* remain for the subject. [34]

In another place he explains that "Ideation", therefore, means to grasp the essential modes and formal structures of the world through a single case only, independent of the number of observations and inductive references which belong to intelligence. [35] Psychic technique which seeks control over the *external* environment, is a-rational in nature. It is not tied to any permanent structure of reason, such as Kant described, nor does it seek to capture the world in a mesh of rational categories. Rather, "The capacity to distinguish between essence and existence", exercised in this technique, "is a basic characteristic of the human spirit; and that upon which all reason and priori knowledge depends. [36]

Through psychic technique of non-resistance one eliminates suffering *internally* by allowing oneself to be *overcome by* it, by *not* resisting the impingements of the "external" world. Through the suspension of world reality, one at the same time suspends suffering. Thus in it, "the goals of health, salvation, and philosophic cognition strangely intersect" [37]: it is necessarily a manner of essential viewing *and* of eliminating suffering simultaneously. Scheler describes the singularity of this process in this way:

> ... what it means is to suspend, at least tentatively, the *moment of reality itself*, or to annihilate the entire, indivisible, powerful impression of reality together with its affective correlates. What it means is to remove the "anguish of earthly existence" which Schiller wrote, is overcome only "in those regions where the pure forms dwell". For all reality, because it is reality, and regardless of what it is, is a kind of inhibiting, constraining, pressure for every living being, and its correlate is "pure" anxiety (anxiety without any object). If existence means "resistance", the can-celling of reality can only be the kind of "ascetic" act by which we suspend the operation of the vital-urge in relation to which the world appears as resistance, and which is the precondition for all sensory experience and its accidental qualities. [38]

Psychic technique of non-resistance is thus not merely one technique among many but can encompass a whole style of living, an entire ethical stance toward the world, a whole manner of dealing with the world and its suffering, as exhibited in the extension of its principles into politics — political passivism and "passive resistance" [39] — and its embodiment in a person like Buddha or, more recently, Mahatma Gandhi.

Scheler offered three primary examples of psychic technique of non-resistance: Buddhism, Socrates' original understanding of philosophy, and phenomenology. All three are rooted, to varying degrees, in essentially the same technique and may bring about the same result, viz. simultaneous essential insight and the elimination of suffering.

Buddhism, Scheler suggests, represents the highest form of psychic technique of non-resistance. It, like virtually every mystical tradition, is an attitude toward suffering, an ethics of suffering, which teaches that one can only eliminate suffering by first accepting it, by cancelling all resistance to it. The Buddhist scholar Daisetz Teitaro Suzuki confirms this when he writes that "The value of human life lies in the fact of suffering, for where there is no suffering, no consciousness of karmic bondage, there will be no power of attaining spiritual experience and thereby reaching the field of non-distinction. Unless we agree to suffer we cannot be free from suffering".[40] Indeed, Buddha's conversion experience occurred when he encountered one poor man, one sick man, and one dead man and from this occasion he saw and accepted suffering as an essential condition of the reality of the world, despite having been protected from such experiences in his father's palace. This cancelling of all resistance to suffering is often described as an "emptying of the self" and an extinguishing of all desires. This emptying of the self is not, however, an absolute nothingness but an absolute fullness: the self is emptied of all pre-occupation with *things, entities,* existence, including itself, and thereby receives the fullness of Being and becomes a nondifferentiated part of a mystical One. [41]

Christianity, too, teaches us "Do not resist suffering", and this ethic of non-resistance is exemplified by such doctrines as "turning the other cheek" and "loving one's enemy" (doctrines which a thoroughly Greek Nietzsche found to be resentful and contemptible[42]) and in Jesus's refusal to defend himself before the Romans.[43] Thus the dogma that "Christ died for our sins" and that acceptance of him means *being released and protected from* suffering is highly inadequate because it would mean, based upon what has been said above, that Jesus would thereby become a means for *avoiding* suffering and that acceptance of him would thereby *deprive us* of our only means to genuine salvation. Rather, the word of the Cross means, as Thomas Merton writes, "to be nailed to the Cross with Christ", to suffer *with* him, to *increase* our own suffering by accepting his suffering *as our own*, and only in this act of open acceptance of suffering does the ego-self, the individualized self as an entity, dissolve itself. Merton writes: "To receive the word of the Cross means the acceptance of a complete self-emptying of Christ.[44] Such emptiness is often described in Christianity as "poverty" — "Blessed are those who are poor in spirit". Meister Eckart explains, "he is a poor man who *wants* nothing, *knows* nothing, and *has* nothing". Such a state is possible only when one is "empty of self and all things".[45] In Christianity, as in Buddhism, only through the acceptance of suffering and emptying of the ego-self can one attain salvation from suffering and receive the "riches" of God's heaven.[46]

While eliminating suffering Buddhism also offers essential insight, enlightenment, through its non-resistance to the world. That enlightenment occurs only with extinguishing of desires, as illustrated by the earliest Zen poem:

> The perfect Way [Tao] is without difficulty,
> Save that it avoids picking and choosing,
> Only when you stop liking and disliking
> Will all be clearly understood.
> A split hear's difference,
> And the heaven and earth are set apart!
> If you want to get the plain truth,
> Be not concerned with right and wrong.
> The conflict between right and wrong
> Is the sickness of the mind.[47]

One attains enlightenment when one ceases to see the world as a collection of things and oneself as an ego-self entity within that world — as one *thing* among many — when one ceases to impose upon the world's preconceived categories of thinking, preconceived categories of what there is possible to be, but allows the world to come forward, to show itself in its fullness, and to be experienced in its simple, singular, concrete wholeness, or pure presence — *Nirvana*. Suzuki illustrates this simple concreteness as follows:

A Zen Master was once asked:

Q. What is Tao? (We may take Tao as meaning the ultimate truth or reality.)

A. It is one's everyday mind.

Q. What is one's everyday mind?

A. When tired you sleep: when hungry you eat.[48]

And C.G. Jung notes that Buddhism's distinct characteristic is its radical *lack of presuppositions (Voraussetzung).*[49]

Enlightenment thus requires that one suspend one's rational apparatus. Suzuki writes: "Zen is decidedly not a system founded upon logic and analysis. If anything, it is the antipode to logic, by which I mean the dualistic mode of thinking ... Zen has nothing to teach us in the way of intellectual analysis; nor has it any set doctrines which are imposed on its followers for acceptance".[50] Reason — logic, analysis — is good for the grasping of *particular things*, but Buddhism aims at "a comprehensive grasp of the whole and this intuitively".[51] "Personal experience, therefore, is everything in Zen".[52] And Jung adds, "The complete destruction of the rational intellect aimed at in the training creates an almost perfect lack of supposition of the consciousness".[53]

This suspension of rational thinking entails the suspension of our linguistic symbols for interpreting the world. Alan Watts writes, "Our problem is that the power of thought enables us to construct symbols of things apart from the things themselves. This includes the ability to make a symbol, an idea of ourselves [viz., the "self"] apart from ourselves . . . For this reason the masters talk about Zen as little as possible, and throw its concrete reality straight at us".[54] Moreover, rational categories and language fragment, distort, and finally lose the fundamental unity of pure presence (*Nirvana*). So Suzuki writes, "because the human tongue is not an adequate organ for expressing the deepest of truths of Zen, the latter cannot be made the subject of logical exposition; they are to be experienced in the inmost soul when they become for the first time intelligible".[55] Buddhism thus uses language sparingly, e.g., through the convention of the *koan*, to help us overcome language: it fully appreciates the silence of an "eternal abyss",[56] the comprehensive fullness of Being, out of which language emerges. "Zen uses language against itself", Merton observes, "to blast out these preconceptions and to destroy the specious 'reality' in our minds so that we can *see* directly". Zen is saying, as Wittgenstein said, "don't think: Look!"[57]

There is in the Christian tradition, too, a tendency to separate that kind of knowing based upon rational categories and consisting of words and statements from wisdom that is a direct intuition of the divine essence. For example, in the first two chapters of his Epistle to the Corinthians, St. Paul distinguishes the "wisdom of speech" from spiritual wisdom. Spiritual wisdom is paradoxical, experiential, beyond reason, and to attain it one must become liberated from the "wisdom of speech", "the wisdom of the wise" (viz., those who are popularly thought wise), by the "word of the Cross".[58] The "word of the Cross" Merton interprets as "a stark and existential experience of union with Christ in His death [i.e., in His suffering] in order to share in His resurrection.[59] St. Augustine also illustrates this distinction in the following passage: "when the soul deserts the wisdom (*sapientia*) of love, which is always unchanging and one, and desires knowledge (*scientia*) from the experience of temporal and changing things, it becomes puffed up rather than built up. And weighted down in this manner the soul falls away from blessedness as though by its own heaviness".[60]

St. Thomas Aquinas, too, distinguishes natural knowledge, based upon natural reason, from supernatural knowledge, based upon faith, and argues the former is subordinate to and incapable of leading one to salvation without the latter.[61] This "spiritual wisdom" or "supernatural vision of God", to which rational knowledge is subordinate, is, I submit, a manner of essential viewing rooted in an attitude of non-resistance, an attitude whereby one's self becomes emptied through acceptance of the suffering of Christ as one's own, thereby preparing one to receive the fullness of Divine grace, of Being.[62] This attitude is perhaps, as Scheler suggests, not as highly developed as, but not unlike that found in Buddhism.

Although there are certainly some major differences between it and the mysticisms of Buddhism and Christianity, Socrates's original understanding of philosophy as "love of wisdom" contains a kernel of psychic technique of non-resistance. To begin with, Socrates does indeed describe in several places the ascent to wisdom as a process of suffering.[63] Also, Socrates, to the astonishment of his students, offers no resistance to death after being sentenced by the city of Athens, but like Buddha, he dies in the midst of quiet conversation with his students.[64] Granted, Buddha, unlike Socrates, probably would not have offered any type of public defense of himself had similar charges been brought against him, nor would he have tried to argue his students out of their fears of death. Insofar as he does so, Socrates remains in that Greek heroic tradition which resists suffering by seeking change in the external world. But, more important, Socrates describes the attaining of wisdom as a process of "dying",[65] of release from the body, its senses and desires: wisdom requires the blocking of vital desires through a special technique of the soul, which de-realizes the world and the self. Socrates "knew this", Scheler claims, "when he envisaged the intuition of forms as a turning away of the soul from the sensory world, and the return of the soul to itself [i.e., the "re-collection" of the soul] in order to go back to the original nature and source of things".[66] Indeed, Socrates describes the attainment of wisdom in this manner:

> *Socrates.* And were we not saying long ago that he should when using the body as an instrument of perception ... is then dragged by the body into the region of the changeable, and wanders and is confused; the world spins round her, and she is like a drunkard, when she touches change?
> *Cebes.* Very true.
> *Socrates.* But when returning into herself she reflects, then she passes into the other world, the region of purity, and eternity, and immortality, and unchangeableness, which are her kindred, and with them she ever lives, when she is by herself and is not let or hindered; then she ceases from her erring ways, and being in communion with the unchanging is unchanging. And this state of the soul is called wisdom?[67]

Wisdom, the in-gathering of the soul, occurs through dialogue, and the process of dialogue, by which one's soul is led from the multiplicity of the bodily senses to the *agathon*, which is the One (*to en*), is essentially a technique of non-resistance, although ambiguously so. Socrates explains in the *Theaetetus*, for example, that he no longer gives birth to ideas; he no longer puts forward ideas of his own as he did in his younger days, described in *Parmenides*; he no longer claims to know anything. Rather, his role is simply that of midwife: he merely facilitates an idea's birth, and rather than refuting any idea, resisting its coming forth, Socrates allows every idea to come forward and show itself in the light of the *logos*. (Dr. John C.H. Wu translates this term as "Tao" in his Chinese translation of the New Testament, a translation to which Thomas Merton gives his full assent.[68]) Socrates criticizes the sophisticated lawyers, who abuse arguments as weapons to win without regard for truth. Indeed, Socrates fully realizes that the Good, which is the One, can never be captured by the categories of reason nor by language: it remains the unknowable and the undefinable, which, like the sun, can only be glimpsed briefly and momentarily. Hence the "Socratic irony": Socrates's wisdom lies in his knowing that he does not know. Knowledge is a necessary step toward the unknowable. The processes of reason and discourse, within the dialogue, reveal their own limits, our own ignorance, and, like the Buddhist *Koan*, turn language upon itself. Wisdom lies where the dialogue ends: in silence.[69] The successful dialogue dissolves our predisposition, our intellectual resistance, to the world, empties us of our opinions about things and ourselves — the world as we think it to be[70] — and into the emptiness allows the fullnes of Being, an experience which Theaetetus describes as one of "dizziness".[77] The genuine "philosophical technique of cognition" — "*sophia*", as Socrates understood it — Scheler contends, "is not only different from, but wholly *antithetical* to, the positive-scientific attitude of cognition of laws pertaining to apparent spatio-temporal coincidence (of the "*hic-nunc*" of what is)", laws which may be used for the technological control of nature.[72] Although the dialogue does not bring us "knowledge" of the positive type, its value, Socrates tells Theaetetus, is that "you will be soberer and humbler and gentler to other men, and will be too modest to fancy that you know what you do not know",[73] qualities which describe those for whom non-resistance is a style of life.

Surely the observation that phenomenology has certain things in common with mysticism is not new.[74] But comparative studies along these lines virtually all restrict themselves to the superficial description of certain common characteristics and aims. What Scheler provides us with in his later thought is a position from which we can observe the *essential* similarity among all psychic techniques of non-resistance, whether they be Buddhistic, Christian, philosophical, or phenomenological.

The nature of phenomenology as a psychic technique of non-resistance is well captured in Heidegger's repeated formulation of it as a manner of "letting appear that whose nature it is to appear in itself", viz., phenomena.[75] To this formulation Husserl and Scheler would both assent. Indeed, Scheler saw psychic technique of non-resistance as lying at the very heart of Husserl's "phenomenological reduction": "Husserl meant the same thing" as Buddha and Socrates, Scheler claims, "when he based the intuition of essences upon a phenomenological reduction, a "cancelling" or "bracketing" of the accidental coefficients of things in the world in order to bring out their essences. While I do not agree with Husserl's theory of reduction in its details, I do believe that it refers to the essential act by which the human spirit must be defined".[76] Scheler, then, does not so much oppose Husserl's notion of phenomenology as he wishes to extend it and make it even more radical by rooting it not merely in consciousness, but in the very becoming of life-urge itself, which makes anything like consciousness possible. Phenomenology should be more than a "logical methodology" or "bracketing" procedure[77] that suspends "the existential *judgment* which is inherent in every natural act of perception". Rather, to be truly radical, phenomenology must aim "to suspend, at least tentatively", the very experience, "the very moment of reality itself, or to annihilate the entire, indivisible, powerful impression of reality together with its affective correlates".[78] Such a radical de-realization of world experience requires a vital-psychic technique that cancels the very point of world resistance, and this means extending phenomenology into a whole ethic of suffering, a whole vital-psychic disposition toward the world.

To be sure, Scheler's insights help illuminate many areas of interest to phenomenology. For example, he provides a new level for understanding Heidegger's interest in such mystics as Jacob Boehme and Meister Eckart, an area which has already received a great deal of attention. Indeed, Scheler provides an important link in understanding the movement of phenomenology from Husserl to Heidegger. His insights also help explain the interest in phenomenology on the part of such Buddhist scholars as Suzuki and Kitara Nishida.[79] These connections could well be the subject of an entire book and will only be noted here. But another aspect of phenomenology for which Scheler provides new depths of understanding and which deserves brief discussion here, is hermeneutical method.

Scheler's notion of phenomenology as psychic technique of non-resistance — sketchily presented though it is — strikes me as thoroughly consistent with Heidegger's and Gadamer's descriptions of hermeneutical method. For example, in his *Introduction to Metaphysics*, Heidegger tells us that the disclosure of Being occurs only in the process of questioning — what he later terms "openness" — and never in one's setting forth of answers.[80] Where thinking loses its open responsiveness to the world, it restlessly seeks to master it, to technologize it.[81] And in his *Disclosure on Thinking*, he states that "we should *do* noting, but rather wait and listen".[82]

Gadamer, too, in his *Truth and Method*, tells us that hermeneutics has its dialectical fulfillment "not in definite knowing, but in that openness to [further] experience, which is itself set in free play by experience itself". "Experience" refers to a non-objectified and largely non-objectifiable accumulation of "understanding" which we call "wisdom". Experience often suggests the pain of growth and new understanding. It has constantly to be acquired, and nobody can save us from it. "Experience is a matter of multisided disillusionment based on expectation; only in this way is experience acquired. The fact that 'experience' is preeminently painful does not really color experience black; it lets us see into the inner nature of experience".[83] "Experience is [always] experience of finitude",[84] or resistance. How then does one gain such insight into the nature of experience? Through the act of questioning and thereby dissolving one's own expectations and prejudices about the world. "In order to be able to question", Gadamer writes, "one must will to *know*, and that means, however, [as Socrates taught] to know that one does not know".[85] "When one knows he does not know", Richard Palmer adds, "and when he does not therefore through method assume that he only needs to understand more thoroughly *in the way he already understands*, then he acquires that structure of openness characterizing authentic questioning".[86] The dialogues of Socrates provide one model of such interchange between knowing and not knowing: only through genuine questioning does one attain "wisdom". The paradigm of hermeneutical experience is that to reading a letter from a dear friend: in reading such a letter one does not adopt a "critical attitude" and immediately pounce on each sentence to determine its truth or falsity, in the manner most of us are taught to read about philosophy. Rather, one sympathetically enters into the worldview of the writer, without resistance, and understands it to the best of one's ability, not in the light of one's own rigid presuppositions, but in the light of its own account.

Now, one might wonder whether one technique for eliminating suffering is preferable to or more "effective" than the other. Scheler gives no direct answer to this, but he does suggest that each technique has its own limitations of their respective dominant techniques for eliminating suffering, and each is looking increasingly to the technique of the other in order to overcome these limitations. Thus, Scheler foresaw a coming together of, and growing exchange between, Eastern and Western cultures and their techniques for eliminating suffering, a reversal of polarities, in what he termed "the world-age of adjustment".[87] Evidence for this development includes the internationalization of sciences and the growing interest among Westerners in Eastern mysticisms, psychoanalytic techniques, and phenomenology. For the first time in human history humankind has a global experience of itself.

The Western technique for overcoming the resistance of the world has demonstrated remarkable successes in eliminating suffering, but the Western technique is uninterested in gaining essential insight into that world and incapable of understanding the *meaning* of the suffering it overcomes. Thus, modern medicine, for example, may prolong human life, but it has nothing to say about the meaning of that life: it may miraculously revive the victim of an unsuccessful suicide attempt, but it has nothing to offer that person that may help him want to go on living — only drugs and surgery to obliterate physically what is essentially a pain of the soul. The Western technique may occasionally be successful in eliminating suffering temporarily, but "this heroic attitude has narrow *limits* to its effectiveness. It breaks down before the more profound suffering of the soul, i.e., the suffering that escapes the control of the aggressive will. It too often buries the fame of its victory over the external suffering of life in the deeper suffering of a hardened heart and cold bitterness. It only *drives* suffering into the *depths* of the soul — out of pride to acknowledge that there is a point where the controlling will is forced to break down".[88]

So greatly has the West, enamoured with the "successes" of its boasted sciences and technology, ignored and repressed the question of meaning, that experiences of meaninglessness, apathy, and detachment — in general, the inability to feel much of anything — are the greatest sources of agony and despair in the Western world today.[89] Suffering has been driven so deep into the human soul that modern humanity seems everywhere on the verge of screaming out, like the figure portrayed by Edvard Munch, or erupting into violence, in ways that are now commonplace. (Hardly anyone seemed surprised when a California high school student gunned down several small children because she was "bored" by Mondays!) Continued one-sided pursuit of this technique will prove disastrous to the West, Scheler warned.[90]

On the other hand, though, the Eastern technique of non-resistance has been increasingly unable to cope with such problems as over-population, and so the East has turned increasingly to Western techniques of economy and technology to overcome suffering in the external world. The task before us, then, in the "world-age of adjustment", Scheler suggested, is to bring together the two major techniques for eliminating suffering: "In all areas where ills may be encountered and in all areas where goods of positive vital values are produced — whether it be for war and peace, disease and health, growth of population and its inhibition for the sake of higher quality, for economy and industry — we must learn systematically to posit *both basic principles of all possible techniques* and their correlate forms of knowledge *simultaneously* and *alternately* in order to restore a meaningful balance of humanity". And he optimistically added, "in Europe and North America a *vigorous epoch of metaphysics and psychic techniques* is likely to follow the positive and technological epoch of so-called 'modern times', while in Asia an epoch of *positive science* and *technology* will replace the strongly one-sided metaphysical epochs of those cultures".[91]

Thus, Scheler's notion of phenomenology as psychic technique of non-resistance must be understood not only, like Husserl's phenomenology, as a response to the "crisis" of Western civilization, but more broadly as a manifestation of the current "world-age of adjustment", wherein new modes of human self-understanding are emerging. As such, it must be grasped in its essential relationship to all other modes of psychic technique of non-resistance. In emphasizing phenomenology's connection with various types of mysticism and Socratic philosophy, we intend in no way to minimize major differences, but only to identify a fundamental point of similarity and departure. By so doing, we can better appreciate the enormous, rich possibilities which Scheler envisioned for phenomenology, possibilities which extend far beyond the egological "method" articulated by Husserl. Phenomenology as psychic technique of non-resistance is not only a manner of essential viewing but much more broadly a comprehensive "attitude" toward the world which also allows us as persons to deal with the world and its sufferings — practically and meaningfully.

147

NOTES

1. Another was Charles Sanders Pierce, whose phenomenology comes much closer to Scheler's than to Husserl's. See Herbert Spiegelberg, "Husserl and Peirce's Phenomenologies: Coincidence or Interaction", *Philosophy and Phenomenological Research* 17 (December 1956), pp. 183–84. And Spiegelberg well notes Scheler's independence of Husserl in "The Phenomenology of Essences: Max Scheler", *The Phenomenological Movement: A Historical Introduction* (The Hague: Martinus Nijhoff, 1960), I, pp. 228–270.
2. E.g., Marvin Farber, *Basic Issues of Philosophy: Experience, Reality, and Human Values* (New York: Harper & Row, 1968), p. 222, and *Phenomenology and Existence: Toward a Philosophy within Nature* (New York: Harper & Row, 1967), p. 20.
3. Scheler, Letter to Adolf Grimme, 4 May 1917, as cited in Manfred S. Frings, *Zur Phänomenologie der Lebensgemeinschaft, Beihefte zur Zeitschrift für philosophische Forschung*, Vol. 24 (Meisenheim am Glan: Verlag Anton Hain, 1971), p. 78f n16. Indeed, Husserl's only significant influence on Scheler seems to have come from his notion of categorical intuition, as presented in the Sixth Investigation of the *Logical Investigations*. See also Scheler's remarks on Husserl in the Preface to his Jena Habilitationsschrift, *Die transzendentale und die psychologische Methode*, 2nd ed. (1922), 3rd ed. in *Frühe Schriften*, ed. Frings, vol. 1 of the *Gesammelte Werke* (Bern: Francke Verlag, 1971), pp. 201–3; Scheler, "Die deutsche Philosophie der Gegenwart" (1922) in *Wesen und Formen der Sympathie*, ed. Frings, vol. 7 of the *Gesammelte Werke* (1973), pp. 259–326; David R. Lachterman, "Translator's Introduction" to Scheler, *Selected Philosophical Essays* (Evanston: Northwestern University Press, 1973), pp. xix–xx; "Max Scheler: A Descriptive Analysis of the Concept of Ultimate Reality", *Ultimate Reality and Meaning* 3 (1980), p. 135.
4. Frings, "Foreward" to *Max Scheler (1874–1928) Centennial Essays*, ed. Frings (The Hague: Martinus Nijhoff, 1974), pp. vii–viii, and *Max Scheler: A Concise Introduction into the World of a Great Thinker* (Pittsburgh: Duquesne University Press, 1965), pp. 23–24; Lewis Coser, "Max Scheler: An Introduction", in Scheler, *Ressentiment*, trans. William W. Holdheim (New York: Free Press of Glencoe, 1961), p. 10.
5. E.G. Aron Gurwitsch, *Studies in Phenomenology and Psychology* (Evanston: Northwestern University Press, 1966), pp. 110–11; Farber, *Basic Issues of Philosophy*, pp. 212, 222–29, and *Phenomenology and Existence*, pp. 4, 20, 33, 75.
6. "Phänomenologie und Erkenntnistheorie", *Schriften aus dem Nachlass*, vol. 1, *Zur Ethik und Erkenntnislehre*, ed. Maria Scheler, vol. 10 on the *Gesammelte Werke* (1957), p. 380; "Phenomenology and the Theory of Cognition", *Selected Philosophical Essays*, p. 137.
7. "Probleme einer Soziologie des Wissens", *Wissensformen und die Gesellschaft*, 2nd ed., ed. Maria Scheler, vol. 8 of the *Gesammelte Werke* (1960).
8. Scheler thus claims that his *Sociology of Knowledge* is propaedeutic for his metaphysics. *Wissensformen und die Gesellschaft*, p. 12. In this regard the work of Max Weber was very influential on Scheler, for he demonstrates that not only does economics influence religion, as Marx argued in *The German Ideology* (New York: International Publishers, 1963), esp. pp. 27–43, but also religion influences economics by providing it with a "spirit" of "ethos". Weber writes: "But it is, of course, not my aim to substitute for a one-sided materialistic [e.g., Marx] an equally one-sided spiritualistic causal interpretation for culture and of history. Each is equally possible, but each if it does not serve as the preparation, but as the conclusion of an investigation, accomplishes equally little in the interest of historical truth". The *Protestant Ethic and the Spirit of Capitalism*, trans. Talcott Parsons (New York: Scharles Scribner's Sons, 1958), p. 183; also see p. 27.
9. *Ideen zu einer reinen Phänomenologie und phänomenologischen Philosophie*, Bk. 1, *Allgemeine Einführung in die reine Phänomenologie, 1st–3rd eds.*, ed. Karl Schuhmann, Vol. 3, No. 1,

148

of Husserliana (The Hague: Martinus Nijhoff, 1976), trans. W.R. Boyce Gibson (New York: Collier, 1962), pp. 72–73.

10. "Idealismus – Realismus", *Späte Schriften*, ed. Frings, Vol. 9 of the Gesammelte Werke (1976), p. 190; "Idealism and Realism", *Selected Philosophical Essays*, p. 295. Such a comment is not intended to discount the insights of philosophies and phenomenologies centered in egological consciousness and thus does not constitute an *ad hominem* argument. Rather, it is meant to call our attention to the fact that part of our essential understanding of a philosophy or phenomenology is seeing it within its proper socio-historical setting.

11. *"The sociological nature of all knowledge* is indubitable". *Wissensformen und die Gesellschaft*, p. 58; *Sociology of Knowledge*, p. 72. Also see *Wissensformen*, pp. 60–63, and *Sociology*, pp. 73–75. "The natural world-view is essentially the intuition of a human community". *Schriften aus dem Nachlass*, vol. 1, p. 404; "Phenomenology and the Theory of Cognition", p. 168.

12. Scheler, *Schriften aus dem Nachlass*, vol. 2, *Erkenntnislehre und Metaphysik*, ed. Frings, vol. 11 of the *Gesammelte Werke* (1979), pp. 156ff.

13. Only secondarily does this single becoming tendency differentiate into force centers and vital centers, which in turn become objectified into inorganic and organic nature. Frings, *Max Scheler*, p.33, and "Max Scheler", pp. 138, 140. Such a view, long dismissed by biologists, has been supported recently by Max Delbruck, 1969 recipient of the Nobel Prize in Physiology and Medicine. See his "Mind from Matter?" *The American Scholar* 47 (Summer 1978), pp. 339–353.

14. *Späte Schriften*, p. 230; "Idealism and Realism", p. 344.

15. *Späte Schriften*, p. 239; "Idealism and Realism", p. 354.

16. *Die Stellung des Menschen im Kosmos* (1928), in *Späte Schriften*, p. 43; *Man's Place in Nature*, trans. Hans Meyerhoff (New York: Noonday, 1961), p. 53.

17. *"Erkenntnis und Arbeit"*, *Wissensformen und die Gesellschaft*, p. 372.

18. 15th ed. (Tübingen: Max Niemeyer, 1979), p. 73; *Being and Time*, trans. John Macquarrie and Edward Robinson (New York: Harper & Row, 1962), p. 103. Emphasis in the original.

19. I am indebted to Professor A.G. Pleydell-Pearce of the University of Birmingham, who suggested to me this connection between Scheler's notion of resistance and Heidegger's description of the being of the tool as present-at-hand.

20. *Sein und Zeit*, p. 137; *Being and Time*, p. 177. Emphasis in the original.

21. *Sein und Zeit*, p. 210; *Being and Time*, pp. 253–54. Emphasis in the original.

22. *Sein und Zeit*, p. 211; *Being and Time*, p. 255.

23. "Beiträge zur Lösung der Frage vom Ursprung unseres Glaubens an die Realität der Aussenwelt und seinem Recht" (1980), *Die geistige Welt: Einleitung in die Philosophie des Lebens*, Pt. 1, *Abhandlungen zur Grundlegung der Geisteswissenschaften*, 4th ed., Vol. 5 of the *Gesammelte Werke*, ed. George Misch (Stuttgart: B.G. Teubner, 1964), pp. 90–138. Indeed, throughout his discussion of resistance in *Sein und Zeit*, Heidegger speaks of Dilthey and Scheler interchangeable, without distinguishing their notions of the term.

24. *Späte Schriften*, p. 260.

25. *Späte Schriften*, p. 260.

26. Frings, *Person und Dasein: Zur Frage der Ontology des Wertseins* (The Hague: Martinus Nijhoff, 1969) is the most extensive comparison of these terms of Scheler and Heidegger. Also see Frings, "Heidegger and Scheler", *Philosophy Today* 12 (Spring 1968), pp. 21–30.

27. *Sein und Zeit*, p. 202; *Being and Time*, p. 246.

28. *Späte Schriften*, p. 262.

29. *Späte Schriften*, p. 261, 266–67.

30. *Späte Schriften*, p. 263.

31. *Die Stellung des Menschen im Kosmos*, pp. 16–17; *Man's Place in Nature*, p. 14; *Schriften*

zur Soziologie und Weltanschauungslehre, 2nd ed., ed. Maria Scheler, Vol. 6 of the *Gesammelte Werke* (1963), pp. 43–44; "*The Meaning of Suffering*", trans. Daniel Liderbach, S.F., in *Max Scheler (1874–1928) Centennial Essays*, pp. 129–30.

32. *Schriften zur Soziologie und Weltanschauungslehre*, p. 36; "The Meaning of Suffering", p. 121.

33. *Schriften zur Soziologie und Weltanschauungslehre*, p. 57; "The meaning of Suffering", p. 145.

34. *Wissensformen und die Gesellschaft*, p. 138; *Sociology of Knowledge*, pp. 141, 215f n 117.

35. *Späte Schriften*, p. 41; *Man's Place in Nature*, p. 50.

36. *Späte Schriften*, p. 43; *Man's Place in Nature*, p. 51.

37. *Wissensformen und die Gesellschaft*, p. 137; *Sociology of Knowledge*, p. 140.

38. *Späte Schriften*, p. 44; *Man's Place in Nature*, p. 54.

39. *Wissensformen und die Gesellschaft*, p. 141; *Sociology of Knowledge*, p. 143.

40. *The Essence of Buddhism*, p. 13, as quoted by Thomas Merton, *Zen and the Birds of Appetite* (New York: New Directions, 1968), p. 94.

41. Suzuki, in *Zen and the Birds of Appetite*, pp. 133–34.

42. Scheler defended Christianity against Nietzsche's criticisms in his *Ressentiment*. There he notes that genuine Christian love of one's enemy is not rooted in weakness but in strength: one is able to take revenge but *prefers* not to do so (pp. 94–95). Non-resistance to suffering because one is *unable* to resist, has no effect. See also *Wissensformen und die Gesellschaft*, p. 141; *Sociology of Knowledge*, p. 143.

43. Jesus's refusal to defend himself is further dramatized by the pacifist Dostoyevsky in "The Grand Inquisitor", *The Brothers Karamozov*.

44. Merton, p. 56.

45. As quoted in Merton, p. 109.

46. Despite these similarities between Buddhist and Christian ethics of suffering, Scheler suggests that Buddhism is the superior. First, non-resistance to suffering "is not as essentially and systematically meaningful for Christianity as it is for Buddhism". Secondly, Christianity lacks specific techniques like those Buddha inherited and developed from Yoga; by contrast to the latter, Christian prayer is a very vague and undisciplined technique. And thirdly, Jesus's personal example is much more ambiguous than Buddha's. Jesus is not altogether non-resistant to suffering, for example, in his clearing the money changers from the temple, in his opposition to the Pharisees, and in his last desperate cry on the cross. *Schriften zur Soziologie und Weltanschauungslehre*, pp. 55–56; "The meaning of Suffering", pp. 143–44.

47. Seng-ts'an, *Hsin-hsin Ming*, as quoted by Alan W. Watts, *The Way of Zen* (New York: New American Library, "Mentor", 1957), p. 116.

48. In *Zen and the Birds of Appetite*, p. 134.

49. "Foreward" to Suzuki, *An Introduction to Zen Buddhism* (New York: Grove, 1964), p. 211. Cf. Husserl.

50. *An Introduction to Zen Buddhism*, p. 38. This does not mean, Suzuki further explains, that Buddhism has nothing to do with the intellect. On the contrary, Buddhism seeks a higher level of intellect than logic can provide.

51. Suzuki, p. 35.

52. Suzuki, p. 33.

53. Jung, p. 20.

54. Watts, pp. 120, 127.

55. Suzuki, p. 33.

56. Suzuki, p. 35.

57. Merton, p. 52.

58. I *Cor* 1: 17–23.

150

59. Merton, p. 55.

60. *De trinitate* xii, 11.

61. "The perfection of the rational creature consists not only in what belongs to it in respect of its nature, but also in what it acquires through a supernatural participation of Divine goodness. Hence . . . man's ultimate happiness consists in a supernatural vision of God, to which vision man cannot attain unless he be taught by God . . . Since man's nature is dependent on a higher nature, natural knowledge does not suffice for its perfection and some supernatural knowledge is necessary". *Summa Theologiae*, Pt. I of Pt. II, ques. 2, art. 3.

62. John Dominic Crossan has shown that Jesus in his parables, like the Buddhist masters in their *koans*, used language against itself, as a vehicle for *seeing* beyond language and reason, and represents the culmination of a long Judaic tradition of iconoclasm. See his *In Parables: The Challenge of the Historical Jesus* (New York: Harper & Row, 1973), *The Dark Interval: Towards a Theology of Story* (Niles, I11..: Argus Communications, 1975), *Raid on the Articulate: Cosmic Eschatology in Jesus and Borges* (New York: Harper & Row, 1976), and *Finding Is the First Act: Trove Folktales and Jesus' Treasure Parable* (Philadelphia: Fortress Press, 1979).

63. Plato, *The Republic* VII, 515.

64. Scheler, *Schriften zur Soziologie und Weltanschauungslehre*, p. 66; "The Meaning of Suffering", p. 156.

65. *Späte Schriften*, p. 44; *Man's Place in Nature*, p. 54.

66. *Späte Schriften*, p. 42; *Man's Place in Nature*, p. 52.

67. Wittgenstein showed deep appreciation for the importance of silence for philosophical insight when he so beautifully wrote: "Sometimes the voice of a philosophical thought is so soft that the noise of spoken words is enough to drown it and prevent it from being heard, if one is questioned and has to speak". *Zettel* (Oxford: Blackwell, 1967), no. 453. See also Brian Klug, "On Doing, Teaching and Studying Philosophy", *Studies in Higher Education* 4 (1979), pp. 243–54, an important contribution to the rethinking of philosophy.

70. Indeed, Theaetetus, through his dialogue with Socrates (*Theaetetus* 210), is emptied of all opinion and left silent:
    Socrates. And are you still in labor and travail, my dear friend, or have you brought all that you have to say about knowledge to the birth?
    Theaetetus. I am sure, Socrates, that you have elicited from me a good deal more than ever was in me.
    Socrates. And does not my art show that you have brought forth wind, and that the offspring of your brain are not worth bringing up?
    Theaetetus. Very true.

71. *Theaetetus* 155.

72. *Wissensformen und die Gesellschaft*, p. 139; *Sociology of Knowledge*, p. 139.

73. *Theaetetus* 210.

74. Those of the analytic tradition, for exampe, have long accused phenomenologists of "mysticism"! Like those of Socrates' day who accused philosophers of seeking death, such critics do not understand the truth they utter.

75. E.g., *Sein und Zeit*, pp. 27–31; *Being and Time*, pp. 49–55.

76. *Späte Schriften*, p. 42; *Man's Place in Nature*, p. 52.

77. *Wissensformen und die Gesellschaft*, pp. 138–39; *Sociology of Knowledge*, pp. 140–41.

78. *Späte Schriften*, pp. 43–44; *Man's Place in Nature*, pp. 53–54.

79. *Fundamental Problems of Philosophy: The World of Action and the Dialectical World*, trans. David A. Dilworth (Tokyo: Sophia University, 1970), *Intelligibility and the Philosophy of Nothingness: Three Philosophical Essays*, trans. Robert Schinzinger (Honolulu: East–West Center Press, 1958), and *A Study of Good*, trans. V.H. Viglielmo (Japanese National Commission for UNESCO, 1960); Merton, pp. 67–78.

80. Trans. Ralph Manheim (New Haven: Yale University Press, 1959), p. 143.
81. Richard E. Palmer, *Hermeneutics: Interpretation Theory in Schleiermacher, Dilthey, Heidegger, and Gadamer* (Evanston: Northwestern University Press, 1969), pp. 145–146.
82. Trans. John M. Anderson and Hans Freund (New York: Harper, 1966), p. 62.
83. *Wahrheit und Methode* (Tübingen: J.C.B. Mohr [Paul Siebeck] 1960), p. 338; *Truth and Method* (New York: Seabury, 1975), p. 319.
84. *Wahrheit und Methode*, p. 339; *Truth and Method*, p. 320.
85. *Wahrheit und Methode*, p. 345; *Truth and Method*, p. 326.
86. Palmer, p. 198.
87. "Der Mensch im Weltalter des Ausgleichs", in *Späte Schriften*, pp. 145–170, esp. pp. 159–161; "Man in the Era of Adjustment", *Philosophical Perspectives*, trans. Oscar A. Haac (Boston: Beacon Press, 1958), pp. 94–126, also reprinted as "Man in an Age of Adjustment", in *Classic Social Theory*, ed. Hendrik M. Ruitenbeck (New York: E.P. Dutton, 1963), pp. 385–414, esp. 402–5.
88. *Schriften zur Soziologie und Weltanschauungslehre*, p. 66; "The Meaning of Suffering", p. 156.
89. E.g., Rollo May, *Love and Will* (New York: Dell, 1969), especially pp. 27–33. Economist E.F. Schumacher concurs with this observation: "Science cannot produce ideas by which we could live ... That study has its own value which I am not inclined to belittle; it tells (a person) a great deal about how things work in nature or engineering: but it tells him nothing about the *meaning* of life and can in no way cure his estrangement and secret despair". *Small Is Beautiful: Economics As If People Mattered* (New York: Harper & Row, 1973), p. 80. (Emphasis added.)
90. "The Western technicism of outer nature and its correlate in the realm of knowledge, positive science, threatens man with enmeshment into the mechanism of things that it intends to control *to such an extent* that this process without the counter-balance of the two completely *opposite* principles of knowledge *and* power, essentially belonging to one another, can end only in the certain fall of the Western world". *Wissensformen und die Gesellschaft*, p. 140; *Sociology of Knowledge*, p. 142. Schumacher concurs with the judgment when he writes, "The resulting confusion is indescribable. What is the *Leitbild*, as the Germans say, the guiding image, in accordance with which young people could try to form and educate themselves? There is non", because a one-sided scientism is inherently incapable of providing one (p. 92).
91. *Wissensformen und die Gesellschaft*, p. 140; *Sociology of Knowledge*, p. 142. Schumacher provides a model for such a synthesis of Eastern and Western techniques in his notion of "Buddhist Economics", pp. 50–58.

The Self In Question
by
Hugh J. Silverman

For Dostoevsky's Underground Man, the problematic of the self is central, but the self *per se* escapes centrality in the act of questioning itself. In Heideggerian fashion, I propose to introduce the question of the self so that it might demonstrate its own decentering. The Underground Man's self-questioning arises from his self-doubts and leads to what Michel Foucault might call an archaeology of the self. By following the path of this discursive practice, which involves self-dividing — the subject from its foundations — without ever attaining division of self from itself, the Underground Man's identity will show itself in its diversity and dispersal. What will become evident is the impossibility of unification and hence contentment. All that remains are questions.

In the *Notes from Underground*, we find the following imperative: "Gentlemen, I am tormented by questions; answer them for me".[1] The Underground Man is continually confronted with questions, but what is their character and origin? They present themselves from the outside, the surface, from above ground. They come from a certain basis — the ground of reason. The Underground Man, however, is *under*-ground. He is without basis or grounding, for to be underground is to be separate from the surface. When we first encounter him, the Underground Man has been underground for at least sixteen years. From the perspective of a forty-year-old, he recounts the circumstances of his initial conditions of alienation, which occurred at the age of twenty-four. "Even then", he writes, "I already had the underground in my soul".[2]

The questions which torment the Underground Man plague him in his underground. But they come from the outside. The underground is not totally isolated from the ground. Questions pierce through; they must be dealt with. Who is to deal with them? The Underground Man claims that he will not! Either he refuses or he is incapable. Hence he writes: "Gentlemen, I am tormented by questions, answer them for me".

These "Gentlemen" are presumably part of the outside. Since the questions are grounded, someone who is also grounded should answer them. That would

W.S. Hamrick (ed.) *Phenomenology in Practice and Theory.*
© 1985 Martinus Nijhoff Publishers, Dordrecht/Boston/Lancaster
ISBN 90 247 2926 2. Printed in the Netherlands.

154

be the most reasonable solution. In such matters, one should go to "primary causes". Reason is surely bound up with "primary causes". When Aristotle claimed along with Plato that man is a rational animal, he associated reason with the four causes or types of explanation. The four causes are ways of explaining the nature of things – *physis* – nature – the laws (*logoi*) of nature. Hence primary causes are grounded in the laws of nature. Others who have reason (*logos*), like these Gentlemen, will surely be able to answer the questions.

The Underground Man cannot answer them, because he still has doubts. His knowledge is not founded in a particular set of laws of nature. His primary causes are vulnerable – they are open to alteration. When one has doubts, one has difficulty acting; and answering questions is a form of action. So he says, "To begin to act, you know, you must first have your mind completely at ease and without a trace of doubt left in it. Well how am I, for example, to set my mind at rest? Where are the primary causes on which I am to build? Where are my bases? Where am I to get them from? I exercise myself in the process of thinking, consequently with me every primary cause at once draws after itself another still more primary, and so on to infinity".[3]

The Underground Man's primary causes are unstable. They have no core, no essence, no center. They are continually in flux. With respect to his primary causes, he is like the people stranded on Gericault's "Raft of the Medusa" in the middle of the ocean – without mooring, without a point of reference.

"I exercise myself in the process of thinking", he says. But in so doing, he does not answer my questions. The self is exercised in the process of thinking but the self is not engaged in answering questions. The self is at sea; the self does not have a center. Only through thinking is the self brought into play. The process of thinking puts the self in question. Thinking calls up that which thinks. Descartes' *cogito* is the establishment of an *ego sum*. For the Underground Man, *cogito* leads only to an *ego me quaero*. This is not to say that the Underground Man spends his time placing his self in question, as does, for example, Samuel Beckett's Malone in *Malone Dies*. The Underground Man is less concerned with his identity than with his relation to well-founded rational primary causes, which are based in the laws of nature. To focus upon personal identity is a problem for reason and is answerable by grounded Gentlemen.

The Underground Man's relation to primary causes is a question of will or desire. He is concerned that will or desire might be reduced to the laws of nature, to systems of reason: "you see, gentlemen, reason, gentlemen, is an excellent thing, there is no disputing that, but reason is only reason and can satisfy man's rational faculty, while will is a manifestation of all life, that is of all human life including reason as well as all impulses".[4]

Associating "impulses" with what he also calls "feeling" we have the three aspects of the self – of human life: (1) will or desire, (2) reason, and (3) feeling. The Underground Man is not particularly concerned with feeling. He mentions it only a few times. And he reveals feeling perhaps only when he was convincing Liza of the future despair that she would undergo as a prostitute. What we might take as synonymous with feeling, i.e. impulse, reveals itself much more readily. The Underground Man is often impulsive, e.g. when the police officer moves him aside, when he decides to slap Zverkov, when he rejects Liza the day she goes to him. But his impulses are held back or delayed by some combination of reason and will.

He understands reason and will to be opposed to one another – or at least will must complement reason and impulse in order to have full human life. Reason however tends to impose itself, just as urbanism imposes itself on Goethe's Werther when he says that "the town itself is disagreeable; but then all around it nature is inexpressably beautiful",[5] and on Wordsworth when he seeks to recollect his childhood or his moments when he is interfused with nature. Nature for Dostoevsky's Underground Man is not that with which one seeks fusion. The self must refuse Nature and its laws. There is an antinomy between will and reason or its counterpart: the laws of nature. The true core of the self is not the rational part of the soul as Plato might have claimed. The Underground Man's conception is purely Christian – more of the Renaissance humanist type than the Augustinian variety however. The true core of the self is the will – the free will which can refuse the dictates of reason. The self is particularly irrational and antinomian; that is, it opposes laws (*nomos*) and conventions; it defies $2 \times 2 = 4$; it refuses to be a stop in an organ always ready to be played upon: "What is a man without desire, a man without free will and without choice, if not a stop in an organ?"[6]

But the minute that he makes this claim, he adds, "What do you think? Let us consider the probability – can such a thing happen or not?"[7] The self is antinomian, but it always defines itself in relation to *nomos*, to conventional laws. Probability is an outgrowth of reason. The Underground Man is prepared to submit his desires or free will to the calculus of reason: "Some day they will discover the laws of our so-called free will – so joking aside, there may one day probably be something like a table of desires so that we really shall choose in accordance with it".[8]

Fifteen years before writing *Notes from Underground*, Dostoevsky was arrested and condemned to execution for participating in a revolutionary group that read the works of the utopian writer Charles Fourier. Fourier had proposed a theory of personality in which all desires could be specified and harmoniously combined. Now Dostoevsky has his Underground Man question such a prospect. At the same time that the Underground Man extolls freedoms of the will and of desires, he compromises them by applying reason to them. Like Fourier, he suggests the probabilities of systematizing desires just as

Newton claimed that Nature can be systematized. Yet he resists a resolution of the opposition between reason and desire: "You shout at me . . . that, after all, no one is depriving me of my will, that all they are concerned with is that my will should somehow of itself, of its own free will, coincide with my own normal interests, with the laws of nature and arithmetic".[9]

They — an amorphous "they" — want his will to coincide with their norms, conventions and laws. But free will is not simply desiring what will be, as defined and elaborated by reason. Free will is not simple conformity with reason. Free will is an "advantage" — man's only advantage. Only with free will can man break down classifications and "shatter systems evolved by lovers of mankind for the happiness of mankind".[10] Free will interferes with all possible constructs of reason. But at the same time that it opposes law, free will accounts for a certain despair. Just as Kierkegaard's Abraham must refuse reason and ethical choice in order to make a leap of faith, to will the impossible, to define his true self through faith, the Underground Man defies reason only after he is aware of it.

One cannot go underground until one has become conscious of the limits of reason, just as an innocence through revelation is not possible in Blake unless one has gone through both pure innocence *and* experience. The Underground Man is intelligent, perhaps too intelligent. The only way for someone to go underground is to become aware of reason and its limits. Free will can be asserted against reason (*anti-nomos* and *anti-logos*). One cannot go underground without consciousness *of* — consciousness of law, of reason, of system. However, withdrawing to the underground, one isolates the self. When one begins to write from underground one places the self in question. From such a perspective it is the self and only the self that can be brought to the fore.

The underground is a man's final retreat. Where Pascal and Kierkegaard appeal to silence as the realm of faith — faith cannot be assessed externally — Abraham's leap can only be *felt* by him — the Underground Man's retreat is nothing so exalted. For the Underground Man, the underground is as small, dingy, and dark as his apartment. The unfurnished apartment — his privacy, his shell, his cave in which he conceals himself from all mankind[11] — is the physical analogue for his psychological retreat. In the same way that he retires to his appartment, he writes, "if you won't deign to give me your attention, then, after all, I won't speak to you, I do have my underground".[12] In a way, the underground is his sole possession. It is what is most truly his. His security and his last resort lie here.

All the rest is perhaps sham and appearance. What he presents to others — the officer, his old schoolmates, Liza — is at most a mask. With them he is a person, but in the etymological sense of the word — a role, a *persona*. Wordsworth in the "Ode on Intimations of Immortality", stanze VII, speaks of life as that which is played by the little Actor donning another part, but done "with

all the Persons''. But the ''moments in the being of eternal Silence'' (stanza
IX), where the eternal Soul appears, are an escape from the conventions of
vocation. For Wordsworth going underground is a recollection of eternal bliss.
For the Underground Man it is the last outpost, the depths of despair. With
Wordsworth, the presence of moments of silence and absence is a time of hope;
the Underground Man clings to underground, his mask, as his only mode of
self-affirmation. Like Wordsworth, however, the external self is only a false
double presented to society. Blake's vision, Wordsworth's intimations of immortality, Kierkegaard's leap of faith, and Nietzsche's *Uebermensch* are all a
step beyond the present system of things. The Underground Man's
underground is a step *under*. None of them seeks to build a utopian Crystal
Palace. Although all of them deal with the self, only the Underground Man's
self is placed in question. His true self is on the fringe; the selves of Blake,
Wordsworth, Kierkegaard, and Nietzsche go beyond. Each is a rebel, but only
the Underground Man cannot face others.

What price consciousness? Hegel proposed in his *Phenomenology of Mind*
that self-consciousness arises only from the desire of others. As Fichte would
put it, Ego follows from the positing of non-Ego: ''I am sure man will never
renounce real suffering, that is, destruction and chaos. Why, after all, suffering is the sole origin of consciousness''. [13] The dialectic of suffering and consciousness of that suffering is far better than simple conformity − identity −
with the laws of nature. Only by suffering does one become aware that self is
other than these laws of nature. This is not a joyful consciousness − the
wisdom brought about by consciousness of suffering is a dismal, humiliating
experience. Yet it is an awareness of selfhood. The self can only arise by opposition, by refusing to accept simply that 2 x 2 = 4:

> How much better it is to understand it all, to be conscious of it all, all
> the impossibilities and the stone walls, not to resign yourself to a single
> one of those impossibilities and stone walls if it disgusts you to resign
> yourself; to reach, through the most inevitable logical combinations, the
> most revolting conclusions on the everlasting theme that you are yourself
> somehow to blame for the stone wall, through again it is as clear as day
> you are not to blame in the least, and therefore grinding your teeth in silent
> impotence sensuously to sink into inertia, brooding on the fact that it
> turns out that there is even no one for you to feel vindictive against, that
> you have not, and perhaps never will have, an object for your spite ... [14]

The Underground Man lives on spite. In the very opening of the *Notes*, he
identifies himself as ''sick'' and ''spiteful''. Spite is his mode of existence. He
cannot affirm that he exists except by way of spite. Spite is the character of his
refusal. All consciousness, as one learns in Husserl's phenomenology, is consciousness *of*. The Underground Man is conscious of others. But the way in
which he is conscious of others is through spite. Spite is his manner of placing

his self in question. Spite is his awareness of suffering and the expression of his free will. He is spiteful of the police officer who moves him out of the way. The most the Underground Man can do to reassert himself is to bump into the policeman in the park. Yet the moment that the other confronts him, he steps aside. Nevertheless, the Underground Man maintains his spite against the policeman – thereby asserting himself, making his self the contrary of the policeman, bringing his self into focus for his own *Notes.*

When he has dinner with his old schoolmates, he vows to assert himself – to make them know his own suffering. By inviting himself to dinner he makes his presence known. The expression of his contempt, however, is limited to getting drunk and pacing beside the table for three hours. He is full of spite against Zverkov and the others, but the best he can do is to apologize and to admit to them that he had insulted them. However, Zverkov even refuses to accept that he had been insulted. The Underground Man is too insignificant to be in a position to insult Zverkov. Even though he is a nobody for the others, their very refusal of him is enough for him to suffer and to bring his self into question. By suffering, he becomes spiteful. Consciousness of suffering *qua* spite is self-affirming. If there were no ground, he could not go underground. His selfness is possible because "they" – those men of reason, – those who abide by convention, – reject him.

His encounter with Liza almost destroyes it all. He becomes someone in that he affects her. He communicates with someone else in a non-spiteful fashion. Yet in so doing, he is placed in a position of helping her, helping her to rise up out of her servile state. But he cannot help, since he has no rational function with respect to the laws of nature. Just as Sonya is Raskolnikov's hope for salvation in Dostoevsky's *Crime and Punishment*, which he published three years later, Liza is the Underground Man's possibility of hope. She comes to him after three days. He refuses her; he brings her to the full consciousness of her suffering – that no one can help. At most, she will live in a house of prostitution with a letter from a man who expressed his love to her – not the Underground Man but another. "Which is better – cheap happiness or exalted sufferings?"[15] he asks. Like Goethe's Werther, he chooses the latter! Liza would not even accept money from the Underground Man. He was thrown back entirely into his own underground world, where his only self-affirmation is to write notes about himself.

He deceives himself, and lies to himself, just as he presents a front to others, sometimes lying to them. This, however, is also his comfort. By lying to others, he can define himself, by distinguishing his will from their rationality, their system of rules and laws, their moral codes which prohibit lying. By lying to and deceiving himself, he attempts to find the very core that is truly his self. Self-deceit is his way of asserting a self which can be deceived:

I want to try the experiment whether one can be perfectly frank, even with oneself, and not take fright at the whole truth. I will observe, parenthetically, that Heine maintains that a true autobiography is almost an impossibility, and that man is bound to lie about himself. He considers that Rousseau certainly told lies about himself in his confessions, and even intentionally lied, out of vanity. I am convinced that Heine is right; I understand very well that sometimes one may, just out of sheer vanity, attribute regular crimes to oneself, and indeed I can very well conceive that kind of vanity. But Heine judged people who made their confessions to the public. I, however, am writing for myself, and wish to declare once and for all that if I write as though I were addressing readers, that is simply because it is easier for me to write in that way. It is merely a question of form, only an empty form − I shall never have readers. I have made this plain already.[16]

The "Gentlemen" are fictitious. Yet they represent the ground − those who would be − as Montaigne says to his readers: "unreasonable to spend your leisure on so frivolous and vain a subject".[17] Montaigne also recognized that the reader comes from a base of reason. For this same reason, the Underground Man does not want any readers − even though he offers at the beginning: "I will talk about myself".[18] He would prefer to maintain his underground self in its nameless isolation. In fact, the "I" − the self − of the editor indicates that the "paradoxalist's" notes do not end where the novel ends. The notes and hence the spiteful sufferings presumably still continue − underground. But who then is the editor? Is it Dostoevsky? Or is it a narrated self who, like a voyeur, has peered into the traces of an underground self? Such peering, such an archeology of the self, is perhaps at most the bringing to light of a certain self − making known the question of its existence as it places itself in question.

NOTES

1. Dostoevsky, *Notes From Underground*, trans. Ralph E. Matlaw (New York: Dutton, 1960), p. 29.
2. Dostoevsky, p. 42.
3. Dostoevsky, p. 16.
4. Dostoevsky, p. 25.
5. Goethe, *The Sorrows of Young Werther*, trans. Victor Lange (New York: Holt, Rinehart, and Winston, 1949), p. 2.
6. Dostoevsky, p. 24.
7. Dostoevsky, p. 24.
8. Dostoevsky, p. 25.
9. Dostoevsky, p. 28.
10. Dostoevsky, p. 20.
11. Dostoevsky, p. 100.
12. Dostoevsky, p. 32.
13. Dostoevsky, p. 31.
14. Dostoevsky, p. 12.
15. Dostoevsky, p. 114.
16. Dostoevsky, p. 35.
17. Michel de Montaigne, "To the Reader", *Essays*, trans. Donald M. Frame (Stanford: Stanford University Press, 1957), p. 2.
18. Dostoevsky, p. 6.

Existential Phenomenology and Applied Philosophy
by
Thomas Attig

> When Eudamidas saw the aged Xenocrates and his
> disciples in the Academy, engaged in seeking for the
> truth, he asked: "Who is this old man?" And when he
> was told that Xenocrates was a wise man, one of those
> occupied in the search for virtue, he cried: "But when
> does he then propose to use it?"
> – Kierkegaard[1]

The philosopher loves wisdom for its potential contributions to meaningful living. The wise person is mindful of the means to refinement of concepts and ideas and aware of the possibilities of their use, misuse and abuse. He strives to minimize distortion, disrespect and compromise of the integrity and uniqueness of the objects of conceptualization and ideation and to maximize truthfulness. He is ever aware of the need for, and yet sensitive to the limits of, the application of static concepts and ideas to a flowing experience of a dynamic reality. He has a will to sustain the dialectical tensions between the abstract and the concrete, the necessary and the contingent, the universal and the particular, the collective and the individual, theory and experience, and theory and practice. Ultimately, the wise person has the virtue of discernment, creativity and humility in making claims to truth in science, religion, morality, social and political thought, aesthetics and everyday living.

I believe that existential phenomenology both continues and enriches the philosophical tradition of pursuit of such wisdom. In this essay I shall show how existential-phenomenological methods can be used to promote the ends of applied philosophy, where the latter is defined as the cultivation *and* exercise of the understandings, skills and virtues which come with wisdom. I shall do so, in part, through an existential-phenomenological analysis of the love of wisdom. This analysis will serve both to demonstrate the applicability of the methods and to characterize further the peculiar calling of the philosopher.

W.S. Hamrick (ed.) *Phenomenology in Practice and Theory*.
© 1985 Martinus Nijhoff Publishers, Dordrecht/Boston/Lancaster
ISBN 90 247 2926 2. Printed in the Netherlands.

1. Existential Phenomenology as Applied Philosophy

Existential phenomenologists maintain that there can be nothing which is philosophically more important than the careful and detailed exploration and description of the wide range of human experiences. In and through experience persons are involved in the world. They experience the surrounding environment, themselves and other experiencing beings. Their experiences include perceiving, exploring, doubting, reflecting, judging, evaluating, knowing, learning, imagining, remembering, creating, decision-making, feeling, communicating, cooperating, empathizing, befriending and loving. The texture of human involvement in the world is luxuriant. Persons are already involved in experiencing the world even as they begin to develop scientific or philosophical theories about what they encounter. Existential phenomenologists reject abstract theorization which is not scrupulously attentive to its experiential beginnings. They seek to recover full appreciation and understanding of the otherwise taken-for-granted subtleties and nuances of the experiencing which comprises everyday living. On the one hand, if it is through experiences that we come to know the world, then it is plausible that exploring and describing experiences is crucial for understanding the foundations of knowledge. On the other hand, if one of the most central features of human existence is experiencing the world, then exploring and describing the broad range of such experiences leads both to self-discovery and mutual understanding.

Existential phenomenologists are applied philosophers in their preoccupation with the problems of maintaining humility before the richness of experience which is to be captured in a conceptual net if persons are to live mindfully. The phenomenological tradition is one of investigation of the laws, structures or meanings of the phenomena, i.e., that which is experienced *as* it is experienced "as opposed to the way that" it is in itself. It is sustained focusing upon and systematic exploration and articulation of the experiential roots of all theories, be they logical, mathematical, scientific religious, moral, social-political or aesthetic. As such, phenomenology is dedicated to development and refinement of well-wrought concepts grounded in thorough-going attentiveness to what is being conceived, i.e., experience itself.

The existential tradition is one which insists upon the integrity of the existing person. One must live mindfully while not losing sight of the lives of particular persons in their uniqueness which are supposedly illuminated by thought. In Kierkegaard's words,

> Two ways, in general, are open for an existing individual: *Either* he can do his utmost to forget that he is an existing individual, by which he becomes a comic figure, since existence has the remarkable trait of compelling an existing individual to exist whether he wills it or not ... *Or* he can concentrate his entire energy upon the fact that he is an existing in-

dividual. It is from this side, in the first instance, that objectives must be made to modern philosophy; not that it has a mistaken presupposition, but that it has a comical presupposition, occasioned by its having forgotten, in a sort of world-historical absentmindedness, what it means to be a human being. Not indeed, what it means to be a human being in general: for this is the sort of thing that one might even induce a speculative philosopher to agree to: but what it means that you and I and he are human beings, each one for himself.[2]

In short, the insights generated by philosophers must speak to the human condition or they are worthless.

Existential phenomenology is a fusion of the phenomenological and the existential traditions. The means to the recovery of human experience are the phenomenological methods which are to be characterized and illustrated below. The locus of application of the methods is human experiencing existence itself. Existential phenomenology is a movement in philosophy dedicated to sustaining the dialectical tensions between concepts and the existence they are to illuminate in the best sense of the wisdom tradition sketched above. Moreover, being philosophical, as understood within this movement, is a matter of personally appropriating philosophical insight into one's mode of existence as a lover of wisdom. I shall elaborate on this experience of appropriation in what follows.

II. The Love of Wisdom: An Existential-Phenomenological Analysis

Thus far, my treatment of existential phenomenology and its relation to applied philosophy has remained on a purely conceptual plane. If existential phenomenological philosophy has the application which I have claimed for it, then this could be shown best through a more detailed treatment and illustration of the methods in use. I should like now to offer a beginning phenomenological analysis of the experience of being a lover of wisdom, i.e., the experience which I have placed definitionally at the heart of what it is to be a philosopher. I shall (a) focus upon a specific experience where wisdom can make a difference and have a value, (b) explicate the phenomenological method as a key to the cultivation of wisdom in such a case and (c) further illustrate the use of the method to highlight existentially significant elements of the experience of loving such wisdom.

An experience in an intensive care unit. Consider the experience of a man who awakens in an intensive care unit. Asked if he is awake, he asks if it is his wife who addresses him, and he wonders out loud what has happened. The male nurse tells him that he is in the hospital and assures him that his wife is waiting outside. He introduces himself as the one responsible for watching over

164

him in the unit. The patient is still not clear about what is being done or exactly why he is where he is. He is told that his blood pressure is being checked and that he should relax and try not to move. He is in the hospital because he appears to have had a heart attack. The crushing pain is now a vivid memory for him. He says he now only feels weak. In saying as much, he notices that his voice is muffled and slow. For a moment he wonders if he is dying. What could all of the gadgets, wires and tubes be for? He marvels at the large nose of the nurse.

His mental agitation is mirrored in his being physically ill at ease. He is told to keep his arm still, that the tube attached to it is giving him fluid which his body needs. The nurse explains more about his surroundings. The machine that looks like a T.V. with poor programming is helping the staff to keep a close watch on how his heart is beating. The tubes over his ears and leading to his nose are giving him a little more oxygen. Another machine helps his heart to beat regularly and is connected to him with wires. He is again urged to realize that his body needs rest.

Yet, he remains agitated. What will happen next? He is afraid to move his arm. He longs for his wife to be by his side. He is afraid his heart is going to stop. His current state seems worse than dying. His mind races, though his body is rigid with fear.

The nurse notices his frightened look and says it is understandable that he would feel as he does. He promises comfort as he relaxes and gets to know his surroundings. He explains the unit routine further. The nurse will check his blood pressure regularly and help him in turning over. He will have to cough periodically and breathe deeply in order to keep his lungs clear. He will be taught how to cough with a minimum of pain.

He can't believe he will ever let himself cough again. The pain would be unbearable. He might hurt his heart. He is not confident that he can trust the nurse to do the right things.

The nurse then informs him that he will be awakened every two hours for the coughing and that he will have no prolonged periods of rest for the next forty-eight hours. His mind again rushes ahead. He realizes he will likely be where he is for a long time. What about his job? He doubts he'll be able to hold it after this attack. What about his relationship with his wife? He wonders if he will be an invalid, whether he will be able to have sex, whether he will ever be the same.

Again, the nurse notices that he is worried. He recognizes that the patient likely has a lot of questions and assures him that they will talk again in a little while. He insists that the patient rest and not talk. He asks if the patient would like his wife to come in to sit beside him.

Anti-reductionism in phenomenology. This case will illustrate some of the need for phenomenological method and attentiveness to the detailed structures of experience. After suffering the trauma of a heart attack, the patient is encountering a new environment, undergoing transformations in his social relationships and sensing his own finiteness and limitations. In beginning to cope with the changes in his life, he seeks reflective clarity about both the nature of his experiences and about their meaning for the life he must now lead. Persons, such as the patient in this case, stand to gain in self-understanding on the basis of phenomenological reflection on the cognitive-affective dimensions of such experiences. Others, such as the nurse and his wife in this case, can become better able to respond sensitively to human needs as they come to understand the diverse experiences people may have and the meanings which they may attach to them.

As descriptive rather than explanatory, phenomenology is decidedly anti-reductionistic, e.g., in its anti-sensationism in theorizing about perceptual contact with the world. To understand the ongoing processes of experiencing, knowing, and living in the world, the philosopher must overcome any predisposition to believe that experience *has to* be a certain way. A principal watchword of Husserl was, "to the things themselves". It is an admonition to sustain a focus upon the subject matters which theories of all kinds are to illuminate. The philosopher must return to careful and detailed scrutiny of experience itself through disciplined reflection upon it. The conceptual net must be complex (*contra* those too ready to employ Occam's razor) in order to capture the fullness of experience, in whatever sphere the philosopher wishes to examine. Any encounter or involvement of consciousness with itself or its surroundings is an occasion to genuine experience susceptible to description. Persons encounter not only physical objects but also such things as relations, propositions, numbers, meanings, values, restictions and obligations, other persons, a wide range of cultural phenomena, including words of art, technologies and institutions, and their own selves. These encounters are cognitively and affectively complex. Important aspects of the patient's experience of hospitalization following his heart attack would simply be neglected if the philosopher were to limit reflective and descriptive attention to his sensations.

Wisdom here is the determination not to dismiss as insignificant the complexity of the patient's experience. The love of such wisdom involves, minimally, the appreciation of the value of the discernment and sensitivity which anti-reductionism entails. The love here is a mode of caring about and commitment to the cultivation of such wisdom. Moreover, it is a mode of experiencing which has its own specific contours to be explored in sections to follow. The love of wisdom is not reducible to (a) the wisdom itself, (b) the mere seeking of wisdom or (c) the experience of loving the patient in question. One can love wisdom and not be wise. One can be wise and not love wisdom. The latter love is the peculiar passion of the philosopher which involves the self-conscious profession of the values of wisdom.

Intentionality. The intentionality of experience is one of the complexities disclosed by the descriptive, reflective methods of phenomenology. To say that experience is intentional is to say that processes of experience refer beyond themselves, or are directed toward objects of which they are experiences. To describe an experience is not the same as to describe the object which is experienced as it is independent of experience. Rather, it is to describe a complex consisting of (a) the process of experience together with (b) the object of that experience *as* it is experienced. Thus, for example, to describe both the process of remembering, as, e.g., difficult, hazy or fleeting, and the remembered object *as* it is remembered, e.g., a ballplayer's batting average as it is remembered to have been twenty years ago. That in fact the batting average was exactly .329 is not part of the description of the memory experience when the memory is that the ballplayer batted .229. Similarly, in order to describe one of our I.C.U. patient's fears fully one must not simply note that he is fearful but also describe the object of that experience *as* it is feared. His fear that he will never have sex again is an agonized conception *of* a future sex life experienced *as* if it were possible never to be enjoyable.

To say that the experience of the love of wisdom is intentional is to say that the loving process refers beyond itself to the wisdom which is loved. The loving is not a free-floating affective state attached to nothing in particular. Nor is the description of the experience of loving wisdom a description of wisdom as it is in itself independent of the experience of loving it. Rather, it is a description of a complex consisting of (a) the process of loving in various modalities and (b) the virtue of wisdom *as* it is loved. The loving may be half-hearted or whole-hearted, inconstant or constant and the like. Persons may love wisdom *as* a virtue witnessed in the loves of others and aspired to, e.g., as in a student nurse's loving admiration for the skills of a gifted R.N. Or they may love wisdom *as* practiced by others tending to their personal needs, e.g., as in the loving gratitude of the patient for the sensitivities of his nurse. Or persons may love wisdom for its contributing to the meaning of their own personal or professional lives, e.g., in a wife's or nurse's sense of fulfillment in approximating to wisdom as an ideal.

Bracketing existence. In characterizing the method of describing the intentionality of experience in this way, I have in passing treated a procedure which phenomenologists call "bracketing". By this they mean that in exploring and describing experiences, the philosopher should suspend judgment about the existence of that which is experienced and about the validity of the experience. This is in fact accomplished in passing as the focus of reflective attention is (a) directed away from making judgments about the objects of experience as they are in themselves and (b) directed toward describing the objects of experience *as* they are *taken to be* within the experiencing process under description. This is the fundamental sense of the phenomenological *epoché.* It remains possible that part of the description of many experiences will include statements that within those experiences objects are taken *as* being real, e.g., the nurse's big nose is taken as real. But if one says that, e.g., within the hallucinatory experience of seeing pink rats climbing the walls the rats are taken as real, one is describing an element of the experience itself, and not saying that, independent of the experience, the rats really exist. Thus, in describing the hallucination of the pink rats, the existence of the rats has been bracketed (we are not concerned with whether they are real). Similarly, in describing our patient's fear about his future sex life, we bracketed the matter of the truth or falsity of his suspicion. It is only indifferent future experiences that such fears may be confirmed or dispelled.

In describing the experience of the love of wisdom, one turns away from consideration of wisdom as it is in itself and turns toward how it is taken to be in the experience of the lover of it. The nurse who is attentive to the presence of fear, or perhaps guilt, in the life of his I.C.U. patient is sensitive to the patient's feelings as the patient experiences them, even if he is confident that neither the fear nor the guilt is well-founded. In this sensitivity, the nurse displays the wisdom grounded in the phenomenological procedure of bracketing as he becomes attuned to the recovery of his patient *as* the patient experiences it. The admirer of such sensitivity, as an instance of wisdom, takes it to be a worthy virtue. In loving the wisdom, the wisdom is experienced as an attainment of the highest value which could hold a prominent place in professional life or in interpersonal relations in general. In thus describing the love of wisdom, the value of wisdom in itself has been bracketed (we are not concerned with whether it really has the character ascribed to it within the experience). It is only in subsequent experiences of the lover that this confidence in the worthiness of wisdom will be sustained and deepened or possibly shaken or dissipated.

Modes of appearance. As one describes experiences one can also focus upon the modes of appearance of that which is experienced. As objects become established within experience they are encountered (a) under different aspects, (b) from different perspectives and (c) with lesser or greater clarity. For example, the patient perceives the machine which is monitoring his heartbeat from the side which has the screen which looks like a T.V. on it, as versus its top or its back. He has an unusual perspective on the tubing leading into his nose which is quite different from the perspective of the nurse. He comes to know only the professionally concerned aspects of the personality of the nurse and from the point of view of a patient as versus that of a fellow nurse or a physician. Much of his experience is one of achieving greater clarity. His perceptions are initially hazy, presumably due to the lingering effects of anaesthesia or other medication. It is not clear to him, in addition, just what sort of institutional setting he is in nor just what his future life will be, given the heart attack he has suffered.

One can also focus upon the modes of appearance of wisdom within the experience of the lover of it. The love may embrace any of a number of aspects of the complex phenomenon which is wisdom. Persons may attend lovingly to the mindfulness and sensitivity in the exercise of wisdom, e.g., the understanding and skills of the nurse in interacting with his patient. Or they may attend to aspects attendent to its exercise, e.g., the contribution to the well-being of the patient or the manner in which the virtue pervades the character of the nurse. Wisdom may be experienced quite differently in the loving of it depending upon whether one's perspective is that of the neophyte, the fully initiated or the jaded philosopher. The contours of wisdom can be known with varying degrees of clarity. A superficial infatuation with wisdom vaguely perceived as an attractive accomplishment, if one could but attain it, can give way to a more profound appreciation of its precious subtleties as worthy of a lifetime of cultivation. This in turn may evolve into the ambivalence of the lover who comes to know with greater clarity the elusiveness of wisdom and the frustrations of one who would sustain the pursuit of it in day to day dealings with the world.

Synthesis in experience. Phenomenology also attends to the complex synthetic structures of experience, i.e., the ways in which experiences combine with one another. These synthetic structures are found throughout the range of experiences of physical and cultural environments, other persons and oneself. One manner of combination, or synthesis, unites temporally distinct phases of experience of an object into an experience of an identical object. Over time, several encounters are experienced as encounters with one and the same object. Thus, this mode of combination with experience is called an *identifying synthesis*. As the I.C.U. patient begins to adjust to the heart attack, he encounters the hospital setting, the nurse and others and his own new physical and emotional state. The machinery and the procedures described by the nurse come to be perceived as all part of the *same* treatment. He is learning the manners and dispositions of the nurse, and he identifies them as aspects of one and the same personality. He recognizes that the crushing pain and his current discomfort are all part of the same heart attack experience. As he worries about his current disabilities, he identifies himself as the same person who once enjoyed a lifestyle which may be no longer possible. These are all examples of identifying synthesis.

Within the experience of the love of wisdom, the many aspects of wisdom are understood as aspects of the same phenomenon. The assurance offered by the nurse, his patience and honesty in orienting the patient to his new situation, his sensitivity to the patient's feelings, and his gentle, yet firm, insistence that the patient rest are all understood as manifestations of the same virtue. All reflect the mindfulness appropriate to good nursing practice. More generally, knowledge and understanding of the uses, misuses and abuses of concepts and ideas, the will both to cultivate mindfulness and to sustain dialectical tension, the exercise of powers of discernment and creativity, and humility in their exercise are all aspects of the singular virtue which is wisdom, and they may be loved as such.

Another type of synthesis within experience takes place when aspects of "one and the same object" are intended simultaneously. There is a layering of multiple modes of experiencing as well as a multiplicity in the modes of appearance of aspects of phenomena. Each present experiencing is combined with retentions of and anticipations of other experiences which present different aspects of the same object. In this way, present experiences of objects refer beyond themselves to horizons of other possible experiences, both past and future, of other aspects of the same objects. This synthesis within present intending is called *horizontal synthesis*. The patient's experience is also filled with horizontal synthesis. His present experience of his surroundings is combined with (a) retentions of past experiences of illness and dependence and past encounters with institutional settings and (b) anticipations of continued dependence upon the life-support system due to his present illness and confinement within a hospital which, he likely expects, has features much like those of other hospitals he may know about. He further anticipates the routine of being awakened every two hours and the inducing of coughing. His present wish that his wife were present is combined with memories of their marriage prior to the attack and fearful anticipation of the effects of the attack upon the relationship between them. As he experiences his own present weakness and pain, he is poignantly aware of the contrast with his feelings prior to the attack, and he anticipates more of the same weakness and pain while also confusedly speculating about implications of the heart attack for his future well-being and his lifestyle.

The present appreciation of the wisdom of the nurse in the I.C.U. may be experienced against the horizon of past encounters with comparable sensitivity or of past encounters which were sharply contrasting. The present appreciation may also be combined with hope for continued mindfulness on the nurse's part or fearful anticipations of reversion to all too common insensitivity. Loving attempts to appropriate wisdom as one's own may be experienced against the horizon of past witnessing to and admiration for its exercise. Loving nurturance of its development in oneself or others may be experienced as combined with an ongoing resolve and commitment which extends from the past into the indefinite future; horizons of the value of wisdom as it contributes to the meaning of the lives it touches.

Constitution in experience. Phenomenologists frequently maintain that "experiences constitute the experienced". It is a mistake to take this as meaning that processes of experience produce or create the objects of experience. Such matters of causal origin are bracketed in phenomenological analysis. To describe the constitution of an object with experience is, rather, to describe the range of both actual and potential encounters with the object within which one can come to be familiar with it. It is to describe the experiential pattern of coming to know the object. Constitutional analyses, then, yield descriptions of the distinctive manners in which objects of different types "take shape" within our experience.

There is great diversity in the ways in which objects of experience are constituted with experience. As examples, contrast the processes of (a) becoming acquainted with existential phenomenology or applied philosophy through hearing or reading this paper; (b) coming to know a tree in a yard by periodic observation throughout its seasonal changes and growth cycle; (c) becoming familiar with a strange city as one comes for specific, short-term business purposes *or* as one comes to establish permanent residence; (d) becoming oriented to life at a large university; (e) observing the contours of a conversation; (f) establishing a friendship; (g) learning a new language; (h) coming to adopt the mores of a foreign culture; or (i) reaching a major decision in one's life. Within each of these experiences the objects are constituted through combinations of experiences peculiar to the types of object experienced.

It is important to note that constitution is a combination of receptive and spontaneous processes. Experience is a mixture of undergoing and doing: it is not simply a matter of passive reception of that which presents itself. Even in experiences where receiving seems to dominate, there are elements of accepting, or making oneself ready and responsive to, that which is presented in experience. Such "active passivity" is illustrated by the careful and attentive listening practiced by many professional helpers. Other experiences involve much initiative and deliberate exploration, including searches with specific ends in view, e.g., confirmation of scientific hypotheses through experimentation.

Much description of our patient's experiences would focus upon the interconnected experiences within which such things as (a) the hospital setting, (b) the intesive care unit routine, (c) the personality of his nurse, (d) the newly defined relationships with his wife and job and (e) a new self-concept are constituted. His experience is initially very much one of taking in, if not being overwhelmed by, his new and strange situation. Yet, it is plausible that as he grows stronger he will begin to be more active as he explores and questions his hospital surroundings, his relations with others and his own capabilities.

Part of the wisdom of the well-trained nurse is sensitivity to these constitutional processes as components of the experiences of patients. In coming to be aware of this and other sensitivities of the nurse, both the patient and his wife may come to a deep appreciation of them. In these experiences, the nurse's wisdom is constituted as valuable in the admiring witness of it. But this admiration of wisdom is not yet the love of it.

To describe the constitution of wisdom peculiar to the loving of it is to describe the range of both actual and potential encounters with wisdom within which one can come to be familiar with it as an object of loving attention. The manner in which wisdom is established in the experience of the lover of it is in many ways parallel to the manner in which friends and lovers come to be known as such. The knowing here is not a mere acquaintance with or tolerance of what is loved, though, to be sure, these are involved. Nor is it a simple admiration for or valuing of what is loved. There is an overcoming of distance between oneself and the object of one's love. The constitution here is conative as well as cognitive. Wisdom comes to be recognized as something which is both precious and to be cherished. The love of wisdom is an experience within which wisdom comes to be established as something which one cares about and is committed to.

This commitment to wisdom entails that the lover of wisdom strives diligently to grow in understanding of the nature of mindfulness, discernment, creativity and humility in making conceptual and ideational contact with reality. The philosopher actively cultivates an appreciation of the varied potential of wisdom for enriching human living. The commitment also entails that the lover of wisdom becomes sensitive to the fragility and vulnerability of this most precious human capacity. Both the exercise of and the growth in wisdom may be hindered, delayed or undermined in circumstances where this sensitivity is lacking. The cultivations of the understanding and sensitivity I have mentioned thus far are relatively active processes within which wisdom comes to be established in the life of the philosopher, at least when compared to the passivity of witnessing or even admiring wisdom as it informs the behavior of others.

Yet, the experience of loving wisdom is not as passive as simply understanding or appreciating certain characteristics of wisdom. The commitment in the love of wisdom entails that the philosopher will strive to act in accord with the understanding and appreciations he acquires. To the extent that the philosopher is capable of wisdom, it will come to be established in his experience through a process of appropriation. The understandings and appreciations will come to have the force of what Kierkegaard called "subjective truth". They will give direction and meaning to the philosopher's actions and life projects. The philosopher, moreover, will seek to minimize interference in the exercise or development of wisdom in the live of others. Indeed, the true lover of wisdom will dedicate much time and energy to actively encourage and facilitate its exercise and development at every opportunity. Wisdom will be further established in the experience of the lover of it as this commitment is tested, sustained and renewed.

Interpreting the significance of experience. Some phenomenologists maintain that all of the foregoing modes of description can be complemented by an attempted interpretation of the significance of the experiences so described. In particular, they are concerned to define the place of the experiences in leading a meaningful life by the person who has them. Such hermeneutic phenomenology has been met with some skepticism within the phenomenological tradition inasmuch as its methodology is more speculative than purely descriptive. However, it is widely accepted as an integral part of *existential* phenomenology. Techniques of interpretation are powerful tools with great potential usefulness. Nevertheless, the prudent philosopher will proceed with caution and offer interpretations of experiences with an appropriate tentativeness.

In the case of our patient, interpretation of his experience would involve, in part, interpreting the change in his experiences of embodiment. (a) In and through his body he has access to more or less meaningful environments. As he is confined, he encounters a strange and antiseptic hospital setting in which he finds little that has had meaning in his life. (b) In and through his body, he exercises control over his environment and acts out his own decisions. He is now in circumstances where much of that control has been taken out of his hands. Moreover, he is afraid to perform such simple actions as raising his arm. (c) It is also through his body that he expresses himself through speech and other non-verbal behavior, including sexual behavior. His experience is transformed here as well, in that his normal gesturing is limited, his speech is distorted by the lingering effects of medication and the tubes in his nose, he has been instructed to rest rather than to talk, and he anticipates future problems of sexual expression. Surely all of these changes in his experience of his body will have a significant impact on whether and in what manner his life continues to be meaningful.

Interpreting the significance of loving wisdom would involve interpreting the transformations (a) in the character of the lover of wisdom, (b) in his interactions with others and (c) in his mode of being in the world at large. Each such transformation can introduce new meaning into his life. There is a new integrity which informs the life of the philosopher. One loves with one's whole being. Thus, love brings with it a sense of wholeness in commitment to that which is loved. The love of wisdom, then, is more pervasive than an understanding or skill which the philosopher uses intermittently or a practice which the philosopher engages in on occasion. This consistency, coherence and sense of wholeness and purpose which can come with the love of wisdom comprise a significant part of the meaning of meaning of the experiences of the philosopher.

The philosopher who, as such, professes the values implicit in the love of wisdom, experiences the hopes and frustrations attendant to the desire that the virtue might color all of his personal and professional relationships. Personal relationships with colleagues, friends, marriage partners and children can all be enriched by the love of wisdom within them. The love of wisdom can inform the manner in which one cares about and nurtures the development of others.

Of special interest is the meaning of the love of wisdom for the philosopher who undertakes the professional responsibility of teaching others. He strives to minimize the adverse effects on his teaching upon the development of wisdom in his students. He actively establishes an environment within which students can mature through their mistakes, refine their powers of discernment and creativity no matter the subject matter of the teaching, and come to see the value which mindfulness and wisdom have. Such teaching fosters an appreciation of the value of and encourages the flourishing of wisdom in non-academic environments, e.g., in the intensive care unit which has been the focus of the ongoing example in this paper.

In regard to his mode of being in the world at large, the philosopher will recognize and appreciate the viability of many possible perspectives on reality, including the scientific, the technological and the religious. His life will be enhanced as he comes to understand the experiential roots of, the motivations to, the purposes of, and the power and limitations of the concepts and ideas generated within such perspectives. His sense of exhilaration in coming to know his own capacities for experience and understanding may be matched by senses of awe, reverence or mystery in the face of the complexity of nature and the cosmos which ever escapes his firm conceptual and ideational grasp.

Essential characteristics of experience. Not only may phenomenology focus upon the various aspects of particular experiences which I have been outlining above, but many believe it is possible to provide descriptions of the essential characteristics of types of experiences. To describe an essential characteristic of a type of experience would be to describe one which is invariably shared by all possible examples of that type. That is, the characteristic would be shared not as a matter of accident but rather as a matter of necessity. No experience lacking the feature would be of the type in question.

The method of discovering such essential features of types of experiences involves attending to what one takes to be clear examples of the type in question while paying special attention to the features of the experiences which one suspects make them the examples which they are. One then undertakes a thought experiment in which one exercises one's imagination, trying to discover any other examples of the same type of experience which lack the features in question are possible. If this process of "imaginative variation" discloses that a particular feature is invariably present in all imagined examples, then an essential feature is thought to have been discovered.

This method of imaginative variation was the pivotal element in Husserl's attempt to transform philosophy into a "rigorous science". This was both a systematic and a critical ideal. He envisioned a community of phenomenological researchers undertaking a systematic investigation of the essential characteristics of all possible cognitive experiences. He held that this mode of reflection could lead to apodictically certain insights about the structures of experiencing the world, including insights into the limits of human knowing. The resultant phenomenological theory of evidence would undermine simplistic preconceptions of the experiences of coming to know mathematical and logical truths, the physical world, God, other persons, institutions and cultures, and oneself. Husserl was a foundationalist both in his insistence upon exploration of the experiential bases of theories and in his confidence that certainty is attainable in phenomenological investigation. Other phenomenologists, e.g., Scheler, Pfänder, Heidegger, Sartre, Merleau-Ponty, Ricoeur, have rejected Husserl's pretensions to certainty here. They have also extended the application of phenomenological method to encompass non-cognitive experiences as well as the cognitive. As they see it, attempts to discover essential characteristics of experiences can only be tentative and approximate. The virtual inexhaustibility of experience dictates a necessarily open texture in the concepts and ideas which illuminate it. This abandonment of the goal of apodicticity by these phenomenologists entails an ongoing refinement of insight into human experiences through dialogue. This difference with Husserl also places them outside of the foundationalist tradition and squarely in that of contextualist, or network, theorists who hold out for a rationality which both overcomes relativism and yet falls short of indefeasibility.

Much of the discussion in the foregoing has centered on features which many phenomenologists take to be essential characteristics of experiences, e.g., its intentional, synthetic and constitutional structures. Rather than describing such features of experience in general, one might attempt to describe the essence of specific kinds of experience, e.g., perception, memory, imagination, anticipation, judgment, volition, fear, hatred and the like. Or one might attempt to describe the essence of the experiences of particular types of objects, e.g., experiences of physical objects, human beings, social units, or cultural objects.

As I have discussed the experiences of the I.C.U. patient, I have focused upon the particular circumstances and experiences of his life. However, I have also intimated that there may well be features of his experience found in all similar hospitalization experiences, or, at least, which may be essential possibilities in such experiences. In a similar manner, I have focused upon what may be construed as essential features of the love of wisdom.

The existentialist, who insists that thought must meaningfully inform the experience of existing individuals *qua* individuals, may not be satisfied, however, with the generalizations of even the most acutely sensitive phenomenologist. Insights into the general structures of types of experiences remain precisely that, i.e., generalizations. The tension between phenomenology and existentialism in existential phenomenology is an uneasy one grounded in the dialectical tensions mentioned earlier.[3] I think it is safe to say that such generalizations as the phenomenologist might generate are not irrelevant to the experiences of individuals, though, to be sure, they never capture all that is important in those experiences.

Consider, for example, attempts to describe essential features either of the experiences of dying persons (perhaps our I.C.U. patient) or of the grief of their survivors. It is useful to cultivate insight into the general contours of such experiences so that one might know what it is reasonable to expect in interaction with the persons involved and so that one may be more empathetic. It does not follow that expression of the general insights need be part of the actual communication with the person in question. Rather, the insight may be used as a kind of mind-frame which enables one to more rapidly become attuned to the uniqueness and specific details of the dying and grieving in question. In dealing with the dying or the bereaved it turns out, paradoxically, that they want both (a) the reassurance that their experience is not entirely unique, that they are not alone in undergoing such experience and (b) the empathy of others who fully appreciate the freshness and perhaps even the unprecedentedness of the occurrence of such experiences in their individual lives.

III. Conclusion

The anti-reductionism of phenomenology together with the methods of exploring and describing the intentionality of experience, the modes of appearance of the phenomena, the synthetic structures of experience, and the constitutional processes within which objects come to be established in experience promote our appreciation of the complexity of human experience. They heighten our sense of the inexhaustibility of the perspectives through which we encounter our world and foster understanding of dynamic adventure which is our experiential involvement in the world. The methods of bracketing, interpreting the meanings of experience and imaginative variation provide critical perspective on the precariousness of all of our trans-subjective claims to knowledge and, in particular, our attempts to generalize about experience. Taken together, these phenomenological methods constitute a basis for mindfulness (a) in providing a means to focusing upon the ongoing, pre-reflective experience philosophers mean to be mindful about and (b) in discouraging the prejudicial imposition of conceptual and ideational frameworks upon that experience. Wisdom, as the cultivation of such mindfulness, is, then, well served by the methods of phenomenology.

The wisdom of the existential phenomenologist is the virtue of cultivation of insight into the structures of human experience through phenomenological methods in combination with humility in the application of those insights, bearing in mind the poignancy of the human existence which is to be informed by those insights. It is a wisdom which encompasses mindfulness about the full range of human experience, not simply its cognitive aspects. It is a wisdom which recognizes that all motivation for reflection and theory arises within the broader field of experience of the world.

Existential phenomenology, in promoting such wisdom, falls squarely within the tradition of humanistic philosophy. It contributes to our understanding of what it is to be human by illuminating our being as experiencers of the world. It contributes to our understanding of what it is to be humans through cultivation of a mindfulness which can ground the sensitivities essential to empathetic response to the experiencing lives of others. Within each of us there is an ongoing experience of the world with unique contours and integrity worthy of our respect.

But, as applied philosophy, existential phenomenology is not simply a matter of understanding certain things. Rather, it is living in accord with the understandings as a lover of the wisdom which it promotes. Understanding the love of wisdom, as I have tentatively described it in the foregoing, is a simple thing. But applied philosophy is a passionate commitment. The true challenge of existential phenomenology is to make the moves of the lover of wisdom in one's own unique life circumstances. This is challenging enough for anyone. As Kierkegaard once said,

> No generation has learned from another to love, no generation begins at any other point than at the beginning, no generation has a shorter task assigned to it than had the preceding generation, and if here one is not willing like the previous generations to stop with love but would go further, this is but ideal and foolish talk.[4]

To be sure, it is likely that Kierkegaard had a love other than the love of wisdom in mind. Yet, his words apply to the current generation of philosophers. It is not applied philosophy which betrays the tradition. Rather, it is any would-be philosophy which has lost touch with its experiential foundations or which dismisses the significance of the distinctive manner of being of the philosopher as the lover of wisdom.

NOTES

1. Sören Kierkegaard, *Concluding Unscientific Postscript*, trans. David F. Swenson and Walter Lowrie (Princeton, New Jersey: Princeton University Press, 1968), p. 34.
2. Kierkegaard, p. 109.
3. See the first page of this essay.
4. Sören Kierkegaard, *Fear and Trembling*, trans. Walter Lowrie (Garden City, New York: Doubleday Anchor Books, 1954), p. 130. In this context, it is important to point out that this paper would not have the applied emphasis which it has were it not for the influence of Herbert Spiegelberg's constant but gentle insistence upon the importance of *doing* phenomenology. I have owed him an essay on this subject for a dozen years, and I'm pleased to be able to submit it to him in the present context.

III. AESTHETIC, ETHICAL, AND RELIGIOUS VALUES

The Good and the Beautiful
by
Robert Bernasconi

I

Plato calls beauty *to ekphanestaton* – the most apparent. As such it provides an exemplary topic for phenomenology understood, as it sometimes is in the works of the later Heidegger and the later Merleau-Ponty, as the vision of the invisible within the visible. Because we find that more appears than appears to appear, phenomenology in this sense investigates, tracks to its lair, an excess. Being is the excess for Heidegger. Phenomenology seeks out this excess, negatively by avoiding reductive analysis, positively by attempting to be true to experience, that is to preserve the experience as experience. What experience means here should become clear in the course of what follows.[1]

In this essay the beautiful always means the beautiful human being, and the first point to notice is that the beautiful human being stands out. He or she is arresting, attracts our gaze, takes up our usual perfunctory glance and holds it so that we withdraw our interest from whatever was occupying us. The beautiful takes us by surprise. We are drawn out of ourselves, taken out of the world of our concerns and brought into a different orbit. To say that the beautiful transports us outside ourselves is not to imply that we were previously locked within ourselves in a Cartesian sense. It means rather that we are taken beyond the limits of a world which we organize.

Before the beautiful, responding to him or her, we become transformed. For a moment at least, we lose our foothold, the stance we have taken up in the world. For that moment we no longer seek confirmation of our self-certainty.

The experience of the beautiful may be treated as only an adventure or interruption, an invitation to indulge in a moment's reverie before we take a grip on ourselves and return to what we are doing. It would not be unlike other interruptions. But we may instead open ourselves to the evidence of the beautiful human being. Only then is the experience of beauty experience in the proper sense. Then we no longer indulge ourselves in beauty but hear its challenge, its provocation. It opens us to new possibilities and offers the possibility of new

W.S. Hamrick (ed.) *Phenomenology in Practice and Theory*.
© 1985 Martinus Nijhoff Publishers, Dordrecht/Boston/Lancaster
ISBN 90 247 2926 2. Printed in the Netherlands.

180

determinations of that which is — a new ordering of our world. The beautiful
serves to disrupt our world while yet preserving a sense of overall significance.
Things lose their fixity. What was thought important is no longer pursued.
What previously held sway falls by the way. We become carefree. And yet this
does not mean that the beautiful is found to be merely pleasing; face to face
with the beautiful we do not feel at ease. It is upsetting and disturbing.

The beautiful takes hold of us. We find ourselves in its grip. We are brought
before something to which we can be alive only in a way different to that which
we are accustomed. The beautiful human being conveys a sense of
transcendence. With hesitation, it can be given its provisional title: the good.
The beautiful awakens us to the good; the good announces itself in the
beautiful. It does not emerge through inference; its presence is not a conclusion
we might arrive at after a process of analysis. It is the excess belonging to the
beautiful.

The beautiful human being seems self-sufficient, harmonious, in unity with
his or herself:

> That the beautiful is complete and thus perfect, that the beautiful in-
> vites us to put aside our preoccupations so that it is attended for its own
> sake, that the beautiful in its disclosure draws our desire, our longing, —
> these notions gathered from an account of the experience of the beautiful
> human being support the tendency in Western thinking to think of the
> good and the beautiful together. We could say in the manner of a Hegelian
> speculative proposition, the beautiful is good. Perhaps better, and in
> keeping with the way speculative propositions are to be read, the truth of
> the beautiful is the good.

> The conjunction of the good and the beautiful cannot be conveyed so
> readily or so accurately in any assertion conforming to the ordinary stan-
> dards of understanding.

II

The speculative proposition "the beautiful is the good" cannot be reduced
to an assertion to be presented before common understanding that the
beautiful human being is good. To be sure, we may have a feeling that the
beautiful human being is good and in a confused manner we may understand
this goodness as in some sense akin to virtue. But we would readily
acknowledge that this is an illusion and that the good-looking person is in fact
likely to be no better than anyone else.

The formula "beauty is skin deep" is presumably meant as a warning to that
effect. And yet the formula prevents us from being led astray only by denying
the evidence of the experience. It might serve as an illustration of the maxim

Hegel taught us that "what calls itself the fear of error reveals itself as a fear of truth", (*Phenomenology of Spirit*, Introduction, second para.). We can show this very readily. The good still addresses us in the face of the good-looking even when he or she does not adhere to "the moral code". Beauty is not a sign which may or may not be deceptive, and the beautiful face can never be reduced to a facade. The discovery of "moral" deficiency in the bearer of good looks does not disillusion us. It was only an illusion if we took looks to be a measure of virtue. Beauty does not point to the good within. The good which features on the face of the good-looking is transcendent; it is excess.

The experience of the good in the beautiful needs protection. It may suffer at the hands of understanding, be misunderstood. But it cannot suffer disappointment, or through some discovery give way to disillusionment. The claim that the beautiful makes on us is not of such a kind that a new perception can displace it, so reducing it to the status of an illusion. Instead of the discovery of ethical deficiency in the good-looking showing up the superficiality of beauty itself, as understanding insists, the discovery only serves to challenge the conception of the good presented by the understanding. The good which the beautiful announces has nothing to do with conformity to a code of moral behaviour.

As experience always takes place within the context of a specific understanding, so a change in understanding affects not only understanding's interpretation of the experience, but the character of the experience itself. As understanding becomes ever more inclined to disregard the good in the beautiful, so for the experience of the beautiful the essential adherence of the beautiful to the good becomes more striking.

A second formula, that "beauty is in the eye of the beholder", also serves to veil the evidence of the experience of the beautiful. This notion wins ready acceptance because it serves as a means of resolving disputes when one person finds someone beautiful that a second person does not. I say the person is beautiful and I am told that this means that the person looks beautiful to me. The two assertions may look equivalent, but the underlying subject of the experience has ceased to be recognised as the beautiful human being and becomes the beholder. In securing the autonomy of the aesthetic judgment, the experience of the beautiful has been lost sight of. Referring the beautiful to the one who judges, so that the beautiful human being is fundamentally and one-sidedly beholden to the beholder is to distort the nature of an experience which removes us from the standpoint of subjectivity. In the face of the beautiful there can be no question of maintaining a conviction that our standpoint is one of mastery of self-sufficiency. The affirmation of the beautiful does not await our judgment; it is always already there before us.

When the experience of the beautiful breaks down our subjectivity, it does so by transforming human being, by letting us become who we are. We do not lose ourselves in the beautiful as we lose ourselves in our preoccupations. We find ourselves lost in the beautiful.

How so? Taken over by it, we yet must respond to it — and the proper response clearly must be at the human level. It would not be proper to stand before a beautiful human being and examine his or her face as we might a face in a painting or photograph. We would not be seen staring. Nor would it be proper to kneel before the beautiful as before a God. Because we are face to face with somebody who as most apparent seems most alive, we sense a heightening, a quickening of ourselves.

In the beautiful human being our self-certainty is challenged and we are confirmed in our responsiveness. The beautiful human being calling us into accord with his or her self, strikes a chord in us. A genuine conversation arises between the good manifest in good looks and the good which it unveils and releases to those under its spell. The beautiful as good addresses us as good and awakens hidden depths in us. As the most manifest it is the most immediately loveable:

> "Beauty alone has this quality that it is what is most apparent and
> loveable". (Plato's *Phaedrus* 250d)

The beautiful summons love. In our response to the good looking we discover our responsibility, our capacity for response.

It is possible to refuse this response to the beautiful, to protect oneself from it. Such protection is pervasive in our times. The understanding of beauty as in the eye of the beholder or as skin-deep guards against this response. The beautiful may also be made an object and be incorporated into the everyday world. For example, in beauty contests the beautiful is surveyed by a foreign look which brings it under the rule or standard of the understanding. Judging the beautiful, whether deriving it from the subjectivity of the observer or seeking to possess it, refuses its calls.

III

So there is a tendency today to consider beauty as bearing only on surfaces. The term "the good" has also long since lost the depth of meaning that once belonged to it; for example when it is taken to mean conformity to certain prescribed standards. Understood in this way beauty and the good are properly thought of as entirely distinct and if their conjunction is recognised at all, it is considered accidental. But the proximity of beauty and the good was known to philosophers and poets until fairly recent times.

Indeed it might be said that Plato's remarkable accounts anticipate or provide the basis for a phenomenological description. No sense can be made of Plato's saying that "the power of the good has fled into the nature of the beautiful" (*Philebus* 64e) so long as a moralistic conception of the good and an aesthetic concept of the beautiful are retained. Both this passage and that quoted from the *Phaedrus* earlier challenge conventional conceptions while being open to a phenomenological reading. So is Kant's recognition of the ideal of the beautiful human figure as "the expression of the moral" (*Critique of Judgment*, sec. 17). Any number of statements could be drawn from the history of philosophy affirming that beauty and the good belong together.

We must beware supposing that there is a basic phenomenological core onto which each thinker projects a metaphysical overlay, and that reading Plato we need only strip off the references to Ideas, or reading Kant those to *Zweckmässigkeit*, to discover the underlying phenomenon all confirm. This would be a reductionism as serious as those which have been examined above. Again the experience of the beautiful offers its own corrective.

Take the Greek work *to kalon*. It carried with it connotations of both goodness and beauty, and affirms their unity. But this usage, which may be found still vibrant in Aristotle's *Ethics*, cannot be said to anticipate a phenomenological description of the good and the beautiful such as might be carried out in this century — precisely because our understanding knows nothing of this unity as unity and must discover it as something foreign.

The different presentations of the character of the relation of beauty and the good in their difference from each other are "metaphysics", but not in the sense, which is sometimes given to the world, of something arbitrary which can be dismissed. The relation of beauty to the good and hence also the way in which the good announces itself in the beautiful human being is historical. This history is not a tale of a growing separation of the good from beauty. It is not a history which can be turned into a story. We gain access to this history through the sayings of the poets and the philosophers. "Analytic understanding", knowing nothing of an adherence of the good to beauty, conceals the testimony of the tradition and its history, and yet that is itself not a mistake, a failure in understanding, so much as another moment in this history. And yet beyond that, it is only when the adherence of beauty to the good sinks into oblivion, is completely lost, that the historical character of that adherence comes to light. For then the experience of the beautiful is most apparent, most striking in its appearance, arising against the background of the world of preoccupations and setting us free from them.

The adherence of the good to beauty is preserved in the beautiful human being. The experience of the beautiful brings the revelation that understanding has lost sight of this adherence. This separation and its recognition as a separation are both historic events (which is not to say that they can be dated). If the separation is called "the danger", then the recognition of the danger as danger is the passage out of oblivion. In Hölderlin's phrase, which Heidegger loved to quote:

184

> "But where danger is, grows
> the saving power also".
> "Wo aber Gefahr is, wachst
> das Rettende auch". (*Patmos*)

Heidegger looks to the arts to foster the growth of the saving power. This is most marked in *The Question Concerning Technology*, and in *Building, Dwelling, Thinking*. Heidegger adds that to save is not only to snatch something from danger but to set it free in its own presencing. So at a time when *poiesis* (bringing forth) is obstructed, Heidegger looks to the arts which are also a *poiesis* to awaken and renew our vision of that which sets free, that which grants. By looking to the arts, Heidegger, who has brought out better than anyone the dominant place of *techne* within the history of metaphysics, reaffirms *techne*.

But in reaffirming *techne*, does not Heidegger stay, in Levinas' phrase within the neutrality of Being? Does not the beautiful human being also emerge as a site for the experience of Being as *Ereignis* — while enriching the responsibility towards human being of this new thinking?

The experience of the adherence of the good to beauty is experience of that which grants. This adherence is preserved in the beautiful human being and the experience of the beautiful human being is preserved in love; in love we stay with the experience, albeit staying in love is no easy matter. Phenomenological description shows that the truth of the beautiful before understanding, the experience itself brings us to the historic recognition that the beautiful is the truth of the good. "The truth of the beautiful" is that which the beautiful reveals. "The truth of the good" is the historical play of the concealment and the unconcealment of the good in the beautiful.

NOTES

1. An earlier version of this paper was presented to the Annual Conference of the British Society for Phenomenology in April 1980 in Oxford.

The Retributive Attitude and the Moral Life
by
Francis N. Dunlop

I. Introduction

In this paper I want to try and show that the retributive attitude is an essential
and necessary part of the moral life. If I am right it follows that moral agents
are sometimes obliged to express their moral disapproval of the wrongful acts
of other people, and to make their indignation "felt" by the wrongdoer. Moral
agents are bound, that is, to make the wrongdoings of others their own concern, to some extent; it would be morally wrong for everyone to ignore the bad
behaviour of others as "none of their business". In other words again, all
members of a moral community ought to be to some extent moral watchdogs,
ready to uphold the moral "universe" (as locally interpreted), and to see that
others do so as well. Unless this is in general done, I shall try to show, human
beings deny an essential part of their nature, community (and society)
disintegrates, and the moral life, which is virtually a synonym for "human
life", becomes impossible. The retributive attitude is an essential part of
human life.

II. Methodological Preamble

I shall first say a little about the sort of method I shall be following, which
I should be happy to describe as phenomenological. I would firstly express
general agreement with those who say that the phenomenological approach is
one in which an attempt is made to give an account of essences and essential
connections. The difficulty is to say exactly what is meant by this. But it is important for what follows to see that retribution is essentially different from
vengeance. In the end this can only be "seen", and never verbally proved, but
various sorts of arguments can be used to help the reader to attain this insight.
The best way of doing this is by making distinctions, and this is done by calling
to mind situations or occasions when people are acting retributively, or feel

W.S. Hamrick (ed.) *Phenomenology in Practice and Theory*.
© 1985 Martinus Nijhoff Publishers, Dordrecht/Boston/Lancaster
ISBN 90 247 2926 2. Printed in the Netherlands.

they ought to take retribution of someone, and contrasting them with occasions or situations when people are acting vindictively, or feel they ought to avenge themselves. It can also be done by recalling the different sorts of things one would want to *say* in these different situations, and so on. But underlying this sort of procedure is an assumption that retribution and vengeance are "given" as distinct phenomena; that the difference in nomenclature reflects a difference in the "things themselves". Another way of putting this is to say that any being whatsoever that shares man's rational and animal natures is bound in the end to "confront" these "things" as separable items in the furniture of the world.

"But", it might be objected, retribution and vengeance are things we *do*. They are not like trees or stars, "there" whether we like it or not. We have a clear *choice* as to whether to act retributively or vindictively, and hence the "existence" or "being" of these things is up to us, in a way that that of trees or stars is "not". However, in the first place, as I shall explain more fully later, the beginnings of retribution and vengeance precede our conscious choice. Certainly we must choose whether to let vengeance and retribution "take their course", since this *is* up to us — but there is an important sense in which we *do* "confront" the two as distinct phenomena *within ourselves*, just as we confront, say, love and hate. We find these things "welling up" in us; our choice lies in the question of whether and how we are to encourage or discourage their further development.[1]

In the second place retribution and vengeance are experienced in terms of the realisation of values that lie above the subjective sphere of pleasure and pain.[2] We are not aware of them as things invented by man that it might be merely satisfying or interesting to do, or as answering some want or desire that he merely happens to have, or even as institutionalised *ways* of meeting value-demands, like punishment, but as things that are primarily given as "to be done" or "not to be omitted" in themselves. Thus, the claim that there are "essences" of retribution and vengeance is intimately bound up with the claim that Humanity feels a legitimate requirement to exact retribution and vengeance in certain circumstances.

This is part of a general claim that *we have moral experience*. This is an extremely important point, failure to appreciate which has led to the denial — even by some who have taken a sympathetic interest in the phenomenological method[3] — that the phenomenologist can, *qua* phenomenologist, contribute to ethics. But unless we have a common moral experience which is, to some extent, self-authenticating, there cannot really be a moral philosophy at all. Instead we are confronted with ever more ingenious and sophisticated *arguments* to show that we *must*, if we are rational, behave in certain ways. But firstly these "certain ways" would never in the first place be selected as significant and to-be-justified unless they were already *recognised* as to-be-justified independently of any argument, and secondly, if these arguments are to have prescriptive force they must at some stage appeal to values, to something, that is, simply "given" as valuable and hence to-be-cultivated. Thus intuition must have the logical primacy, and, if it is thought to be subjective and inadequate, can only be replaced by more "objective" (that is, less personally biased) and more adequate intuition. No transcendental arguments to the effect, for example, that a man ought to speak the truth, or respect a person, have ever come near to replacing the experienced *insights* into the disvalue of mendacity and the value of person that inspire these arguments. But if we have the insights, then of what use are the elaborate and often suspect arguments to "justify" our claims that truth and persons should not be slighted? Certainly there is an "apologetic" or pedagogical task to perform here. There is always a new generation to teach, some of whose representatives will not, or say they do not, share our insights. It is clearly necessary to appeal to reason where insight is lacking. But beyond this, it often seems to me, the insistence that all moral philosophy is about "justifying" the basic insights (understood as a matter of "deriving" them logically from one or a handful of basic principles) is sheer arbitrariness and mystagogy — a prison from which phenomenological ethics provide a merciful escape.

The phenomenological approach to moral philosophy, then, is centrally concerned with an analysis of moral experience. This involves, as I have tried to show, the analysis of "essences", but it also involves the analysis — or rather the display — of essential connections. This is in fact by far the most important end. I myself will try to bring to light the essential connections between the retributive attitude and moral community, between it and moral concern, and between it and living a properly human life. It is not easy to say what is meant by an "essential connection" without using terms that raise just the same sort of puzzlement in a different form. Thus it may not help much (though again, it may) to say that if x and y are essentially connected then the connection between them is not arbitrarily or contingent (though it may be added that it certainly need not be necessary in the individual case, and no tautologies need be involved in stating it), or that it is in the nature of x to manifest y, or that, given x, y is *a priori* likely, other things being equal, and so on. Nor may it help to say that we do not come to *know* about the connection by purely empirical means, since the term "empirical" is itself extremely unclear. The charge is often made against some phenomenologists (e.g., Scheler) that they confuse the necessary and the contingent, the *a priori* and *a posteriori*. It may well be that this is bound to be the case where human being and human life are the subject of philosophy on the one hand, and that of psychology and sociology on the other. But it seems to me more important to say what impresses itself on one as true than to worry unduly about such metaphilosophical matters. Let it suffice to say that I myself think this to be an essay in phenomenologically based philosophical ethics, and that, though I can say *something* of what the method involves, I cannot say very much.

As for the latter, it will be clear from what I have said above that my argument cannot have any clear "linear" or deductive form. The general aim is to appeal to moral *experience*, and thus "get the reader to see what can in the end only be seen", in Scheler's words. To this end the subject matter is approached from various angles; examples are produced in the attempt to illuminate experience from different points of view. What I try to do is to produce a coherent and self-justifying picture that is not internally contradictory and that should impress itself on the unbiased contemplator of experience as broadly speaking right or correct, despite an undeniable fuzziness in some of the details. This, I think, is all that one can in the end do in any part of true philosophy (as opposed to formal logic). But no *account* of what I think I am doing can be a substitute for doing it. The method is useless unless it yields useful results.

III. Retribution Opposed to Vengeance

In attempting to show a distinction between retribution and vengeance, one may at times appeal to the evidence of linguistic usage, but one is not concerned primarily to analyse concepts (unless concepts are assumed to be in a one-to-one relationship with essences). Linguistic usage is very imprecise in this area, and a great many people use either word to mark nearly all the phenomena which can be plausibly covered by both. There is, however, one clear exception to this. The word "vengeance" always refers to the visiting on someone of something unpleasant for the injury he is taken to have brought about, never (as "retribution" perhaps still does) of some reward for some good he is taken to have caused. I shall ignore this rewarding aspect of retribution in the present paper.

Both words, then, refer to ways of responding to harm, injury, or evil-doing. But unlike moral indignation or anger, the responses in question have an essential connection with practice. Moral indignation or anger may well be the *foundations* of retributive or vindictive responses or attitude, but are, in themselves, merely self-enclosed responses in feeling. One may without a sense of logical strain think of them as denied any kind of symbolic expression (though one may well feel they are bound to have some physical or bodily manifestation). However, because the moral agent *cannot* in the end be thought of purely as an isolated individual, I think this self-containedness of moral indignation or anger *does* have something odd about it. They seem almost of necessity to "press on" towards some kind of expresssion, or to some kind of "cancelling" or inhibition by another spiritual act, but nevertheless they can be analysed as self-contained responses.

It is otherwise with retribution and vengeance. These, or their foundational feelings, must be themselves *founded* on moral indignation, anger, or some other pure feeling response, but in themselves they denote *practical* responses to the source of injury, evil or wrong. There is at the very least a wish that the evil-doer be made to suffer for the evil he has brought about and in a great many cases a determination to contribute to this "suffering" should be suitable opportunity arise, or at any rate to participate spiritually in its imposition. Essential here is the looking forward to the practical "answer".

We must now try to distinguish between retributive and vindictive attitudes. Although linguistic evidence does not unequivocally support this division, a good case can be made out for the claim that by and large our language *does* witness to a real distinction. I shall therefore proceed to discuss the difference between te retributive and vindictive attitudes without the use of tentative or suggested invented commas. There are distinct phenomena "there", I am claiming, even if they are not completely separable, and much evidence to suggest that my nomenclature is widely presupposed.

The chief difference between the retributive and the vindictive attitudes concerns the degree of impersonality involved. An individual, it is often said, takes "his" revenge, or a group avenges "itself"; one cannot, in English, talk of anyone exacting "his" retribution. This distinction is important, though it must not be taken too far. Many primitive tribesmen experience the call to avenge themselves or their group as a sacred or a moral duty; failure to perform it is itself sometimes the occasion of retribution; men have sometimes to summon up their courage and resolution to its performance as to a disagreeable but morally indispensable task. Conversely, though retribution be experienced as a thoroughly impersonal demand emanating from "justice" or "the moral order", the original moral indignation may be closely associated with a sense of personal affront or outrage, and the exacting of retribution, either directly or "through" a group's representatives, or the individual expression of retributive attitudes, may produce a satisfaction that is far more personal than that expressed by the bare thought that "justice has been done".

It might, however, be thought that the obvious difference between retribution and vengeance is in the nature of the injury. One avenges, it might be insisted, injuries or wrongs conceived of as done to *oneself* or one's own *group*; one exacts retribution for injuries or wrongs that violate the moral order. Isn't it here that the "personal" reference of vengeance as opposed to retribution is most unequivocally apparent? There is much truth in this, but again qualifications are necessary. Certainly it would make no sense for me to *avenge* x's insult to y where I do not feel closely bound up with y to a degree to which I do not feel bound to x, but nevertheless if I am to *avenge* my injury I must see it as an *injury* and not merely as pain or discomfort or suffering caused by someone. The proper reaction to this would be either mere avoidance or flight, or else a blind hitting back or attempt to put a stop to the pain. If I take *revenge* it is clear that some higher sphere of values than that of mere pleasure and pain is involved — namely that of dignity or honour, the value possessed by my person or my group as such. If x injures y — deliberately, that is — he humbles or humiliates him. It is not just that y receives a hurt; his own value as a power in the world, or as a source of independent action and will, is brought into question. He can only hold up his head again if his own value is reasserted, and this can only be done through vengeance. And yet we cannot talk of this as "purely personal" as opposed to the impersonal value of the restoration of the moral order (see below). X's value is not experienced as self-bestowed; it is "given". X "finds himself to be of value", a finding implicitly acknowledged by all who respond to him as to a person as opposed to a physical object or animal. The same goes for the value of x's group (his family, clan, tribe, village, or whatever). In reasserting his own or his group's value in the world he is responding to a call that issues from the sphere of values itself. And again, there is the all but inevitable communal reference in vengeance. This is quite openly acknowledged in most primitive societies where an insult to x will always be interpreted as an injury to his family, or clan or tribe. But even in more advanced cultures the cummunal reference is there. If it is not his family who shares his sense of injured dignity (or he who experiences his injury in the first place as one to the kinship group of which he is a member) it is his circle of friends, peers or colleagues. Always there is the tendency to see the counter-stroke as reasserting the value (which the individual sees himself as representing) of a collective, something essentially supra-personal. Hence the ease with which people *participate* in spirit in acts of vengeance. Thus though in vengeance the injury is necessarily conceived of as personal in one way (one must either be injured in one's own person or "identify" with one who is), it is clearly *im*personal in another (in that values that transcend the subject are involved). Nevertheless, though it is the nature of value that leads one to talk of the impersonal element of vengeance, one's relation to the value is something more akin to possession (it is almost one's *property*, at one's *disposal*) than that of allegiance or respect. The value of my person or my group may be something to which I ought to respond, but nevertheless, it is not as impersonal a value as those comprising "the moral order". This is why revenge is said to be "sweet".

Retribution, on the other hand, bears an obviously more impersonal note. When a displays a retributive attitude towards x for his injury of y (by withholding the customary greeting, say, or publicly denouncing him), he need feel no special closeness to y that he does not normally feel to x as well. He is simply indignant at x's disregard of y's rights, and concerned that x should not be allowed to get away with it. The values under attack here are those of justice or the moral order, which a conceives as equally binding on himself as on x and *y*. There is no idea here of the values of the moral order as being somehow *a's property*, or his being "bound up with their fate in a way that other people are not. The moral order is *any*one's concern. And yet, in a way, there *is* an element of this. When *a* indignantly repudiates *x's* ill-treatment of *y* by withdrawing his custom or patronage, or cutting him at a ceremonial occasion, he does so as upholder and champion of the values that *x* has disregarded. *A* experiences himself as "charged" or "commissioned" to "stand up for" certain standards. What is more, because people must *choose* between values, a choice that is bound to be heavily influenced by one's group or community, however much it may also be true that not *any* choice is as good as another and that *some* value-choices are almost bound to be approved by all people as such, any individual championing of values in the world is bound to be partial and selective. Thus, when *a* takes up a retributive position towards *x* for his treatment of *y* he does so as representative of an ethos, of a certain pattern of values acknowledged and values preferred. Hence, once more, the retributive attitude can never have that complete and God-like impersonality it aspires to. Though the values reaffirmed in vengeance are in a more obvious way "one's own", there is thus a sense in which those upheld in retribution also are. But whereas the relation between the individual and the values in vengeance is one of quasi-ownership — implying a virtually "automatic" and normal "effortless" defense of them (or desire to defend them) when under attack — the relation in retribution is far more directly one of "allegiance" and "respect", a championing of something that is "not oneself", given as "to-be-cultivated" even when, as is at times almost certain, this goes against the grain.

Further reflection on retribution and vengeance brings to light a different "rationale" operating in each. In vengeance, as we have seen, the injury is experienced as a threat to the value, or dignity of myself or my group as such. The counter-stroke, or continual readiness to take counter-measures, can thus be depicted as directed outwards from the city walls of my group, as it were. As a result of this stroke, honour may be satisfied. Our city may hold up its head again as a power in the land. What happens to the enemy on whom vengeance is taken is immaterial. Logically speaking, he is annihilated. The situation is vastly different with retribution. Here a common allegiance to values standing over against and making demands on all three parties is presupposed. The offender here is looked on not as someone "beyond the pale" but within a common frontier — a confederate but rebellious city, as it were. The offender, by his act, has threatened to break up the federation, has begun to loosen the bonds of mutual trust that tie its members together. Already by his very act, he has cut himself off from the rest. But this cannot be allowed to go further; he himself longs for reconciliation in his heart of hearts. Thus community must be upheld. The solution is the retributive response. The offender must be made to suffer, not primarily to bring satisfation to those members of the group who have "kept their bond", but that he himself may eventually be reclaimed, and received once more as an equal partner with the federation. Retribution thus presupposed the breaking and eventual restoration of relationship among those sharing a common ethos. Vengeance certainly would not make sense where there was no general appreciation of the value and dignity of agency, will and choice, of being "a power in the land" (however small), and thus presupposes the appreciation of some values. But there is no real concern here for the high values that make real community possible, no sense of a fragile spiritual superstructure that must be protected and fought for if human life is not to degenerate. Vengeance is far more conceivable among animals than retribution.

IV. The Indispensability of the Retributive Attitude in the Moral Life

It would be absurd to claim that one should *always* make one's moral disapproval "felt" when confronted by wrong-doing. My claim is that one should be prepared in general to do so, and that if this duty is completely disregarded, the moral life becomes impossible because community disintegrates. It should be clear that this claim goes counter to much that is thought and spoken by philosophers in the Western world. Here tolerance, "pluralism" and a refusal to "meddle" in other people's affairs are increasingly taken for granted and state punishment is denied its retributive meaning. I do not, I hasten to add, *deny* a value to tolerance and the spirit behind "pluralism" and "live and let live". A complete social and moral philosophy would be bound to investigate their claims and "logic" in detail. But retribution in all its forms has been under philosophical attack for a long time now. It is no accident, in my view, that community (which is essential to Humanity) has been at the same time collapsing, and that more and more Englishmen and Americans have begun to experience themselves as lonely and isolated individuals in a world of increasingly threatening and untrustworthy strangers.

But I wish first to forestall one criticism that might be made of my general claim. What people really dislike, it seems to me, is a certain caricature of retribution, which they see as irretrievably barbaric and primitive, and associate with savage and brutal treatment of offenders, with an absence of all pity and sympathy, and with all the more subjective elements of self-assertion that go with vengeance. On the other hand, they may well accept the need to denounce other people on occasion, or to cold-shoulder them for particularly anti-social behavior, and of course to deliver them to the processes of law and state punishment. Their ploy is to deny any genuinely retributive significance to these things. But this is a mistake which arises from a failure to observe how these responses are inevitably experienced. It is absolutely fundamental to human beings to wish to be confirmed or approved in their actions. In the normal way this confirmation or approval is indicated by continued association and solidarity. But if I denounce someone, or suddenly start to avoid him, or even deny him the friendly and affirming glance that I am accustomed to give him, this is bound to be interpreted in retributive terms unless there are obvious indications of some other cause. Retribution does not require me to knock a person down or refuse him help when in danger of his life, since I can indicate my retributive attitude and make a person smart by raising my eyebrows or by a slight movement or turning away from him on his approach. Not that these tokens of disapproval will always suffice. All I am concerned to insist on here is the immense scope of expressions of the retributive attitude. There is something pre-eminently "natural" about all this.

"But what is natural is not necessarily right", it will be objected. Although this is not the place to discuss it, I think it can be plausibly argued that there is a sense of "natural", indeed the proper sense, according to which what is natural is right, except when the claims of still higher values make themselves felt. The nature of a human being is complex, but we begin to understand it from the idea that he is both spiritual and animal, and that life on the animal level must hence be given its due. Broadly speaking, a person acts spiritually when his actions are coloured by his response to transcendent values, "naturally" when his acts are shaped by a less clear-sighted, perhaps almost blind, response to values that are at least partly immanent. Thus, what is "natural" in Humanity, in the sense in which retribution, and indeed vengeance, is natural, is nevertheless still value-impregnated, even though a spiritual response may be superior.

The "naturalness" of retribution can also be grasped by recalling that its beginnings lie at a lower stratum of personality than that of conscious decision. The "retributive attitude" is not really something one can switch on or off at will. Suppose that I witness an act of inexcusable cruelty or callous disregard of someone's rights on the part of an acquaintance whom I had been perhaps on the point of considering as a friend. I still wish to cultivate his acquaintance further because we have interests in common. But the knowledge of what he has done has created a barrier between us. I cannot now look him in the eye with trust and freedom I once felt; my smiles freeze on my face; there is a wariness and decrease of warmth in my approach that I cannot possibly disguise. Perhaps I have still not consciously "given way" to any retributive feelings, have still not stamped them with the *fiat* of my willing, purposive self and thus given them full rein. Nevertheless the unmistakable message has been understood. My acquaintance already feels the smart induced by my cooling off and my withdrawel. The process of retribution has begun even before my "central self" has had any say in the matter.

Its "natural" and "proper" end is the restoration of full relations, which

will certainly be possible provided that all parties accept the justice of the situation and agree that the "suffering" is not out of all proportion to the harm
done.[4] The wrongdoer must "expiate" his wrong — that is, suffer for it —
before the barriers to his reincorporation into the moral community have
disappeared. And it is worth emphasising that where the delinquent does feel
himself to be part of the moral community he himself will feel the need to atone
for his misdeed. There is no room here to discuss expiation.[5] It must suffice
to say that suffering *does*, in the normal case, bring about a restoration of community, and that all parties to the relationship experience this as right, proper
and "natural". What needs to be "justified", however, is not so much the
natural process: offence — breakdown of community — expiation — restoration of community as it is the conscious and deliberate "consent" of the central
self to be "made a party" to this process, its willed acceptance and reinforcement of the retributive attitude and its realisation that, except in certain un-
typical circumstances, to fight against it is both unavailing to some extent,[6]
"unnatural" and wrong.

The importance of the retributive attitude (as fully realised), and its indispensability can be best seen by means of an example. Suppose you follow
a man into a small shop. The person serving there begins, for no apparent
reason, to treat your fellow customer with a sort of casual rudeness. It is plain
that they have not met before, and that the rudeness of the shop assistant is as
surprising as it is repellant to the other person. You begin to share his indignation. Now the question is — what are you going to do about it? The customer
is by now — in vain — demanding to be treated with more politeness and consideration, and both men keep looking your way. Whether you like it or not
you are being drawn into the business. The shop assistant no doubt hopes you
will take his part against the other customer, whose accent and manner proclaim him a stranger. The customer hopes, from your respectable and kindly
appearance, that you will support him in condemning the boorish behaviour
of the shop assistant. But the crucial thing is that you are being asked to declare
yourself, to take sides.

What can you do in such a situation? You can ignore their appeal — not
openly (which would itself put *you* in the wrong as arrogantly assuming an
Olympian detachment), but by pretending you have not heard. This might even
be the commonest response today. But this would entail letting down the
customer, who deserves our moral support, betraying values which in other
easier circumstances we might vigorously defend, and denying our common
allegiance to human decency in the face of a boorish attack which, if repeated
often enough and in more and more situations, threatens to drag Humanity
down to the level of sub-humanity. Are we not then compelled by the situation
itself to take sides?

Suppose we simply take the shop assistant aside and talk to him, get him to see the error of his way by sweet reason, perhaps? But in this way we are (assuming the course to be at all feasible) in danger of assuming a *super-human*, God-like position again, of evading the issue by trying to rise above it, or by attempting to thrust the shop assistant himself down beneath us to the level of a child. Naturally the shop assistant will resent the attempt to judge and instruct (we have no warrant to act the pedagogue towards him), and the affronted fellow-customer will rightly feel that we have belittled him by ignoring his complaint and, as much as the shop assistant, resent our improper intervention. The fact is that only by taking sides can one respond as a fellow human being bound up in the struggle for good against evil, as an agent inescapably and equally involved in the moral life.

Let me dwell for a moment on this matter of "taking sides". Moral philosophers are fond of talking about the making of moral judgments, which they tend to conceive of as working out the answers to problems. There is a kind of tacit assumption that moral judgment takes place in some ideal realm of mind which is completely removed from the sphere of human action and passion. Thus the idea of taking sides is abhorrent to most of them. Yet the making of a moral judgement in the course of the moral life (as supposed to the seminar room or academic office) *is* a matter of taking sides. Through such an action I ally myself with all those who share my ethos (or alternately I let them down by betraying the values concerned), I show my allegiance to certain values, show myself prepared to stand up for *these* values against others. In pronouncing "this is wrong", or implying it by my behaviour, I *ipso facto* denounce this sort of conduct, I deliver an implicit rebuke to all those who show by their deed that they either disagree or have failed to conform, and thus − at the very least − deny them the satisfaction of having their actions confirmed or assented to by my continued complaisance.[7]

Since a great many moral situations resemble the one exemplified above the moral life is inevitably a matter of taking sides. During the ordinary course of one's life one is constantly being drawn into situations where one is not directly involved but in which one is "required" by the exigencies of the case to show one's hand. And "showing one's hand" is frequently bound to entail the display of a retributive attitude. A male acquaintance, let us say, openly boasts of having frequently travelled on the railway without a ticket. Are we simply to carry on as though nothing has happened? We may feel it is none of our business. Yet it *is* our business. His boasting is an appeal − covert, of course − for confirmation of the deed. He, being human, needs this confirmation, both to assuage his guilt and as a sign that he can still consider himself in moral community with us. Our own position as upholders of the values of honesty and justice is being challenged (indeed his very boast in our presence may insult us by its seeming to take our complicity for granted). We are surely bound to express our disapproval, and *ipso facto* make him smart. We may merely deny him the confirmation he is looking for by our awkward silence and abrupt change of subject. Or we may move away, and avoid him in future as much as possible as an undesirable acquaintance. We may also tell him to his face that we condemn his behaviour. Whichever of these things we do we are expressing a retributive attitude.

Let us look more closely at the situation which results from my *connivance* at the man's wrong. I react to his boasting about having frequently evaded the vigilance of the railway staff purely as though this were some exploit involving daring and skill. I assume — indeed, must assume — that we are in some significant sense both members of a group whose ethos includes awareness of and general disapproval of the disvalue of dishonesty. Though his boast, and the action itself, imply allegiance to certain vital or "life" values, it is an implicit rejection or betrayal of other higher values, reinforced now by my own failure to stand up for these values.

Now the moral life is largely a struggle between life values (whose predominant theme is the securing of the necessities and comfort of life, both physical and mental, for oneself and one's own kin) and spiritual values (which set not always easily rationalisable limits to such activity and offer new and wider goals to be aimed at "for their own sake"). Individual men and women, unless they are saints, cannot conduct this struggle alone. Indeed, outside a community of people bound together in some way by their shared allegiance to spiritual values (or a certain range of them), such a struggle is virtually inconceivable. It follows that people, as individual moral agents, *need* the support of spiritually inspired institutions and individuals in order to fight the moral fight (which, in the last resort, *is* the individual's struggle) in his own person. Hence comes the moral obligation we all share to confirm others in the good and steer them away from evil. It is the tacit but universal recognition of this situation that tends to make habitual evil-doers such hypocrites. Groups of people who band together to commit acts of injustice, or who connive at such acts, almost always invent ways of dressing up their wrongs in presentable disguises. Evil-doers are rarely prepared to acknowledge their deeds openly even within groups of people equally prepared to flout moral standards in practice. Such phenomena are eloquent testimony to the fact that we all are, in some way, "our brother's keeper", all charged with the responsibility of upholding the common standards and helping others to do so, and all ashamed to admit our defection. Thus again, failure to denounce or blame, either by word or deed, or by those numerous subtle signs that can betray a retributive response, the wrong-doing we directly encounter, inexorably leads to the undermining of *other's* ability to withstand temptation as well as our own, and thus again to a loosening of the bonds of community and the break-up of society.

These points about society must be particularly emphasised. What holds people together in a community and enable them to *experience* themselves as members of a group, is largely the allegiance to and hence readiness to uphold a common stock of values. Take any group of people at first loosely associated or thrown together in pursuit of some purpose or end that they all happen to share. So long as they continue to experience their association in terms of utility in relation to their purposes ("I can only get this thing I want if I associate with these other individuals") no real sense of community or belongingness will come into being. For this to happen a sense of common *dedication* must emerge that quite transcends the notion of getting what one has previously desired. A person who continues to regard the group merely as a useful clubbing together of individuals for a clearly-defined purpose now feels very much on the edge of things. If he is to feel really part of the group he must to some extent submit to a new set of value emphases and preferences which will, perhaps, subtly alter the emphasis of his original purpose, and give him new and subsidary purposes that are now charged with meaning and significance.

These considerations may lead one in two directions. On the one hand "society" at large must share these features of small group life if it is not to disintegrate. On the other hand, the individual person must belong to one or more communities if he is to be complete as a human being. Either consideration leads to a deeper understanding of the indispensability of the retributive attitude in human life.

It is fashionable today to emphasise the differences between modern Western societies, which are characteristically "open", and the small, closed groups familiar to us from the works of anthropologists. But the "laws" of community must in the end be the same for all. All social groups of whatever size are made up of individuals, whose desires and purposes and ends are sanctioned by the general moral consensus. This situation, where a collection of potentially divisive elements has to be held together, can only in the end be stabilised where there is shared voluntary allegiance to an ethos. Public policy everywhere must be to some extent concerned (whether deliberately or not) with preserving this ethos, or at least protecting it from too much or too rapid change, since this shared allegiance — with its corollary of a readiness to defend it — is the condition of community's existence. The situation is disguised in our own large, loosely structured and "open" societies by the fact that there are so many sub-communities (any individual may belong to dozens) with their own sub-ethos, and by the fact that the disintegration of large-scale community is a long and gradual business. Because it is always easy for an individual to "withdraw" from one sub-group (thus obviating the need for the individual to sanction his or her involuntary retributive attitudes in defense of the common sub-ethos) and join another group with a slightly different ethos, one's social perspective shortens, and one forgets that Western societies, and the numerous sub-groups within them, are still held together by a common allegiance to (most of) the values of mediaeval Christendom. Many of these values are, of course, protected by our laws, and hence it may well seem that the burden of retribution has been lifted from the individual and placed in the hands of the officers of the law. But such people are still merely our agents and representatives, and unless state punishment continues to be, among other things, "the emphatic denunciation by the community of a crime", the break-up of society and the weakening of the individual's allegiance to the values of his community will continue. Besides, there are numerous values which are not defended by law, or only defended in part or in certain circumstances, and it is imperative that these are still supported by the retributive responses of individuals if the common allegiance to these values is not to decay utterly.

The other aspect of the breakdown of community is the decay of an aspect of human personality. A human being is by nature a social being: part of this self is necessarily embedded in one or more groups to which he is ready to refer on appropriate occasions as "we". Phenomenologically speaking this is so whether or not other people are *actually* present. Isolates, recluses or hermits experience themselves as members of groups whose other members are all absent, or with whom they could resume contact only if things were different. This is why the break-up of a community (for example an institution that has become "part of a person's life") always brings a sense of personal loss to its members, not in the superficial sense that they have lost something that brought them satisfactions but that they themselves are diminished by its demise. Thus once again the failure to reinforce a group or social ethos by ignoring or setting aside retributive responses to attacks on the ethos amounts to a gradual destruction of Humanity itself. It is a myth that a human being can exist as such outside a community (though his being and significance are far from being exhausted by community membership).

My previous reference to the values of Christendom and to the possibility of preferring other, higher values to those of retribution on occasion might prompt the questions: are not forgiveness or mercy always better? Is it not unworthy of a human being to content himself with the sordid business of hitting out at a wrongdoer when there may be other and superior ways of reclaiming him? These are undoubtedly *cris de coeur*, cries, what is more, of a sensitive heart, but they result from muddled thinking and a refusal to look the facts in the face, I *cannot* forgive or have mercy on x for his ill-treatment of y (unless perhaps y is my child or perhaps my spouse) since forgiveness and mercy relate to the withholding of those responses to wrongs inflicted on myself that are properly "mine". But in so far as I feel morally indignant at one stranger's treatment of another, and feel "injured" or "affronted" myself as "representative" of the values thus slighted, I feel all this − or should properly feel it − as a member of the moral community that includes us all, not as a private individual, and have no business to act for the group in the suggested ways. Even in the case of injuries deliberately inflicted on oneself a general policy of forgiveness outside a framework of religious belief and practice would seem highly dubious. The line dividing forgiveness from condonation is perilously narrow. [8]

The fact is that there *are* no "higher" alternatives that can be adopted in the normal case. If I am of a situation where x acts unjustly to y my options are limited to taking sides, withdrawing, or arrogating to myself a false position "above" (God-like or pedagogical) or "below" the proper level of equality under the moral law. The idea that there is some always legitimate "higher" way of reacting to wrongdoing than the retributive proves chimerical. Of course, as I have already conceded, "turning a blind eye" may occasionally be the right policy, and tolerance of different value-perspectives and preferences is clearly essentially bound up with respect for human individuality and the realisation that Humanity cannot be conceived in the end merely as social beings. But there must be a limit to such policies. These refusals to sanction the retributive response must not be too frequent; some values are too important or urgent to be denied the reinforcement of retribution. There is simply no proper alternative to a *general* readiness to sanction one's spontaneous retributive feelings and to cultivate them where they are lacking, though again this is not incompatible with the existence within society of a certain number of exceptionally loving or charitable individuals who are − in religious terms − prepared to love the sinner while hating his sin.

One further criticism must be answered here. I have tried to show that retribution is only in place when all three parties to the transaction are assumed to be in moral community with each other. But how can one assume this in a modern "open" society? Would not my previous assertion that the peoples of the Western world are still held together in moral community by the values of Christianity be widely challenged? This question raises many extremely complex issues that cannot possibly be touched on here. But firstly the objector may be challenged on his own theoretical ground by pointing to the values that are taken for granted in discussion of public policy at local, national and international level. These are still in manifest continuity with the values of mediaeval Christian Europe, though of course there have also been changes, some of value-content, others of interpretation, emphasis and scope of application. Again one may point to the fact that a citizen of, say, the United Kingdom may feel at home in all these countries (granted some knowledge of the language). It is still the case that a tourist or business-traveller may take certain standards of interpersonal behaviour for granted on his travels, not only in the West, but in other parts of the World as well. There is something like an "ethos of humanity" which all travellers take for granted, an idea that lies behind the continuing interest in "natural law".

But the objector may also be challenged for his "judicial" assumptions. Moral experience teaches us that we are not to judge each other (which entails the *withholding* of judgment where the evidence is insufficient), but to take the side of good against evil. We have to live as moral agents in moral community with each other (all equally subject to the moral law), because this is the only way we can fully realise our nature as human beings. To withhold a retributive response towards a wrongdoer because of a doubt about whether he acknowledges the same moral standards as I do is to *deny* him moral community, to proclaim my moral separation from him.[10] But the displaying of retributive reactions may be itself a way of creating community, of reclaiming the person who is, as it were, on the way out by including him in the same moral "fold" as myself. I do not deny the many practical problems that arise here. The wrongdoer may be apparently "beyond recall" and react to my retributive response as to an original injury. There are genuine diversities of ethos that would be foolish to deny and arrogant to condemn (though moral experience itself forces on us a distinction between necessary "foundational" values that *must* be fought for, and other, higher, more supererogatory values that are more properly encouraged then enforced). These practical issues are by no means simple or clear-cut.

Let me also try to make one other point clear. It might be thought that my defense of retributive responses as to be encouraged "on occasion", as not being invariably but only sometimes appropriate, and so on, betrayed a lurking Utilitarianism. Thus, one might argue, retributive responses would only be justified when we had "good reason to believe" that they would lead eventually to the restoration of community. This implies that we regard retributive responses as means to an end, and that, if we had good reason to think that they were *not* contributing to this end we should proscribe them. But it is part of my claim that the retributive response is a natural expression of our human nature that we directly experience as right and proper. Its intimate link with the formation, preservation and restoration of human community may help us to see its propriety (and indeed its indispensability), but are not themselves "the reasons" that make it "right". But what is really wrong with the Utilitarian position is not that it takes account of consequences (any sensible agent will do this) but its general *attitude* to life, which stems ultimately from an obsession with technology, giving rise to the idea that Humanity can be master of its fate and, in particular, that people can bring about fundamental changes in their own nature. I claim that a clear-eyed and unbiased examination of moral experience, and the human condition in general, shows this attitude to be both unwise and indeed hubristic in much the same sense as the one that is the theme of many ancient Greek tragedies. A human being can only live a properly human life — and that entails a properly satisfying life — if he accepts his nature, with its limitations, and the deliverances (which are not all completely "justifiable") of his moral conscience. This means that he must sometimes do things whose rationale is not completely intelligible. Thus, though by and large the consequences of acting retributively *are* good (we believe), we must not respond retributively in order to produce certain results but because this is the natural and proper thing for human beings immersed in the moral life to do. It is an appropriate expression of humanity, not a device for achieving an end. There is an ineliminable opaqueness about the moral life, a sort of fog of residual unintelligibility surrounds it; were everything to be made absolutely clear-cut and rational it would cease to be a "life" at all, but something utterly different. A human being can only find himself by submitting to its claims, even though this means at times that he must allow something more like a blind instinct than reason.

All this may seem completely repugnant to the modern mind, which demands the clarity and finiteness of technology or mathematics. I am myself painfully aware of the deficiencies of my exposition in these respects. All philosophy must of course strive towards clarity and intelligibility. But it must also keep in close touch with experience, otherwise it becomes an elegant but misleading extravagance. It is, to my mind, the mark of the true phenomenologist that he gives more weight to truth, to the representation of experience, than to the task of reducing it to rational order and pattern. Phenomenology is also predominantly theoretical, concerned, that is, to lead people to see how things *are*, whereas much modern philosophy, with its obsession with justification, has a markedly practical slant. But practical philosophy is useless if it is based on a false idea of the human condition. It is out of concern to try and illuminate one obscure and lowly corner of this that this paper has been written.

NOTES

1. The best phenomenological description of the self that I know is to be found in the works of Alexander Pfänder. See especially his *Zur Psychologie der Gesinnungen*, Ch. IV, in *Jahrbuch für Philosophie und phänomenologische Forschung*, III.

2. Those who are horrified at the claim that vengeance can be itself the bearer of value are recommended to read Alexander Solzhenitsyn, *The Gulag Archipelago*, Part VI, Ch. 4, the last two pages.

3. E.g., Peter Heath, "The Ideal of a Phenomenological Ethics" in Edo Pivcevic, ed., *Phenomenology and Philosophical Understanding* (Cambridge: Cambridge University Press, 1975).

4. For a discussion of what this might mean, see my unpublished doctoral thesis, *Retribution and Punishment* (University of London, 1974), Ch. 4.

5. I have already briefly discussed this unjustly neglected topic in "Scheler's Theory of Punishment", *Journal of the British Society for Phenomenology*, Vol. 9, No. 3, October 1978. See especially pp. 171f. See also Ch. 3 of *Retribution and Punishment*.

6. It might conceivably be the case that one could so train oneself to deny retributive responses free rein that they "dried up" altogether. My point is that one would at this point have totally withdrawn from humanity — either in an upward, "God-like", direction or in a downward "beastlike" one.

7. This is why so few genuine moral judgments seem to be made in moral philosophy seminars!

8. See especially Aurel Kolnai's paper "Forgiveness" in his *Ethics, Value and Reality* (Indianapolis: Hackett Publishing Co., 1978). It is this point that I would like to refer the reader to Kolnai's papers in general. Kolnai was a superb exponent of phenomenological ethics as I understand it.

9. In Kolnai's terms, the Moral Consensus of Mankind. See the paper "Moral Consensus" in Kolnai.

10. See, too, Strawson's line of argument in "Freedom and Resentment", a British Academy lecture reprinted (among other places) in P.F. Strawson, ed., *Studies in the Philosophy of Thought and Action* (Oxford: Oxford University Press, 1968). For Strawson, not to resent an injury may imply that we do not consider its originator a moral *agent* at all.

Kindness[1]
by
William S. Hamrick

Toward the beginning of his poem, *Tintern Abbey*, Wordsworth wrote approvingly of

> ... that best portion of a good man's life;
> His little, nameless, unremembered acts
> Of kindness and of love ...

For profesional philosophers, and especially for those in ethics, Wordsworth's observation is apt to be a bit unsettling. This is so because kindness is an almost totally neglected subject of ethical writings. Both classical modern and contemporary philosophers who have dealt with "the passions" and feelings generally have not examined what Wordsworth not only praised, but called "best". Nor is the *lacuna* any better filled in phenomenology, even by those thinkers most closely concerned with ethics, Max Scheler and Nicolai Hartmann, where the German expressions of "kindness" would be "Güte" or "Freundlichkeit". Perhaps the closest approximation is to be found in Gabriel Marcel's notion of disponibilité,[2] about which more will be said below.

It would, of course, be extremely odd if all these writers were ignorant of the nature of kindness or took it to be unimportant. Rather, it seems more likely that the lack of discussion is due to a combination of at least three different sorts of things. The first of these is language. Philosophies tend to develop in tandem with, or at least reflect, the way language is used in their cultures, and it is significant that "kind" as usually signifying something morally praiseworthy is a rather late development (since the Renaissance), at least in English. Before that time, "kind" was employed to refer more nearly to natural kinds, qualities of nature, and so forth. For example, Spencer wrote in the *Faerie Queen* (I. iii. 28):

The earth shall sooner leave her kindly skill
To bring forth fruit, and make external dearth,
Than I leave you, my lief, y-born of heavenly birth.

W.S. Hamrick (ed.) *Phenomenology in Practice and Theory*.
© 1985 Martinus Nijhoff Publishers, Dordrecht/Boston/Lancaster
ISBN 90 247 2926 2. Printed in the Netherlands.

204

Here "kindly" refers to natural ability. Thus also Hamlet, after taking his mother to task for her immorality and after killing Polonius, says to the Queen (*Hamlet*, Act III, Sc. 4):

I must be cruel, only to be kind;
Thus bad begins, and worse remains behind.

In this instance, "kind" is apparently intended to refer to Hamlet's fulfilling his natural duties as a son. It also appears that "kindness" and "kindly" tended to work their way into the language as an alternative to this sense of "kind" − as a way of expressing what we think of today as the morally praiseworthy sense of kindness.[3]

The second possible reason for the lack of due attention to kindness is that it has been uncritically identified with benevolence, beneficence, or even love, and this synonymity is faithfully reported in a variety of English, French, and German dictionaries. Finally, the third possible reason for the lack of discussion of kindness is that the main concern of the last two hundred and fifty years or so of ethics has been to assess the morality of actions or rules by themselves − act-and-rule utilitarianisms and deontologies − as opposed to an interpretation of actions within a morality of being. But, as William Frankena points out, kindness is much more at home in the latter approach to morality:

> Throughout its history morality has been concerned about the cultivation of certain dispositions, or traits, among which are "character" and such "virtues" (an old-fashioned but still useful term) as honesty, kindness and conscientiousness. Virtues are dispositions or traits that are not wholly innate; they must all be acquired, at least in part, by teaching and practice, or perhaps by grace. They are also traits of "character", rather than traits of "personality" like charm or shyness, and they all involve a tendency to or certain kinds of action in certain kinds of situations, not just to think or feel in certain ways. They are not just abilities of skills, like intelligence or carpentry, which one may have without using. In fact, it has been suggested that morality is or should be conceived as primarily concerned, not with rules or principles as we have been supposing so far, but with the cultivation of such dispositions or traits of character. Plato and Aristotle seem to conceive of morality in this way, for they talk mainly in terms of virtues and the virtuous, rather than in terms of what is right or obligatory.[4]

In this context, then, the purpose of the present essay is not only to exhibit a concrete use of the phenomenological method, but much more importantly, to chart something of the moral significance of a very much neglected virtue. Before beginning, however, the reader should bear in mind that this paper is only a limited essay in phenomenology. It is very far from a developed moral theory or even the foundations of one.

1. The *Epoché*

The first step in our method is the *epoché*, putting into parentheses ("bracketing") our previous beliefs about kindness. As part of our "natural attitude" of everyday life, they will be "untested indeed but also uncontested", as Husserl said in *Ideas I*.[5] The aim is to slacken the ties of feelings, beliefs, and prior judgments which bind us to the world of the natural attitude so that we may better understand both them and the resulting purified evidences in our investigations. This is the fundamental move from mere thinking to reflection, from an interested to a disinterested consciousness and, as Richard Schmitt has correctly pointed out, "It is here, in reflection, that the distinction between true belief and knowledge is first drawn".[6] In the end, it may not be possible to free ourselves totally from the powerful emotional investment that we have in our beliefs the phenomena, and certainly phenomenologists themselves have written much on this difficulty or impossibility. Nevertheless, for the reasons that Professor Schmitt indicates, it is crucial that we try.

In terms of kindness, the *epoché* will not pose a great problem for ethicists and other professional philosophers since, as noted above, the difficulty is the absence of substantive discussion rather than an excess of it. But at least we can bracket value judgments such as those of Wordsworth with which we began – that kindness is (always) good and the best part of morality. We can also suspend our judgment in the belief that it is synonymous with benevolence, beneficence, and so forth. Still more obviously, we can bracket tentative answers to several typical questions in ethics such as whether kindness can be commanded as a duty or is more nearly like what Kant referred to as "pathological love", and correspondingly, whether kindness is a function of reason, of feeling, of will, or of some combination of all these. In a similar way, we also need to bracket beliefs about whether kindness is a given part of our temperament and character and/or an achievement.

II. The Phenomenological Reduction

Once the brackets are in place, however securely, let us attempt to get back to "the things themselves", in Husserl's well known phrase, and try to describe the appearing of the phenomenon of kindness as it appears. In *this* sense of the phenomenological reduction,[7] the goal is to describe the phenomenon, now purified of uncritical interpretations, as it is given to us in and of itself. One attempts to faithfully describe both that which appears, i.e., the objective side of phenomenon (the noematic element), as it manifests itself in all its concrete and rich diversity, as well as the activities of consciousness (the noetic element) in and through which the noematic element is given and its sense constituted. In what follows, then, we shall first examine the noematic side of kindness, that in various experiences which is called "kind", and then proceed to the noetic.

In terms of the noematic aspect of the phenomenon, how then does kindness present itself? The first thing to notice is that there are essentially different presentations depending on one's perspective – whether one is the object of an act of kindness or the agent doing a kindness. As the object of a given kindness, the latter presents itself to me mediately, or perhaps indirectly. What is immediately and directly presented are those things we call "kind", that is, people's actions, laws, rules, administrative policies, and so on. When I see these as kind, it is so mediately – mediated by a judgment about what is immediately present to me when I am the agent doing a kindness – a particular type of motive, about which more will be said below.

On the other hand, when people themselves, as distinct from particular actions, present themselves to me as kind, their acts are perceived immediately as kind. This is so because the past reflective judgment about the type of persons they are is pre-reflectively taken up in the present experience, conditions it, and is presupposed by it. How I form the judgment itself will be considered below.

What is the noematic basis for judging that a particular action, rule, law, and so forth, is kind? That is, how does the phenomenon appears so that I am led to judge it to be an act, say, of kindness? First, it is presented as something done for me. It is in my interest, for my welfare. It is a fundamentally helping gesture, and it is believed to be motivated by care and concern, of which a vast spectrum of seriousness is possible. That is, there are monetary or passing, "casual" kindnesses such as opening doors for persons heavily laden with packages and, at the other end of the spectrum, very important, crucial acts of kindness requiring a greater investment of time. Examples of these latter might include such activities as consoling survivor victims of suicides, spending time talking with wretchedly lonely elderly people, and so forth.

Acts of kindness therefore present themselves to me as embodying some type of caring relationships and, as Milton Mayeroff indicates,[8] caring involves, *inter alia*, the following features of experience. There is, first of all, knowledge. This means that the person doing a kindness for someone is believed to be making a free, deliberate choice. His action is not accidental, random, or determined in a sense that would exclude the presence of free will. Second, the act of kindness in caring has a "basic pattern" of "helping the other grow".[9] This establishes, or helps to establish, what David Garrick perhaps had in mind long ago (*Prologue on Quitting the Stage in 1776*) in referring to "A fellow-feeling (which) makes one wonderous kind". And finally, caring involves a certain humility in the sense that one avoids a dominating control and manipulation of the other. Kindness presents itself to me as involving this fundamental respect for the other which Mayeroff expresses as follows:

The union with the other in caring differs in another way from that found in parasitic relation. Instead of trying to dominate and possess the other, I want it to grow in its own right, or, as we sometimes say, "to be itself", and I feel the other's growth as bound up with my own sense of well-being. The worth I experience in the other is something over and above any value it may have for me because of its ability to satisfy my own needs . . . . In other words, I experience what I care for as having worth in its own right. [10]

Of course, not all acts of kindness incarnate a caring relationship with the other in the same way. There is a wide variety of possibilities depending on the location of the act in the spectrum of seriousness described above; giving up one's seat in a crowded bus evidences a different degree of care for the other than helping someone recover from a great tragedy. And at its deepest levels, the care involved in kindness can develop into a loving relationship. As Erich Fromm reminds us in almost exactly the same words which were to appear much later Mayeroff, "Beyond the element of giving, the active character of love becomes evident in the fact that it always implies certain basic elements, common to all forms of love. These are *care, responsibility, respect*, and *knowledge . . . Love is the active concern for the life and the growth of that which we love*". [11]

Responsibility and respect are as crucial in a loving relationship for Fromm as they are in one of caring for Mayeroff, and they are equally central to the appearance of kindness. It is a question of avoiding all that Nietzsche described as bad uses of the will to power and of recognizing the independent worth of the other. In Kantian language, the other is treated as an end in himself rather than merely as a means to an end. Or, as Fromm expresses it, "Today responsibility is often meant to denote duty, something imposed upon one from the outside. But responsibility, in its true sense, is an entirely voluntary act; it is my response to the needs, expressed or unexpressed, of another human being. To be "responsible" means to be able and ready to "respond" . . . . Responsibility could easily deteriorate into domination and possessiveness, were it not for a third component of love, *respect* . . . . Respect means the concern that the other person should grow and unfold as he is. Respect, thus, implies the absence of exploitation". [12]

Even when kindness is not part of a loving relationship, it is still the case that the former appears in such a way as to include responsibility and respect for the other. This is clearly evident in the manifold pictures of *un*kindness described in Eric Berne's *Games People Play* most of which occurs at the unconscious rather than conscious level. Consuder, for example, the marital game called "Corner":

> *Thesis.* Corner illustrates more clearly than most games their manipu-
> lative aspect and their function as barriers to intimacy. Paradoxically, it

208

consists of a disingenuous refusal to play the game of another.

1. Mrs. White suggests to her husband that they go to a movie. Mr. White agrees.

2a. Mrs. White makes an "unconscious" slip. She mentions quite naturally in the course of conversation that the house needs painting. This is an expensive project, and White has recently told her that their finances are strained; he requested her not to embarrass or annoy him by suggesting unusual expenditures, at least until the beginning of the month. This is therefore an ill-chosen moment to bring up the condition of the house, and White responds rudely.

2b. Alternatively: White steers the conversation about to the house, making it difficult for Mrs. White to resist the temptation to say that it needs painting. As in the previous case, White rudely responds.

3. Mrs. White takes offense and says that if he is in one of his bad moods, she will not go to the movie with him, and he had best go by himself. He says if that is the way she feels about it, he will go alone.

4. White goes to the movies (or out with the boys), leaving Mrs. White at home to nurse her injured feelings.[13]

As the author notes, these can be two hidden agendas in this game. In the first (A), Mrs. White knows from past experience that she should not take seriously Mr. White's distress and that what he really wants is for her to show her appreciation for his work. Then they could go off to the movies together quite happily. But this she does not do, leaving him let down. Filled with resentment he leaves alone and she remains at home looking victimized, but secretly enjoying her victory.

In the second hidden agenda (B), Mr. White also knows well from past experience that he should not take seriously his wife's fussiness and that, if he were especially nice to her, they could then go off together cheerfully. But he refuses to do this while knowing that his refusal is dishonest. He knows she wanted to be honeyed out of her pique, but pretends that he does not. So he leaves by himself in a cheerful mood, but looking the victim, and this leaves his wife full of resentment. As Dr. Berne remarks, "In each of these cases the winner's position is, from a naive standpoint, irreproachable; all he or she has done is take the other literally. This is clearer in (B), where White takes Mrs. White's refusal to go at face value. They both know that this is cheating, but since she said it, she is cornered".[14]

The *antithesis* for the game depends on the players. Since Mrs. White has the initiative, she can simply "change her mind, take her husband by the arm, smile and go along with him (a shift from Child to Adult ego state)".[15] The situation is more difficult, however, for Mr. White, "but if he reviews the situation, he may be able to coax her into going along with him, either as a sulky Child who has been placated or, better as an Adult".[16]

Returning now to kindness from unkindness, it is also the case that the former presents itself to me as motivated by something besides duty, at least in a Kantian form which is either necessarily or contingently opposed to inclination. The type of responsibility evident in a kind act, policy, and so forth, is an ability to respond in a personal, rather than purely formal, way, and involves feeling and desire in addition to reason. This contrast of motives of kindness with those of duty so conceived is clearly part of what Marcel was thinking of in contrasting *"disponibilité"* and "creative fidelity" with the "constancy" of duty: "fidelity as such can only be appreciated by the person to whom it is pledged if it offers an essential element of spontaneity, itself radically independent of the will".[17]

Fromm makes a similar point about love in which, as we have seen, kindness sometimes finds expression. He writes that "the Jewish-Christian norm of brotherly love is entirely different from fairness ethics. It means to love your neighbor, that is, to feel responsible for and one with him, while fairness ethics means *not* to feel responsible, and one, but distant and separate; it means to respect the rights of your neighbor, but not to love him ... the practice of love must begin with recognizing the difference between fairness and love".[18]

On the other hand, even practising Kantians can do their duty in a kind way. They perhaps need not do so to satisfy the categorical imperative, but they could let kind feeling enter into the structure of a particular *action* which embodied a willing out of respect for the moral law. Also, there is no evidence so far that it is always one's duty — or anyone's model of duty — to be kind or to act in a kind way, although Kant might well say that actions motivated by kindness are "in accord with duty, but not from duty". Neither immoral nor moral, they would be a-moral.

Correlatively, on other models of duty in which inclination and duty are synthesized, when one does a kindness spontaneously as a duty, then the appearance of it could be indistinguishable from that of duty. This would be the case for both the person to whom a kindness is done as well as for the agent himself or herself.

So far we have considered the kindness of particular actions, rules, policies, and the like. But we have not yet succeeded in pinning down what is singular about the phenomenon of kindness. This is so because kindness presents itself as having particular style which has not been captured in the above description of generally benevolent or beneficient behaviour. It is true that, if one does a kindness for someone, then one invokes some type of caring relationship with an intent to help the other. And it is true that some modes of kindness can embody the elements of love as Fromm described them, namely, care, responsibility, respect, and knowledge.

But I am also aware that the converse is not the case. That is, it does not follow from the fact that, if one is kind one is also benevolent, that if one is benevolent then one is also kind. In other words, kindness is a particular mode of benevolent approach to the other which is distinguishable from other types, and there are several readily available examples in which this is the case. For instance, teachers and parents may sometimes find themselves in situations of being harsh taskmasters in which benevolent care and concern for the other can only be effected unkindly. There is also a legitimate sense to the expression "righteous anger". Likewise, judges and doctors can and do find themselves in situations in which benevolence and kindness are incompatible. Or, in a different sort of case, suppose a heavy habitual smoker whom I know to be unreformable asks me for a match. If, as an officious and moralizing friend, I refuse it on the grounds of benevolence, it may still be unkind of me to do so.

To find, therefore, what it is that distinguishes kindness from other modes of benevolence, we shall examine first the kindness of particular actions and then that of the persons themselves. These in turn will be easier to explicate by moving from the noematic side of the phenomenon of kindness to the noetic activities of consciousness involved in (1) perceiving an act of kindness and relating to kind people and (2) actually doing acts of kindness.

When I perceive an act of kindness, I see the other as somehow influencing my life. I am simultaneously aware of myself as in need of the particular service performed. But I also judge the other's intervention as an act of generosity or of courtesy. I interpret it as a commitment to lighten my burdens coupled with a respect for my feelings. In other words, based on this judgment, I am aware of the other in basic sympathy with me, wanting to help me in the same manner in which I would help myself were it possible. The agent of the kindness takes my part as an actor unobtrusively slips into a role − in a nondominating and nonmanipulative way. In the same gesture, acts of kindness also become acts of gentleness with the latter being conceived as a moderation or, perhaps, a reasoned control in the use of power. [19]

Correlatively, when I am the agent doing an act of kindness, I take up a situation by responding to a lack. [20] Either someone needs something I can provide and recognizes in me a source of help, or I perceive someone in need for which I can provide the remedy. Or, I can do something for someone before it is even recognized as a need. I exist in a power relationship with the other such that, in intervening in his or her life, I do so in a way that avoids manipulation and exploitation. This respect coupled with polite consideration involves on my part both motive, will, and action.

My purpose to be kind to someone also involves an adequate knowledge of him or her because I am aware that I can wrongly believe that I am doing that person a kindness. That is, I can intend to be kind to someone and then that action misfires. This need not imply any moral weakness or other fault on my part. I may, rather, simply reflect the fact that our knowledge of the needs of the other is apt to be limited be circumstance or for other reasons.

When, however, I perceive the other as being himself kind, this meaning is constituted in consciousness in a more complicated way. That is, whether a given individual is presented as kind or not is distinct from whether one of his actions should be so labelled. For as Alexander Pope pointed out in his *Moral Essays* (*Epistle* I, line 109):

Not always actions show the man, we find
Who does a kindness is not therefore kind.

And Wordsworth finds more pathos in the experience of such a difference. As he tells us in *Simon Lee*:

I've heard of hearts unkind, kind deeds
With coldness still returning;
Alas! The gratitude of men
Hath oftener left me mourning.

How, then, is a person presented as kind in a way phenomenologically distinguishable from the kindness of a particular action? When someone so appears to me, I have evidence, as noted above, his actions and a belief about his motives in behaving in certain ways. I perceive the individual's actions toward me as involving something more than will in the sense of a reflective, deliberative choice. I am also aware of a spontaneity born out of a given disposition toward me — the other presents himself as "set" to behave in certain ways. The other becomes "available" to me, *disponible* in Marcel's sense, and on a more enduring rather than transitory plane.

For Marcel, the being who is really *with* me, who is truly *disponible*, is genuinely present to me in a way that transcends mere physical presence and may or may not be conjoined with it. As Marcel once expressed the difference, "The most attentive and conscientious listener can give me the impression of being unavailable (*indisponible*); he brings me nothing, he cannot really make a place for me in himself whatever be the material services which he will perhaps heap upon me. In reality, there is a way of listening which is a way of giving; there is another way of listening which is a way of refusing, or *refusing oneself*. The material gift and the visible action are not necessarily a witness of presence".[21]

Marcel points out also that "in reality, we will always find at the heart of unavailability a certain alienation",[22] and that "the being available to me is he who is capable of being completely with me when I have need of him. The being unavailable to me is, on the contrary, he who seems to offer me a sort of temporary borrowing from the ensemble of resources which he can provide".[23] This must not be taken to mean that he who is unavailable to me is necessarily against me. It is only that he is not *totally* with me.

The significance of this fact for the phenomenon of kindness is that it seems to be at least an important part of the distinction between kindness and kindliness, and is perhaps the sense of Wittgenstein's remark about G.E. Moore that he was kindly but not kind.[24] The judgment that I make about the "kind-

212

ly" person, then, as opposed to he who is "kind", is that the former is not totally with me in lightening burdens and respecting my feelings, but it is also true that he is not against me either in the sense of taking up a posture of thwarting my desires.

In addition to this fact, however, my consciousness relates to the kind person as so disposed not exclusively in my direction, but toward others as well. Just as the kind other does not attempt to manipulate or dominate me, I am similarly prevented from establishing a possessive relationship with him. Thus Shakespeare, in *The Merchant of Venice* (Act III, Sc. 2), has Bassanio describe his friend Antonio as:

> The dearest friend to me, the kindest man
> The best-conditioned (of the best disposition)
> and unwearied spirit
> In doing courtesies . . .

But how did Bassanio arrive at such a judgment in the first place? What activities of consciousness are necessary for anyone to constitute such a meaning? At least part of what is essential in arriving at such a belief is the perception of a temporally enduring pattern so that we become anticipatively "set" to perceive someone as kind who is himself "set" or disposed to believe in appropriate ways. One or two actions, gestures, and the like would not suffice for making such an induction. But if I perceive an appropriate consistency in someone's conduct over a period of time with no significant stretches of contradictory behavior, then I feel justified in concluding that someone is kind. Perfect consistency indeed is not necessary, for I am aware of (all?) people whom I believe to be kind, just, benevolent, and so forth, who are subject to moral weakness and other temporary lapses. But on balance, the pattern must be present for me to feel justified in saying that a given individual is kind.

The activities of consciousness which culminate in such a judgment are analogous to those of those of the "passive synthesis" of perspectival appearings of perceptual objects. Despite the clear difference of active, reflective judgment in the first instance and passive, pre-reflective perception in the second, there are marked similarities between the exploration of perceptual objects and making sense of a person's character through perceiving a coherent pattern arise across the individual's actions. In the case of a perceptual object, say, a house I see while passing on the road, what appears to me is that house from this perspective. If I decide to see more of it, I move around it and the primordial datum is again that house from a certain point of view. I am justified in believing that the house is indeed there in the way I perceive it if all the perspectival appearings cohere with one another without falsifying ruptures (For example, when I go around it, I do not find that it has no back or that it is two-dimensional like a clever stage set). Similarly, in the case of judging someone to be a kind person, I can have confidence in such a judgment if my several experiences of him fit together coherently over a significant period of time as described above.

Of course, the experiences are also disanalogous in certain ways, as for example with reference to the evidence required for falsification. That is, in perception one discordant perspective, absent any evidence of distorting environmental conditions or those pertaining to the state of the observer, would count seriously or decisively toward falsifying a belief that one is having a veridical perception. But this is not the case for judgments of character, as we saw in terms of moral weakness. There appears to be no perceptual equivalent to moral weakness but it is still true on balance that for all our experiences in the life-world – including, therefore, those of coming to see someone as kind – Maurice Merleau-Ponty was right in saying that "Rationality is exactly measured in the experiences in which it reveals itself. There is rationality, that is to say: perspectives match up, perceptions confirm each other, a meaning appears .... The phenomenological world is not pure being, but the meaning which shows through at the intersection of my experiences and at the intersection of my experiences and those of the other".[25]

The importance here of the perception of pattern entails also, I believe, a critique of Marcel's notion of *disponibilité*, at least as far as the latter overlaps kindness. Immediately after the passage cited above which distinguishes real presence from physical presence and of being totally with the other as opposed to a partial, momentary relationship, Marcel adds another claim which is far more debatable: "Let us not speak of proof here", he says; "the word itself is inappropriate. Presence is something which reveals itself immediately and incontrovertibly in a look, a smile, an accent, a shaking of hands".[26]

This, I believe, is wrong. *Disponibilité* and the kindness that embodies it are not immediately obvious in one isolable action. If they were, they would be phenomenologically indistinguishable from clever deception, fraud, seduction, and so forth. Certainly, something is immediately obvious in the kinds of experiences which Marcel is describing which makes them count as evidence in the establishment of the pattern which is, as above, required to form a judgment about someone's character. But it is not the kindness of *disponibilité* itself when we are first getting to know someone. Rather, it can be immediately obvious only after the pattern has been perceived, judgment made, and this inductive inference conditions my future perceptions of the individual in question.

III. The Eidetic Reduction

Such are, in brief outline, some main features of the experience of kindness. To recapitulate, an act of kindness appears as a benevolent caring and concern for the other. There are many degrees of seriousness possible in the care for the other which kindness expresses, and these range from the casual, passing helping gesture at one end of the spectrum to love at the other extreme. Further, kindness involves a respect for the feelings of the other through politeness, generosity, and gentleness conceived as a moderation in the use of power. In this way, kindness is opposed to a manipulative, exploitative approach to the other. But even without a special reference for feelings through generosity and courtesy for reasons noted clearly by Kant, kindness *qua* mode of benevolence would still be opposed to using the other merely as a means to some end. However, the kind person is responsible to the other in the sense of responsibility referred to in Marcel's notion of *disponibilité* rather than in the sense of the categorical imperative.

But phenomenology is not description of the phenomena for their own sakes. Rather, it is description put in the service of a concern for essences. The essence is the core meaning of a given phenomenon, that which makes it what it is. It is the essential structure of a phenomenon. Now to articulate the essence of kindness, if we adopt the Husserlian technique of imaginative variation and fancy some feature of the experience of kindness changed while the phenomenon remains intact, then that particular aspect will not be part of the essence of kindness. Conversely, if the absence of some element of the phenomenon does destroy its experiential identity, then that element is part of the essence.

In performing our imaginative variations, let us first consider those main features of the experience as recapitulated above and then certain others which the former either presuppose or to which they are otherwise related. Respect for feelings through generosity, gentleness, and courtesy clearly appears to be a necessary ingredient in the essence of kindness because, without it, the power I have to influence the other would be at best unkind benevolence and at worst malevolent exploitation. The latter speaks for itself but as an explanation of the former, we may again consider the sort of example of this given in Part II. A stern parent or teacher, say, might have to teach a child a lesson which, to really "sink in", is judged (rightly or wrongly) to have to be presented in an unkind way. And what would convert this act of benevolence to one of the more restricted type of kindness would be precisely care and solicitude for the child's feelings.

Of course, this does not imply that the qualities of being gentle, courteous, polite, generous, and so on, are sufficient conditions of being kind or of doing a particular act of kindness. And in fact, they are not, as the following sort of case illustrates. In *The Shorter Oxford English Dictionary, On Historical Principles*, under "kindly" (at p. 1155), Archbishop (Archibald Campbell) Tait (1811–1882) is quoted as saying, "Tell him he is an ass, – but say so kindly". The sense of this is probably to gently inform whoever it is of the good Archbishop's judgment of his character, but it is not necessarily a kindness to do so. More dramatic instances of gentleness and courtesy not being sufficient conditions of kindness are also not difficult to find. Crimes, for instance, can be committed with courtesy, as in the cast of Don Giovanni or the English highwayman, Dick Turpin. And more recently, police in the State of Florida managed to catch a man who had raped more than a dozen women. He was dubbed "the courteous rapist" or the "gentlemanly rapist", or some such title not only for the presumable style with which he committed his crimes, but also for his practice of carrying a box of contraceptives.

Of course, what is missing in the case of crimes, even gentle ones, is the fundamental motive of respect (for the victims) in the Kantian sense. For, benevolence must be typified by such respect to avoid manipulation and domination of the other, and kindness *qua* particular mode of benevolence must follow suit. Thus the notion of being "good willed" is also an indispensable part of the essence of kindness, and this becomes evident when we imaginatively vary situations to eliminate this sense of respect. We then realize that the external results of one's actions would be indistinguishable from, in the closest possible resemblance, various forms of clever fraud.

Now a possibly competing claim has recently been urged by Philip Hallie[27] in detailing the background of his study of cruelty and power relationships. He considers both the Nazi persecution of the Jews, to which I shall return towards the end of this paper, as well as slavery in America. And he situates his concern for the latter in the context of Frederick Douglass's great autobiography, *Life and Times*. In relevant part, Hallie tells us that:

> In studying slavery in America and the concentration camps of central Europe I found that kindness could be the ultimate cruelty, especially when it was given within that unbalanced power relationship (of the domination of the victim by the victimizer). A kind overseer or a kind camp guard can exacerbate cruelty, can remind his victim that there are other relationships than the relationship of cruelty, and can make the victim deeply bitter, especially when he sees the self-satisfied smile of his victimizer. He is being cruelly treated when he is given a penny or a bun after having endured the crushing and grinding of his mental and bodily well-being. As Frederick Douglass put it:
> The kindness of the slave-master only gilded the chain. It detracted nothing from its weight or strength. The thought that men are for other and better uses than slavery throve best under the gentle treatment of a kind master.[28]

Does it follow, then, that one can do a kindness for someone without respecting that person as an end in himself? Can it ever be that being kind is ever exploitative? I still think not. But at the same time, I hasten to note that I would not have the temerity to substitute the philosopher's perspective for that of the victims of such chilling and starkly horrifying experiences to which Hallie and Douglass refer. Rather, I would venture some different interpretations, or at least precisions, of the language cited above to describe the relationship of cruelty to kindness.

In the first place, Hallie is quite right that "kindness could be the ultimate cruelty" for the reasons he gives, viz. such kind treatment reminds the victim in an excruciatingly painful way of the cruel institution to which he is bound. But it does not follow from this that doing a kindness for someone can involve acting in a cruel way or without a Kantian-like respect. Indeed, it would *appear as* kindness only to the degree that it does involve respect in this sense, or at least tries to approximate it as much as the cruel institution will permit. For that matter, something like this happens constantly in impersonal, mechanical bureaucracies. It is the kind and respectful functionary – rather than philosophers, theologians, or sociologists – who often serves as the most forceful critic of the dehumanizing aspects of modern society, precisely by being a contrast to it. Not only should we be willing to grant the logical possibility of such a sincerely kind person, even if his actions remind us of the degraded state of "mass man", but also the reports of several victims of Hitler's death camps referred to the occasional, kind S.S. guard who through kindness tried to relieve the horror.

Second, Hallie speaks of one and the same S.S. guard or overseer as later being kind to his victim – i.e., by giving him or her "a penny or a bun" – after first having acted cruelly toward the victim. This is puzzling. There is nothing in this passage to suggest that either the guard or the victim would perceive the giving of the penny or bun as a kindness. As we have seen above, we must distinguish outward, observable behavior from intention and motive which we believe – rightly or wrongly – to lie behind the behavior. I cannot understand how kindness could phenomenologically appear through "the self-satisfied smile of his victimizer". As McTaggart once observed somewhere, providing refreshments in the intervals between tortures does nothing to prove the humanity of the torturer.

It is also true, though, that a Kantian sort of respect is not a sufficient condition of being kind to someone, as Kant's own discussions of crime and punishment show very clearly – particularly in regard to capital punishment. And in quite a different context, even in the non-dehumanizing aspects of our urban, technological civilization we relate to a variety of people each day in terms of their social functions. They serve as means to our ends without being degraded into *mere* means to an end, and in the former case, a Kantian-like respect can still manifest itself. Yet, kindness need not be present, and in some cases cannot be. There are, for instance, interrelationships with anonymous functionary others in institutions. Also, when, say, I am going into surgery, I may be confident that I will be respected and also be quite sure that the very last thing I want is for the doctor to relate to me personally, considering feelings in his work as a surgeon, and so forth.[29]

But it also appears to be true that the type of responsibility embodied in kindness is very different from that which is invoked by the Kantian view of respect. For kindness, as an exercise of care and concern, transcends a purely formal calculation of the requirements of the moral law. As with Marcel's *disponibilité*, kindness rests on a spontaneous, fully personal response to the other which is as much rooted in a commitment of feeling and sympathy as it is in reason. To put another way, kindness is a type of caring or concern *for* the other and not simply a way of recognizing and respecting someone's rights.[30]

For the same reason, the Kantian sense of respect by itself is much more readily correlated with justice than is kindness, and this leads to the next imaginative variation. Namely, is kindness essentially good? Here, fancying various possibilities leads me to see in kindness itself something good and therefore worth cultivating. But at the same time, I can also envisage situations in which (a) one can be morally blameless even if one can be kind and chooses not to, and (b) it would not always be morally good or right to do a kindness for someone. An example of (a) would occur if, other things being equal, I refuse to give someone my symphony ticket. And in terms of (b), we may again consider the examples cited above in which a given individual could act benevolently toward the other only in a unkind way. Let us say, therefore, that kindness should always be prized but not always praised.

This perception leads directly to the question of what knowledge of the facts of a given situation is required for doing an act of kindness? From all that appears, the answer seems to be that such knowledge is indispensable for actually doing them but not necessary for intending to do them. This is so because, in the case of a misperception of relevant facts, the best intentions can misfire with a practical result of actual harm done. Thus I see that such knowledge about what is really in the best interests of the object of my kindness is a necessary part of giving my intention real effect.

Tightly related to this claim, one may also ask whether action itself is required to constitute the essence of kindness, and one would further need to disentangle two very different meanings concealed in phrasing the question in this way. The first meaning would be whether, in kindly influencing the other, I must positively intervene in his or her life — actually do something for him or her — or whether I can also do him or her a kindness by refraining from doing something. Here, there is no doubt that I can do someone a kindness in the latter fashion as well as in the former, and this is so because sometimes, as in the case of grief in the face of tragedies, the best way to respect the feelings of the other is to respect his or her privacy.

The second possible meaning of this question is more significant and involves a more complicated response. That is, is it possible for someone to be a kind person and yet not express that kindness in concrete action? For Kant, it would appear, the agent can fulfill his moral commitment by *willing* in the correct way and by that only. Whether or not that will finds expression in action is a contingent and empirical matter which, by definition, lies beyond the nature of the practical use of pure reason. Certainly Kant would have doubted the practical utility of such an individual, but it is still the case on his theory that action is not necessary for being good-willed.

With kindness, on the contrary, the opposite result obtains. If I imaginatively vary action out of given situations, not only do I no longer have any evidence of the presence of kindness, but also – and much more significantly – the agent's honest self-knowledge could include no such reference. That is, a given individual may claim on the basis of an alleged private and incorrigible access to his own "mind" or "self" that he is kind. But if an inspection of that person's behavior reveals that he never gives tips or practices any other generosities, is persistently harsh and even cruel in dealing with others, we may rightly be suspicious of his putative self-knowledge.[31]

There is also an important corollary of the necessity of including both concrete action and knowledge of the relevant facts within the essence of kindness. That is, while kindness by itself is always to be prized, the kind person whom we praise is not a man or woman of good principles merely, but also someone who has both the requisite factual knowledge to put them into play and the determination to do so. (One must be "wise as a serpent and simple as a dove".) No better example of this can be found than Pastor André Trocmé who, together with his fellow villagers of Le Chambon-sur-Lignon in France, opened their hearts and homes to Jews fleeing Nazi persecution.

In his remarkable book, *Lest Innocent Blood Be Shed: The Story of Le Chambon and How Goodness Happened There*, Philip Hallie describes Trocmé as follows:

> He was a good man according to the classic conception of good and evil, but he was more. Essential to his goodness, central to his decency, was what he did with and for other people, and what he did against them. In part he was good because he resisted the people who were doing harm and because he helped save the lives of those they were seeking to harm, the refugees. He was good because he diminished evil in the world. The evil he diminished was harm-doing, and the evil he diminished was suffering. ... When Darcissac and Trocmé praised the Chambonnais, they were praising not only what was happening within the souls of the Chambonnais; they were praising what happened in the presbytery, in the temple, in the boardinghouses, in the funded houses, and on the farms. The classic conception of good and evil as inward conditions of the mind or the soul is not totally wrong. It points up one of the important forces in

ethical actions: respect for the demands of ethics despite fear, despite indifference, and despite all the other passions that tend to debilitate and destroy action. In Le Chambon, at least, there was more to being good than this deep inward respect for the demands of ethics.[32]

It is also significant that Hallie contrasts Trocmé's approach to the world with Kant's ethics in a way that reinforces the above reasoning designed to show that action is indispensable to kindness:

> Another great builder of the classic conception of ethics is Immanuel Kant. He opens his *Metaphysical Foundations of Morals* with perhaps the most memorable statement of an inward government ethic that has ever been written: "Nothing can possibly be conceived in the world, or even out of it, which can be called good without qualification, except a GOOD WILL". And he goes on to say that a good will is good "not because of what it performs or effects" but because it respects the moral law. This respect for the law means that the good person will not allow his own passions to overcome his reason and throw his inward government into anarchy, Kant is very careful to point out — and this care makes him one of the greatest figures in the history of the classic conception of ethics — that what we do to or for others is not central to ethics; the orderly condition of our own souls, our character, is what ethics seeks to achieve, and praises when it succeeds.[33]

Finally, let us conclude with one additional imaginative variation which can extend our view of the utility of kindness. In terms of the object of kindness, we can imaginatively vary the spatiality and temporality of situations to see that the other need not be immediately present or even fully cognizant of the agent's intentions in order that an act of kindness be performed. For example, John Dryden once implored a friend (in his *Epistle to Congrève*, at line 72):

> Be kind, to my remains, and oh defend
> Against your judgment, your departed friend!

Also, one can be kind to dead poets by not misquoting them. And different sorts of examples of kindnesses done without the immediate presence of the other and/or his or her cognizance would include anonymous kindnesses, kindnesses to babies, kindnesses to lower forms of animal life, and so forth.

In conclusion, then, this paper has been an attempt to phenomenologically delineate the essence of kindness. It has not attempted to specify the significance of kindness in ethical theory or to make even farther reaching claims about the preferability of a morality of just doing the decent thing to and for people as opposed to (1) utilitarian calculations of moral scores of action, rules and the like, and (2) dutifully following moral laws. These are larger questions for future and hopefully fruitful inquiries.

NOTES

1. A preliminary version of this paper was presented to the annual meeting of the British Society for Phenomenology in St. Edmund Hall, Oxford University, April 1981. I wish to thank all present who helped me with criticism which have hopefully been done justice in the final version.

2. This notion, which one finds throughout several of Marcel's works, is difficult to translate into English. It is an amalgam of "availability", "disposibility", and − most awkward of all − a "disposition to be with the other". See generally his *Position at approaches concrètes du mystère ontologique*, Deuxième Edition (Louvain: Editions Nauwelaerts, 1967).

3. Cf. William Shakespeare, *The Tragedy of Hamlet, Prince of Denmark*, edited and with notes by George Lyman Kittredge (Boston: Blaisdell Publishing Company, 1939), p. 142. In glossing Hamlet's retort to his uncle, the King, "A little more than kin, and less than kind"! (Act I, Sc. 2), Kittredge points out that Hamlet "is applying to his own case an old proverbial antithesis", of which Steevens and Collier quote three good examples: "The neerer we are in bloud, the further wee must be from loue; and the greater the kindred is, the lesse the kindness must be" (Lyly, *Mother Bombie*, iii, 1; ed. Bond, III, 195); "In kinde a father, not in kindliness" (*Gorboduc*, i, 1, 18); "I would he were not so neere to us in kindred, then sure he would be neerer in kindness" (Rowley, *A Search for Money*, 1609; Percy Society ed., p.5). Cf. Bastard, *Epigrams*, 1958, iii, 29: "Neuer so many cousins: so fewe kynde"; Webster, *Duchess of Malfy*, iv, 2, 288−290 (ed. Lucas, II, 101).

4. William Frankena, *Ethics*, Second Edition (Englewood Cliffs, N.J.: Prentice-Hall, Inc., 1973), pp. 62−63.

5. *Ideas I*, trans. W.R. Boyce Gibson (London: George Allen & Urwin, Ltd., 1969), p. 111.

6. "Husserl's Transcendental-Phenomenological Reduction", *Philosophy and Phenomenological Research*, Vol. XX, December, 1959, No. 2, p. 243.

7. There are, of course, a variety of views on the nature of the phenomenological reduction and its relation to the *epoché*. For a concise summary of some of the more interesting ones, see Herbert Spiegelberg, "Is the Reduction Necessary for Phenomenology? Husserl's and Pfänder's Replies", *Journal of the British Society for Phenomenology*, Vol. IV (1973), 3−17, and especially " 'Epoché' Without Reduction: Some Replies to my Critics", *Journal of the British Society for Phenomenology*, Vol. V (1974), 256−261.

8. *Caring* (New York: Harper & Row, 1971).

9. Mayeroff, p. 5.

10. Mayeroff, p. 6.

11. Erich Fromm, *The Art of Loving* (New York: Harper & Row, 1962), p. 26.

12. Fromm, pp. 27−28.

13. Eric Berne, M.D., *Games People Play* (London: Penguin Books, 1964), pp. 80−81.

14. Berne, p. 81.

15. Berne, p. 81.

16. Berne, pp. 80−81. Dr. Berne also notes (at pp. 81−82) the possibilities inherent in this game for the whole family and, tightly related to this its relevance to psychiatric problems: "Corner is found in a somewhat different form as a family game involving the children, where it resembles the "double-bind" described by Bateson and his associates. Here the child is cornered, so whatever he does is wrong. According to the Bateson school this may be an important etiological factor in schizofrenia. In the present language, then, schizophrenia may be a child's antithesis to "Corner". Experience in treating adult schizophrenics with game analysis bears this out − that is, if the family game of "Corner" is analysed to demonstrate that the schizophrenic behaviour was and is specifically undertaken to counter this game, partial or total remission occurs in a properly prepared patient. An everyday form of "Corner" which is played

by the whole family and is most likely of affect the character development of the younger children occurs with meddlesome "Parental" parents. The title boy or girl is urged to be more helpful around the house, but when he is, the parents find fault with what he does − a homely example of "damned of you do and damned if you don't". This "double-bind" may be called the Dilemma Type of "Corner".

17. Gabriel Marcel, *Creative Fidelity*, trans. Robert Rosthal (New York: The Noonday Press, 1964), p. 155.

18. Fromm, p. 130.

19. This conception of gentleness is to be distinguished from that of Aristotle and is closer to the French tradition of *gentillesse*. In Aristotle's view, "Gentleness is the mean in feelings of anger. Although there is no name for the person occupying the median position and hardly even for the extremes, we apply the term "gentleness" to the median, despite the fact that it inclines toward the deficiency, which has no name either. The excess may be called something like "short temper". For the emotion is a feeling of anger, which is brought about by many different factors. Now, a man is praised for being angry under the right circumstances and with the right people, and also in the right manner, at the right time, and for the right length of time. He may be (termed) gentle, since gentleness is used as a term of praise. For being gentle means to be unruffled and not be driven by emotion, but to be angry only under such circumstances and for as long a time as reason may bid. But he seems to be more prone to going wrong in the direction of deficiency: a gentle person is forgiving rather than vindictive". *Nicomachean Ethics*, trans. Martin Ostwald (Indianapolis: The Library of Liberal Arts, 1962), pp. 100−101.

20. Cf. Jean Paul Sartre, *L'Etre et le néant* (Paris: Gallimard, 1943), p. 508. The similarity here is more than unsettling from the point of view of kindness owing to the nature of intersubjectivity as Sartre describes it in that particular work.

21. *Position et approches concrètes du mystère ontologique*, p. 83.

22. *Position et approches concrètes du mystère ontologique*, p. 84.

23. *Position et approches concrètes du mystère ontologique*, p. 83.

24. I am indebted for this reference to Herbert Spiegelberg, who located it in Morton White's review of Paul Levy's *Moore: G.E. Moore and the Cambridge Apostles*, in *The New York Review of Books*, Vol. XXVIII, No. 5, April 2, 1981, pp. 35−37. The remark cited is at p. 37. I am not making any claim about what Wittgenstein meant in saying this. Nor would I wish to deny that someone could use "kindly" in a non-pejorative sense. (Cf. John Henry Newman's *The Pillar of the Cloud* which begins "Lead, kindly Light, amid the encircling gloom, /Lead thou me on"!

25. *Phénoménologie de la perception* (Paris: Gallimard, 1945), p. xv.

26. *Position et approches concrètes du mystère ontologique*, p. 83.

27. "From Cruelty to Goodness", *The Hastings Center Report*, Vol. 11, No. 3, June 1981, pp. 23−28.

28. Hallie, p. 35.

29. Cf. Harvey Cox, *The Secular City* (New York: The Macmillan Company, 1966), pp. 48−49. Cox argues in the same way in trying to make a case for an urban, technological society still being a hospitable milieu for a religious commitment. But Cox nowhere directly considers the significance of such a society being a very unkind place to live.

30. This point is distinct from one made by Joel Feinberg, and is partially inconsistent with it. Feinberg, in considering whether there are any absolute rights, takes up "A third possibility [which] is the right not to be subjected to exploitation or degradation even when such subjection is utterly painless and therefore not cruel. It is possible to treat human beings with drugs, hypnosis, or other brain-washing techniques so that they become compliant tools in the hands of their manipulators useful as means to their manipulators' ends, but with all serious purposes of their own totally obliterated .... It would be good business as well as good morals to treat

them kindly (so long as they are obedient), for that way one can get more labor out of them in the long run. Clearly, kindness and "humanity", while sufficient to satisfy the rights of animals, are not sufficient for human beings, who must therefore have ascribed to them another kind of right that we deliberately withhold from animals". *Social Philosophy* (Englewood Cliffs, N.J.: Prentice-Hall, Inc., 1973), pp. 96–97. If the arguments in the present essay are correct that kindness involves a respect in a Kantian sense, "kindly" and "kindness" in the above passage should be replaced by "gently" and "gentleness" and other kindred words.

31. Cf. Gilbert Ryle, *The Concept of Mind* (London: Hutchinson & Co., Ltd., 1949), pp. 174ff. I have argued elsewhere that Merleau-Ponty holds the same view ("Whitehead and Merleau-Ponty: Some Moral Implications". *Process Studies* V, No. 4 (Winter 1974), pp. 235–251).

32. Philip Hallie, *Lest Innocent Blood Be Shed: The Story of the Village of Le Chambon and How Goodness Happened There* (New York: Harper & Row, 1979), pp. 279–280.

33. Hallie, p. 278.

The Phenomenology of Symbol: Genesis I and II
by
Frank K. Flinn

The following essay, which is divided into three parts, is a phenomenological interpretation of the two accounts of creation which open the Book of Genesis. In the first part below, I discuss the problem of interpretation stemming from the current use of the term "myths" for the creation accounts. In the second part, I examine a problem peculiar to modernity − critical consciousness along with the demystification and demythologization which may block us from interpreting symbolic discourse. These two parts then provide a dialectical framework for the third − the phenomenological approach to the texts about the "Beginning" in the Book of Genesis.

The essay takes its cue from a statement by Paul Ricoeur that "the first account of creation is actually *the theological reading of a phenomenology of perception*" and "the progressive portrayal of the theatre of our existence".[1] Extending this statement, I suggest that, if the first account of creation presents a phenomenology of the *theatre* of human existence, the second account presents a phenomenology of *drama* of human existence that commences on the stage which gets unfolded in the first. As will become clear below, I read these two accounts as dialectical articulations of one another.

Before proceeding to my main task, however, I wish to say a word about both phenomenology and hermeneutics. The Book of Genesis is an example of religious discourse, a text that speaks of the Holy or Sacred. The Holy or the Sacred, however, does not appear directly the way a tree appears in a garden, but as "a *highly impressive* and *extremely exceptional* 'Other'".[2] Thus speech about the "Other" connotes more than it denotes, by way of symbols and metaphors. Ordinary language must be used in an extraordinary way to express the appearance of the Sacred. Thus, when Jesus says that, "the Kingdom of God is like a mustard seed", he has brought into the same constellation of meaning both something from the everyday experience of horticulture − the growth of a tree from a tiny seed − and something from beyond that everyday experience − its likeness to the sudden appearance of the coming Kingdom of God. Ordinarily, we do not live eschatologically, nor

W.S. Hamrick (ed.) *Phenomenology in Practice and Theory*.
© 1985 Martinus Nijhoff Publishers, Dordrecht/Boston/Lancaster
ISBN 90 247 2926 2. Printed in the Netherlands.

do we experience ordinary things like mustard seeds as symptoms of the coming Kingdom. But symbolic language, such as the Parable of the Mustard Seed, both reverses the perception of the everyday world and challenges one's being-in-the-world.

The phenomenology of religious language seeks to detect the symbolic doubleness of religious experience. It seeks to open up the horizon of meaning at the intersection of the ordinary and the extraordinary, the "letter" and the "spirit", the familiar and the "Other" and the profane and the sacred. The very doubleness of this horizon, however, necessitates the task of hermeneutics. In symbolic expression, a primary, literal meaning gives rise to second meaning. The relation between the primary and secondary meaning — for example, the symbolic conjunction of a mustard seed and the Kingdom of God — is obscure and dense, resulting in a risk of distortion, dislocation and falsification. Hermeneutics is the art of deciphering ambiguous meanings and of unmasking false connections ("rationalizations") between the primary and secondary meaning of symbols.

Beyond this first task of hermeneutics lies another, perhaps more important, task. Because the accounts of creation in Genesis have come down to us from an ancient culture, we may bestow upon them a "false antiquity". The historico-critical method of exegesis falls prey to this danger. The quest for the original author(s) and audience(s) often displaces the ideality of meaning which any text, ancient or modern, intends. Conversely, literalistic interpretations, often associated with the religious phenomenon of "fundamentalism", tend to bestow a "false modernity" on the text, presuming that its horizon of meaning is immediately accessible to a consciousness shaped by modernity. If this problematic may be transposed into Gottlob Frege's categories, historicist interpretations stress historical representation (*Vorstellung*) at the expense of meaning (*Sinn*) whereas literalistic interpretations do the opposite.[3] This second hermeneutical task is, therefore, to confront the problem called the "hermeneutical circle" so that the text retains both its distance and proximity. Only by preserving the delicate balance between representation *and* meaning can the horizon of the text enter into and speak to my own horizon.

I cannot hope to read and interpret a text unless I let that text in some way read and interpret me. Only thus can I approach that ideal of interpretation that Hans-Georg Gadamer calls the merging-of-horizons (*Horizonverschmelzung*) and Paul Ricoeur terms "the second naiveté".[4] In this way, too, interpretation escapes the fate of the hermeneutical circle remaining a vicious circle. This does not mean that I can step outside the circle, but by bringing into question time-bound historical representations — my own and that of the text — the omnitemporality of meaning can appear through the expansion of the circle itself and the enlargement of the horizon of understanding.

I. Myth and the Horizon of Genesis

Today it has become fashionable to refer to the opening accounts of creation in the Book of Genesis as myths or legends. There is nothing necessarily sinister in this usage, yet there is a need for hermeneutical caution. If the primary step in the hermeneutical task is to enter into the world of representation of a text and to first interpret it as it interprets itself in terms of its own categories, symbolic expressions, etc., then it is not proper to use the word "myth" when speaking of biblical texts. One reads many books and articles about biblical myths, legends, tales and sagas, but there are not equivalents for these terms in biblical Hebrew. There is the category of *haggadah* (tale, story) but this term is found only in post-biblical Hebrew and reflects a time when Judaic culture came into contact with Hellenistic civilization. There are biblical words for "song", for "proverb", and for "laws and ordinances", but none for the genres, oral or written, that go by the names of myth, legend, tale or saga.

In speaking about biblical myths, therefore, we need to be forewarned that we may be bestowing a false horizon on the text. This caveat alerts us to the pre-understanding of our own horizon and to the fact that the understanding of myth does not issue from the Jerusalem side of our heritage. Two aspects of this pre-understanding need further inquiry.

Myth and History. Today many scholars, including biblical scholars, are in the habit of making a distinction between myth and history in the belief that this distinction comes down to us as an Athenian inheritance. If we still understood "history" as an "inquiry into causes and origins", that belief would be partially correct. In biblical hermeneutics, the distinction between myth and history has been used to elevate certain texts and lower others on the grounds of "historicity".

But singling out of "the historical credo" as the core of the Hexateuch and the emphasis on the "God-who-acts-in-history" have the effect of reducing the texts about creation to *ein blosses "Dass"*, a mere "That" which has no content and which serves as a prelude to "the real", i.e., the historical call of Abraham, the historical Exodus, etc.[5] Creation takes on the characteristics of *Natur*, the primeval *Urgrund* or *Ungrund*, in the dialectic Nature/History or Nature/Spirit or German Idealism. Thus Hegel saw the emergence of the historical Spirit and the demythologization of Nature in Jewish religion: "The Spiritual speaks itself here absolutely free of the Sensuous, and Nature is reduced to something merely external undivine".[6]

Again, our sense of hermeneutical caution ought to come into play. There is no biblical equivalent for the concept of "nature". There are the "heavens and the earth", but there are no comprehensive concepts, like the Aristotelian *physis* or *kosmos*, in the Old Testament. Nor is there a biblical concept that

226

goes by the name of "history". There are "generations" and "events of the day" (= Chronicles), but no formal concept which coincides with what we mean by history.

Mythos and Logos. Since the distinction myth/history runs so much of a risk of bestowing a false horizon on the text, it behooves us to inquire more deeply into the true opposite of myth. Here our best guide is none other than Plato. In the *Republic*, Plato draws out the elaborate proportion, poetry: mythos: philosophy: logos. Myth is narrative that does not escape the ambiguities of becoming, the region of the passions. It is a mixture of falsehood, deception and concealing (*to pseudon*) and of truth, verity and deconcealing (*to alethinon*). Logos is speech which aims at being. Through dialogue and dialectic, the philosopher seeks to separate false opinion from right opinion and to replace right opinion with knowledge of true being.

In its account of the world of becoming, myth portrays gods and men doing unjust deeds in extreme passion. The passions are the religion of Eros and the body, and can lead to the conviction that there is no cosmic support for virtue in the soul. As an example of extreme passion, Socrates cites the speech Achilles' shade makes to Odysseus (*Odyssey* XI. 489–92, cited at *Republic* 386c):

I would rather be on soil, a slave to another,
A man without portion, whose sustenance is meager,
Than rule over the dead who have perished.

Socrates considers that Achilles' speech could leave the impression that the distinctions between freedom and slavery, courage and cowardice, justice and injustice in this life do not make a difference because of the meaninglessness of the afterlife.

The overriding theme of the *Republic* is the search for a reasoned account, a logos, of justice in the soul and the city, which is the soul writ-large. For there to be justice, the logos demands virtuous acts of gods and humans in the tales told to the young. Under the severe gaze of the logos, myth is forced to undergo a purgation, and Plato gives an example of a purged myth in Book X of the *Republic*. Socrates' Myth of Er is a "dis-implication" of the Myth of Alcinous or Odysseus' account of his journey to Hades (*Odyssey* IX–XIII). The myth is grounded on a "proof" of the immortality of the soul and the assumption that the soul is non-composite. In his journey to the other world, Er is given a vision of justice which sustains the whole cosmos and in light of which it is demonstrated that the souls of humans choose their own destinies in this life and the next, such that "God is blameless" (617e). Significantly, Achilles is absent in Er's tour among the shades of the dead (620ff.).

The myth of Er may be called philosophic poetry. But in order to attain the luminous clarity of the vision of the whole, Plato is compelled to abstract from the body and Eros. The positing of the soul's absolute freedom and complete accountability is grounded on this abstraction which parallels exactly Kant's abstraction from human propensity (*Hang*) and inclination (*Neigung*) in search for the idea of the morally pure will.[7] However, the argument of the *Republic* does not reach its goal − the definition (*logos*) of justice in itself. Likewise, the "proof" of the immortality of the soul remains inconclusive because the compositeness or non-compositeness of the soul is left undecided (612a).

These reasons compel us to read the *Republic* not in isolation, but in light of the dialogues which directly engage the theme of the *metaxu*, the In-between, which appears in the symbols of the soul as "composition", "*mélange*", "mixture" and "absolute mean".[8] The very deduction of the soul at the end of the *Republic* absolves the gods, the cosmos, and the body itself of accountability for the origin of evil. Prior to the origin of evil there was justice in the whole. This very deduction, however, renders the origin of evil and injustice inexplicable. It remains a mystery how the soul which has had a glimpse of the ideas, and whose ether is justice itself, can be deflected toward injustice. Prior to any "fall" − whether this be interpreted gnostically as a fall "into the body" or ethically as a fall into bad will or religiously as a fall into sin − there was the prior "incarnation" of fragility in the soul.

Here the logos encounters a limit − what St. Paul calls "the mystery of iniquity" and Kant, "the inscrutability of radical evil". The moment I posit my accountability for my evil acts (my freedom), I posit, too, my propensity toward evil (my non-free inclination toward it). The origin of evil resists decoding into clear and distinct signs. It cannot be factored out into "This plus that" or "That, therefore this". Any attempt to lay hold on one side of the antinomy (accountability/propensity) opens up the chasm of reductionism − either a rigid doctrine of predestination or a doctrine of a radically capricious will. The mystery of the origin of evil resists conceptualization.

The inscrutability and impassibility of the origin of evil motivates the return of logos to mythos. The last word of the *Republic* is: "Thus, Glaucon, mythos was saved and not lost (621 b−c)". In Plato, the dialogue alternates dialectically between clear and univocal signs − the medium of the discourse proper to logos − and dense, multivocal symbols − the discourse proper to mythos. It is the power of symbol to say more than can be said in philosophy. Thus, for example, Paul Ricoeur and Victor Turner have discussed how the symbol, in contrast with the sign, can hold in unity meanings which are even opposite in signification.[9] This power of the symbol, at once opaque and laden with meaning, is to provide access to the inscrutable while thwarting the hubris of absolute knowledge. Yet what the symbol takes away from knowledge it offers to thinking. The purgation of myth in Plato does not lead to the abrogation of symbol because in the later dialogues we witness the process of resymbolization. The symbol of the two-souled Eros, offspring of Penia (Impoverishment) and Poros (Surfeit), in the *Symposium* (201d ff.), is a token for recollecting why the soul, forgetful of the Truth, must gorge itself on the meager fodder of Opinion. At the same time, the symbol of Eros is a beacon of future meaning which illumines, if only by indirect lighting, the dynamic of the logos' own quest for the clarity of the Eidos. As thinking precedes knowledge, so mythos precedes logos.

The Platonic dialectic of mythos and logos can serve as an appropriate modality for approaching the narratives of creation in Genesis. When set against their Near-Eastern background, the accounts of creation manifest the same aspect of purgation and resymbolization as do the Platonic myths. But before we can show how this is so, we must first confront the project of modernity which implies not only a purgation of myth, but also the annulment of symbol.

II. Demystification and Demythologization

Paul Ricoeur had detected two conflicting currents in modern hermeneutics. He captures this conflict in the sentence, "Thus idols must die — so that symbols may live".[10] The first mode of hermeneutics he calls "the hermeneutics of suspicion" which seeks to reduce the illusion and idols of false consciousness with which the human species is beset. This mode is associated with thinkers such as Freud, Nietzsche, and Marx. The second mode he calls "the hermeneutics of the restoration of meaning" which strives to approach again the sacred through the understanding of symbol. Ricoeur himself attempts to mediate the conflict.

Ricoeur also makes a distinction between demystification and demythologization.[11] Demythologization is the critique of religious discourse arising from within the sacred sciences. Demystification is the critique arising from outside. Now for our purposes in this essay, Ricoeur's typology of the critique of the sacred needs amplification and deepening in order to show in precise detail how the project of modernity has involved both a purgation of myth and an annulment of symbol. The hermeneutics of suspicion was a long time arriving, and it coincides with modernity which has twin roots in the Reformation and the modern empirico-analytic sciences. Modernity may well be defined as the age of "de-", for it has undergone successive waves of de-allegorization, deidolization, disenchantment, dekernelling and demystification, disillusionment and decipherment, and finally, demythologization.

The Reformational hermeneutic begins with the reduction of the medieval fourfold sense of scripture (the literal, the allegorical, the moral and the analogical) to the literal or historical sense. Although medieval exegesis provided the template for the *interpretatio naturae et historiae*, it could also surpass and pass by the plainness of the primary meaning in a fantastic web of typologization and allegorization. Luther sought to de-allegorize the scriptures by a return to the letter and the establishment of the principle that *scriptura suae ipsius interpres*.[12]

There is a hidden connection between Luther's de-allegorization and Bacon's project of de-idolization and establishment of the correlate principle that *naturae suae ipsius interpres*. Just as the Reformers reduced the biblical text to a set of evidences for faith, so Bacon's return to things themselves (*ipsissimae res*) reduced the Book of Nature to an array of instances which humanity could control and master through the new "active science". .

The twin roots of modern faith and modern science led to what Friedrich Schiller called "the disenchantment of the world". The representation of the world as a living cosmion, which proferred symbolic links between the rhythms of nature and human existence, gave way to the representation of the world as a mechanical cosmos or system of calculable forces by which nature could be put "under constraint . . . forced out of her natural course, and squeezed and molded".[13] This marked the great hermeneutical reversal of modernity: instead of scripture providing the template for the interpretation of nature and history, history and nature became the criteria for the interpretation of scripture.[14] In biblical circles, this gave rise to the historico-critical enterprise known as "higher criticism".

The turn to history marked the second way of modernity. Hegel envisioned history as a dialectic between nature and spirit (*Geist*) which terminated in the rationally free spirit of the secularized and bureaucratized state. The rational concept first exists as a "kernel" in "limitless wealth of forms, appearances and configurations" of the "variegated rind" of mythical consciousness.[15] History is a process of progressive de-husking (*Enthüllung*) and demystification whereby absolute spirit becomes both in itself and for itself through the rational concept. In biblical circles, the Hegelian hermeneutic of history provided the schema for the separations and classifications of the various literary strands in the Bible:

THESIS	ANTITHESIS	SYNTHESIS
JE (Yahwist-Elohist, ca. 1000 B.C.)	D (Deuteronomist, ca. 700 B.C.)	P (Priestly, ca. 500 B.C.)
natural religion	historical	legal
polytheism	henotheism	monotheism
harvest ritual (Matzoth)	historical (Passover)	sacrificial (Yom Kippur)

230

Marx, for his part, as one knows well, radicalized and inverted the Hegelian dialectic. He argued first that the Idea does not determine the material conditions of existence, not the reverse. Thus in his critique of religious representations, he argued that religious suffering is an "expression of real suffering" which, nonetheless, becomes the "opium of the people" when it is deflected and mystified by being transfixed into an imaginary "Heaven" where all wrongs will be righted.[16] Secondly, Marx's critique of "holy" illusions laid the groundwork for his critique of "unholy" illusions which becloud the secular domains of law, politics and economics.

With Nietzsche's project of disillusionment (*Enttäuschung*) and Freud's task of decipherment (*Entzifferung*), the de-structive aspect of the hermeneutics of suspicion reached its pinacle. As disenchantment was to the world as object, so disillusionment and decipherment is to the world as subject. Nietzsche unmasked the religious representation of Christianity as a revenge of the weak against the strong (Christianity as "Platonism for the masses") and as *ressentiment* against the becomingness of the world.[17] In sum, for Nietzsche, religion is one of the lower forms of the naked will-to-power.

Freud, on the other hand, dethroned the modern Ego, initially so confident of its inwardness in faith (Luther) and certainty in doubt (Descartes), by ciphering it out into an economy of drives (Unconscious, Preconscious, Conscious) and, alter into a topography of competing domains (Id, Ego, Superego). According to Freud, religious representation is a systematic illusion which never rises above the imperialism of the infantile wish.[18]

Faced with the disillusionment of destructive hermeneutics, post-modern faith could no longer find a footing on the ground of naive religious representation. Thus the search for critical faith was to appear in Karl Barth's dialectical theology and Rudolph Bultmann's demythologization of scripture. Barth makes a radical distinction between faith and the cultural representation of it in religion. Faith is the encounter with the KRISIS of God in the proclamation of the gospel (*kerygma*). Critical faith − or faith under KRISIS − is in no way grounded on the human capacity to represent the divine, but reveals cultural religion as the supreme illusion and narcotic.[19] Critical faith is faith in faith itself.

Bultmann, on the other hand, applies dialectical theology to the faith situation of those who find themselves committed to a scientific world-view. As Hegel and Marx sought to extract the rational kernel from the mythical rind, so Bultmann sought to extract the nucleus of faith − the kerygmatic event of the Word of KRISIS addressed to our existential depth − from the cultural vehicle of mythological representation in which it was originally embedded. Demythologization is not an accommodation of the biblical text to suit the prejudice of modern science, but the attempt to enucleate the authentic *skandalon* of the biblical Summons to humanity as humanity in the word of the cross. The mythical cloak of the original revelation, according to Bultmann, is a "false stumbling block".[20]

Demythologization irretrievably removes the function of myth as explanation. From the perspective of scientific explanation, for example, the accounts of creation can only appear as science-*manqué*. This de-structive consequence, however, has a restorative side. The accounts of creation can now reappear as poetry-*plus*. Tillich has therefore suggested that demythologization ought to be called deliteralization, for it recovers for us the scripture as symbolic language.[21] Only in symbol and through symbol can one approach the double horizon of the *arche* and the *eschaton* of ultimate meaning. In this sense, the path through the fiery furnaces of demystification and demythologization becomes the necessary rite of passage for the reappearance of the symbol and the recovery of the sacred.

In this situation, the example of Second Isaiah is instructive. The prophetic author of Isaiah 40—55 announces the extreme of iconclasm and the smashing of idols (see Is. 44.1 ff.) and yet also the recrudescence of mythic symbol. Vitriolic demythologization is co-joined with the lyrical interweaving of the symbolic themes of Creation, Exodus, Exile; inverted motifs from Near Eastern cosmogonic myths, vignettes from everyday life, and the historical events surrounding the reign of Cyrus. And in the most surprising symbolic reversal of all, the texts about the First Things (*ta prota*) are inverted and resignified to speak about the Last Things (*ta eschata*) in an incomparable paean on creation as recreation (Is. 40: 1—31).

III. The Beginning: Genesis I and II

Since the rise of higher criticism in the modern age, scholars have recognized that the Book of Genesis begins with two different accounts of creation. The first account (Gen. 1:1—2; 4a) has been assigned to the Priestly literary tradition which came to fruition sometime during or shortly after the Exile (ca. 587—39 B.C.). The second account (Gen. 2:4b—3:22) has been assigned to the Yahwist literary tradition which flourished around the time of David or a little after (ca. 950—900 B.C.). For the sake of convenience I shall call these two accounts Genesis I and II. It is not my purpose to retrace the steps of the documentary hypothesis and form critical method which have been applied to these texts. These methods divide the text diachronically into earlier and later sources with their respective *Sitzen im Leben*. My intent is to read the two accounts synchronically as texts which dialectically speak about the "Beginning".

GENESIS I. Not everything about the opening account of creation is strange, i.e., so laden with mythological language as to impede our meeting the text on its own level. Genesis I speaks about the appearance of the Beginning, but it also speaks of things which are still plainly evident to the proverbial man from Missouri — light and darkness, dry land and seas, birds, fishes and cattle, etc. Thus we are cautioned against understanding the Beginning as something merely "back then" or creation as an "effect" of which the Creator is taken to the "cause". However, we are forced to confess that something strange does meet us in the first two verses.

In verse 1 we are told that in the beginning God created first the heavens and then the earth. We are not told who says this and how this person has come to know this. It is simply announced. Modern biblical grammarians interpret verse 1 and the protasis or introductory clause to verse 2: "When in the beginning ..., the earth was ...". This implies that there was something "prior" to God's act of creating. This *aliquid prior*, like Plato's "Receptacle" for all things, does not admit of direct reason, but can only be imagined by symbol or what Plato calls "bastard reasoning" (*Timaeus* 51a–52b). In Genesis I, this priority is expressed in the phrase *tohu-wa-bohu*, which is often translated as "formless void".

We know something of what *tohu-wa-bohu* is like and unlike. On the one hand, the primal condition is associated with darkness and "the deep" (*tehom*). On the other hand, it is contrasted with the motion of "the spirit/breath of God hovering over the surface of the waters". Darkness is associated with indistinction and the deep is associated with confusion, random motion and wetness. The contrast of images tells us something of the steps of creation, if not its nature, and the sequence of events can be represented in a crude schema:

$$\frac{\text{breath of God hovering}}{\text{tohu-wa-bohu}} \rightarrow \text{bara'} \rightarrow \frac{\text{heavens}}{\text{earth}}$$

The sequence proceeds from a contrast between (1) "hovering" — an image of orderly motion or "motion-at-rest" — and *tohu-wa-bohu*, an image of disorderly motion, to (2) the creative act of which seems to be some kind of separation, and finally, (3) to created things which are distinct, the heavens and the earth.

Scholars are undecided whether to interpret these verses mythologically by relating *tehom* to Ti-amatu, the Mesopotamian dragonness of the deep, and *bohu* to Baau, the Phoencian goddess of darkness, or to interpret them more philosophically by rendering the terms with privities ("without shape or form") in keeping with Septuagint translation: *aoratos kai akataskeusatos*, "unhorizoned and unstructured". Against a straight mythological interpretation, we note the absence of any cosmogonic struggle or themachy by personified powers in the Bible. The philosophical rendering on the other hand, takes away positive intention of the phrase *tohu-wa-bohu*. The problem is to steer a course between mythological retroduction and philosophical rationalization.

The best course is to understand the phrase *tohu-wa-bohu* as a reinterpreted symbol. On Mesopotamian cylinder seals, Ti'amatu is represented as a hydra-like being that has seven serpentine heads moving confusedly in all directions. The writhing heads in turn are attached to a feline body.[22] As a fantastic being, Ti'amatu represents a congery of anomalous motions and parts. In the *Enuma Elish*, the Babylonian creation epic, she is represented as the personified generative force of sea water which brings forth all things by mingling with the underground fresh water, personified by Apsu:

"When heaven above was not (yet even) mentioned, firmset earth below called by no name; (when) but primeval Apsu, their begetter, and the matrix, Ti'amat — she who gave birth to them all — were mingling their waters in one".[23]

Genesis I demythologizes the cosmic generative forces of nature as personified powers, yet the polysemic vectors of meaning attached to the primeval given — mingling, confusion, moistness (a mixture of the dry and the wet), congery, etc. — are retained. The symbolism of directionless motion leads me to translate verse 2 in a way that retains the onomatopoeic doubleness of the Hebrew original: "And the earth (perhaps, nether-world) was slithering-and-writhing".

Within the paradigmatic structure of Genesis I, the symbolic figure of the Seven-headed Dragonness of the Deep has been demythologized and resignified. It functions as a symbol measured in the same unit but opposite in value to the single Lord of the Seventh Day, the day of rest. Opposed to the confused motions and parts of the primal Slitherer-and-Writher is the Lord of the Sabbath by whose creative action ordered motion and distinct things are brought into being. Phenomenologically speaking, the primal givenness of *tohu-wa-bohu*, "the always already there", looms in the background of the appearance of motions and things that are increasingly distinct.

The notion of creation in Genesis I is not fully articulated as *creatio ex nihilo*, but rather symbolized as an act of discontinuous separation coeval with the ongoing background of *tohu-wa-bohu*. Creation is a separation by that which is separate, i.e., Wholly Other. This is stressed by the verb *bara'*, which is used about God alone in the Old Testament. The root meaning of the verb seems to be "to divide" or "to incise in two halves", a sense which is retained in the Hebrew Pi'el verb form. The notion of separation is reinforced by *badal*, "to distinguish, separate, divide". The verb *bara'* is not, as some scholars claim, used in opposition to *'asah*, the common word for making, but rather serves of the semantic carrier of all the other verbs in Genesis I. All doing, making, producing, increasing and multiplying is to be done "each according to its own kind'', i.e., in such a way that the principle of separation and indistinctions is maintained. Yet behind the distinction remains the possibility of *tohu-wa-bohu*, the ''always already there''.

The reciprocally articulated symbols of *tohu-wa-bohu* (anomalous motions, parts) and the Lord of the Seventh Day (ordered motions, distinct things) are the *termini a quo* and *ad quem* of the six-day creation. The six ''days'' which intervene are further divided into two sets of *tridua* based on two parallel principles: the separation of non-moving things (division) and the distinguishing of moving things or things which can separate from their places (local motion). The creation of light initiates the first set and the creation of the sun initiates the second. We also note that God names some things but not all, that some divisions are called good but not all, and that some things are given a blessing or positive command (''Be fruitful, increase, and multiply'') besiders being seen as good. These complex differentiations can be abbreviated in a diagram:[24]

	SEPARATION: LIGHT		LOCAL MOTION: SUN
DAY 1	Light-Darkness *day / night* (good)	DAY 4	Greater Light/Lesser sun / moon / stars (good)
DAY 2	Waters Above/ Below *heavens/***** (****)	DAY 5	Birds/Sea Animals (good; blessing)
DAY 3	Congealed Seas/ Dry land *seas / earth* (good)	DAY 6	Cattle/Reptiles/ Wild Beasts (good)
	Verdure/Plants/ Trees (good)		Humanity masculine/feminine (blessing)

LEGEND 1. – things named by God
2. () things seen as good and or blessed by God
3. – – double creation on one day
4. **** incomplete distinction

Perhaps the most important thing that can be said about the creation days
— which are not the same as sun days — is that there is nothing particularly
mythological about them. The world that comes into appearance and comes
to appear progressively distinct is a world which is plainly perceptible and accessible to all humans as humans, believers and non-believers alike. The creation account addresses the world as we know it, as humans have always known
it and will continue to know it — a heavens and earth composed of stable
regions which serve as the background of moving things. Yet just as the creation account is not a mythological cosmogony, so it is not a scientific explication. Rather, it addresses my pre-understanding (*Vorverstehen*) of the theatre
of existence prior to any explication, mythical or scientific.

To return to the above diagram, it seems necessary to read the days of creation dialectically. Creation does not appear as a conglomeration of isolated
things, but as an ensemble of relations between backgrounds and foregrounds,
stable regions and moving things. As noted above, there are no comprehensive
concepts in the Bible like *physis* or *kosmos*, but relations such as heavens and
earth, seas and dryland, and so on. We are invited to read Day 1 in relation
to Day 4, etc.

Days 1/4. On Day 1 the background regions (light/darkness, day/night) for
the things which will move in them (sun, moon, stars) are created and
distinguished. It is somewhat surprising to see Genesis I speaking about light
before speaking about the sun. We know light chiefly via the sun, moon and
stars. But there is also the light that comes naturally in lightning and artificially
in fire. The priority of light seems to be based on our presupposing it for
distinguishing all other things we see. In this sense, light is an absolute beginning. The light and sun are compared and contrasted. As light provides the
principle of distinction for things which have place or occupy regions (heavens,
earth, seas, plants), so the sun provides the distinction for moving things, i.e.,
things which separate themselves from their places (heavenly bodies, birds, sea
animals, land animals, humans). The divisions are seen as "good" but not
"holy". Creation implies a distinction between goodness and sacredness. The
sun, moon, and stars are not to be worshipped as gods, nor are they con-
templated as models of perfect, circular movement (Plato, *Laws* 897b, ff.).
The earth does not serve the heavenly bodies, but the heavenly bodies benefit
the earth by marking out the seasons for plants and animals and the festivals
for mankind. The heavenly bodies separate from their places but do not depart
from their courses.

Days 2/5. The most noteworthy aspect of Day 2 is that, after dividing the
waters above from the waters below, God does not see this division as good.
Day 2 is not seen as good because the division is not complete until the waters
below are further divided into congealed seas and dry land (Day 3). Creation,
then, implies not only separations, but separations which are complete and

whole. Only then can something be seen as good. Corresponding to the division between the heavens and the waters below are the living beings which fill those regions — birds and sea creatures (Day 5). In contrast with the heavenly bodies, living things cannot only depart from their places, but also from their courses. Genesis I seems to make a distinction between growing and static things (Day 3) and living and moving things (Day 5). Life is seen preeminently as a kind of motion or action. Living beings are not only seen as good, but are also given a threefold blessing or positive command: "Be fruitful, increase and multiply". Life is precarious, particularly the life of moving beings that can alter their courses. Genesis I wants to stress that the Creator is on the side of life. In addition, the Creator addresses living beings in the second person, whereas the earth on Day 3 had been addressed in the third: "Let the earth bring forth verdure . . . ." In the sequence of the days of creation, seeking holds a lower rank than speaking and hearing. Hearing will become a dominant theme in the Bible, e.g., the call to Abraham. Speaking and hearing are somehow closer to life than seeing.

Days 3/6. The remarkable feature of the third and sixth days is that there is a double creation on both of them. Once the waters below are divided into seas and dry land, the three distinct regions (heavens, earth, seas) are seen as good by God. After the dry land is separated from the seas and can be called the earth in the narrower sense, there is an appropriate region for the land animals of Day 6 to occupy. The earth is the last thing named by God. Retrospectively we notice that God has named only the most general things (day/night, heavens/seas/earth). More particular things will be left to be named by Adam in Genesis II. There is a similar treatment of divine and human naming in Plato's *Cratylus*.

In the second half of the double creation on Days 3/6, a correlation is made between vegetation and human beings. At first sight this seems strange. Vegetation ranks as the most distinct of the non-moving things. There seems to be a progression of distinctness among the various forms of vegetation. Verdure does not give the appearance of making seeds or fruit; seed-bearing plants such as wheat produce seeds which need further making — e.g., planting, winnowing, grinding, and so forth. And finally, fruit trees make a fruit that is whole, complete, and separable from the tree and without needing any further making. Vegetation in general gives the appearance of being monosexual when compared to animals. Parallel to the rank of fruit trees, human beings head the list as the most distinct of moving things. The heavenly bodies can separate themselves from their places but cannot depart from their courses. Animals can separate themselves from their places and depart from their courses but cannot depart from their "ways" (instincts). Humans can separate themselves from their places, depart from their courses *and* — here an ambiguity erupts — depart from their ways.

The parallel between vegetation and humanity gives way to contrast on a deeper level. Vegetation appears as monosexual, but humanity is obviously comprised of two distinct sexes. Vegetation cannot separate itself from the earth, but humanity is separable in the highest degree. The fruitmaking tree, the highest form of vegetation, makes things which are whole, complete and separable from the tree itself, but humanity makes things which are not separable from itself, namely, words and deeds. In some way humanity appears to be fully responsible. Finally, the contrast between humankind and vegetation is at its sharpest when God sees the makings of the vegetative realm are good but humanity is given only a blessing.

Why is humankind not seen as being good? Perhaps humans do not need to be called good because they are created in the image and likeness of God. Genesis I seems to stress humanity's special status in the order of the heavens and the earth by triply using the verb *bara'* with respect to humans (Gen. 1:27). Here, we should note that both masculinity and feminity are said to be equally in the image and likeness of God. There seems to be a plurality in God who is yet single and one. Human sexual differentiation is unlike that of the animals, for it is attached to the image and likeness of God.

The terms for the sexes in Genesis I (*zakar* and *neqebah*) should be rendered "masculine and feminine" and not "male and female". The terms are not linguistic cognates in Hebrew, as are the English terms. Genesis I wishes to stress equality-in-difference. "Male and female" or "Man and woman" are appropriate for the terms used in Genesis II (*'ish* and *'ishshah*).

The creation of humankind in the image and likeness of God underscores the high part of humanity. Perhaps, too, humanity is not seen as good because of its special status in the order of creation. Human beings are not only told to be fruitful, increase and multiply but also given dominion over the earth (Gen. 1:26−28). This theme inspires the wonder of the author of Psalm 8 which depicts mankind as "a little less than the gods" (Ps 8:6).

Yet the moment human supremacy is asserted, a dark note creeps in. Although human beings are promised dominion − or, as we would say today, technical control over nature − they are given only the vegetative realm for food. This limitation stands in contrast to the powerful verbs used to express dominion (*radah*, to trample down; *kabash*, to tread upon, subjugate). The verbs point toward the ceaseless inquietude humans must exert in order to have dominion and by which they can be impelled, as it were, to overstep the limits. Although Genesis I concentrates on a phenomenology of all that is distinct, separate, complete and good, there suddenly arises the ambiguous possibility of humanity: destined toward the good in terms of the whole, yet capable of evil. This ambiguity becomes the explicit theme of Genesis II.

Day 7. Day 7 does not have a parallel in the days of creation. But, as noted above, the repose of the creation Sabbath stands in opposition to the disordered motion of *tohu-wa-bohu*. The creation Sabbath is not the same as the ritual Sabbath in the Book of Exodus (Ex. 31:12–17), for it is not hedged in with taboos, i.e., negative commands. Rather, the creation Sabbath marks the completion of distinct things by God. In contrast to all that went before, the seventh day is not only blessed but also made holy. God sees that the whole is "very good". Genesis I leaves unspoken whether or not a part can become evil. It seems that only God can make something hold. Created things cannot be "made" holy by humankind. On the other hand, creation according to Genesis I is good and not "neutral". This challenges moderns who, having passed through the disenchantment of the world, can no longer touch the goodness of the created order but rather reduce it to "neutral objects" and "raw material" in the quest for technological mastery.

In conclusion, we see that Genesis I orders the creation days according to a principle of division – or, as Plato says in the *Sophist, diairesis* – division by two. The divisions we encounter in Genesis I are grounded on a theological phenomenology of the "heavens and earth" as the arena of human existence. The ground of this phenomenology is that the theatre of existence "signifies" before human beings begin to interpret and classify the "messages". This is no less true for us who classify biological species on the microscopic and submicroscopic level (RNA, DNA, etc. as message systems) than it is for "primitives" who classify on a macroscopic level according to concrete phenomena which present themselves to consciousness. No one system of classification is more "logical" than another. The essential difference is that the ancients (and "primitives") make a symbolic leap between the cosmological, ethical, religious and epistemological orientations to the theatre of existence, whereas we moderns have raised walls between them.

Such a symbolic connection we see later in Genesis. After the Fall and Flood, God once again renews the blessing on humanity. The Flood reduces creation to the primal state of *tohu-wa-bohu* after which there is a recreation. This time, however, humans are allowed to eat meat, provided they separate the "nonliving" part (the flesh) from the "living" part (the blood). This is the beginning of the *Kashrut* or the laws of clean and unclean foods. Later in Leviticus 11 and Deuteronomy 14, these laws are expanded. The laws separating the clean from the unclean follow according to the phenomenological taxonomy layed out in Genesis I. Corresponding to the three orders of the heavens, the earth and the seas are three "ideal" types of creatures with distinct parts – birds with wings, cattle with hooves, fish with fins – which move through their respective orders without mixing either parts or motions.[25]

For example, both the camel and the pig are taboo, the first because it has a "cloven" stomach (an ungulate) but not a cloven hoof, the second because it has a cloven hoof but not a "cloven" stomach. The paradigm of the unclean are the "treeping" things which move every which way. The food laws are reinforced by other secondary laws, e.g., not mixing meat products with dairy products, not sowing barley with wheat, not yoking an ass with an ox, not weaving linen with wool, etc.

The system of the clean and unclean, then, is not an arbitrary aggregate of customs, but a well-formed semiological system derived from the theological phenomenology of Genesis I. Maintaining the principle of *Habdalah* (Separation/Distinction) is the way to focus attention on the one, separate Lord of the Seventh Day and to preserve order in creation. The counter-principle is the possibility of *Tebhel*. This word is translated as "foul" or "perverse" but the Hebrew root (*balal*) points in the direction of mixing and confusion, such as the confusion of tongues of men at Babel. Anything which possesses *Tebhel* points backward toward the primeval confusion *tohu-wa-bohu*. The entrance of the counter-principle into the human drama is central theme of Genesis II.

GENESIS II. Scholars have noted both differences and contrasts between Genesis I and II. Modern higher criticism has attributed these differences and contrast to the diverse social conditions which the authors were addressing. However, from the viewpoint of the Redactor(s) of the literary traditions, these discrepancies must have appeared as more than mere differences and contrasts; rather, they manifest themselves as symbolic contradictions. These contradictions cannot appear until one discovers that the surface details of the twofold account of creation give evidence of a contradiction on the deep level of the narrative structure. The Redactor(s) have given us many clues.

Creation and Adam. The first thing we notice about Genesis II is that YHWH-Elohim "makes" (*'asah*) first the earth and then the heavens in contradistinction to Genesis I. God's creative activity is understood more in terms of "fashioning", "molding" and "transforming" than in terms of "creating/dividing". Secondly, Genesis I begins with everything wet and moist, whereas in Genesis II everything begins dry and is later watered by the Source. Finally, humankind is the last thing to be made in the first account, but the first in the second account. In Genesis I, the stress is placed on humanity's high position, the image and likeness to God. In the second account, this high view of humanity is "corrected" by emphasizing its low origin from the dust of the soil. In Genesis I, human beings are depicted "a little less than the gods" (Ps. 8:5); in Genesis II, human beings are portrayed as a little more than brutes.

The Garden and the Tree. In Genesis I we noticed the attention given to vertical distinctions (heavens, earth, seas, etc.), whereas in the second story attention is paid to horizontal transformation, e.g., the one source dividing into four streams outside the garden, just as later the generic or androgynous "mankind" (Adam) becomes transformed into "man" and "woman". Many commentators claim that the reference to the four streams has no essential connection with the story. However, the streams flow into four regions noted for their exotic minerals. The opposition seems to be between the luxury that comes with civilization as opposed to the simplicity of a tiller of the soil. This theme is repeated in variant form in the opposition between the simple shepherd Abel and the sophisticated farmer Cain, who becomes the ancestor of the city dwellers and artisans. God seems to take notice of Adam's simple state by planting a garden. Adam needs only to till and tend the soil. This is in marked contrast to Genesis I where humankind is destined to master and subdue the earth. The original simple state is symbolized by Adam's "mono-sexual" existence in the garden. Corresponding to this lowly state is the single prohibition not to eat of the fruit of the tree of knowledge of good and evil in the midst of the garden. Again we note the difference with Genesis I where humankind is given only positive commands and God gives *all* the vegetative realm to humans and animals for food. Adam possessed sufficient knowledge to name the animals and woman when they were made. What Adam was denied − or lacked − was knowledge of good and evil, i.e., the knowledge sufficient to guide human life and find the right way.

Animals and Woman. In the first account, only the good, complete and whole aspects of creation were pointed out. Those things which are evil or am-biguously good were not so much denied as evaded. In Genesis II, though, we discover the dawning of an awareness that for humans there cannot be good without some evils, just as there cannot be light without some darkness. Adam seems content inside the garden, and it is God who recognizes that "it is not good for a human to be alone ("monosexual") yet fertile, but Adam, though he has "whole life" (immortality), is infertile. More precisely, Adam *could* have been immortal, for there was no prohibition against eating from the tree of life.

The passage on the transformation of Adam into man and woman is most difficult. Why the deep sleep and why the making of woman from Adam's rib? Why, indeed, the fashioning of woman after the animals? As indicated above, Genesis I looks to what is high in humanity, whereas Genesis II centers our attention on what is low. Genesis II considers the likeness to the animals as what is low in human beings, but rejects that as a reason. This is so because God makes the animals to be "co-workers corresponding to the human". Adam names them, but does not see that they are good, as God does in Genesis I. It is God and not Adam who sees that the animals do not correspond to a human.

The lowness of humanity, therefore, must be something specific to humans as humans. It seems that, though Adam is alone, leading a simple life, and has at least the possibility of immortality, he-she is a mixed being. Adam seems to possess "whole life", including the potencies of both sexes, but lacks the characteristic which marks goodness according to Genesis I: distinctness. Even after woman is separated from man and fashioned out of his rib, the distinction between "man" and "wo-man" is not complete or clear. The Hebrew stresses this by using *'ish* and *'ishshah* which points to a fundamental identity despite difference. In the second account, the man cannot be distinguished from the woman, for he cleaves to her in a way that their destinies are ineluctably intertwined. The potential for evil, which was left unspoken in Genesis I, looms into the foreground in Genesis II. Neither Adam nor Eve can be "low" alone, since in their very being they essentially refer to each other. They can be neither totally good nor totally evil by themselves, since evil arises out of reciprocal relations. This is a limit to reason.

With the appearance of humanity in Genesis II, there is the simultaneous appearance of ambiguity, confusion and disorientation. Humanity cannot be "placed" as could the heavens and earth in Genesis I. At the deeper level, the juxtaposition of Genesis I and II uncovers the contradiction that the theological phenomenology of the heavens and the earth in the first account cannot serve as the ground of the theological anthropology in the second. In the second account, there is the eruption of something radically other – evil. We do not know its origin. On the one hand, it is not something inherent in humans as humans. They are created as good and must be tempted to it. On the other hand, it invades human existence in a way that they are held accountable for it.

Serpent and Temptation. One of the most striking features of Genesis II is that the symbol of the Serpent is *not* demythologized. In any answer to the question "Whence evil?", therefore, one is driven to a two-fold reflection. On one side, it is something for which we humans are unaccountably responsible. On the other, evil belongs to the "always already there" as the human propensity to evil. Evil cannot be ontologized and made external; nor can it be existentialized and reduced to pure subjective guilt. The symbol of the Serpent encompasses the ambiguity hedged in by both these limitations.

In Genesis I we saw the progressive depiction of the heavens and the earth moving forward toward ever greater distinction and ordered motion. In Genesis II we encounter the drama of human existence which impels a counter-movement backwards. There is a striking affinity between this theme and the myth of Plato's *Politicus* (269c ff.) which narrates the forward movement (the age of Chronos) and the counter-movement (the age of Zeus) of the cosmos. According to Plato, these two movements establish human life as a "mean" between the extremes. Genesis II detects not so much the mathematical balancing act of the "mean" as it does the confusion and rupture attached to the mixedness of being human. We encounter this confusion and rupture in the "dialogue" between the Serpent and the woman. The "dialogue" is marked by dissimulation, innuendo, indirection and half-statement. As Plato saw in the *Cratylus, Sophist,* and *Theatetus,* within the self-same possibility of the orderly interweaving (*symplokè*) of the finite, static noun and the infinite, kinetic verb lurked also the possibility of "mixture" and "jumbling" (*symmixis*).[26] The capacity for truth is identical with the capacity for error. In contrast with Adam's simple "naming", the theological phenomenology of language in Genesis II shows the possibility of Eve's "speaking" reaching backwards toward the "confusive" *tohu-wa-bohu*. The same motif reappears in the scrambling of human tongues at the Tower of Babel.

We never meet the Serpent alone nor do we ever detect its motives. It is described as possessing a low kind of wisdom ("cunning"). Verbal dissimulation is implied in the Serpent's question to the woman: "Did God say that you were not to eat from *any* tree of the garden?" The Serpent puts God's single simple prohibition about one tree into the region of the indefinite. Echoing the multidirectional ambiguity of the question, the woman immediately doubles the prohibition: "Of the fruit of the tree in the midst of the garden God said: 'Thou shalt not eat of it or touch it lest you die'" (Gen. 3:3). In the woman's mind there was only one important tree, whereas earlier God had distinguished the tree of knowledge of good and evil from the tree of life. Furthermore, God has *not* prohibited Adam from *touching* the tree. The woman quotes God directly, whereas God had spoken only to Adam. The first exegesis, as it were, was open to distortion. The entire dialogue between the Serpent and Eve takes place in a hermeneutical fog.

Meanwhile the woman's vision becomes riveted on the tree of knowledge. Beguiled by words, the eye becomes mesmerized. The tree is not only "good to eat" and "delectable to the eyes" like all the other trees in the garden but also "covetous to gaze at" (Gen. 3:6). In Romans 7:7–24, Paul taught us much about the meaning of this text. Paul shows how the single precept (*entolè*) became the "starter propellent" (*aphormè*) for the proliferation of Law and Sin in Genesis 3–11 (Rom. 7:7). Secondly, Paul demythologizes – almost – the figure of the Serpent. The Serpent is "Sin" (*hamartia*). Though Romans 7 has often been subjected to existential interpretations (guilt, dread, *Angst*), the Ego of which Paul speaks is not the Ego of existentialism or psychoanalysis but the Adamic Ego, destined toward good, yet propelled into sin. In a paraphrase of the Septuagint version of Genesis 3:13, Paul is not even above appropriating Eve's rationalization: "For Sin, getting its propulsion through the percept, tricked me and struck a deathly blow" (Rom. 7:11). Finally, it is also Paul who shows us that the first commandment to be breached was in fact the last of the decalogue (Rom. 7:7, Ex. 20:17). There has always been an exegetical bias to reduce the primal sin to some sort of sexual deviation. Genesis II, however, points to the polydirectionality of deviation.

The connection between Genesis 3:6 and Exodus 20:17 is lost when the root *hamad* ("to covet, lust after") is translated by "tempting" or "desirable". The commandment "Thou shalt not covet ..." has a potentially infinite number of objects to which it may apply. It strikes the humanity at its weakest point. We, who have experienced the disillusionment of Freud and Marx, are perhaps better able to comprehend the inner connection between sexuality and economics. The vision of the fruit opens upon the infinitude of desire which can mesmerize humanity into the idolatry of money fetishism.

The woman gave the fruit to the man who took and ate for he was cleaving to her. There seems no hesitation on the part of man. The story seems to want to convey the inarticulable feeling that the violation of the prohibition was avoidable yet inevitable. Here we touch upon the theme of tragedy which is both close to the theme of the Fall, yet distant from it. Not depicting the high part of humanity, Genesis II does not portray defiant hubris on the part of the first parents. They are rather shown drifting into sin by forgetting the prohibition.

Prophetic Indictment and Curse. It is important to note that Adam and Eve's shame precedes the interrogation and curses by God. Shame is something like an unaccountable internal indictment. There is a similar analysis in Plato's *Gorgias.* As Sin cannot be reduced either to a subjective state or to an objective condition, so shame, which surfaces suddenly in the physical blush, represents a dialectic of inwardness and outwardness. This dialectic gets lost the moment the "body" is accused of being the "case of sin". The moment the spirit turns accusingly toward the flesh as the vehicle of Sin, it encounters contradiction: the priority of goodness in both material and spiritual creation.

The inarticulable effect of shame motivates the clearly ennunciated prophetic lawsuit by God. Strangely, the Serpent is absent from the interrogation and yet is the only creature cursed. Adam and Eve are punished but not directly cursed. Cain is the first human to be cursed by God (4:11) and there is an increase in punishment with the growth of civilization (Gen. 9:6). The singling out of curses and punishments in Genesis II is in sharp contrast with Genesis I where there were only blessings. Likewise the dominion foreseen in Genesis I stands in opposition to the structures of domination which erupt after the Fall. At the same time, the curses partake of the in-between. They are negative bearing positives. Adam loses "whole life" but gains multiple life through Eve, "the mother of all those who live" (Gen. 3:20). Eve stands as the counter-image of the single tree of life. Likewise the curse of death — "Dust thou art ..." is reversed in the promise to Abraham: "I will make your offspring countless as the dust of the earth" (Gen. 13:16).

Exile and Wandering. The man and the woman are cast from the garden which is mythically sealed as a place of return by the avenging angels. On the one hand, God assumes a certain externality in sin and punishment. On the other hand, humans are said to become like God, knowing good and evil. It seems that humans cannot know the good purely and simply, but only good mixed with evil. Kant spoke of this in his remarkable commentary on the opening chapters of Genesis.[27] It is woman and not man who makes the first practical employment of reason. By eating of the fruit, Eve makes a distinction between edible and inedible plants. But this first use of reason was also its abuse for it violated the prohibition.

244

The ambiguity of knowledge places a veil over what we have come to know as culture and civilization. Modern theories of the origin of society envisage an undeterred line of progress from the state of nature (animality) to the state of culture (humanity). The Book of Genesis challenges this view. In the Antedeluvian period (Gen. 4–9), humans are on their own without the law. During this time there is an increase in the arts and civilization but also an increase in lawlessness. The first art, weaving, arose as a consequence of shame. Cain, the ancestor of artisans and founders of cities (Gen. 4:19–23), is also guilty of fratricide, as was Romulus, the founder of another great city. The invention of viticulture leads to its misuse (Gen. 9:20–25). Genesis II stresses that piety and civilization are two different things. The instant of the use of reason is also the instant of its abuse. We post-moderns, who have suffered through what Max Horkheimer calls the "irrational rationality" of technical reason are perhaps better able to hear the prophetic voice that comes through this passage.

Genesis II concludes with the expulsion of the man and woman from the garden. Outside the garden there is death but also the continuation of life. Adam and Eve receive the blessing of offspring only after the expulsion. Here we may detect a subtle biblical joke or inversion of the Babylonian Epic of Gilgamesh. In his quest for the secret of immortal life, Gilgamesh sets out to find Utnaphistim, the hero of old to whom the gods had granted immortality. After a perilous journey. Gilgamesh finds the former warrior and his wife. Utnaphistim is lying prostrate on his back. The picture is one of an isolated, old, and enfeebled man for whom immortality does no good.[28]

Genesis II begins where the Epic of Gilgamesh ends. Where the latter finds disillusionment, the former finds hope, despite the mixture of evil and good in human existence. Perhaps this is why in the Book of Genesis there is no quest for immortality nor even a hint of nostalgia for paradise. Humans are destined to wander in order to find the way. In the uncertain world of the desert steppe, humanity will encounter curses, toil, and hardship mixed with moments of blessing, rest and ease. Humans will need faith that this journey is not on the side of death, but of life.

IV. Some Reflections

From the perspective of historic-critical analysis, the problem of the two stories which open the Book of Genesis is "solved" by history itself. Though the documentary hypothesis of literary strands and the formcritical method can tell us that the second account (Genesis II) dates from an earlier time than the first (Genesis I), they cannot account for the strangeness of why there should be two accounts of the Beginning or why the later version should be put first. "Historicist" interpretation rests on the presupposition that the world of representation of a text receives its meaning from its relation to the social conditions to which it was addressed. In this regard, the above interpretation of Genesis I and II sides with a "logicist" interpretation. From this perspective, the two accounts of the Beginning are not simply addressing different audiences under different circumstances. They are not, as texts, simply, next-to-one-another, but reciprocally addressing one another and only thereby addressing different *Sitzen im Leben*.

I believe that the phenomenological approach to the texts, in allowing the surface details of the story to appear in their full intentionality, lets us discover in the deep structure the appearance of contradictions when speaking about the Beginning. These contradictions can be briefly summarized as follows:

Genesis I	Genesis II
1. God "creates" the heavens then the earth.	1. YHWH – God makes the earth and then the heavens.
2. In the beginning all is moist.	2. In the beginning all is dry.
3. The story proceeds from confused *motion* (*tohu-wa*-bohu) to *rest* (Sabbath).	3. The story proceeds from *stasis* (settled life in the Garden) to *kinesis* (wandering in the steppe).
4. Distinct things come to be by *separation*, e.g.: a) salt water vs. fresh b) "masculine" vs. "wo-man".	4. Different things be by *division* and come to *fashioning and transformation*, e.g.: a) one Source becomes four Rivers. b) "man" and "feminine".
5. God names the most general things.	5. Adam names specific things (animals and woman).
6. Humans created according to a high part (image/pattern of God).	6. Adam made according to a high part (breath of life from Yahweh God) and a low part (dust of the earth).
7. The whole is very good.	7. Evil emerges in one part.
8. Humanity is destined to *dominion* over the earth.	8. Humanity becomes subject to structures of *domination*.

The oppositions make clear that the two accounts of creation are not two unrelated texts, but two articulations about the ambiguity of the Beginning.

Claude Lévi-Strauss has defined mythic narrative as "a logical model capable of overcoming a contradiction" but he adds that this may be "an impossible achievement, if, as it happens, the contradiction is real".[29] The structural analysis of Genesis I and II above has, I believe, uncovered an insuperable contradiction which gives rise to equivocation. This equivocation, however, is not an equivocation by *default* but an equivocation arising from the *surplus* of meaning.[30] In logic-technical discourse, such equivocation would be intolerable. Logical argument depends upon the transparency and stability of the terms, i.e., on univocal of meaning. But logico-technical discourse abstracts from the texture of existence, from the existential thickness of finding oneself in the environment of a heavens and earth which are good, yet within which the eruption of evil has occurred. Only the multivocal symbol can encompass the polysemic contradiction of the Beginning: the priority of distinctness, purity, wholeness and goodness in the theatre of existence *and* the co-instantaneous eruption of mixture, defilement, incompletion and evil in the human drama.

This leads me to define the mythical story, not so much as a logical model for overcoming contradiction, but as a symbological model for encompassing the contradictions of existence with a view to the teleology of meaning. The contradiction encompassed by symbolic speech is, on the analogy of the *felix culpa* proclaimed in the Christian Easter liturgy, a *felix contradictio*. The myth of Eros as the offspring of Penia gives rise to the myth of Eros as the forgotten and lost child of Poros. While the technical sign peels away the layers of false consciousness ("idols") by offering transparency and clarity to knowledge, it threatens to close down meaning in a perpetuity of the same, as, for example, in the reduction of the heavens and the earth to a system of calculable forces ("facts") which humans can exploit, but in which they can find no meaning ("value"). At this moment of closure of meaning the symbol, chastened and purified by critical consciousness, reappears as the promise of future meaning. Even within demystifying and demythologizing discourse one discovers the re-emergence of symbolic discourse. The Freud who reduces the psyche to neurotic drives is the same Freud who has recourse to the symbols of Eros and Thanatos, Ananke and Logos. The Nietzsche who unveils the religious motive as the will to power is also the Nietzsche who speaks of *amor fati* and the Eternal Recurrence. The Marx who unmasks religion as the opium of the people is also the Marx who envisons a Classless Society free from the structures of ideology and domination. The Hegel who seeks to extract be rational kernel from the mythical shell is also the Hegel who describes *Absolutes Wissen* in religioso-symbolic terms as the reconciliation of consciousness to itself.

Thus, too, the phenomenological reduction − an "archeology" of meaning, as it were − of the stories about the Beginning, and the disclosure of the contradiction of being created as good yet inclined toward the evil, propels us toward a teleology of the symbol. The demythologization of the drama of the "first" Adam calls forth resignification in the drama of the "second" Adam, just as the story of "sin abounding" hearkens to the story of "grace superabounding" (Rom. 5:12–21). The sequence of prior goodness and evil erupting produces its own symbolic inversion of restored fallenness which can behold a "new" heavens and a "new" earth (Rev. 21:1).

If the *explication du texte* above is indeed a "saving of the myth", it is not because I have understood the authors of Genesis I and II better than they understood themselves. It is, rather, overt in the act of interpretation, the text to be explicated has entered into my horizon and has become also a *texte de l'explanation*.

NOTES

1. Paul Ricoeur, "The Language of Faith", *The Philosophy of Paul Ricoeur: An Anthology of His Work*, ed. Charles E. Reagan and David Stewart (Boston: Beacon Press, 1978), p. 228.
2. G. van der Leeuw, *Religion in Essence and Manifestation*, trans. J.E. Turner (New York: Harper & Row, 1963), p. 25.
3. Cf. Paul Ricoeur, *Interpretation Theory: Discourse and the Surplus of Meaning* (Fort Worth: The Texas Christian University Press, 1976), pp. 89–95.
4. Hans-Georg Gadamer, *Truth and Method* (New York: The Seabury Press, 1975), pp. 273–4, 337, 338; Paul Ricoeur, *The Symbolism of Evil*, trans. Emerson Buchanan (Boston: Beacon Press, 1967), pp. 347–57.
5. Rolph Rendtorff, "'Machet euch die Erde untertan': Mensch und Natur im Alten Testament", *Evangelische Kommentare* 10/11 (1977), pp. 659–61. See my redaction of this article in *Theology Digest* 27/3 (Fall, 1979), pp. 213–16.
6. G.F.W. Hegel, *The Philosophy of History*, trans. J. Sibree (New York: Dover Publications, 1956), p. 196.
7. Immanuel Kant, *Fundamental Principles of the Metaphysics of Morals*, trans. Thomas K. Abbott (Indianapolis: The Library of Liberal Arts, 1949), p. 49.
8. Cf. Paul Ricoeur, *Fallible Man*, trans. Charles Kelbley (Chicago: Henry Regnery Co., 1965), p. 19 ff.; Simone Weil, *Gravity and Grace*, trans. Arthur Wills (New York: G.P. Putman's Sons, 1952), pp. 200 03.
9. Paul Ricoeur, *Freud and Philosophy: An Essay on Interpretation*, trans. Denis Savage (New Haven: Yale University Press, 1970), pp. 28–32; Victor Turner, *The Forest of Symbols: Aspects of Ndembu Ritual* (Ithaca: Cornell University Press, 1967), pp. 27–9. Ricoeur's distinction between sign and symbol corresponds to Kant's distinction between the schema and the symbol: "Schemata contain direct, symbols indirect, presentations of the concept. Schemata effect this presentation demonstratively, symbols by the aid of an analogy, judgment performs a double function" – *The Critique of Judgment*, trans. James Creed Meredith (Oxford at the Clarendon Press, 1952), Part I: The Critique of Aesthetic Judgment, p. 222. The schematism allows for the direct application of the category to the appearance or the conceptual organization of a field of experience which brings about knowledge (cf. *The Critique of Pure Reason*, trans. Norman Kemp Smith [New York: St. Martin's Press, 1965], A 137/B 176–a 147/B187, pp. 180–87). Symbols do not provide direct knowledge by food for reflection arising from the indirect analogy of two unlike things, e.g., a hand-mill and a despotic state (*The Critique of Judgment*, p. 223). Kant suggests all religious discourse is symbolic in this sense.
10. Ricoeur, *Freud*, p. 531.
11. Ricoeur, "The Critique of Religion" in *The Philosophy of Paul Ricoeur*, pp. 213–22.
12. Cf. Martin Luther, *Bondage of the Will in Martin Luther: Selections from his Writings*, ed. John Dillenberger (New York: Doubleday Anchor Books, 1961), pp. 172–73.
13. Francis Bacon, "The Great Instauration" in *The New Organon and Related Writings*, ed. Fulton H. Anderson (Indianapolis: The Library of Liberal Arts, 1960), p. 25.
14. Bacon hints that nature or the "book of God's works" is a "second Scripture" almost on an equal basis with the book of God's words – "Aphorisms in the Primary History", Aphorism ix, in Bacon, p. 282. Spinoza wrote that "the method of interpreting Scripture does not widely differ from the method of interpreting nature – in fact, it is almost the same". Cf. Benedict Spinoza, *Theopolitical Treatise and a Political Treatise*, trans. R.H.M. Elwes (New York: Dover Publications, 1951), p. 99.
15. Hegel, preface to *The Philosophy of Right* in *The Philosophy of Hegel*, ed. Carl J. Friedrich (New York: The Modern Library, 1954), p. 225.

16. Karl Marx, "Toward a Critique of Hegel's Philosophy of Law: Introduction" in *Writings of the Young Marx on Philosophy and Society*, ed. Lloyd D. Easton and Kurt H. Guddat (New York: Doubleday Anchor Books, 1967), pp. 250–51.

17. Cf. esp. Friedrich Nietzsche, *Beyond Good and Evil: Prelude to a Philosophy of the Future*, trans. R.J. Hollingdale (Harmondsworth: Penguin Books, 1973), Part Three: The Religious Nature, pp. 56–71.

18. Cf. Sigmund Freud, *The Future of an Illusion* (New York: W.W. Norton & Co., 1961), pp. 30–31. It is important to note that Freud distinguishes sharply between illusions, errors and delusion.

19. Karl Barth, *The Epistle to the Romans*, trans. Edwyn C. Hoskyns (London: Oxford University Press, 1968), pp. 150, 236–44.

20. Rudolph Bultmann, *Jesus Christ and Mythology* (New York: Charles Scribener's Sons, 1958), p. 36.

21. Cf. Paul Tillich, *A History of Christian Thought*, ed. Carl E. Braaten (New York: Touchstones Books, 1968), p. 524.

22. See, e.g., James Pritchard, *The Ancient Near East: an Anthology of Texts and Pictures* (Princeton: Princeton University Press, 1958), fig. 170.

23. Thorkild Jacobsen, *The Treasures of Darkness: A History of Mesopotamian Religion* (New Haven: Yale University Press, 1976), p. 168.

24. This diagram represents an abbreviation of the discussion by Leo Stauss, "Jerusalem and Athens, Some Introductory Reflections", *Commentary* 43/6 (June, 1967), pp. 45–57.

25. On the phenomenological "taxonomy" of the laws of the clean and unclean, cf. Mary Douglas, *Purity and Danger: An Analysis of Concepts of Pollution* and *Taboo* (Harmondsworth: Penguin Books, 1966), pp. 53–72; Jean Soler, "The Dietary Prohibitions and the Hebrews", *New York Review of Books* (July 14, 1979); and Robert Alter, "A New Theory of Kashrut", *Commentary* 43/2 (August, 1979), pp. 46–52.

26. Cf. Ricoeur, *Fallible Man*, pp. 26–57.

27. Kant, "Conjectural Beginning of History" in *Kant on History*, ed. Lewis Beck White, Robert E. Anchor and Emil L. Fackenheim (New York: The Library of Liberal Arts, 1963), pp. 55 ff.

28. The Epic of Gilgamesh (XI.6) in Pritchard, p. 66.

29. Claude Lévi-Strauss, "The Structural Study of Myth" in *Structural Anthropology*, trans. Claire Jacobsen and Brooke G. Schoeff (New York: Doubleday Anchor Books, 1967), p. 226. Lévi-Strauss comes close to reducing symbols to logico-technical signs but pulls himself up short.

30. Ricoeur, *The Philosophy of Paul Ricoeur*, p. 234.

Epilogue:
For the Third Generation of Phenomenologists Contributing to this Volume
by
Herbert Spiegelberg

This brief epilogue to your work is not meant to be the critical review which I owe you individually as a minimum of personal appreciation for each one's special contribution, of which thus far I merely have had a preliminary preview. But before doings so, I would like to offer you a few general reflections about your enterprise from the vantage (and disadvantage) point of a going-gone earlier generation in the hope that you may find them encouraging in your own work.

In principle I confess that I am prejudiced against the idea of a person-centered *Festschrift* – and I am grateful that your brave editor has avoided this Germanic label for a ceremonial mass burial of scholarly work in places mostly ignored by the wider scholarly community, both in review and bibliographies. All the more happy am I that, thanks to Bill's innovative initiative, you are giving me the sense that my name was able to act as a catalyst for so much original phenomenology in you. I am thinking particularly of those who did front line phenomenology by going to the *Sachen* with or without the model of my collection of essays *on* and *in* phenomenology, but also of those who contributed largely interpretive studies of the first-hand work of other well-known phenomenologists or by applying phenomenology to literary works, as long as this did not result in mere "metaphenomenology", i.e., studies *of* phenomenology.

What I want to do here is to reflect on what I see as the significance of the work in phenomenology of your generation to me who is now one of the few survivors of an older generation with the unearned privilege of having outlived its leaders, John Wild, Aron Gurwitsch, Dorion Cairns and Alfred Schutz (in chronological order). I am referring to them as the second generation of phenomenologists as distinguished from the first generation of the "founder", i.e. primarily Edmund Husserl, with Alexander Pfänder, Adolf Reinach, Moritz Geiger and Max Scheler as his associates and Martin Heidegger and Oskar Becker as those who joined them a little later.

What makes the difference between these three generations? How far is the

W.S. Hamrick (ed.) *Phenomenology in Practice and Theory*.
© 1985 Martinus Nijhoff Publishers, Dordrecht/Boston/Lancaster
ISBN 90 247 2926 2. Printed in the Netherlands.

division into separate generations merely artificial, if not arbitrary? Clear answers to such questions would presuppose a phenomenology of the phenomenon of generation, which to my knowledge does not yet exist. So I would improvise it. I shall do so only to the extent that it may shed light on your particular situation and only in the spirit of opening up another phenomenological frontier for solid research after my preliminary scouting.

What is a generation? The only book known to me in this connection is that be a German art historian, Wilhelm Pinder, on *Das Problem der Generation in der Kunstgeschichte Europas* (1926 and 1961). While this book drew attention to the fact previously overlooked that the art of each period is the output of several generations working simultaneously. Pinder did not try to determine the nature of a generation by anything but by the common birth years of its members. In particular, he made no attempt to relate the phenomenon of a generation to their consciousness of generational solidarity. Indeed one may wonder whether such a consciousness existed before the nineteenth century. There is an informative article on the concept of generation by Julian Marias in the *Encyclopedia of the Social Sciences* of 1968 which refers to other works and incidental discussions such as those by Wilhelm Dilthey in "Die geistige Welt" (*Gesammelte Schriften* 5, pp. 31–73) which contains the following illuminating characterization of the social phenomenon: "Those who in the years of susceptibility experienced the same guiding influences jointly make up a generation". But even Dilthey did not apply this conception to the history of philosophy. Besides, no attempt is made to determine the difference between first, second and subsequent generations.

What is needed here is a clear conception of what a generation means in philosophy. Why not leave it simply at a dictionary definition to the effect that generation is determined by "the average time interval between the birth of parents and the birth of their offspring" (*Heritage Dictionary* under Generation [5], which among humans amounts to about thirty years.) While such an objective biological characterization may be sufficient in most contexts, especially where strict genealogy is at stake, the matter is somewhat different if one applies the concept of generation to philosophy. Here the decisive criterion would be the relation not between child, parent and grandparent etc., but the analogous one between a student — his teacher and his teacher's teacher etc. In this sense I designate the oldest generation in the case of a movement or a school as the first generation, that of their direct students as the second generation, and that of the latter's students as the third generation. Thus in the case of phenomenology I would consider Edmund Husserl and his associates as the first generation. Among the second-generation phenomenologists are primarily their students, especially those who wrote Ph.D. theses under their supervision, beginning in Husserl's case at Göttingen with Karl Neuhaus 1908, in Pfänder's with Hedwig Conrad-Martius (in this case for technical reasons, her main work having been done at Göttingen). But all that is really needed in this case is the personal contact of having taken part in seminars or at least attended lectures with the *Meister*, the inner circle's affectionate nickname for Husserl, or his associates. In this lesser sense I myself consider myself a second-generation student of Husserl and Becker, but mostly of Pfänder, who supervised my Ph.D. thesis. Any attempt to collect the names of all those who stood in this relation to the first generation would now be almost hopeless and serve no useful purpose.

This would probably also be the case with all the third generation phenomenologists, thinking especially of the world-wide expansion of Phenomenological Movement in recent decades. What must not be overlooked in this context is that from the very beginning a good many philosophers came to phenomenology not by way of personal contacts with the first or second generation of teachers and/or students but on the basis of their extensive study of the phenomenological texts, examples: Felix Kaufmann, Alfred Schutz and H.L. Van Breda. This seems to be particularly true of the first original French phenomenologists such as Gabriel Marcel, Jean-Paul Sartre and Maurice Merleau-Ponty.

However, even these relatively objective facts are not what I consider really relevant about the situation of the three generations of phenomenologists. What matters is the kind of typical experience each of them had, compared with that of the other generations. I would like to sketch here very briefly what seems to me characteristic differences, along with the common heritage they share, and weigh their significance especially in considering emphathetically the situation of the third generation from the perspective of the second.

For the first generation of phenomenologists, that of the "founders", there was clearly no problem. They had no start from scratch by going to the *Sachen*. They might of course begin by setting themselves off from their predecessors in other traditions, and at times they even did so to the extent that such "polemics" (*Auseinandersetzung*) grew out-of-hand. But this did not change the basic picture of the landscape for the pioneers facing the wilderness. They could not but be "original" in the sense of doing phenomenology without the threat of metaphenomenology.

The situation was a lot different for us − if I may speak here for at least some of the members of the second generation. We grew up under the shadow of the founders, who provided sometimes, if not always, overpowering models at that, even when they tried not to influence us. We could not help seeing the phenomena and problems through their eyes. Our first move was mostly to ask: what has the "master" said or what would he have to say on the subject? Only where he had remained silent did we feel the right to move on our own. This does not mean that we did not at times feel the need to rebel, and especially that we were not eager to strike out independently in territories new or not suf-

254

ficiently cultivated by the pioneers. But even then, we could not ignore the "giants" under whose shadows we had grown up. Our phenomenological field was no longer open country but a half-cultivated landscape. The privilege of having been in contact with the first generation carried with it the price of being no longer free to go straight to the *Sachen* without passing first the structures which the protagonists had erected.

Here I see the basic potential difference in the situation of the third generation. In trying to outline it imaginatively I do not want to minimize the privilege that we of the second generation enjoyed who were still in touch with the originators of the Movement with all their strengths and weaknesses. Seeing some of these weaknesses could at least protect us from uncritical hero worship.

The survival of a third generation of phenomenology and in fact its spread over the globe is of course in itself a testimony to the vitality and significance of the Movement. This development calls for explanations, in fact there could be too many of them. Short of painstaking verification (and falsifications!) I shall refrain from indulging in this exercise. In any case, the situation is much too complex to allow for one single simple answer.

What I would like to do instead is to reflect on the meaning of the new situation of the third generation as I envisage it and the special opportunities which it involves. One of the major advantages of the third generation seems to me that it can again phenomenologize "under the open sky", as it were. While aware of its ancestors, especially through their works, it no longer will be diverted by personal factors and allegiances. In this respect you could enjoy again some of the freedom of the first generation in approaching the *Sachen* themselves without intermediaries. You no longer need to study the phenomena under the shadow of the historical authorities, not even the authorities of the founders of phenomenology. But you are also free to avail yourselves of their genuine and tested insights. You can phenomenologize closer to the *Sachen* than could we of the second generation, unless we applied a special historical "reduction" suspending belief even in the voices of our teachers. The third generation no longer hears these voices. It merely hears their messages, but owes them no longer any unexamined belief any more than any other thinkers of the past and present. My happy impression is that the essays of the present collection contain some first fruits of this new freedom on which I want to congratulate you in the spirit of a renewed solidarity of all the generations of a soberly advancing phenomenology.

Index

257

258